A Course in Public Economics

A Course in Public Economics explores the central questions of whether or not markets work, and if not, what is to be done about it. The first part of the textbook, which is designed for upper-level undergraduates and first-year graduate students, discusses the two theorems of welfare economics. These theorems show that competitive markets can give rise to socially desirable outcomes, and describe the conditions under which they do so. The second part of the book discusses the kinds of market failure – externalities, public goods, imperfect competition, and asymmetric information – that arise when these conditions are not met. The role of the government in resolving market failures is examined. The limits of government action, especially those arising from asymmetric information, are also investigated. A knowledge of intermediate microeconomics and basic calculus is assumed.

John Leach is Professor of Economics at McMaster University, Hamilton, Ontario, Canada. He has published articles in leading refereed journals such as the *Journal of Political Economy*, the *Journal of Economic Theory*, the *Journal of Public Economics*, the *International Economic Review*, the *Canadian Journal of Economics*, the *Journal of Labor Economics*, *Canadian Public Policy*, and the *Journal of Economic Dynamics and Control*. Professor Leach's current research focuses on tax competition between regions seeking to attract firms by setting favorable rates.

A Course in Public Economics

JOHN LEACH

McMaster University, Canada

PUBLISHED BY THE PRESS SYNDICATE OF THE UNIVERSITY OF CAMBRIDGE
The Pitt Building, Trumpington Street, Cambridge, United Kingdom

CAMBRIDGE UNIVERSITY PRESS
The Edinburgh Building, Cambridge CB2 2RU, UK
40 West 20th Street, New York, NY 10011-4211, USA
477 Williamstown Road, Port Melbourne, VIC 3207, Australia
Ruiz de Alarcón 13, 28014 Madrid, Spain
Dock House, The Waterfront, Cape Town 8001, South Africa

http://www.cambridge.org

First published 2004

Printed in the United States of America

Typeface Minion 10.5/13.5 pt.   *System* LATEX 2_ε [TB]

A catalog record for this book is available from the British Library.

Library of Congress Cataloging in Publication Data

ISBN 0 521 82877 5 hardback
ISBN 0 521 53567 0 paperback

It is not from the benevolence of the butcher, the brewer, or the baker that we expect our dinner, but from their regard to their own self interest.

Adam Smith, in *An Inquiry into the Nature and Causes of the Wealth of Nations, 1776*

Some of us see the Smithian virtues [of competitive markets] as a needle in a haystack ... Others see all the potential sources of market failure as so many fleas on the thick hide of an ox, requiring only an occasional flick of the tail to be brushed away. A hopeless eclectic without any strength of character, like me, has a terrible time of it.

Robert Solow [60], in his presidential address to the American Economic Association, 1979

Resources for Instructors

Additional resources, including the solutions to the textbook problems, are available to instructors using this book in their courses. Information on obtaining access to this material is available at:

www.socsci.mcmaster.ca/leach

Contents

Asymmetric Information and Efficiency

Asymmetric Information and Income Redistribution

List of Figures

Preface

You will put it in the proper Whitehall prose, scabrous, flat-footed, with much use of the passive, will you not? I may have allowed something approaching enthusiasm to creep in.

Dr. Maturin, in Patrick O'Brian's *The Yellow Admiral*[1]

Do markets work, and if they don't, what should be done about it? This question has been at the center of microeconomics since Adam Smith proposed, in *The Wealth of Nations* (1776), that each individual's self-interested participation in the market system often promotes the greater good of society. Providing a comprehensive answer to this question has been no easy task. The way in which markets work was not fully articulated until Walras outlined the first general equilibrium model in the early 1870s, and the sense in which market outcomes advance society's interests was not defined until Pareto published his major work in 1909. The principles set out by Walras and Pareto formed the basis of a research program that continued into the second half of the twentieth century, culminating in the Arrow–Debreu model of general equilibrium. This model precisely describes the conditions under which free markets yield a socially desirable outcome. These conditions are very restrictive, leading Stiglitz ([63], p. 29) to comment that "in a sense Debreu and Arrow's great achievement was to find the almost singular set of assumptions under which Adam Smith's invisible hand conjecture is correct."

Adam Smith would not have been surprised by this finding. He is often portrayed as an unrelenting advocate of free markets and an opponent of government intervention, but this portrayal is inaccurate. Certainly, he was opposed to some types of government intervention: *The Wealth of Nations* is in large part a criticism of the mercantile system, under which the government conspired with merchants to develop powerful trading monopolies. But he did not believe that the government should never intervene in economic

---

[1] Published by Harper Collins, 1997.

matters. Indeed, he argued that the government has three essential duties, including

> the duty of erecting and maintaining certain public works and certain public insti-
> tutions, which it can never be for the interest of any individual, or small number of
> individuals, to erect and maintain; because the profit could neither repay the expense
> of any individual or small number of individuals, though it may frequently do much
> more than repay it to a great society.[2]

John Stuart Mill, writing almost a century later, displayed an equal ambivalence toward
free markets. He argued that "*laissez faire* . . . should be the general practice; every
departure from it, unless required by some greater good, is a certain evil," but had little
difficulty in identifying justifiable interventions, including the regulation of education.[3]

More than a century after Mill, the attitude of mainstream economists is little
changed. They oppose monopoly power. They recognize Smith's "public works" as
public goods, or as goods with strong positive externalities, and would agree with his
call for government action. They might even find in Mill's rationale for the regulation
of education – that the consumer is not able to judge the nature of the commodity –
an intimation of modern informational economics. They endorse the market system
while remaining aware of its shortcomings.

The issue of whether markets work, and what should be done if they don't, forms
the core of public economics. While this book is intended to be a textbook in public
economics, it examines only this core issue. It excludes a number of topics normally
found in public economics textbooks, such as tax incidence and cost–benefit analysis.

This book is also intended to act as a bridge between two modes of economic analysis.
Undergraduate students tend to rely upon graphs and simple verbal arguments. By
contrast, graduate students rely heavily on extended logical and mathematical analysis.
This kind of analysis is also routinely employed by academic economists, and to a lesser
degree, by private and public sector economists. The first kind of analysis is employed at
the beginning of the book, but there is an increasing reliance on mathematics thereafter.

Let me emphasize, however, that this is not a book in which sophisticated mathematical tools are either taught or applied. I have assumed that you can do the sort of
things that anyone who has survived a university course in calculus should be able to
do. Specifically, I have assumed that you can

- calculate the derivatives of functions of one or more variables, and understand the
  meaning of these derivatives;
- manipulate an equation to isolate a single variable;
- solve a system of simple equations by recursive substitution.

---

[2] This quote is from chapter 9 of book IV of *The Wealth of Nations*. The other duties are maintaining
the armed forces and the judiciary.
[3] The quote is from chapter 11 of book V of *Principles of Political Economy*. Under *laissez faire* (literally,
"let do"), the government does not attempt to constrain individual decisions, especially economic
decisions.

I believe that you can learn a great deal about economics by formulating issues as mathematical problems and *applying the skills that you already have* to solve them.

Knowing how to drive a car is quite different from actually driving it: there is no substitute for time behind the wheel. The same thing is true of problem solving. You might know how to calculate a derivative, but that's not the same as knowing when to calculate one and what to do with it when you've got it. I hope that this book will provide you with "time behind the wheel." The chapters are really extended examples of the way in which mathematics can be applied to economic issues. As well, there are questions at the end of the chapters, so you will be able to try your hand at problems that are similar to the ones described in the chapters themselves.

You might be less bothered by the mathematics than by the sheer *length* of the arguments presented here. In most undergraduate texts, a one-page explanation is a long explanation. Here, mathematical models of the economy are developed over several pages and their solutions are described over several more pages. Reading this kind of material requires a great deal of concentration.

A lack of concentration was my problem when, in the first year of graduate school, I began to read articles in academic journals. I eventually adopted the following strategy, and use it still:

1) When I read an article for the first time, I read it relatively quickly. I try to understand the issue that is being addressed and the way in which the author intends to address it. If I come across verbal arguments or bits of mathematics that I don't readily understand, I skip them.

2) I read the article again, more slowly. I check to make sure that I understand the issue, and I try to develop a more detailed understanding of the author's arguments. I try to figure out all of the mathematical bits, but if they are really tough, I skip over them again.

3) If I feel that I have to understand the article completely, I read it a third time. I have a pretty good understanding of it by this time, so I can read it quite quickly, slowing down only in the neighbourhood of the tricky bits that I hadn't understood the last time through. (I find that reading *only* the parts that I hadn't previously understood is generally not a useful practice. It is often the case that the tricky bits are tricky because I haven't entirely understood something earlier in the article – I'm missing a piece of the puzzle. Reading the entire article gives me a chance to pick out the missing piece.)

The virtue of the method is that skipping over is always better than stopping. If you find yourself tempted to give up on any of these chapters, you might give this method a try.

This book emphasizes problem solving at the expense of other things. Specifically,

• It is not *comprehensive*. There is a very large literature on almost every subject covered in this book, and I have largely ignored it. Instead, I have tried to present simple and coherent models from which the principal insights of the literature can be derived.

- It is not *general*. I use simple models, and I almost always use specific functional forms for such things as utility functions and production functions. As a rule, economists prefer general models to very specific models,[4] but general models require a little more mathematical sophistication. More general versions of all of the models presented here can be found elsewhere in the economics literature, and in most cases, their major implications are not significantly different from those of the models presented here.

I hope that I have managed to avoid scabrous and flat-footed prose, and that some evidence of my enthusiasm for this subject has crept in. In any case, I have done what I can. Now it's your turn. Good luck.

I should like to thank Richard Arnott, Neil Bruce, and Dan Usher for their encouragement of this project in its early stages, and my colleagues John Burbidge and Les Robb for carefully reading large parts of the manuscript.

I think that in some ways I have written a better book than I thought I could write. Much of the credit for this happy outcome belongs to the readers chosen by Cambridge University Press. They are David Andolfatto (Simon Fraser University), Richard Arnott (Boston College), Robert Gilles (Virginia Polytechnic Institute and State University), Paul Soederlind (Stockholm School of Economics), Bent Sorensen (State University of New York at Binghamton), and Oved Yosha (Tel Aviv University). I should like to thank them all for their suggestions. Finally, I should like to thank Scott Parris of Cambridge University Press for overseeing this project.

---

[4] A result proved for one kind of utility function might not hold for other kinds of utility functions. Economists like results that are general (i.e., apply to the greatest possible number of cases) so they prefer to employ general functional forms rather than specific ones in their analysis.

1

Introduction

There was a little girl, she had a little curl,
Right in the middle of her forehead;
And when she was good, she was very, very good,
And when she was bad, she was horrid.
                    Henry Wadsworth Longfellow

Competitive markets seem to have a great deal in common with the little girl who had a little curl. When they are good, they are so very good that our participation in them becomes part of our unconscious daily routine. If I want broccoli for supper, there is broccoli waiting for me at the grocery store. Down the aisle are the green peppers, locally grown in summer and Mexican in winter. The bananas are from Ecuador and the apples are from as far away as New Zealand. The presence of each item on the grocer's shelves is the result of a complex chain of decisions made by the grocer, the wholesaler, the shipper, and the farmer. Their actions are co-ordinated by prices, and this fact has important implications for the way in which specialized knowledge is utilized. The farmer does not need to know anything about shipping or the grocery business or the making of fertilizers, nor need he communicate to anyone his specialized knowledge of farming. He need know only the prices at which various crops can be sold, and the prices at which factors of production can be purchased. He makes his production decisions by combining information about these prices with his own knowledge of farming; and if he makes these decisions so as to advance his own interests, he does all that the market system requires of him. Similarly, the grocer, wholesaler, and shipper do not communicate detailed information about their own activities, but simply decide whether they are willing to trade at the prevailing prices. If their decisions are made in their own self-interest, they too are doing all that the market system requires of them. I'm at the end of the chain: all that I have to do is to decide whether I'm willing to pay a dollar for this particular bunch of broccoli. I hardly ever think about how the broccoli came to be there because, after all, it's always there.

And when they are bad, competitive markets can be truly horrendous. For example, self-interested economic decisions have led to any number of environmental tragedies. It was observed in 1956 that many people living near Japan's Minimata Bay were suffering from a degenerative neurological disease. In 1968, this disease was officially identified as mercury poisoning caused by eating fish contaminated by industrial waste. The Japanese government has officially recognized in excess of 12,500 victims. In 1954 in the state of New York, the community of Love Canal was constructed on top of a former disposal site containing some 20,000 tons of toxic waste. Mounting evidence of miscarriages and birth defects led to the evacuation of 239 homes in 1978, and in 1980, evidence of chromosomal damage among the inhabitants led to the total evacuation of the community. The example of Love Canal led the American government to establish the Superfund Program, which subsequently identified hundreds of abandoned toxic dumps.[1]

While such experiences have taught us not to dump garbage in our own backyards, we are still reluctant to apply this lesson globally. Progress on the control of ozone-depleting chemicals and carbon dioxide emissions – key factors in global warming – has been slow and halting. The logging and clearing of rain forests continues unabated, reducing the planet's ability to draw carbon dioxide from the atmosphere and replenish its oxygen content. The Food and Agricultural Organization reports that, of the seventeen major fisheries in the world, nine are in serious decline and four others are already commercially depleted.

These examples illustrate just one of the problems encountered by market systems (specifically, the presence of externalities) and there are a number of other problems. They are sufficient, however, to establish the following proposition. There is nothing either scientific or sacred about the market system. It is an institutional arrangement that has persisted and evolved over the past few hundred years because it has contributed greatly to our economic well-being. It isn't perfect, however, and in some situations, our economic well-being can be raised by regulating it or even by side-stepping it altogether.

The purpose of this book is to describe the circumstances under which markets perform well, and the circumstances under which they do not. The role of the government in correcting the faults of the market system is also examined.

1.1 TWO THEOREMS

Every economy must address three problems. Which goods are to be produced? How should they be produced? Who gets the goods once they have been produced? One way of solving these problems is to allow people to trade in competitive markets. The

---

[1] It should be emphasized that these tragedies have their origins, not in the market system, but in the pursuit of narrowly defined interests. Countries that do not use markets to allocate resources have encountered similar, and often worse, environmental problems. In the last half of the twentieth century, for example, the communist countries of eastern Europe experienced far worse pollution than the market economies of western Europe.

The value of the market system is that it can often make individual self-interest serve society's ends. Its failing is that it cannot *always* do so.

TIME AND THE TWO THEOREMS

Although economic models often imagine that people are making choices at a single moment of time, many important economic problems involve choices through time. Should you begin work now, or attend school for another year? Should you buy a house now, or wait until you have scraped together a bigger downpayment? How much of your income should you put aside for retirement, and how will that choice affect the timing of your retirement? It is therefore important to know whether the two fundamental theorems continue to hold in an intertemporal environment. By and large, they do, with an important exception. The two theorems hold for these economies:

1) The economy consists of a fixed number of people, who are alive in the current period and who will continue to live for T periods (where T might be infinite). These people trade in commodity markets during each period of their lives.
2) The economy will last for T periods, where T is some finite number. Some people are alive in the current period. In this period and in every future period, some people will be born and some will die, so that the identities of the people living in the economy are constantly changing. The death rate and the birth rate are not necessarily equal, so the population could change through time. This economy is called a **finite-horizon overlapping generations economy.**

An **infinite-horizon overlapping generations economy** has the same structure as its finite-horizon counterpart, except that it never ends (that is, T is infinite). The two theorems fail in this economy. Thus, the theorems hold in an economy in which there is an infinite horizon, or in an economy in which successive generations overlap, but not in an economy with both of these characteristics.

two fundamental theorems of welfare economics show that this solution is *potentially* a very good one.

The **first theorem** demonstrates that, under certain well-specified conditions (we'll return to these conditions shortly), there is no better solution than the one generated by competitive markets. Specifically, any alternative solution that makes someone in the economy better off must also make someone else worse off. The reasoning behind this argument is simple. A system of competitive markets ensures that all mutually beneficial trades take place, so that every remaining trade – every adjustment of the solution – benefits one person only at another's expense.

If a solution has the property that any other solution can only make someone better off at someone else's expense, it is said to be **Pareto optimal.** Arguably, we would not wish to accept a solution that is not Pareto optimal, for there would then be an alternative that makes someone better off without harming anyone else, and we would certainly prefer this alternative to the original solution. However, the observation that a particular solution *is* Pareto optimal doesn't mean that we need not consider alternatives.

There are many Pareto optimal solutions, and by definition, a move from one to another changes the distribution of economic well-being. If A and B are Pareto optimal solutions, and a move from A to B involves robbing Peter to pay Paul, then a move from B to A involves robbing Paul to pay Peter. Our ideas about equity or fairness might cause us to prefer one or the other of these solutions.

Competitive markets generate a Pareto optimal solution, but that solution isn't necessarily an equitable one. Does it follow that competitive markets must be abandoned if a more equitable outcome is to be attained? The **second theorem** implies that there is no such necessity. This theorem shows that, if certain well-specified conditions are met, the government can shift the economy from one Pareto optimal solution to another by redistributing purchasing power and then allowing people to trade in competitive markets. There is a redistribution that takes the economy to any desired Pareto optimal solution.

An economy that reaches a Pareto optimal solution is commonly said to be efficient. The first theorem argues that competitive markets can be the vehicle that takes the economy to an efficient outcome. The second theorem argues that, in a competitive economy, there is no conflict between reaching an efficient outcome and reaching an equitable outcome.

1.2 MARKET FAILURE

Willem Buiter coined the term "the economics of Dr. Pangloss" in a critique of macro-economics. Dr. Pangloss, a character in Voltaire's *Candide,* taught that "all is for the best in the best of all possible worlds." Encountering a series of misadventures, he was repeatedly forced to choose between abandoning the belief that he lived in the best of all possible worlds, and acquiescing to the idea that every unfortunate incident was somehow for the best. The resilient Dr. Pangloss remained true to his beliefs. Buiter argued that some present day macroeconomists, having idealized the nature of our economies, were constantly confronted with the same dilemma, and proving equally resilient.

Had he not employed the term elsewhere, Buiter could have applied it to the world of the two fundamental theorems. These theorems first imagine that we live in the best of all possible worlds, and then conclude that, indeed, all is for the best. The assumptions that underlie this best of all possible worlds include:

1) Each person's welfare depends only upon the goods that he consumes, and each firm's profits depend only upon its own use of the factors of production.
2) There are established and enforceable property rights over every good.
3) There is a market for every good.
4) Firms behave competitively, and in particular, believe that their own actions have no appreciable effect on market prices.
5) Participation in markets is costless.
6) All market participants have the same information about the nature of the good and the circumstances under which it is traded.

If one or more of these assumptions does not hold, the market system does not give rise to an efficient outcome (i.e., the first theorem does not hold). These inefficient outcomes are called **market failures.** The principal types of market failure are discussed below.

1.2.1 Public Goods

A public good is one whose consumption benefits more than one person or firm. Some of these goods are **non-rivalrous,** in the sense that providing the good to one person necessarily allows the good to be provided to every other person at no additional cost. The lighthouse is one of these goods. If its warning beacon can be seen by one boat, it can be seen by every boat. The lighthouse's successor, the global positioning system (GPS), also has this property. The signals of the GPS satellites are beamed to the earth, and if they are available to one person, they can be made available costlessly to every other person.[2] Other goods are only partially non-rivalrous, in the sense that the quality of the benefit provided to each person diminishes as the number of people to whom it is provided rises. These goods are said to be **congestible,** and are much more common than non-rivalrous goods. Examples of congestible goods include parks and recreational facilities, police and fire protection, and roads and bridges. Every public good involves a violation of assumption 1.

Some public goods also have the property that, if they are provided to one person, they are automatically made available to everyone. Such goods are said to be **non-excludable.** The lighthouse is one example of a non-excludable public good. The GPS, by contrast, is not in principle non-excludable. Its signals could be sent in code, and the provider of the system could sell decoding devices to the manufacturers of GPS receivers. The provider would then be able to limit the number of users by limiting the number of decoders sold. The provider of the GPS (the U.S. defence establishment) has not chosen to do so, and hence the GPS is in practise non-excludable.[3]

A **pure public good** is both non-rivalrous and non-excludable, and hence violates assumptions 1 and 2. Competitive firms are unable to provide sufficient quantities of these goods. Non-excludability means that the firms are unable to set a fee for the use of the public goods that they provide, and hence can only cover their costs if the users make voluntary payments. This situation gives rise to the **free rider problem.** Each user is confronted with the following choice: he can contribute to the provision of the public good and enjoy its benefits, or he can keep his money in his pockets and enjoy its

---

[2] The satellite transmissions are non-rivalrous, but the electronic gadget that receives and interprets the signal is not. If the signals are available to you on your yacht near Fiji, they are also available to me on my yacht near Tahiti. However, your possession of a receiver does me no good whatsoever.

[3] The American military initially reserved for its own use a part of the satellite signal, so that military units could determine their positions more accurately than members of the public could. Very precise positioning is a good from which potential users can be, and at one time were, excluded.

benefits anyway. Not surprisingly, people faced with this choice prove to be reluctant to part with their money.[4] Total contributions are relatively small, so only a small quantity of the public good is ultimately provided. Every person would be better off if everyone could be forced to give a little more. Governments, when they finance the provision of public goods through taxes, are therefore engaging in a socially beneficial form of coercion.

While the under-provision of public goods takes its most dramatic form when the public good is "pure," the provision of less-than-pure public goods is also problematic. If a good is non-rivalrous but excludable, a private provider of that good can only remain in business by charging the users a positive price. This practice results in the exclusion of some potential users. The provider's interests are at odds with those of society, because society's welfare is maximized by excluding no one.

If the good is congestible and excludable, by contrast, society's welfare is maximized by excluding some users from each facility. Decisions about exclusions and the facility size must then be made simultaneously.

1.2.2 Externalities

An externality can occur when a person's utility is affected by another person's consumption or by a firm's production activities. As well, an externality can occur when a firm's profits are affected by another firm's production activities or by an individual's consumption. However, not all such interactions constitute externalities. An externality only occurs when appropriate monetary compensation is not made. Appropriate compensation induces the generator of the externality to take into account the effects of his actions on others, so that he curtails harmful activities and extends beneficial ones. For example,

- You are harmed if your neighbour throws noisy parties that prevent you from sleeping. Your neighbour is not required to compensate you for the harm done to you, so he doesn't take your interests into account – the parties are long and loud. An externality is present here.
- The small stores at a shopping mall benefit from the presence of a large department store. The department store draws customers to the mall, creating additional business for the small stores. The leases signed by the stores reflect this benefit: the department store often pays no rent, and the small stores pay higher rent than they would pay in the absence of the department store. This arrangement shifts the burden of rent from the department store to the small stores, so that the department store implicitly receives compensation. No externality occurs.

Although externalities can occur only if assumption 1 is violated, violations of some of the other assumptions can also be important.

---

[4] In North America, and perhaps elsewhere, this phenomenon is familiar to us from the fund-raising campaigns of public television and radio stations.

Coase [17] has emphasized the importance of clearly defined property rights in determining appropriate compensation. Suppose, for example, that two farmers are drawing water from the same river. If the up-river farmer increases his water consumption by so much that the down-river farmer cannot obtain sufficient water for his needs, who should pay whom? If the up-river farmer has the right to draw as much water as he likes, the down-river farmer must bribe the up-river farmer to induce him to take less water. If the down-river farmer has the right to sufficient water, the up-river farmer must compensate him for his loss. But if the property rights are not clearly established (i.e., if the farmers cannot agree as to whose rights have been violated), compensation is unlikely to be paid and an externality is likely to occur.

Compensation will not necessarily be paid even when property rights are clearly established. Suppose that a firm pollutes the air, to the detriment of everyone living downwind. Suppose also that the firm has the property rights. An externality is prevented only if people band together to bribe the firm to reduce its emissions; but if the harm done to each person is small relative to the individual cost of negotiating the bribe, no one will bother to negotiate. Compensation will not be paid and an externality will occur. Thus, violations of assumptions 2 and 5 can also play a role in externalities.

Another interpretation of externalities is that they occur because some markets are missing. A steel producer knows the market price of steel, so it can evaluate the reward for additional production. It also knows the market prices of labour, iron ore, and fuel, so it knows *some* of the costs of additional production. It increases production if the reward exceeds the sum of these costs. However, one of the costs of additional production is a decline in air purity. Since there is no market for air purity, the firm is not forced to bear the cost of degrading the atmosphere, and does not include this cost in its profit calculation. Under this interpretation of events, an externality occurs in part because assumption 3 is violated. While most non-economists would regard this view of pollution as exceedingly baroque, some economists believe that it is a useful way to analyze the problem. They argue that externalities can be eliminated by constructing artificial markets in which emissions permits – entitlements to pollute – are traded.[5]

Some externalities, such as the noisy party and the polluting firm, are easily recognized. Other externalities are less readily recognized. Two important examples of well-disguised externalities are common property exploitation and co-ordination failure.

Common Property Resources

A common property resource is a good which is not owned by anyone. Individuals acquire ownership of a common property resource simply by taking it. Self-interested individuals are likely to take as much as they can as quickly as they can. Early photographs of the Oklahoma oil fields show a virtual forest of oil derricks erected by competitors

---

[5] These markets are artificial in the sense that the general public does not participate in these markets, but is instead represented by the government. Chapter 7 describes the workings of permit markets.

attempting to gain a greater share of the oil. The "land rush" depicted in so many Hollywood westerns is another example of this kind of behaviour.

In the case of renewable common property resources, the rush to be first can lead to the exhaustion of the resource. Many fisheries have been commercially depleted, and others are threatened with depletion. The commercial values of the whale, the rhinoceros, the elephant, and the sea turtle are great enough to threaten these species with extinction.

Co-ordination Failures

Co-ordination failures are a particular form of externality, and therefore involve a violation of assumption 1. They are treated here as a separate phenomenon only because they have some distinctive and interesting features.

In an efficient market economy, market prices convey everything that each economic agent needs to know about every other economic agent. Consider, for example, the markets for consumer goods. Each consumer believes that he can buy at the prevailing price as much of each good as he likes, and this belief is validated by the fact that he can, in fact, buy exactly the goods that he wants. Each firm believes that it can sell at the prevailing price as many units of goods as it wants, and is in fact able to do so. The transactions that consumers and firms want to make depend only upon prices, and they are able to carry them out.

Keynesian economics argues that this picture of the workings of the market economy is deficient. The quantity of goods that consumers want to buy is determined by their income, which is in turn determined by the quantity of labour that they can sell. Similarly, the quantity of labour that firms buy is determined by the quantity of goods that they can sell. A recession, the Keynesians argue, is a situation in which consumers do not buy goods because they cannot sell labour, and firms do not buy labour because they cannot sell goods. If this view is correct, each agent's behaviour is influenced by quantities as well as prices.

Similarly, an agent's decision to trade in a market might be influenced by his estimate of the probability that other agents will trade in that market. Multiple equilibria are then possible. There could be an equilibrium in which few people trade because few people are expected to trade, and another in which many people trade because many people are expected to trade. Since trading is mutually beneficial, welfare is higher when more people trade.

1.2.3 Imperfect Competition

A competitive firm expands its production until the price of the last unit of output is just equal to the market price of the resources needed to produce that unit. If the other firms in the economy are also competitive, the market price of these resources is just equal to the market value of the other goods that could have been produced with these same resources. In these circumstances, consumers learn about their options by examining prices. If a good's price is high, they are warned that consumption of this good requires them to forgo other goods that they themselves believe to be valuable. If a good's price is low, they are told that the consumption of this good requires them to forgo something, but not something of any great value. Consumers use these signals to decide which goods they should consume; specifically, they consume expensive goods sparingly and cheap goods freely. This mechanism – Adam Smith's "invisible hand" – causes the economy's limited resources to be allocated to the production of the goods that consumers most want.

This mechanism tends to break down if some firms are large enough to appreciably affect the prices at which goods are bought and sold. The most extreme case is monopoly, in which there is only one seller of a particular good. The price set by the monopolist is greater than the good's marginal cost of production (i.e., greater than the value of the goods that must be given up to allow its production). Consumers respond by buying fewer units of the good than they would if its price reflected its marginal cost of production.

Perfect competition is the only form of market organization under which a good's price is certain to be equal to its marginal cost. Hence, any violation of assumption 4 is likely to cause the free market outcome to diverge from the competitive outcome.

Arguably, imperfect competition is a symptom rather than a cause. The presence of imperfect competition suggests that something has prevented sustained competition among firms. One possibility is that production is characterized by increasing returns to scale, meaning that output more than doubles when the use of all factors of production is doubled. The largest firm is then able to produce and sell goods more cheaply than its competitors, and will eventually drive them out of business. Once it is alone in the market, it will behave as all monopolies do, restricting its output and raising its selling price. A second possibility is that entry into the industry involves such high set-up costs that potential competitors are unable to raise the necessary financial capital.[6] Finally, it might be that a necessary patent is possessed by only one firm, ensuring its position as a monopolist.

1.2.4 Asymmetric Information

The price system is an important mechanism because it is **decentralized,** that is, because every economic decision is made by the people or firms directly affected by that decision. Each farmer knows which crops grow best on his own land, and he decides which crops will be grown there. Each firm knows which goods can be produced at its manufacturing plants, and the various ways in which these goods can be produced, and it makes decisions on exactly these issues. Each consumer knows his own tastes better than anyone else, and decides which goods and services he will purchase. All parties base their own actions on their own information and their knowledge of market prices.

---

[6] High set-up costs can only lead to imperfect competition if there is some flaw in the capital markets that makes lenders unwilling to provide the necessary capital. Asymmetric information, which is discussed in the next section, can give rise to this kind of behaviour.

Consequently, they do not need to communicate detailed information about tastes and production processes to each other.

The value of the price system lies precisely in its ability to exploit information that is not widely known, but it can only do so if two essential kinds of information are known to everyone.

First, the market participants must be equally well informed about the *nature* of the good being traded. The purchase of a new computer, for example, would be a relatively simple matter if computers could be completely described by a small number of characteristics, say, processor speed and disc capacity. Computers with a particular speed and capacity would then differ in price only because their manufacturers were more or less efficient. A manufacturer which managed its inventory better, or more conscientiously sought out better deals on components, could offer its product at a lower price. Everyone would buy from this manufacturer, and the less efficient manufacturers would ultimately be driven from the market. The price system would work as it should. However, not all of the characteristics of computers are readily observable, and hence price differences are not easily understood. An inefficient producer might match the low prices of his more efficient competitors by substituting low quality components for higher quality components. If consumers were unable to discover the difference between these products, the less efficient producers would not be driven from the market.

Second, the market participants must be equally well informed about the *circumstances* under which the good is traded. Here are two situations that satisfy this condition:

- We meet on a rainy day, and you have an umbrella while I do not. I might offer to buy your umbrella, and after some haggling, you might agree to sell it. This trade would be mutually advantageous, in the sense that each of us would place a higher value on the thing received than on the thing given up. Both of us know the circumstances of the trade (specifically, that the person without the umbrella will get wet), and our haggling establishes that my aversion to getting wet is greater than yours.
- It's not raining when we meet, but the clouds look threatening. Neither of us is certain that an umbrella will be needed, but we are looking at the same grey skies, so we are equally well informed about that possibility. Any trade that occurs between us will again be mutually advantageous.

There are many situations in which the participants are not equally well informed, and the market outcome in these situations might not be efficient. Trades which are mutually advantageous might not take place, and trades that take place might not be mutually advantageous. Suppose that you have a toothache. You go the dentist believing that you need minor dental work, but the dentist instead suggests some major (and expensive) reconstruction. How do you know that this work actually needs to be done? How do you know that he is not simply creating a little extra business for himself? If you agree to the work, and if the work is largely unnecessary, the trade between you and your dentist is not mutually beneficial. If you are suspicious of his motives and refuse his advice, and the work is necessary, a trade which would be mutually beneficial does not take place. Similar situations arise when you deal with doctors, lawyers, stock brokers, and garage mechanics. They have better information than you do, but you might be uncertain as to whether they are advancing your interests or their own.

1.3 INFORMATION AND THE SECOND THEOREM

The second theorem argues that the government, if it wishes to achieve a more equitable distribution of income, need not concern itself with the manner in which individual goods are allocated within the society. Instead, the government need only transfer income from the economically advantaged to the economically disadvantaged. The price system, operating in the wake of these transfers, will ensure that the allocation of goods within the society is efficient.

This statement of the theorem hides the complexity of the government's task. The transfers cannot be based upon market behaviour. Gearing an individual's transfer to his income or education, or to the frequency of his visits to Palm Springs, would alter his behaviour in ways that prevent the price system from generating an efficient outcome. Instead the transfers must be based upon the innate characteristics that determine each individual's success in the market economy. This requirement is sometimes easy to fulfill. People with certain mental or physical disabilities are unlikely to be successful in the market economy, and should be the recipients of transfers. It is, in other instances, impossible to fulfill. The distinctions between moderately successful people and very successful people might not be apparent to themselves, let alone to the government.

This informational requirement is so severe that governments are, in practise, forced to impose transfers that are partly based upon market behaviour. Taxes, for example, are levied on the purchases of goods and the receipt of income. Welfare payments are made to those who have no other source of income. The claim of the second theorem, that income redistribution does not adversely affect the efficiency of the economy, cannot be accepted without reservation under these circumstances. Indeed, the design of redistributive programs is strongly influenced by the need to reduce the associated efficiency loss.[7]

1.4 THE USEFULNESS OF THE TWO THEOREMS

Although the logic of the two theorems is impeccable, they are premised upon conditions quite unlike those that exist in actual economies. It follows that their claims have no obvious applicability to the economies in which we live. Why should we bother with them?

First, they alert us to the potential of the price system. Solving the fundamental economic problem – what goods are produced how and who gets them – requires a

---

[7] The size and nature of the efficiency loss is also an important feature of the political debate over redistribution. The rich often argue that the poor "exploit" redistributive programs. The poor, on the other hand, imagine that the incomes of the rich accrue to them without particular effort or self-sacrifice, so that they can be taxed away without adverse consequences.

staggering amount of information. Thousands of goods are produced for the benefit of millions of consumers. The information required to produce any one of these goods is enormous, and a complete description of the preferences of any one person, under each of the contingencies that he faces, is simply not imaginable. The first theorem tell us that this information does not have to be collected, that there is a decentralized system that yields a solution to this problem.

This solution is, of course, imperfect. Every society is faced with a choice: it can try to patch up the problems that arise under the price system, or it can jettison the price system in favour of some other economic system. Western societies generally concluded that, whatever its flaws, the price system is likely to be better than any realistic alternative. They adopted a "grease is cheaper than parts" philosophy, and the twentieth-century history of eastern Europe suggests that this decision was a wise one.

The second thing that the theorems tell us is the circumstances under which patches are going to be required. Specifically, the first theorem describes the minimal conditions under which competitive markets give rise to an efficient outcome. Any violation of these conditions will lead to inefficiencies, so policies must be designed to deal with the consequences of these violations. This view of the market economy suggests that, at the very least, governments should provide public goods, regulate externalities and maintain the competitiveness of markets.

Third, the observation that market solutions are often good ones suggests that problems can sometimes be fixed by creating artificial markets. Externalities, in particular, might be regulated by creating permit markets.

Finally, the theorems provide the context for a serious consideration of income redistribution. The second theorem describes the conditions under which any desired distribution of income can be obtained without compromising the efficiency of the economy. These conditions will not be satisfied in an actual economy, so redistributive policies will have efficiency effects. An understanding of why redistribution affects economic efficiency will ultimately allow us to design better redistributive policies.

1.5 THE ROLE OF THE GOVERNMENT

It is one thing to use the two theorems to discover the things that need to be fixed, and another thing to fix them. The task of correcting market failures generally falls to the government. In some instances, the government need only regulate the behaviour of the private sector. Competition policy and environmental policy are two examples of the government's regulatory function. In other instances, the government involves itself in the production and distribution of goods and services. There are many kinds of pure and congestible public goods, and many of these are provided by governments.

Governments are also involved in the provision of some kinds of **private goods,** that is, goods that are completely rivalrous in consumption or nearly so. Among the private goods commonly provided by governments are health care, education, and housing. A government might provide these goods to correct a market failure. The allocation of health care and health care insurance, for example, is profoundly affected by asymmetric information, and a government might believe that it can achieve a better allocation of these goods if it provides them itself. More commonly, however, a government which provides private goods is responding to a failure of the second theorem rather than the first. This theorem argues that, under certain conditions, a more equitable distribution of income can be achieved without incurring a loss of economic efficiency. The requisite conditions are, however, unlikely to be satisfied. In practice, redistributive policies often entail a loss of economic efficiency. The redistributive policies that minimize this efficiency loss often involve the transfer of private goods as well as cash.

The government can reduce efficiency losses but cannot entirely eliminate them. Its effectiveness is limited by several factors:

- The government must raise revenue to cover the cost of policies that increase economic efficiency. Unfortunately, the act of raising revenue distorts the price system, creating further efficiency losses, and these efficiency losses generally rise with the amount of revenue raised. The social benefit of an additional government policy will, at some point, be offset by the social cost of raising the revenue required to implement the policy. If the government expands the scope of its policies beyond this point, social welfare will fall rather than rise.

- If people and firms were to voluntarily comply with government regulations, appropriate regulations would generate a high level of social welfare. They are often unwilling do so, however, so scarce resources must be used up to monitor their behaviour and punish those who fail to comply. Since these resources could have been used in other socially valuable ways, social welfare is lower than it could have been.

- Asymmetry of information creates problems in some private sector transactions that the government cannot remedy through public policy.

- One of the problems of asymmetric information, the **principal-agent problem**, might well cause governments to behave in ways that do not advance social welfare. This problem arises when a principal employs an agent to act on his behalf. If the principal and the agent have different objectives, and if the principal cannot perfectly observe the agent's actions, the agent will sometimes choose actions that advance his own interests rather than those of his principal. Such situations often lead to irreducible economic inefficiencies. The relationship between government and society is one of those situations. Governments ought to try to maximize social welfare, but the people who constitute government (elected officials, the civil service, and the administrators of government-owned firms) have their own objectives – such as power, wealth, and prestige. To the extent that they can pursue these objectives, rather than society's objectives, without being held accountable for it, they will.

These considerations suggest that the government's actions won't result in the best of all possible worlds – but they can improve on the one that we would have in the absence of government.

Markets

The fundamental task of every economic system is to determine which goods are produced, how they are produced, and who gets them. Economists believe that a system of competitive markets tends to perform this task both cheaply and reasonably well. They recognize, however, that there are some situations in which competition generates unsatisfactory outcomes. In these situations (collectively known as **market failures**), government intervention can lead to better outcomes. The greater portion of this book is devoted to describing the various kinds of market failure and, where possible, the government policies that correct them.

This part of the book, however, deals with a more basic issue. What are the grounds for the economist's belief that competitive markets perform a vital function in our economy? Why are economists unwilling to accept government intervention in the market system unless some cogent justification can be given?

The next three chapters answer these questions through the study of two simple economies. The first economy is the exchange economy, in which existing goods are exchanged but no goods are produced. The second is the production economy, in which goods are both produced and exchanged. In each of these economies, two issues are examined:

- Which ways of allocating goods to people and (in the production economy) factors of production to firms are desirable?
- Which allocations occur when people and (in the production economy) firms trade in competitive markets?

The economist's endorsement of competitive markets follows from the finding that the competitive allocations are the same as the desirable allocations. The economist's acceptance of selective government intervention follows from their recognition that actual economies differ from these model economies in very important ways, and that the match between desirable allocations and competitive allocations is unlikely to occur in reality.

2

The Exchange Economy

Markets range in size and sophistication from neighbourhood flea markets to global currency markets, but every market exists for the same reason. Some exchanges of goods and services between two or more people are **mutually beneficial,** in the sense that they would raise the well-being of every party to the exchange. Markets are a mechanism through which people identify these trades and carry them out.

The simplest mutually beneficial trades involve only two people, for example, a dairy farmer and a poultry farmer who trade cheese for eggs. Underlying these trades is a **double coincidence of wants:** each person wants the goods that the other person is willing to give up. Double coincidences are relatively rare, and a mortician or divorce lawyer who relied upon them to furnish his table would not eat well.

The benefits from trade generally rise with the number of people who are potentially involved in each trade, for two reasons:

- Multilateral trade – trade involving more than two people – might be possible even when bilateral trade cannot occur. For example, if the poultry farmer does not want cheese, there can be no trade involving *only* the dairy farmer and the poultry farmer because there is no double coincidence of wants. A multilateral trade in which the dairy farmer gives his cheese to the barber, who cuts the hair of the poultry farmer, who provides eggs to the dairy farmer, might nevertheless be possible.
- Multilateral trade might be preferred to bilateral trade even when bilateral trade is possible. Suppose that the poultry farmer is willing to accept cheese in trade, but prefers the haircut. If the barber is prepared to trade a haircut for cheese, the multilateral deal offers greater benefits than the bilateral deal, because both the barber and the poultry farmer are better off.

The value of the market system lies in its ability to co-ordinate trades that potentially involve thousands, or hundreds of thousands, of people.

The trades that take place under the market system have these properties:

- Each person, having observed the market prices, decides what he will give up and what he will take. He is prevented from being too greedy by the requirement that he pay for what he takes, so that the market value of the things he takes cannot exceed the market value of the things he gives up.

- The individual decisions are co-ordinated by market prices. If the market participants as a group want too many units of some good, its market price rises, encouraging some people to ask for less and other people to offer more. If the market participants as a group want too few units of some good, its market price falls, inducing some people to ask for more and others to offer less. The market prices ultimately reached have the property that, for each good, the amount given up by some market participants is just equal to the amount taken by the rest.

These trades are generally so large and complex that no one person can identify all of the pieces of the trade. Our failure to apprehend the whole trade sometimes causes us to think of "buying and selling" as an activity different from "trading," but we should not do so.[1]

This chapter examines competitive markets in the context of the exchange economy, in which people seek to trade consumption goods that they already possess. It examines the desirable ways of allocating these goods, and the way in which competitive markets allocate them, and compares the two.

The exchange economy is, of course, much less complicated than any real economy. Its value is that it forces us to think about mutually beneficial trade, and in doing so, provides us with a framework that can be extended to more complex economies.

2.1 THE EDGEWORTH BOX

The **exchange economy** is the simplest of all economies: the people in this economy trade the goods that they already have but do not produce more goods. Furthermore, the exchange economy studied here is the simplest of all economies of this type. There are only two people, George and Harriet, and they possess quantities of only two goods, ale and bread.

An exchange economy's **endowment** is a list of the quantities of each good initially possessed by each person. Let's assume that George has $\overline{a}_G$ pints of ale and $\overline{b}_G$ loaves of bread, and that Harriet has $\overline{a}_H$ pints of ale and $\overline{b}_H$ loaves of bread. The endowment is then the list $(\overline{a}_G, \overline{b}_G, \overline{a}_H, \overline{b}_H)$. Since all of the goods in the economy are initially owned by either George or Harriet, the total quantity of ale, $\overline{a}$, is the sum of the quantities that they own:

$$\overline{a} = \overline{a}_G + \overline{a}_H \tag{2.1}$$

The total quantity of bread, $\overline{b}$, is also the sum of the quantities owned by George and

---

[1] The equivalence of these two concepts is apparent in the stock market. No one can sell a stock unless someone else is willing to buy it, and this simple observation has been responsible for some precipitous declines in stock prices. Similarly, no one can buy a stock unless someone else is willing to part with it.

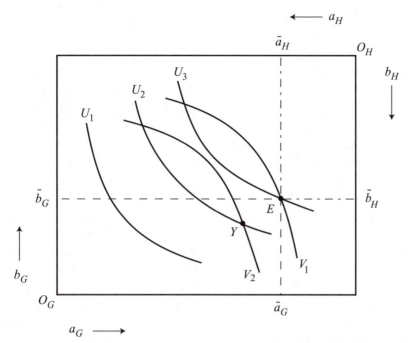

Figure 2.1: An Edgeworth Box. Ale is measured horizontally and bread is measured vertically. Quantities pertaining to George are measured from the bottom left corner, and quantities pertaining to Harriet are measured from the top right corner.

Harriet:

$$\overline{b} = \overline{b}_G + \overline{b}_H \tag{2.2}$$

Any way of dividing up these goods between George and Harriet is called an **allocation.** An allocation, therefore, is another list. It is the list (a_G, b_G, a_H, b_H), where a_G and a_H are the quantities of ale given to George and Harriet, and b_G and b_H are the quantities of bread given to George and Harriet. Every unit of the available goods must go to one of these two people, so

$$\overline{a} = a_G + a_H$$
$$\overline{b} = b_G + b_H$$

Note that the endowment is just a particular allocation: it is the initial allocation.

George and Harriet might decide to consume the goods with which they were endowed; but they might also decide to trade with each other, consuming instead the goods that they possess after trade has been completed. This kind of trading changes the allocation of goods, so that the ultimate allocation is not the same as the endowment.

The **Edgeworth Box** shows all of the possible allocations. This box appears in Figure 2.1. Its width is $\overline{a}$, the total quantity of ale in the economy, and quantities of ale will always be measured horizontally. Its height is $\overline{b}$, the total quantity of bread in the economy, and quantities of bread will always be measured vertically.

Every point in the box represents an allocation, and every allocation can be represented by a point in the box. This is a little bit surprising. A point plotted in a plane usually represents *two* numbers, the point's Cartesian co-ordinates. One of the co-ordinates is a distance measured along the horizontal axis, and the other is a distance measured along the vertical axis. However, a point in the box corresponds to an allocation, so it must represent *four* numbers (a_G, a_H, b_G, and b_H). We are able to infer all four numbers from the position of the point because fixing a_G (or b_G) determines a_H (or b_H) residually. All of the ale must go to someone, so a decision as to how much ale George gets is also a decision as to how much ale Harriet gets – she gets all the rest. Similarly, Harriet gets all of the bread that does not go to George.

Suppose, for example, that we want to find the allocation that corresponds to the point Y in Figure 2.1. George's share of each good is represented by a distance measured from the origin, O_G. The horizontal distance from O_G to Y is George's ale (a_G), and the vertical distance from O_G to Y is George's bread (b_G). Since the quantity of ale available is given by the width of the box, and since Harriet gets what George does not, Harriet's ale (a_H) is represented by the horizontal distance from Y to the right side of the box. Since the quantity of bread available is given by the height of the box, and since Harriet gets what George does not, Harriet's bread (b_H) is represented by the vertical distance from Y to the top of the box.

This procedure treats George and Harriet asymmetrically: Harriet's share of the goods is calculated as a residual and George's share is calculated directly. The same procedure can be used for both people if Harriet is given her own origin (O_H) at the top right corner of the box. Then, for each person and any allocation, the quantity of ale (bread) received by that person is the horizontal (vertical) distance between that person's origin and the point representing the allocation.

A **commodity bundle** for any person is a list showing the amount of each commodity possessed by that person. George's commodity bundle is (a_G, b_G) and Harriet's commodity bundle is (a_H, b_H). Taken together, these two commodity bundles constitute the allocation. Alternatively, each allocation corresponds to a particular commodity bundle for each person.

Indifference curves representing George's preferences over all of his commodity bundles can be drawn inside the box.[2] George's indifference map will have the usual properties because they are drawn with respect to a normal set of axes: the bottom of the box is an axis along which a_G is plotted, and the left side of the box is an axis along which b_G is plotted. Harriet's axes, however, have been rotated 180°. The a_H axis is the top of the box and runs from right to left; the b_H axis is the right side of the box and runs from top to bottom. When indifference curves representing Harriet's preferences over all of her commodity bundles are drawn into the box, these indifference curves will also be rotated 180°. If you find Harriet's indifference map a little puzzling, just rotate Figure 2.1 by 180° (i.e., turn the page upside down) and you will find that both Harriet's axes and Harriet's indifference map look absolutely normal.

---

[2] For a review of indifference curves, see the box on page 21.

A REVIEW OF INDIFFERENCE CURVES

Each person is assumed to have well-defined preferences over alternative commodity bundles. Given the choice between two commodity bundles (call them A and B), he is able to say that he would rather have A than B, would rather have B than A, or that he likes A and B equally well.

These preferences can be described by indifference curves. Each **indifference curve** consists of the commodity bundles that an individual believes to be equally good. Given any two indifference curves for the same person, that person prefers any commodity bundle lying on one of these curves to every commodity bundle lying on the other. Infinitely many indifference curves are needed to describe each person's preferences, and these curves are collectively known as the **indifference map**.

If there are only two goods, commodity bundles can be represented by points in the positive quadrant. If consuming more of either good makes the individual better off, the individual's indifference curve map, drawn in this quadrant, has the following properties:

1) Exactly one indifference curve passes through each point in the quadrant. (An immediate implication of this property is that indifference curves cannot cross.)
2) Indifference curves are downward sloping.
3) Any commodity bundle on an indifference curve farther from the origin (i.e., the commodity bundle containing zero units of each good) is preferred to every commodity bundle lying on an indifference curve closer to the origin.
4) As well, indifference curves are generally imagined to be bowed toward the origin, indicating that the individual prefers balanced commodity bundles to unbalanced ones.

It is assumed in this chapter that George's and Harriet's indifference maps have the basic properties of indifference maps, and two others as well:

- Each person is assumed to prefer any bundle containing at least a little of both goods to any bundle containing only one of the goods. This assumption means that George's indifference curves don't bump into the bottom and left-hand side of the box, and that Harriet's indifference curves don't bump into the top and right-hand side of the box. The allocations that interest us – the desirable allocations and the competitive allocations – then lie in the interior of the box. This assumption is not essential, and is introduced only because it simplifies the discussion.[3]
- Each person's indifference curves are assumed to be bowed toward that person's origin. A person whose indifference curves have this property is said to have **convex preferences.** The convexity of preferences plays an important role in the analysis, and some of the consequences of abandoning it are discussed in the box on page 37.

---

[3] Question 4 at the end of this chapter examines the complexities that arise when this assumption is violated.

In summary, the main ideas underlying the Edgeworth box are these:

- Each point in the box represents an allocation, that is to say, a commodity bundle for each person. Since the total quantity of each commodity is fixed, one person's commodity bundle cannot be changed without changing the other person's commodity bundle.
- Each person's preferences over his or her commodity bundles (and therefore over the allocations) can be described by an indifference map drawn in the box. Each person's welfare rises as he or she switches to commodity bundles lying on indifference curves farther away from his or her origin. In Figure 2.1, for example, Harriet prefers Y to E but George prefers E to Y.

2.2 PARETO OPTIMALITY

Economists generally argue that an allocation is a good one if it satisfies the Pareto optimality criterion. It is perhaps easier to understand what is not Pareto optimal than what is Pareto optimal. An allocation is **not Pareto optimal** (i.e., it is not a good allocation) if there is another allocation at which at least one person is better off and no one is worse off. An allocation is Pareto optimal if no alternative allocation with these properties exists. That is, an allocation is **Pareto optimal** if there is no alternative allocation at which one person is better off and no one is worse off.

The Pareto optimality test provides an "incomplete ordering" of the allocations. It partially orders the allocations because it divides them into two groups, those that are Pareto optimal and those that are not. However, the test does not allow us to rank the allocations within each group.[4]

Suppose, for example, that George and Harriet live in an economy in which there is only one commodity, army surplus rations, and that there are 100 units of these. It is easy to list all of the possible allocations: give n units to George and $100 - n$ units to Harriet, where n is an integer between 0 and 100. Which of these allocations are Pareto optimal? Suppose that we are initially giving 10 units to George and 90 units to Harriet. Harriet can be made better off only by increasing the number of units of rations given to her, but as the additional units must be taken away from George, Harriet can only be made better off by making George worse off. Similarly, George can only be made better off by transferring units of rations from Harriet to George, which makes Harriet worse off. Since neither Harriet nor George can be made better off without the other person being made worse off, the initial allocation (10 units to George and 90 to Harriet) is Pareto optimal. The same argument can be made for any other allocation, so *every* allocation is Pareto optimal. In this example, the Pareto optimality criterion provides no guidance in choosing an allocation because it places every allocation in the same group, the group of Pareto optimal allocations.

The Pareto optimality criterion has nothing to do with fairness or equity. We might agree that splitting the rations equally would be better than giving all of the rations

---

[4] By contrast, a "complete ordering" places any number of items in an exact sequence. An example of a complete ordering is alphabetization, which we use to uniquely order words.

to George, but the Pareto optimality criterion does not distinguish between these two allocations: both allocations pass the test.

Nevertheless, this criterion does perform a very useful function. It asks whether there remain any "free" ways of increasing someone's welfare, that is, any ways of increasing that person's welfare without harming anyone else. If such an action exists, it should certainly be undertaken. Only when all of these "free" actions have been taken, and none remain unexploited, is the Pareto optimality test satisfied. Economists say that an economy in which some "free" actions have not yet been undertaken is **inefficient** (because we could do better). An economy in which no "free" actions remain is said to be **efficient.**

2.2.1 Applying the Pareto Criterion: An Example

Suppose that there are three people (let's call them Fred, Wilma, and Barney) and that there are four possible allocations (call them W, X, Y, and Z). Each of the allocations lists the commodity bundle that will be given to each person. Since the people have different tastes, and since any one allocation can treat the three people quite differently,[5] they might rank the allocations quite differently. Imagine that their rankings are represented by the following lists:

Fred	Wilma	Barney
W	X, W, Z	X, Z
X, Y	Y	W
Z		Y

Fred's list is to be interpreted as follows: Fred likes W best; he likes X and Y equally well, but he likes each of them less than W; he likes Z least. Wilma's and Barney's lists are interpreted in a similar fashion.

Remember that not everyone can have his or her first choice. An allocation specifies a commodity bundle for each person, and we must choose a single allocation – not one for each person. If Fred gets his first choice, Barney cannot get his first choice, and vice versa. The role of the Pareto criterion in this situation is to tell us which compromises are good ones and which are not.

Remember also that our objective is to divide the allocations into two groups – those that are Pareto optimal and those that are not – so we will have to test each allocation separately.

Let's begin with W. Is it Pareto optimal or not? To decide this question, we must ask another:

Is there another allocation at which someone is better off and no one is worse off?

---

[5] It might be that some allocations treat the agents quite equitably while others do not (for example, allocation Z might assign very generous commodity bundles to Wilma and Barney, and a scant one to Fred).

W is not Pareto optimal if the answer to this question is "Yes," and *W is* Pareto optimal if the answer to this question is "No." The only alternatives to *W* are *X*, *Y*, and *Z*. Choosing any of these alternatives would make Fred worse off, so the answer to the above question is "No." We therefore conclude that *W* is Pareto optimal.

Is *X* Pareto optimal? We must again ask the question set out above; *X* is not Pareto optimal if the answer is "Yes" and it is Pareto optimal if the answer is "No." The alternatives to *X* are *W*, *Y*, and *Z*; and choosing any of these alternatives would make someone worse off. (Choosing *W* or *Y* would make Barney worse off and choosing *Z* would make Fred worse off.) The answer is "No" so *X* is Pareto optimal.

Now consider *Y*. The alternatives to *Y* are *W*, *X*, and *Z*. Choosing *X* rather than *Y* makes Wilma better off and makes no one worse off (Fred is equally well off and Barney is better off). Since there is an alternative allocation (*X*) at which someone would be better off and no one would be worse off (i.e., since the answer to the question is "Yes"), *Y* is not Pareto optimal.[6]

Finally, consider *Z*. The alternatives to *Z* are *W*, *X*, and *Y*. Choosing *X* rather than *Z* would make Fred better off without harming anyone (Wilma and Barney would be as well off under *X* as they are under *Z*). Since there is an alternative to *Z* at which someone would be better off and no one would be worse off, *Z* is not Pareto optimal.

In summary, *Y* and *Z* would be poor choices. Choosing either of these allocations would mean that we would be forgoing the opportunity to make someone better off without harming anyone. *W* and *X* are acceptable compromises: choosing either of these allocations would mean that we are not forgoing any such opportunities.

2.2.2 Pareto Optimal Allocations in the Exchange Economy

In our exchange economy, what is Pareto optimal and what is not?

The allocation denoted *X* in Figure 2.2 is not Pareto optimal: there are many alternative allocations such that at least one person is better off and neither person is worse off. We can prove that *X* is not Pareto optimal by finding one of these allocations, and this is easily done. George is indifferent between *X* and any other allocation lying on the indifference curve U_1, and he prefers to *X* any allocation lying above U_1. Harriet is indifferent between *X* and any other allocation lying on the indifference curve V_1, and she prefers to *X* any allocation lying above V_1. (When I refer to an allocation "above" someone's indifference curve, I mean an allocation offering that person a higher level of welfare. For George, these allocations are also above the indifference curve in the spatial sense of the word. For Harriet, these allocations are above the indifference curve in the spatial sense when the page is rotated 180°, so that we are looking at Harriet's indifference curves as we usually do.) These two indifference curves form the boundary of a lens-shaped area, shown in Figure 2.2 as a shaded region. Any allocation in the

---

[6]   In fact there are two alternative allocations with the necessary properties: choosing *W* rather than *Y* would make each agent better off. However, the existence of even one such allocation implies that *Y* is not Pareto optimal, so once we have found one, we can stop looking.

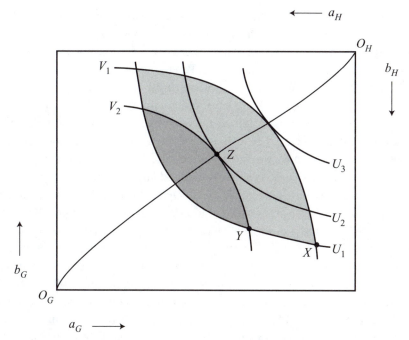

Figure 2.2: Pareto Optimality in the Edgeworth Box. The allocation Z is Pareto optimal, but the allocations X and Y are not.

interior of this area is preferred by both people to the allocation X. Any allocation on one of the boundaries is preferred by one person to the allocation X, and is thought to be just as good as X by the other person. Thus, every allocation inside this lens-shaped area or on its boundary is an alternative allocation that makes one person better off without making the other person worse off. It follows that the allocation X is not Pareto optimal.

Since we can make one person (or both) better off without making anyone worse off, let's do it. Specifically, let's change the allocation from X to Y, giving Harriet all of the benefits of the change. Is the new allocation Pareto optimal? It is not, because there are again alternative allocations which make one person better off without making the other person worse off. These alternative allocations are contained in a new lens-shaped area (darkly shaded in Figure 2.2) bounded by the indifference curves that pass through the new allocation Y.

Clearly, an allocation is not Pareto optimal if the indifference curves passing through it form one of these lens-shaped areas. There are, however, allocations at which the two indifference curves are tangent to each other, so that no lens is formed. Every allocation of this kind is Pareto optimal.

One such allocation is Z, and we can prove that it is Pareto optimal by showing that there are no alternative allocations which make one person better off without making the other worse off. To make Harriet better off, we must choose an allocation lying above (in our peculiar sense of the word) Harriet's indifference curve V_2; but every allocation that lies above V_2 also lies below George's initial indifference curve U_2, so that George would be made worse off. To make George better off, we must choose an allocation that lies above U_2; but every allocation that lies above U_2 lies below V_2, so that Harriet would be made worse off. Since we cannot make either person better off without making the other worse off, the original allocation (Z) is Pareto optimal.

Each of Harriet's (infinitely many) indifference curves is tangent to exactly one of George's indifference curves, so there are infinitely many Pareto optimal allocations. These allocations form a locus of points extending from one origin to the other. This locus is often called the **efficiency locus,** because every allocation on the locus is efficient. However, they do not all have the same welfare implications. A movement along the locus toward O_H causes George's welfare to rise and Harriet's welfare to fall.

There is another way to characterize the efficiency locus. Let the **marginal rate of substitution** (MRS) be the amount of bread needed to exactly compensate someone for the loss of one unit of ale. Alternatively, one unit of ale is exact compensation for the loss of MRS units of bread. ("Exact compensation" means that the compensation returns the person to the level of welfare attained prior to the loss of the specified goods.) Each person's marginal rate of substitution varies with his commodity bundle: the more bread and less ale he has, the more reluctant he will be to give up ale in exchange for bread. The marginal rate of substitution associated with a particular commodity bundle is equal to the negative of the slope of the indifference curve as it passes through that commodity bundle.[7]

The efficiency locus consists of all the points at which one of George's indifference curves is tangent to one of Harriet's indifference curves. Since two curves have the same slope at any point of tangency, the efficiency locus also consists of all of the points at which George's and Harriet's indifference curves have the same slope. Equivalently, it consists of all the points at which

$$MRS_G = MRS_H$$

where MRS_G and MRS_H are George's and Harriet's marginal rates of substitution.

2.3 COMPETITIVE EQUILIBRIUM

Economists use the concept of competitive equilibrium to describe the consequences of trading in competitive markets. They imagine a system of markets with these properties:

- Each good is traded in a single market. The participants in that market believe that they are able to buy or sell as much of the good as they like at the prevailing price.
- Each participant, having observed the market prices, tries to carry out the trades that would make him as well off as possible.

A **competitive equilibrium** has been reached if the prevailing price in each market "clears" that market, in the sense that each trader is able to make his preferred trade.

---

[7] For example, in Figure 2.1, George's marginal rate of substitution when his commodity bundle is $(\overline{a}_G, \overline{b}_G)$ is equal to the negative of the slope of U_3 evaluated at E.

Each trader's belief that he can buy or sell as much as he likes at the current prices is then confirmed by his market experience. No trader walks away dissatisfied, unable to sell the goods that he had intended to sell, or unable to buy the goods that he had hoped to buy.

We are accustomed to thinking about market prices as money prices, but we can equally well think of prices as relative prices. A **relative price** measures the price of a good in units of another good.[8] In an economy in which there are many goods, a complete set of relative prices is obtained by choosing one good to be the **numeraire** (i.e., the measuring stick), and expressing the prices of the other goods in units of the numeraire. Competitive equilibrium determines only relative prices.[9]

There are two goods in our exchange economy. Let bread be the numeraire, so that the only relative price to be determined is the price of a pint of ale measured in loaves of bread. If this price is p, someone purchasing a pint of ale must pay p loaves of bread, and someone selling a pint of ale will receive p loaves of bread.

George and Harriet are endowed with particular commodity bundles. Trade in organized markets allows them to move away from these commodity bundles, to commodity bundles that they like better. We must consider two issues. First, which commodity bundles could George and Harriet get by trading in organized markets? Second, which of these commodity bundles do George and Harriet want most? These issues will be addressed in turn.

The commodity bundles (a_G, b_G) that George can attain through trade at a given price p are represented by a **budget constraint.** George's budget constraint, if plotted in the (a_G, b_G) positive quadrant, has these properties:

- His budget constraint passes through the point $(\overline{a}_G, \overline{b}_G)$. George is endowed with this bundle, so he consumes it if he does not trade.
- His budget constraint has slope $-p$. He gets p loaves of bread for every unit of ale that he gives up, and he gets a unit of ale for every p loaves of bread that he gives up.

Since the a_G and b_G axes form the bottom and left-hand sides of the Edgeworth box, George's budget constraint – or to be more exact, a part of it – can be plotted within the box.[10] It appears in Figure 2.3 as the line segment MN. George acquires commodity

---

[8] Relative prices seem like an abstraction to us, but in most places for most of recorded history, some commodity – most notably, gold – has been used as money. When a commodity circulates as money, money prices *are* relative prices.

[9] Implicit in any set of money prices is a set of relative prices. For example, if a pint of ale sells for $2 and a loaf of bread sells for $1, the price of ale measured in bread is 2 (because you must give up two loaves of bread to obtain a pint of ale). The **quantity theory of money** argues that money prices are proportional to the quantity of money in circulation. An increase in the quantity of money raises all money prices, but leaves the underlying relative prices unchanged. If so, relative prices can be determined without reference to money prices.

[10] George believes that, if he wished to do so, he could sell ale for bread until his endowment of ale is exhausted, or that he could sell bread for ale until his endowment of bread is exhausted. Consequently, his budget constraint extends to the a_G and b_G axes. It will frequently be the case that only a part of this budget constraint is contained within the box. That part will be referred to as his budget constraint, even though it is in fact not the entire budget constraint.

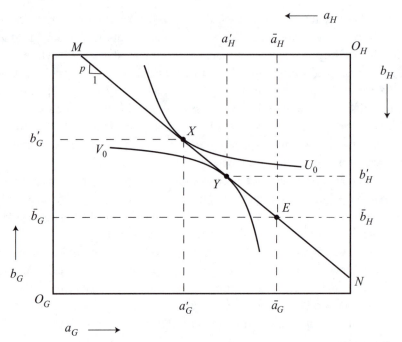

Figure 2.3: This Price is not Market-Clearing. George wishes to consume the commodity bundle X and Harriet wishes to consume the commodity bundle Y. George wants to sell more ale than Harriet wants to buy.

bundles on the segment EN by giving up bread to get more ale, and he acquires commodity bundles on the segment EM by giving up ale to get more bread.

Similarly, Harriet's budget constraint shows all of the commodity bundles (a_H, b_H) that she can attain through trade at a given price p. If plotted in the (a_H, b_H) positive quadrant, it has these properties:

- It contains the bundle $(\bar{a}_H, \bar{b}_H)$ because she can choose not to trade.
- It is a line with slope $-p$ because she gets p loaves of bread for every unit of ale that she gives up, and she gets a unit of ale for every p loaves of bread that she gives up.

Part or all of Harriet's budget constraint can also be plotted in the box. (It is, of course, plotted with respect to her own axis.) In Figure 2.3, it is represented by the line segment MN. Although the *same line* represents *both* budget constraints, the effects of trade are reversed for Harriet. She reaches points on the segment EM by giving up bread to get more ale, and she reaches points on the segment EN by giving up ale to get more bread.

George believes that he can buy or sell as much ale as he likes at the price p. Of all the attainable commodity bundles, the one that he will actually try to obtain is the one that makes him as well off as possible. This commodity bundle is represented by the point X, at which George's budget constraint is tangent to one of his indifference curves.[11] It contains a'_G pints of ale and b'_G loaves of bread. To obtain it, George must sell $\overline{a}_G - a'_G$ units of ale for $b'_G - \overline{b}_G$ units of bread.

Harriet also believes that she can buy or sell as much as she likes at the price p. Her best attainable commodity bundle is Y, at which there is a tangency between her budget constraint and one of her indifference curves. This bundle contains a'_H pints of ale and b'_H loaves of bread. To obtain it, Harriet must sell $\overline{b}_H - b'_H$ units of bread for $a'_H - \overline{a}_H$ units of ale.

Given these choices, is the economy in a competitive equilibrium? That is, is the prevailing price one at which each person's desired trades can be carried out?

George and Harriet are the only two people in the economy, so each of them can only buy what the other is willing to sell, and each of them can only sell what the other is willing to buy. An examination of Figure 2.3 shows that their desired trades cannot be carried out. George wants to buy bread and Harriet wants to sell it, but she does not want to sell as much as George wants to buy. Harriet wants to buy ale and George wants to sell it, but Harriet does not want to buy as much as George wants to sell. There is an excess demand for bread and an excess supply of ale, so Figure 2.3 does not portray a competitive equilibrium.

Now consider Figure 2.4, which shows the choices made by George and Harriet at a *different* relative price.[12] At this price, Harriet wants to sell $\overline{b}_H - b^*_H$ loaves of bread for $a^*_H - \overline{a}_H$ pints of ale and George wants to sell $\overline{a}_G - a^*_G$ pints of ale for $b^*_G - \overline{b}_G$ loaves of bread. An examination of Figure 2.4 shows that Harriet wants to buy exactly the quantity of ale that George wants to sell, and that she wants to sell exactly the quantity of bread that George wants to buy. This price "clears" the market in the sense that George and Harriet are able to undertake their desired trades. Figure 2.4 portrays a competitive equilibrium.

A comparison of these two figures shows the difference between a price that clears the market and one that does not clear the market. Every point in the Edgeworth box represents an allocation, that is, a way of dividing the existing goods between George and Harriet. One person's choice of a commodity bundle necessarily determines the entire allocation. When George is confronted with the budget constraint in Figure 2.3, he wants to change the allocation from E to X. Harriet, confronted with the same budget constraint, wants to change the allocation from E to Y. Since both cannot have their way, this budget constraint corresponds to a price that does not clear the market. By contrast, when George and Harriet are confronted by the budget constraint in Figure 2.4,

---

[11] Every other commodity bundle on MN lies on a lower indifference curve (i.e., one that is closer to his origin) and hence leaves George less well off. Note that the best attainable commodity bundle is unique. This uniqueness is a direct consequence of our assumption that George's indifference curves are bowed toward the origin. If his indifference curves had been "wavy," the highest attainable indifference curve might have been tangent to MN in more than one place – so that there would be more than one best attainable commodity bundle.

[12] That is, Figure 2.4 differs from Figure 2.3 because the budget constraint has a different slope, causing George and Harriet to make different choices.

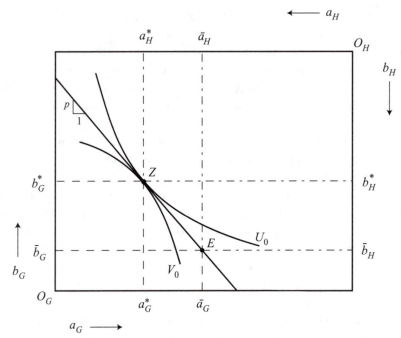

Figure 2.4: This Price is Market-Clearing. Harriet wishes to buy exactly as much ale as George wishes to sell. Their trade will change the allocation from E to Z.

both of them want to change the allocation from E to Z. Their agreement implies that the market will clear at this price.

2.4 MARKETS

Competitive equilibrium professes to describe market behaviour, and yet our depiction of competitive equilibrium doesn't seem to have much to do with markets. There are no demand curves, and no supply curves, and these are the constructs that we usually associate with markets. What happened to them?

The answer is that they are in the box, and we can pull them out if we like, but we don't really need them. Competitive equilibrium describes a situation in which markets are clearing, while supply and demand curves describe both situations in which markets are clearing and situations in which they are not clearing. In effect, the supply and demand curves contain more information than we need, so we can get by without them.

This section shows how a supply-and-demand representation of equilibrium is derived from the Edgeworth box. Only one of the two markets need be described, because the markets are linked together. Every offer to buy (sell) bread is also an offer to sell (buy) ale at the market price. If one person is offering to buy more bread than the other wants to sell, that person must also be offering to sell more ale than the other

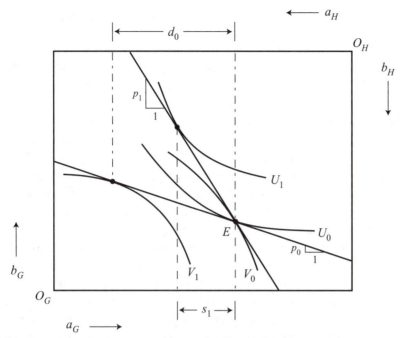

Figure 2.5: Two Prices. At the lower price, Harriet wants to buy ale and George does not want to trade. At the higher price, George wants to sell ale and Harriet does not want to trade.

wants to buy. That is, an excess demand for one good implies an excess supply of the other good. This observation is called **Walras' Law.**[13,14]

Since the relative price that we are looking for is that of ale (measured in bread), let's look at the ale market. The demand curve shows the quantity of ale that people want to buy at any given price, and the supply curve shows the quantity of ale that people want to sell at any given price. To find them, we'll need to know who is offering to buy and who is offering to sell. This information can be deduced from Figure 2.5, which shows

---

[13] Walras' Law states that, in a system of n markets, the last market is clearing if the other $n-1$ markets are clearing.

  Walras' Law explains why microeconomic theory determines only relative prices. Given any price for the first good, the prices of the other $n-1$ goods can be determined by equating demand and supply in their respective markets. If these markets are clearing, so is the first – which means that the price that was chosen for the first good is a market-clearing price, no matter what it was. That is, the *absolute prices* are not uniquely determined. If the price in the first market is set equal to one (i.e., if that good is chosen as the numeraire), the $n-1$ market-clearing prices constitute the complete set of relative prices.

[14] You have already encountered Walras' Law if you have studied intermediate macroeconomics. In the IS/LM model, people are assumed to be able to hold their wealth as either money or bonds. The LM curve describes the circumstances under which demand equals supply in each of these markets, but since a desire to hold more (fewer) bonds implies a desire to hold less (more) money, the bond market clears whenever the money market clears. The LM curve is therefore derived by establishing the conditions under which the money market alone clears.

two budget constraints, corresponding to the prices p_0 and p_1, where p_0 is smaller than p_1. These budget constraints were carefully selected.

The budget constraint with slope $-p_0$ is tangent to one of George's indifference curves (U_0) at the endowment point. If he were allowed to buy or sell ale at the price p_0, he would choose not to do so. There would be no trade that makes him better off. However, if he were allowed to trade at *any* price higher than p_0 (i.e., if he were confronted with a steeper budget constraint), he could reach an indifference curve that is further away from his origin than U_0 by selling ale to obtain bread. If he were allowed to trade at *any* price lower than p_0 (i.e., if he were confronted with a flatter budget constraint), he could reach an indifference curve higher than U_0 by doing exactly the opposite – selling bread to obtain ale. Thus, George wants to sell ale at every price higher than p_0, and he wants to buy ale at every price lower than p_0, and he doesn't want to trade at all if the price is p_0.

Now flip the page around, so that you are looking at Harriet's indifference curves right side up. The budget constraint with slope $-p_1$ is tangent to one of her indifference curves (V_0) at the endowment point. At that price, she would choose not to buy or sell, as any trade that she could make would leave her on a lower indifference curve. If the price were higher, she would be able to reach a higher indifference curve by selling ale to get bread; and if the price were lower, she would be able to reach a higher indifference curve by selling bread to obtain ale.

The quantity of ale offered for sale by George is zero at the price p_0 and positive at every higher price. The quantity of ale demanded by Harriet is zero at the price p_1 and positive at every lower price. If the ale market is to clear, it must do so at a price between p_0 and p_1. Let's sketch the demand and supply curves between these two prices.

George's supply of ale at any of these prices can be found by drawing a budget constraint with a slope equal to the negative of that price. The point of tangency between that budget constraint and one of George's indifference curves is the commodity bundle that George would choose to acquire if he could trade at that price. The quantity of ale that George offers for sale is the difference between his endowment of ale and the quantity of ale contained in that bundle. For example, at the price p_1, George offers to sell s_1 pints of ale.

Performing this exercise at every price between p_0 and p_1 allows us to trace out George's supply curve. George will supply no ale at the price p_0, s_1 pints of ale at the price p_1, and positive amounts of ale at all of the intermediate prices. Furthermore, George's supply of ale will vary smoothly with the price (i.e., there will be no breaks in the supply curve) if his indifference curves have certain basic properties – specifically, if they are downward sloping and bowed toward the origin. We don't know much else about the supply curve, and in particular, we can't be sure that it is upward sloping everywhere.

Similarly, Harriet's demand for ale at any of these prices can be found by looking at the choices that she would make when confronted with alternative budget constraints. She would demand no ale at the price p_1, d_0 pints of ale at the price p_0, and positive amounts of ale at all of the prices in between. The same simple restrictions ensure that

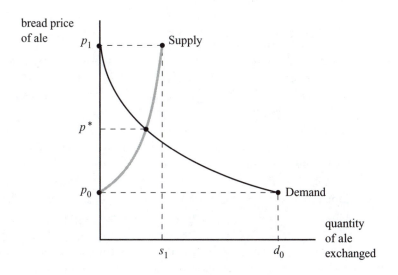

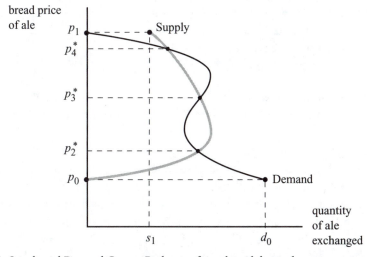

Figure 2.6: Supply and Demand Curves. Both sets of supply and demand curves are consistent with the previous figure. There is only one market-clearing price in the top diagram, but there are three market-clearing prices in the bottom diagram.

there are no breaks in her demand curve, but there are no simple restrictions that ensure that it is downward sloping everywhere.

A market-clearing price is one at which the quantity of ale that Harriet wants to buy is the same as the quantity of ale that George wants to sell. Every intersection of the supply and demand curves corresponds to such a price. You can easily satisfy yourself that, for any pair of unbroken curves with the stated endpoints, there is always at least one market-clearing price. There is, in fact, always an odd number of market-clearing prices.

The top half of Figure 2.6 shows the simplest case, in which the supply curve is everywhere upward sloping and the demand curve is everywhere downward sloping. There is exactly one market-clearing price, p^*. At this price, George and Harriet want

STABILITY

An **equilibrium** is a position of rest: an object which is in equilibrium will remain there unless disturbed by outside forces. An equilibirum can be either stable or unstable. If an equilibrium is **stable**, an object that is not initially in equilibrium will be pushed toward the equilibrium. If an equilibrium is **unstable**, an object that is not initially in equilibrium will be driven away from the equilibrium.

A marble is in equilibrium when it is resting in the bottom of a bowl, and it is also in equilibrium when it is balanced on the top of a globe. However, these positions have very different stability properties. If you throw a marble into a bowl, it will roll around for a while and then come to rest at the bottom: it is drawn to the equilibrium. Getting a marble to perch on the top of a globe is a much tougher task. The smallest error in the positioning of the marble will cause the marble to roll off the globe, bounce across the floor, and come to rest under the couch (yet another equilibrium). The equilibrium in the bottom of the bowl is stable; the equilibrium on the top of the globe is unstable.

Similarly, the market-clearing prices in the bottom half of Figure 2.6 are all equilibria, but the middle one is unstable while the outer two are stable. We do not expect the observed price to be an unstable equilibrium for the same reason that we do not expect to find marbles balanced on the tops of globes.

to take opposite sides of the same trade, so that both of them are able to carry out their preferred trades. At every other price, they are proposing different trades and both cannot be satisfied.

The importance of the price system lies in the fact that George and Harriet can discover the market-clearing price without the intervention of any outside agency. Their own self-interested behaviour will guide them to that price. Specifically, if the current price is not market clearing, one person will be unable to make the trade that he or she would like, and will have an incentive to bid the price upwards or downwards. These price revisions will eliminate the discrepancy between their desired trades. For example, if the price is above p^*, George would like to sell more pints of ale than Harriet would like to buy, so George has an incentive to lower the price at which he would be willing to sell ale. If the price is below p^*, Harriet cannot buy as much ale as she would like to buy, and will have an incentive to bid the price upward. These kinds of pressures move the price toward p^*.[15]

---

[15] The pressures that drive the price toward its market-clearing value are more evident in a market in which there are many buyers and sellers. If the total quantity offered for sale is greater than the total quantity demanded, the buyers will discover that not all of them will be able to purchase as much as they would like at the current price. Each buyer will attempt to make sure that he is himself able to purchase goods by offering a higher price than the other buyers, and their attempts to outbid each other drive the price upward. Similarly, if the total quantity offered for sale is greater than the total quantity demanded, the sellers will discover that not all of them will be able to sell as much as they would like. Each seller will attempt to undercut his competitors to ensure that he is himself able to make his desired sale, and their competition drives the price downward.

The bottom half of Figure 2.6 shows a more complicated situation in which there are three market-clearing prices: p_2^*, p_3^*, and p_4^*. The price will be driven to p_2^* if the initial price is below p_3^*, and to p_4^* if the initial price is above p_3^*. Trade is not likely to occur at the price p_3^*, since the kind of price adjustment described above drives the price away from this value instead of toward it.[16]

2.5 THE TWO FUNDAMENTAL THEOREMS OF WELFARE ECONOMICS

Economists tend to believe that systems of competitive markets allocate resources reasonably well. The theoretical grounds for this belief are contained in the **two fundamental theorems of welfare economics:**

First Theorem: Every competitive allocation is Pareto optimal.

Second Theorem: Each Pareto optimal allocation is the competitive allocation under some distribution of the endowed goods.

The first theorem argues that trading in competitive markets is certain to produce a Pareto optimal allocation. Every "free way" of raising someone's welfare will be exploited. This theorem constitutes a strong endorsement of market economies, but is not in itself decisive. Competition almost certainly generates an allocation in which some people are very badly off. Most of us are endowed only with our own labour, and this labour is what we must sell if we are to provide for ourselves. Its value varies widely from person to person, with the consequence that some people live very well under competition and others live very badly. Some individuals with physical or mental disabilities, and some who have simply made a series of bad decisions, might not be able to sustain themselves. If these inequities could not be remedied within the market system, we might prefer to abandon it. The second theorem deals with this issue. It imagines that the economy's total endowment of goods is fixed, and considers different ways of distributing the endowed goods across individuals.[17] It argues that each Pareto optimal allocation is the competitive allocation under some distribution of the endowed goods. The inference is that there is no need to abandon the market system in the pursuit of equity, because a central authority with the ability to redistribute endowments is able to guide the economy to any Pareto optimal allocation.

2.5.1 Proof of the Theorems

The theorems do not hold under all conditions, but they do hold for exchange economies like the one described here. They are easily demonstrated with the help of Figure 2.4.

---

[16] The prices p_2^* and p_4^* are stable while the price p_3^* is unstable. See the box on page 34 for details.
[17] That is, it considers alternative endowments that satisfy (2.1) and (2.2) for given values of $\overline{a}$ and $\overline{b}$.

The first theorem is very straightforward. Market-clearing in a competitive economy requires that George's and Harriet's indifference curves be tangent to the budget constraint at the same allocation. If they are both tangent to the budget line at this allocation, they are tangent to each other, and this tangency is the defining characteristic of a Pareto optimal allocation. Traders move to a point like Z under competition, and all points like Z lie on the efficiency locus.

Now consider the second theorem. We wish to show that there is an endowment such that a given Pareto optimal allocation can be reached through competition. Suppose that Z is the Pareto optimal allocation to be reached. George and Harriet's market transactions will take them to this allocation if, and only if, (i) the budget line passes through Z, and (ii) the budget line has the same slope as their indifference curves at Z. To satisfy the second condition, note that George's and Harriet's indifference curves have the same slope at Z, and set the price p equal to the negative of this slope. To satisfy the first condition, choose any endowment such that a budget line with slope $-p$ passes through Z.

Note that there are infinitely many endowments under which the competitive allocation will be Z. Aggregate purchasing power in this economy is equal to the market value of the endowments, $p\bar{a} + \bar{b}$. Competition will lead the economy to Z if this purchasing power is appropriately divided between George and Harriet. The form in which each person receives his or her share of the purchasing power – ale or bread or some combination of the two – is irrelevant. The only thing that matters is the shares. Arguably, this observation is what makes the second theorem interesting. A society that is concerned about equity need worry only about the distribution of purchasing power; it need not concern itself with the detail of what each person will consume.

2.5.2 Discussion

The problem with the two theorems lies not in their logic, which is impeccable, but in their premises. The theorems argue that, under certain well-specified conditions, market economies have very desirable properties. These conditions are satisfied in the economy inhabited by George and Harriet, but they are not satisfied in the economies of this world.[18] Consequently, the theorems have no direct relevance to our economies. A system of competitive markets would not, in our world, generate a Pareto optimal allocation. A central authority would not be able to guide the economy to the Pareto optimal allocation of its choice by transferring purchasing power between people.

The theorems are interesting precisely because they do not describe our economies. They describe the properties of an ideal market economy, and we study them to discover why our economies fall short of the ideal and what can be done about it.

---

[18] See Chapter 1 for a discussion of the conditions under which the theorems hold, and the reasons why they are not satisfied in our economies.

CONVEX PREFERENCES AND THE TWO THEOREMS

People often prefer more balanced commodity bundles to less balanced ones. For example, they tend to prefer commodity bundles containing moderate amounts of food, clothing and shelter to commodity bundles that contain large amounts of one of these goods and little of the other two.

The assumption that people have convex preferences converts this tendency into an imperative. It requires that, as a person's consumption of any one good rises, he becomes less willing – or at least no more willing – to give up other goods in order to obtain another unit of that good. Alternatively, it implies that movements down and to the right along any indifference curve are not associated with a steepening of the indifference curve.

This assumption might well be too restrictive, in the sense that it rules out some kinds of normal behaviour. Consider the "mini-addictions" which make it so difficult to have just one potato chip or just one beer. The second potato chip or second beer is more valuable to us than the first, so that our preferences are (locally) not convex. Alternatively, consider vacations. Some people feel that a one-week vacation is not long enough to allow them to psychologically break away from their normal routine, but that a two-week vacation lets them truly relax. They believe that a two-week vacation is more than twice as valuable as a one-week vacation, or equivalently, that the second week of vacation is more valuable than the first. Their preferences, too, are not convex.

Since the assumption that preferences are convex is somewhat suspect, it is important to recognize which results require it and which do not.

1) The argument that there must be a market-clearing price relies on this assumption. Convexity implies that the demand and supply curves are unbroken, which in turn implies the existence of a market-clearing price. (If there were a break in one of the curves, the other curve might pass between the two pieces of the first curve. There might then be no intersection, and no market-clearing price.)

2) The proof of the first theorem does not rely on convex preferences. The first theorem merely describes the properties of a competitive equilibrium if it exists.

3) The proof of the second theorem requires convex preferences. To see why, look again at Figure 2.4. The allocation Z is a competitive allocation because, if George and Harriet are allowed to trade at the price p, they both want to undertake the trade that takes them from the endowment E to the Pareto optimal allocation Z. This outcome will not necessarily occur if preferences are not convex. Consider, for example, the Edgeworth Box pictured below, in which George's preferences are not convex. As before, E is the endowment and Z is a Pareto optimal allocation. If George and Harriet are allowed to trade at the price p, Harriet would still want to reach Z but George would not. He would want to reach the allocation Y, where

(continued)

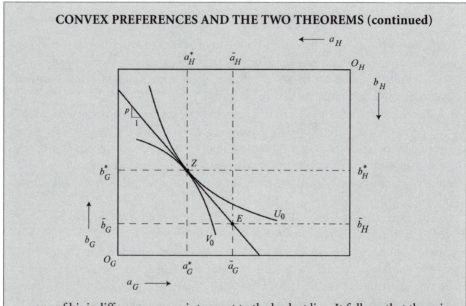

CONVEX PREFERENCES AND THE TWO THEOREMS (continued)

one of his indifference curves is tangent to the budget line. It follows that the price p is not a market-clearing price under the endowment E, and that Z cannot be reached through competition.

The first theorem assumes that the economy does not need to cope with externalities, public goods, and other kinds of market failure. Our economies must cope with these issues. The second theorem assumes that purchasing power can be transferred between people in a way that does not distort their behaviour. In our economies, people will alter their behaviour in the hopes of avoiding taxes or receiving government transfers. Our economies consequently fall short of the ideal. Public economics studies the way in which the *degree* to which our economies fall short of the ideal can be minimized.

2.6 SUMMARY

The exchange economy is a simple economy in which the division of endowed goods between people is to be determined. A way of dividing up these goods is called an allocation. An allocation is Pareto optimal if there is no alternative allocation such that someone is better off and no one is worse off. There are infinitely many Pareto optimal allocations, and a system of competitive markets will lead the economy to one of them. Furthermore, the allocation reached is determined by the division of purchasing power. Every Pareto optimal allocation is reached under some division of purchasing power.

QUESTIONS

1. Draw an Edgeworth box containing an endowment point and a budget line.
   a) Draw an indifference curve for George and an indifference curve for Harriet, both tangent to the budget line, such that George wants to buy ale, Harriet wants to sell ale, and George wants to buy more ale than Harriet wants to sell.
   b) Draw two indifference curves, both tangent to the budget line, such that George and Harriet both want to buy ale.
   c) Draw two indifference curves, both tangent to the budget line, such that the current price is market-clearing but no goods are traded.

2. Let p^* be the price of ale (measured in bread) at which George neither buys nor sells ale. Show that George wants to buy ale at any lower price and wants to sell ale at any higher price.

3. Consider an economy composed of two people, Monday and Tuesday.
   a) There are two possible allocations, and neither Monday nor Tuesday likes these allocations equally well. (That is, each of them believes that one of the allocations is better than the other. They don't necessarily agree as to which allocation is better.) Can both allocations be Pareto optimal? If not, explain why not. If so, give an example.
   b) Now imagine that there are five possible allocations. There are no two allocations that Monday likes equally well, and there are no two allocations that Tuesday likes equally well. Can all of the allocations be Pareto optimal? If not, explain why not. If so, give an example.
   c) Finally, imagine that there 108 allocations. Is it possible that none of the allocations is Pareto optimal? If not, explain why not. If so, give an example.

4. It was assumed in the text that George's indifference curves do not cut the bottom or left-hand side of the box, and that Harriet's indifference curves do not cut the top or right-hand side of the box. The characterization of Pareto optimal and competitive allocations is a little more complex if they do. The next question deals with these complexities.

   Assume that George's indifference curves are linear and have slope -1. Assume that Harriet's indifference curves are linear and have slope -2.
   a) Let X be an allocation in the interior of the box. Show that all of the allocations that both George and Harriet believe to be at least as good as X lie within a triangular or diamond-shaped area.
   b) Show that every allocation on the left-hand side or top of the box is Pareto optimal. Show that no other allocation is Pareto optimal.
   c) Let p be the price of ale measured in bread. Find George's best attainable commodity bundle(s) when p is equal to 1 and when it is greater than 1. Find Harriet's best attainable commodity bundles when p is equal to 2 and when it is less than 2.

d) Show that:

    i) If a budget line with slope -1 cuts the top of the box, then 1 is a market-clearing price.

    ii) If a budget line with slope -2 cuts the left side of the box, then 2 is a market-clearing price.

    iii) If a budget line with slope $-p$ cuts the top left corner of the box, and if p is between 1 and 2, p is a market-clearing price.

3

An Algebraic Exchange Economy

There is a long tradition of graphical analysis in economics, but this method has some severe limitations. The first is that it can only be used in problems that have two or three dimensions. Adding another commodity to our graphical model of the exchange economy would be difficult, and adding a fourth would be impossible. The second is that it is difficult to determine the circumstances under which a result will hold. Perhaps a different result would have been obtained if a line had shifted a little bit further, or if the bend in a curve had been a little bit sharper. The third is that graphical arguments have to be relatively simple. Only so many lines can be placed in a graph before it becomes an unreadable jumble.

Mathematics allows economists to circumvent these restrictions. There are only three physical dimensions, but mathematics allows us to imagine infinitely many dimensions. Mathematics also allows us to quantify things like the shift of a line or the sharpness of a curve. And finally, mathematics is a language designed for extended logical arguments.

This chapter returns to the exchange economy in which George and Harriet trade ale and bread, and to the two fundamental theorems, formulating them in mathematical terms. It is your introduction to a methodology upon which we will increasingly rely.

3.1 UTILITY FUNCTIONS

A person's preferences can be described by an indifference map if he is capable of making pairwise comparisons between commodity bundles. That is, given any pair of commodity bundles, A and B, he must be able to decide whether he likes A better than B, B better than A, or A and B equally well. All of the commodity bundles that he likes equally well lie on the same indifference curve, and commodity bundles that he likes better (worse) than these bundles lie on higher (lower) indifference curves.

A person who likes A better than B might also be able to decide *how much* better than B he likes A. His preferences could then be represented by a **cardinal utility function** that describes the way in which his well-being, or **utility,** varies with his commodity bundle. For example, if he consumes only ale and bread, his utility function u would assign a utility U to each commodity bundle containing a pints of ale and b loaves of bread:

$$U = u(a, b)$$

Introspection suggests that people are unlikely to be able to make this kind of calculation. Exactly how much better off would you be if you won a million dollars? And how much worse off would you be if your house burned down? Yet, in situations involving risk and insurance, people can only make sound decisions if they can make these kinds of calculations.[1] Economists sometimes assume that preferences can be described by a cardinal utility function, but they do so reluctantly.

By contrast, an **ordinal utility function** is simply a compact way of describing an indifference map. Specifically, a utility function provides an ordinal representation of a person's preferences if it can generate his indifference map. It must assign the same utility to commodity bundles that he likes equally well; and in every pairwise comparison of bundles that he does not like equally well, it must assign a higher utility to the preferred bundle. However, there is no presumption that utility actually *measures* the individual's welfare. Utility rises when the individual is happier and falls when he is sadder, but utility does not measure happiness.

An indifference map is like a gauge without a scale. We know when the individual's welfare is rising and when it is falling, but we do not know by how much it is rising or falling. An ordinal utility function is obtained by marking a scale on the face of the gauge. Since we can use any scale that we like, so long as it is increasing, there are infinitely many ordinal utility functions that describe the same indifference map.

3.2 THE MARGINAL RATE OF SUBSTITUTION

The **marginal rate of substitution** (MRS) is the number of loaves of bread that exactly compensates an individual for the loss of one pint of ale.[2] Alternatively, one pint of ale is exact compensation for the loss of MRS loaves of bread. Here, "exact compensation" means that the compensation returns the person to the level of welfare attained prior to the loss of the specified goods.

The marginal rate of substitution will vary from person to person because people have different tastes. It will also vary as any given person's commodity bundle changes. The usual assumption is that each person is more reluctant to part with a pint of ale

---

[1] Policies are often redistributive, in the sense that they raise the utility of some people and lower the utility of others. Evaluating these policies would be easier if we could compare the utility gains with the utility losses. Unfortunately, such comparisons would *not* be possible even if each person's preferences could be represented by a cardinal utility function. An individual with cardinal utility has an internal "measuring stick" that he uses to evaluate alternative commodity bundles, but he has no way of describing that measuring stick to anyone else. He knows how much happier he would be if he had a pint of chocolate ice cream, but he cannot explain it to anyone else. Since individuals cannot compare measuring sticks, they cannot compare utility gains and losses.

[2] Actually, this should be called the "marginal rate of substitution of bread for ale" because there is a marginal rate of substitution between any two goods in the economy. I will avoid the of/for terminology wherever possible, and it is certainly possible when there are only two commodities.

(i.e., has a higher MRS) when he has much bread and little ale than he would be if he had little bread and much ale.

An individual's marginal rate of substitution is measured graphically by the negative of the slope of his indifference curve. It can also be calculated algebraically, and we can deduce the appropriate method by considering a related problem:

Question: Suppose that a pound of cheese is worth \$10 and that a bag of potato chips is worth \$2. If I take from you a pound of cheese, and if I want to compensate you with potato chips for the *financial loss* that you incur, how many bags of potato chips do I have to give you?

Answer: The loss of a pound of cheese knocks \$10 off your net financial wealth. It's not exactly Bloody Monday, but I do want to be fair. I will compensate you with 5 bags of potato chips, because $5 \times \$2$ is \$10. Alternatively, the number of units that must be given in compensation is this ratio:

$$\frac{\text{the value of the thing taken away}}{\text{the value of } each \ unit \text{ of the thing given in compensation}}$$

Since the pound of cheese is worth \$10 and each bag of potato chips is worth \$2, $10/2 = 5$ bags of chips must be given in compensation.

The calculation of the marginal rate of substitution is very similar. Something is being taken away, something else is being given in compensation, and the MRS is the number of units that must be given. The only difference is that the intent is to compensate an individual for his *utility loss,* not his *financial loss,* so each "value" in the ratio must be measured in utility terms. Formally, the utility lost when one unit of a good is taken away from an individual is said to be the **marginal utility** of that good. The marginal utilities correspond exactly to the partial derivatives of the utility function. If MU_a and MU_b are the marginal utilities of ale and bread respectively, and if u is the utility function,

$$MU_a = \frac{\partial u}{\partial a}$$

$$MU_b = \frac{\partial u}{\partial b}$$

Thus, for any person,

$$MRS = \frac{MU_a}{MU_b} = \frac{\partial u}{\partial a} \div \frac{\partial u}{\partial b} \tag{3.1}$$

3.3 PARETO OPTIMAL ALLOCATIONS

The economy is endowed with quantities of ale and bread. For simplicity, assume that there is one unit of each good.[3] Since an allocation describes the division of the

---

[3] This assumption is harmless because we are always free to choose the units in which we measure commodities. Ale, for example, can be measured in drops or pints or kegs or anything else. The assumption that there is one unit of each commodity means that we *define* a single unit of each commodity to be the quantity that happens to be present in the economy.

available goods between George and Harriet, it is a list (a_G, b_G, a_H, b_H) that satisfies
the conditions

$$a_G + a_H = 1 \tag{3.2}$$

$$b_G + b_H = 1 \tag{3.3}$$

Some of the allocations are Pareto optimal and some are not. The Pareto optimal
allocations are characterized by a tangency between one of George's indifference curves
and one of Harriet's indifference curves. Since tangent curves have the same slope at the
point of tangency, and since the marginal rate of substitution is equal to the negative of
the slope of an indifference curve, a tangency occurs at any allocation that satisfies the
condition

$$MRS_G = MRS_H \tag{3.4}$$

Here, the subscripts indicate the person whose marginal rate of substitution is being
evaluated.

Note that this condition is an equation. The marginal rates of substitution are not
constants, but rather depend upon the individual commodity bundles. That is, MRS_G
is a function of a_G and b_G, and MRS_H is a function of a_H and b_H. Thus, a Pareto
optimal allocation is a solution to a particular equation system:

**A Pareto optimal allocation is a list (a_G, b_G, a_H, b_H) that satisfies equations
(3.2)–(3.4).**

The list contains four unknowns, but there are only three equations to determine them.
Such a system will have infinitely many solutions – which is as it should be, because
there are an infinite number of Pareto optimal allocations.

Explicit solutions can only be obtained if the relationship between the marginal
rates of substitution and the commodity bundles has been exactly specified. Suppose,
for example, that George and Harriet have the Cobb–Douglas utility functions

$$U_G = (a_G)^{1/3} (b_G)^{2/3} \tag{3.5}$$

$$U_H = (a_H)^{1/2} (b_H)^{1/2} \tag{3.6}$$

Applying the rule (3.1) gives[4]

$$MRS_G = \frac{1}{2} \left(\frac{b_G}{a_G} \right)$$

$$MRS_H = \frac{b_H}{a_H}$$

---

[4] See the box on page 45 for a simple way of calculating the partial derivatives of Cobb–Douglas
functions.

QUICK COBB–DOUGLAS DERIVATIVES

A **Cobb–Douglas function** expresses the value of a variable as the product of a constant (which can be 1) and two or more power functions. Here is an example of a Cobb–Douglas function in which x and y determine z:

$$z = kx^{\alpha} y^{\beta}$$

The parameters of this function are the constant k and the powers α and β.

Evaluating the partial derivatives and simplifying yields

$$\frac{\partial z}{\partial x} = \alpha k x^{\alpha-1} y^{\beta} = \left(\frac{1}{x}\right) \alpha k x^{\alpha} y^{\beta} = \frac{\alpha z}{x}$$

$$\frac{\partial z}{\partial y} = \beta k x^{\alpha} y^{\beta-1} = \left(\frac{1}{y}\right) \beta k x^{\alpha} y^{\beta} = \frac{\beta z}{y}$$

The final form of the derivatives is particularly simple, involving no powers. The partial derivatives of Cobb–Douglas functions *always take this form*, so you don't need to manipulate cumbersome equations to find them.

Here's a somewhat more complicated example. Suppose that z is determined by the same Cobb–Douglas function, but that y is itself a function of x:

$$y = f(x)$$

To find the full derivative of z with respect to x, apply the usual rule:

$$\frac{dz}{dx} = \frac{\partial z}{\partial x} + \frac{\partial z}{\partial y}\frac{dy}{dx}$$

Evaluating the partial derivatives gives

$$\frac{dz}{dx} = z\left[\frac{\alpha}{x} + \frac{\beta}{y}\frac{dy}{dx}\right]$$

Evaluate dy/dx and you are done.

Substituting these functions into (3.4) gives

$$\frac{1}{2}\left(\frac{b_G}{a_G}\right) = \frac{b_H}{a_H} \tag{3.7}$$

Now (3.2), (3.3), and (3.7) describe the economy's (infinitely many) Pareto optimal allocations.

A particular Pareto optimal allocation can be found by arbitrarily choosing a value for one of the variables and then solving the equation system for the remaining unknowns. For example, suppose that a value is assigned to a_G. Substituting (3.2) and (3.3) into (3.7) to eliminate a_H and b_H gives

$$\frac{1}{2}\left(\frac{b_G}{a_G}\right) = \frac{1 - b_G}{1 - a_G}$$

Rearranging this equation yields

$$b_G = \frac{2a_G}{1 + a_G} \tag{3.8}$$

This equation determines the amount of bread that George receives in the Pareto optimal allocation in which he gets a_G units of ale. Harriet gets everything else:

$$a_H = 1 - a_G$$

$$b_H = 1 - b_G = \frac{1 - a_G}{1 + a_G}$$

Thus, if the economy is endowed with one unit of each commodity, and if George and Harriet have the utility functions (3.5) and (3.6), the following list is a Pareto optimal allocation for any a_G between 0 and 1:

$$\left(a_G, \frac{2a_G}{1 + a_G}, 1 - a_G, \frac{1 - a_G}{1 + a_G} \right)$$

3.4 COMPETITIVE EQUILIBRIUM

Let p be the price of ale measured in bread. Then a competitive equilibrium in our exchange economy consists of a price p and an allocation (a_G, b_G, a_H, b_H) such that

1) George consumes the best commodity bundle that he can obtain by trading at the market price p.
2) Harriet consumes the best commodity bundle that she can obtain by trading at the market price p.
3) The price p clears the market, in the sense that George wants to sell exactly what Harriet wants to buy and Harriet wants to sell exactly what George wants to buy.

Finding a competitive equilibrium is therefore a matter of finding the values of the five variables that satisfy these conditions. We know that five variables can be determined by a system of five equations, so we can find a competitive equilibrium if we can convert these three conditions into such an equation system.

Consider condition 1. For any given price p, the commodity bundles that George can obtain through trade are described by the equation

$$b_G = \bar{b}_G + p\left(\bar{a}_G - a_G \right) \tag{3.9}$$

This equation, which is George's budget constraint, encompasses three cases:

- If his ale consumption is exactly equal to his ale endowment, he is neither buying nor selling ale, and his bread consumption is equal to his bread endowment.
- If his ale consumption is smaller than his ale endowment, he sells his surplus ale to obtain more bread. That is, he sells $\bar{a}_G - a_G$ pints of ale to obtain $p\left(\bar{a}_G - a_G\right)$ loaves of bread. His bread consumption is the sum of his bread endowment and his bread purchase.

- If his ale consumption is greater than his ale endowment, he must sell some of his bread endowment to get the extra ale. The cost of acquiring $a_G - \overline{a}_G$ extra pints of ale is $p(a_G - \overline{a}_G)$ loaves of bread. His bread consumption is the difference between his bread endowment and his sale of bread.

Of the commodity bundles that satisfy (3.9), the one that George likes best is the one at which there is a tangency between his budget constraint and one of his indifference curves. Since curves have the same slope at a point of tangency, this condition can be written as[5]

$$MRS_G = p \tag{3.10}$$

George's marginal rate of substitution varies with his commodity bundle, so MRS_G is a function of a_G and b_G. Since (3.10) is an equation containing the same variables as (3.9), these two equations can be solved to find George's best attainable commodity bundle at the price p.

Likewise, condition 2 can be represented by a two-equation system. For any given price p, the commodity bundles that Harriet can obtain through trade are described by her budget constraint:

$$b_H = \overline{b}_H + p\,(\overline{a}_H - a_H) \tag{3.11}$$

The best of these commodity bundles is characterized by a tangency between her budget constraint and one of her indifference curves, implying that

$$MRS_H = p \tag{3.12}$$

Since her marginal rate of substitution is determined by her commodity bundle, (3.11) and (3.12) constitute a two-equation system in two unknowns, a_H and b_H. Solving this system determines Harriet's best attainable commodity bundle at the price p.

Now consider condition 3. George and Harriet are both able to obtain their desired quantities of ale if the quantity that one person wants to sell is just equal to the quantity that the other person wants to buy:

$$\overline{a}_G - a_G = a_H - \overline{a}_H \tag{3.13}$$

Similarly, George and Harriet are both able to obtain their desired quantities of bread if the quantity that one person wants to sell is just equal to the quantity that the other person wants to buy:

$$b_G - \overline{b}_G = \overline{b}_H - b_H \tag{3.14}$$

This equation is automatically satisfied if (3.13) is satisfied. Walras' Law tells us that these two equations contain the same restriction: either both are satisfied or neither

---

[5] Note that both sides of this equation are measured in loaves of bread per pint of ale. The left-hand side is the number of loaves of bread that George is *willing to give up* to get a pint of ale, and the right-hand side is the number of loaves of bread that he *must give up* to get a pint of ale.

is satisfied.[6] Only one of them needs to be added to the equation system. We'll add (3.13).

Thus, a competitive equilibrium is also a solution to an equation system:

A competitive equilibrium consists of a price p and an allocation (a_G, b_G, a_H, b_H) that satisfies (3.9)–(3.13).

Once again, an explicit solution can only be obtained if the relationship between the marginal rates of substitution and the commodity bundles is known. Let's continue our previous example by assuming that George and Harriet have the utility functions (3.5) and (3.6). Assume also that the economy is endowed with one unit of each commodity, and that this endowment is divided between George and Harriet in some fashion:

$$\bar{a}_G + \bar{a}_H = 1$$

$$\bar{b}_G + \bar{b}_H = 1$$

It really does not matter how we solve a system of five equations containing five unknowns, so long as we end up with the right answer. However, one method allows us to look at the underlying markets, so we'll use that one. This method involves the following steps:

1) Solve the two-equation systems that determine each person's best attainable commodity bundle at any given price p.
2) Find the trades that each person would have to make to obtain this commodity bundle. These trades determine the market supply and demand curves.
3) Find the market-clearing price.
4) Once the price is known, go back and calculate the commodity bundles actually obtained by each person.

3.4.1 Excess Demands

Substituting the expression for George's marginal rate of substitution into (3.10) gives

$$\frac{b_G}{a_G} = 2p \tag{3.15}$$

Solving (3.9) and (3.15) yields George's best attainable commodity bundle when he can trade at the price p:

$$a_G{}^\circ = \frac{1}{3}\left(\frac{\bar{b}_G + p\bar{a}_G}{p}\right)$$

$$b_G{}^\circ = \frac{2}{3}\left(\bar{b}_G + p\bar{a}_G\right)$$

---

[6] You can verify this observation by using (3.9) and (3.11) to eliminate b_G and b_H from (3.14). Simplifying the resulting equation yields (3.13).

Similarly, substituting the expression for Harriet's marginal rate of substitution into (3.12) gives

$$b_H = pa_H \qquad (3.16)$$

Solving (3.11) and (3.16) yields Harriet's best attainable commodity bundle when she can trade at the price p:

$$a_H{}^\circ = \frac{1}{2}\left(\frac{\overline{b}_H + p\overline{a}_H}{p}\right)$$

$$b_H{}^\circ = \frac{1}{2}\left(\overline{b}_H + p\overline{a}_H\right)$$

These are the commodity bundles that George and Harriet would like to consume, and they are generally not the commodity bundles with which they are endowed. Trade allows them to exchange their endowed commodity bundles for commodity bundles that they like better.

Again, Walras' Law tells us that we can look at the trades in ale or the trades in bread, but there is no need to look at both. Let's look at the ale trades.

The amount of ale that each person wishes to buy or sell depends upon that person's endowment as well as the price. Someone who is endowed with no ale, for example, will be a buyer at every price, while someone who is endowed only with ale will be a seller at every price. A person with a more balanced endowment would buy ale at some prices and sell it at others. How are we to find a market-clearing price without knowing who is selling and who is buying?

The answer is to formulate excess demand functions, rather than demand and supply curves. Each person's **excess demand** for ale is the difference between the quantity of ale contained in that person's best attainable commodity bundle and the quantity contained in that person's endowment. More simply, it is the difference between the quantity that he wants and the quantity that he has:

$$ED_G = a_G{}^\circ - \overline{a}_G$$

$$ED_H = a_H{}^\circ - \overline{a}_H$$

In our example,

$$ED_G = \frac{\overline{b}_G - 2p\overline{a}_G}{3p} \qquad (3.17)$$

$$ED_H = \frac{\overline{b}_H - p\overline{a}_H}{2p} \qquad (3.18)$$

Both excess demands fall as the price rises. Both excess demands are positive at sufficiently low prices and negative at sufficiently high prices.

A person who has a positive excess demand for ale at a particular price wants more ale than he has. That person will be a buyer of ale at that price. A person who has a negative excess demand for ale at a particular price has more ale than he wants. That person will be a seller of ale at that price.

The ale market clears when one excess demand is the negative of the other, so that one person wishes to buy precisely the quantity of ale that the other person wishes to sell. Equivalently, the market clears when the excess demands sum to zero:

$$ED_G + ED_H = 0 \tag{3.19}$$

It is easily verified that this condition is equivalent to the original market-clearing condition (3.13).

3.4.2 Equilibrium

The market-clearing price is obtained by substituting the excess demands, (3.17) and (3.18), into the market-clearing condition (3.19) and then solving for p. It is

$$p^\circ = \frac{2\overline{b}_G + 3\overline{b}_H}{4\overline{a}_G + 3\overline{a}_H}$$

Since the economy is endowed with one unit of ale and one unit of bread, the market-clearing price can also be written entirely in terms of George's endowment:

$$p^\circ = \frac{3 - \overline{b}_G}{3 + \overline{a}_G}$$

Note that, in this equation, raising $\overline{b}_G$ (or $\overline{a}_G$) means that some of the bread (or ale) endowment is being *transferred* from Harriet to George. Note also that the form of this equation is determined by George's and Harriet's utility functions.

The equations that describe George's and Harriet's best attainable commodity bundles at an arbitrarily selected price p have already been determined. The commodity bundles actually consumed are found by substituting the market-clearing price into these equations. They are

$$a_G{}^\circ = \frac{\overline{b}_G + \overline{a}_G}{3 - \overline{b}_G}$$

$$b_G{}^\circ = \frac{2\left(\overline{b}_G + \overline{a}_G\right)}{3 + \overline{a}_G}$$

$$a_H{}^\circ = \frac{3 - 2\overline{b}_G - \overline{a}_G}{3 - \overline{b}_G}$$

$$b_H{}^\circ = \frac{3 - 2\overline{b}_G - \overline{a}_G}{3 + \overline{a}_G}$$

For example, if George is endowed with one-half unit of each good, the market-clearing price of ale is 5/7. Confronted with this price, he chooses to sell 1/10 unit of ale to obtain 1/14 unit of bread, so that he is able to consume 2/5 unit of ale and 4/7 unit of bread. Harriet, of course, takes the other side of the trade, so she consumes 3/5 unit of ale and 3/7 unit of bread.

3.5 THE TWO THEOREMS

This section uses the algebraic version of the exchange model to demonstrate the two fundamental theorems of welfare economics. Since it is desirable to show that the theorems hold under a wide variety of circumstances, George and Harriet will not be assumed to have particular utility functions (such as the Cobb–Douglas ones used above). Instead, it is assumed that they have indifference maps in which each indifference curve is downward sloping and bowed toward the origin. Furthermore, each person is assumed to prefer any commodity bundle containing some of each good to a commodity bundle containing only one good.[7]

Each person's marginal rate of substitution is determined by his or her commodity bundle. The relationships between the marginal rates of substitution and the commodity bundles are described by the functions μ_G and μ_H:

$$MRS_G = \mu_G(a_G, b_G)$$

$$MRS_H = \mu_H(a_H, b_H)$$

These functions can be used to reformulate the equation systems:

- A Pareto optimal allocation is an allocation (a_G, b_G, a_H, b_H) in which

$$a_G + a_H = 1 \tag{3.20}$$

$$b_G + b_H = 1 \tag{3.21}$$

$$\mu_G(a_G, b_G) = \mu_H(a_H, b_H) \tag{3.22}$$

- A competitive equilibrium consists of an allocation (a_G, b_G, a_H, b_H) and a price p in which

$$b_G = \overline{b}_G + p\,(\overline{a}_G - a_G) \tag{3.23}$$

$$b_H = \overline{b}_H + p\,(\overline{a}_H - a_H) \tag{3.24}$$

$$\mu_G(a_G, b_G) = p \tag{3.25}$$

$$\mu_H(a_H, b_H) = p \tag{3.26}$$

$$\overline{a}_G - a_G = a_H - \overline{a}_H \tag{3.27}$$

---

[7] These assumptions imply that each person's best attainable commodity bundle is characterized by a tangency between his budget constraint and one of his indifference curves, and that there is only one such tangency.

where

$$\bar{a}_G + \bar{a}_H = 1 \qquad\qquad (3.28)$$

$$\bar{b}_G + \bar{b}_H = 1 \qquad\qquad (3.29)$$

The two theorems describe the match between the Pareto optimal allocations and the competitive allocations. Let's consider them in turn.

The first theorem argues that every competitive allocation is also Pareto optimal. That is, if a particular allocation coupled with a particular price constitutes a solution to the second set of equations, that allocation must also be a solution to the first set of equations. The proof of the theorem hinges upon a demonstration that the first set of equations can be obtained by combining equations contained in the second set. The demonstration itself is quite mechanical:

> Combining (3.27) and (3.28) yields (3.20). Combining (3.23), (3.24), and (3.27) yields the market-clearing condition for the bread market:
>
> $$b_G - \bar{b}_G = \bar{b}_H - b_H$$
>
> Combining this condition with (3.29) yields (3.21). Finally, combining (3.25) and (3.26) yields (3.22).

The implication of this finding is that every restriction imposed by Pareto optimality is also implicitly imposed by competitive equilibrium. Consequently, every allocation that satisfies the restrictions imposed by competitive equilibrium also satisfies the restrictions imposed by Pareto optimality. Every competitive allocation is Pareto optimal.

The second theorem involves a reinterpretation of the second equation system. Our earlier discussion of the exchange economy imagined that the endowments were known, and asked what would happen if people were allowed to trade. What would the market price be, and what commodity bundles would be consumed? Mathematically, a set of endowments that satisfied (3.28) and (3.29) was exogenously specified, and the five-equation system (3.23)–(3.27) determined the price and the allocation. That is, the endowments were exogenous and the allocation was endogenous. The second theorem asks us to reverse this assignment, so that the endowments become endogenous and the allocation becomes exogenous.

Specifically, the second theorem selects one of the Pareto optimal allocations, and asks whether there is a distribution of the available goods such that this allocation would be reached under competitive markets. It argues that there always is such a distribution of goods. In mathematical terms, an allocation that satisfies (3.20)–(3.22) is exogenously specified, and the theorem is proved by demonstrating that there is an endowment satisfying (3.28) and (3.29) that, in conjunction with some price, also satisfies the conditions for competitive equilibrium, (3.23)–(3.27).

At first glance, it seems unlikely that a solution to this system can be found. The equations in a system are said to be **independent** if each equation provides a new restriction on the way in which the unknowns are selected. A system has no solution if it has more independent equations than it has unknowns. Our system contains seven equations and only five endogenous variables, so it will not have a solution if the equations are independent.

If the allocation were arbitrarily selected, the equations would be independent (except by accident) and there would be no solution. But the allocation was not arbitrarily selected: it was chosen to satisfy the conditions for Pareto optimality. This fact implies that the equations in the system (3.23)–(3.29) are not independent. Each equation is not a new restriction on the way in which the unknowns are selected; some equations simply state old restrictions in superficially different ways. Our first task is to delete from the system those equations that impose the same restrictions as other equations in the system.

We first delete (3.27). Here, a_G and a_H are parameters that satisfy (3.20), so (3.27) restricts $\overline{a}_G$ and $\overline{a}_H$ in exactly the same way as (3.28). Now consider (3.25) and (3.26). Equation (3.25) states that p is determined by the commodity bundle assigned to George, and equation (3.26) states that p is determined by the commodity bundle assigned to Harriet. If the commodity bundles were chosen arbitrarily, these equations would generally specify two different values for p. However, the commodity bundles satisfy (3.22), so each equation requires p to be set at the same value. One of the pair can be deleted, so let's also throw away (3.26). Finally, consider (3.24). Substituting (3.28) and (3.29) into (3.23) gives

$$b_G = (1 - \overline{b}_H) + p\left((1 - \overline{a}_H) - a_G\right)$$

But the allocation satisfies (3.20) and (3.21), and substituting these conditions into the above equation reduces that equation to (3.24). Since (3.24) can be obtained by combining other equations in the system, it is not independent and can be dropped from the system.

So, where do we stand? There are now four equations in the system – (3.23), (3.25), (3.28), and (3.29) – and five unknowns. One of these equations, (3.25), determines the price that will prevail in *every* competitive equilibrium which generates the desired allocation. The other three equations describe the endowments under which competitive equilibrium generates that allocation. Of these equations, (3.28) and (3.29) simply state that Harriet's endowment contains all of the goods that are not part of George's endowment. The only actual restriction on George's endowment is therefore (3.23). If George's endowment satisfies this condition (and if both $\overline{a}_G$ and $\overline{b}_G$ are between 0 and 1 inclusive), competitive markets will generate the specified Pareto optimal allocation.

3.6 CONCLUSIONS

The exchange economy has now been studied using both graphical and algebraic analysis. The graphical approach is fast and easy, but the algebraic approach is ultimately more powerful. Subsequent discussions will use both methods, fitting the tool to the task.

QUESTIONS

1. Harold is endowed with 6 pints of ale, 8 loaves of bread, and 10 pounds of cheese. He can consume these goods, or he can trade some or all of them on organized markets. Specifically, he can buy or sell ale at a price of p loaves per pint, and he can buy or sell cheese at a price of q loaves per pound. After trading as much as he likes in these markets, he will consume all of the goods that he possesses. Let a, b, and c be the quantities of ale, bread, and cheese that he consumes.

   Harold's budget constraint can be found by recognizing that his bread consumption is the sum of three amounts: the amount contained in his endowment, the amount that he gets from the sale of ale, and the amount that he gets by selling cheese. (Either of these last two amounts could be negative.) Fill in the blanks below to find his budget constraint:
   a) Harold's endowment of bread is _____ loaves.
   b) If Harold wishes to consume a pints of ale, he is able to sell _____ pints of ale. The bread value of this ale is _____ loaves.
   c) If Harold wishes to consume c pounds of cheese, he is able to sell _____ pounds of cheese. The bread value of this cheese is _____ loaves.
   d) Harold's actual consumption is the sum of these three amounts, so his budget constraint is:
   $$b = \underline{\quad} + \underline{\quad} + \underline{\quad}$$

2. When there are only two people in an economy, the markets clear when the sum of their excess demands is equal to zero. The same rule holds no matter when how many people there are in the economy: the market clears when the sum of the excess demands is equal to zero. Try this three-person example:

   Consider an economy consisting of three people – Athos, Portos, and Aramis. Each of the three is endowed with a certain quantity of bread and a certain quantity of roasted chickens. There is a market in which bread can be traded for roasted chickens; and the prevailing price in that market, p, is the price of a roasted chicken measured in loaves of bread. The excess demands for roasted chicken of Athos, Portos, and Aramis are, respectively,

   $$ED_{At} = \frac{8}{p} - 4$$

   $$ED_P = \frac{4}{p} - 2$$

   $$ED_{Ar} = \frac{12}{p} - 2$$

a) Find the equilibrium price of roasted chickens. At the equilibrium price, who is buying chickens and who is selling them? How many chickens is each person buying or selling?

b) At the equilibrium price, who is buying bread and who is selling it? How much bread is each person buying or selling?

3. Consider an economy in which two people, Dinah Mojo and Dynamo Joe, exchange two goods, ale and bread. Let p be the price of ale measured in bread.

a) Dinah's utility function is

$$U_D = (a_D)^{1/2} + b_D$$

where a_D and b_D are her consumption of ale and bread, respectively. She is endowed with 10 loaves of bread but no ale. Find *i*) Dinah's budget constraint, *ii*) her best attainable commodity bundle, and *iii*) her excess demand for ale.

b) Joe's utility function is

$$U_J = (a_J)^{1/2} + b_J$$

where a_J and b_J are his consumption of ale and bread, respectively. Joe has 18 pints of ale but no bread. Find *i*) Joe's budget constraint, *ii*) his best attainable commodity bundle, and *iii*) his excess demand for ale.

c) Let p be the price of ale measured in bread. Find the market-clearing value of p. Find the quantity of each good traded, and find each person's actual consumption of ale and bread.

4. The goods in the next question are not ale and bread. To solve this question, you are going to have to evaluate the condition

$$MRS = p$$

The price p is defined for you, but you will have to define the marginal rate of substitution for yourself. What ratio of marginal utilities should you use? You will know the answer to this question once you have defined the marginal rate of substitution – that is, decided which good is being given up and which good is being given in compensation. When making this decision, remember that both sides of this equation refer to the same kind of trade. The right-hand side describes the rate at which one good *can be traded* for the other in the marketplace; and the left-hand side describes the rate at which someone *is willing to trade* that good for the other. Thus, the definition of the price determines the manner in which the marginal rate of substitution must be defined.

Pierre lives on red wine and blue cheese. His utility function is

$$U = c^{1/4} w^{3/4}$$

where w is his consumption of wine and c is his consumption of cheese. He is endowed with 4 kilograms of cheese and 8 bottles of wine. He can trade these commodities in a marketplace, where the price of red wine, measured in blue cheese, is p.

a) Find Pierre's optimal consumption of wine and cheese at any given price p.
b) Find the quantity of wine that Pierre would like to buy at any given price p.
c) Suppose that Pierre trades with Gabrielle, whose excess demand for wine is

$$ED_G = \frac{4}{p} - 2$$

Find the market-clearing price.

4

The Production Economy

The exchange economy describes the single most important feature of market behaviour, namely, mutually advantageous trade. It does not, however, incorporate many aspects of our own economy, the actual production of goods being the most obvious of these. This chapter expands the exchange model to include production.[1]

In the exchange economy, George and Harriet were endowed with quantities of ale and bread, and we considered the way in which these goods could be traded. The allocations open to them were described by two equations:

$$\overline{a}_G + \overline{a}_H = a_G + a_H$$

$$\overline{b}_G + \overline{b}_H = b_G + b_H$$

In the production economy, George and Harriet are instead endowed with the factors of production, capital (K) and labour (L), and with the ownership of firms, rather than with goods.[2] Specifically,

- George is endowed with $\overline{K}_G$ units of capital and $\overline{L}_G$ units of labour, and he owns a fraction α of the ale-producing firms and a fraction β of the bread-producing firms.
- Harriet is endowed with $\overline{K}_H$ units of capital and $\overline{L}_H$ units of labour, and she owns the rest of the firms.

The firms use the capital and labour to produce commodities that are ultimately consumed by George and Harriet.

All of the available units of capital and labour are used in either the ale industry or the bread industry. The quantities of capital used in the ale and bread industries are K_a and K_b, respectively, and the quantities of labour used in the ale and bread industries are L_a and L_b. The amount of goods produced in each industry is determined by the

---

[1] Bator [6] provides a quick graphical introduction to the production economy.

[2] Here, capital refers to *physical* capital, such as machines and equipment. The firms are organizations which buy both capital and labour so that they can produce commodities. Part of each firm's revenue is used to pay for the factors of production used, and the rest is returned to the firm's owners as profits.

industry's **production function.** If a and b are the quantities of ale and bread produced, and if f and g are the production functions of the ale and bread industries,

$$a = f(K_a, L_a)$$

$$b = g(K_b, L_b)$$

The production functions are assumed to be "strongly increasing and concave," and this assumption has two immediate economic implications[3]:

- The production functions display either **constant** or **decreasing returns to scale.** The industry's production function displays constant returns to scale if output doubles when twice as much capital and labour is used, and it displays decreasing returns if output less than doubles under the same circumstances.[4]
- The **marginal product** of a factor of production in an industry is the amount by which the industry's output rises when one more unit of the factor is employed. The marginal products correspond exactly to the partial derivatives of the production function; for example, the marginal product of capital in the ale industry is equal to $\partial f / \partial K_a$. The assumption that the production functions are strictly increasing implies that the marginal products are always positive. The assumption that they are concave implies that the marginal products are non-increasing, meaning that the marginal product of each factor in each industry does not rise as more of that factor is used in the industry.

It is also assumed that, in each industry, the marginal product of each factor becomes arbitrarily large as the use of that factor falls toward zero. This assumption ensures that each industry employs both factors of production.

As in the exchange economy, an allocation is a list that shows what is done with each unit of goods. Since there are two kinds of goods in the production economy, namely factors of production and commodities, the list is a little longer. An allocation is a list $(a_G, b_G, a_H, b_H, K_a, L_a, K_b, L_b)$ such that every unit of each factor is employed in one of the industries and every unit of each commodity is consumed by one of the people:

$$\overline{K}_G + \overline{K}_H = K_a + K_b \tag{4.1}$$

$$\overline{L}_G + \overline{L}_H = L_a + L_b \tag{4.2}$$

$$f(K_a, L_a) = a_G + a_H \tag{4.3}$$

$$g(K_b, L_b) = b_G + b_H \tag{4.4}$$

---

[3] See "A Note on Maximization" (pp. 395–404) for a discussion of these concepts.

[4] A production function might also display **increasing returns to scale,** meaning that output more than doubles when twice as much capital and labour are used. If production in an industry is characterized by increasing returns to scale, one firm will ultimately drive all of the other firms out of the industry. Once it has eliminated its competitors, the remaining firm will behave as monopolists always do: it will contract industry output and charge a price higher than marginal cost. This phenomenon is discussed in Section 14.1.

Since increasing returns to scale are inconsistent with a discussion of *competitive* markets, they are not given further consideration in this chapter.

The outline of this chapter is essentially the same as the outline of the last chapter. The Pareto optimal and competitive allocations are described in turn. It is then shown that in this economy, as in the exchange economy, every competitive allocation is Pareto optimal. That is, the production economy satisfies the conditions under which the first theorem holds. It also satisfies the conditions under which the second theorem holds, although this result will not be demonstrated.

4.1 PARETO OPTIMALITY

There are three allocative decisions to be made in the production economy:

- What quantities of ale and bread should be produced?
- How should they be produced? That is, how should the factors of production be allocated between the industries?
- Who should get the goods that are produced?

An allocation is said to be match efficient if the first decision is made efficiently, production efficient if the second decision is made efficiently, and exchange efficient if the last decision is made efficiently. An allocation is Pareto optimal if each of these three decisions is made efficiently.

As in the exchange economy, there are infinitely many Pareto optimal allocations. Moving from one of these allocations to another raises the welfare of one person at the expense of the other.

4.1.1 Exchange Efficiency

Consider the third issue first. Given that certain quantities of ale and bread have been produced, the only remaining issue is who get these goods, and we examined this issue in the previous chapter. An allocation of goods is **exchange efficient** if it cannot be altered so as to make one person better off without making the other person worse off. The characteristic of an exchange efficient allocation is that George and Harriet have equal marginal rates of substitution:

$$MRS_G = MRS_H \tag{4.5}$$

4.1.2 Production Efficiency

Given the available quantities of capital and labour, the combinations of ale and bread that the economy is capable of producing are those that lie on or below the **production possibility frontier** (shown in Figure 4.1). There are two reasons why an economy might produce a combination of goods that lies inside the frontier. First, some of the factors of production might not be employed. Since we have already assumed that all of the factors of production are allocated to one of the two industries, this possibility need not

bread

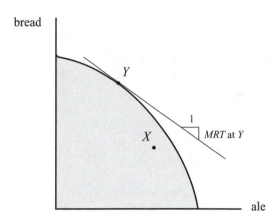

Figure 4.1: The Production Possibility
Frontier. The marginal rate of transformation at any point on the frontier is equal to
the negative of the slope of the frontier at
that point.

ale

concern us.[5] Second, the factors of production could be divided between the industries
in an unproductive manner. It is this possibility that we must consider further.

An economy is **production efficient** if the factors of production are allocated so
that the economy produces a combination of ale and bread lying on the production
possibility frontier, rather than below it. The following test can be used to determine
whether the economy is on or below the frontier:

> **The economy is operating below the frontier if the factors of production can
> be reallocated in a way that increases bread production without changing ale
> production. It is operating on the frontier if there is no way of reallocating the
> factors that increases bread production without changing ale production.**

The point X in Figure 4.1, for example, represents an inefficient allocation of factors.
The frontier lies above it, indicating that there is some alternative allocation of factors
that allows the economy to produce the same amount of ale but more bread. The point
Y, by contrast, lies on the frontier, so that every reallocation of factors that increases
bread production will also reduce ale production.

The consequences of any reallocation of factors depend upon the marginal products
of the factors involved. The marginal product of capital in the ale industry is the amount
of additional ale that could be produced by using one more unit of capital in the ale
industry; and the other marginal products are defined analogously. There are two ratios
of marginal products that have interesting interpretations. Using superscripts to identify
industries and subscripts to identify factors, we have

> MP_K^b / MP_K^a is the amount by which bread production rises if capital is moved
> out of the ale industry, and into the bread industry, until the production of ale
> falls by exactly one unit.

[5] Although this possibility has been set aside here, it is an important issue in reality. Recessions
are periods during which neither capital nor labour is fully employed. As well, the design of the
government's taxing and spending programs influences the amount of work done in an economy.

MP_L^b / MP_L^a is the amount by which bread production rises if labour is moved out of the ale industry, and into the bread industry, until the production of ale falls by exactly one unit.

Consider the first ratio. Moving one unit of capital out of the ale industry reduces ale output by MP_K^a units, so moving $1/MP_K^a$ units of capital out of that industry reduces ale output by the required 1 unit. Since each additional unit of capital in the bread industry produces MP_K^b units of bread, the movement of $1/MP_K^a$ units of capital from the ale industry to the bread industry increases bread production by $MP_K^b \times (1/MP_K^a)$. An analogous argument is used to interpret the second ratio.

These ratios also represent the amounts of bread lost if a factor is moved out of the bread industry, and into the ale industry, until ale production rises by one unit.

Now let's get back to the test of production efficiency. If ale production is to remain unchanged, there are only two kinds of reallocations that we have to consider:[6]

- Move labour from the ale industry to the bread industry until ale production falls by one unit; and then move capital from the bread industry to the ale industry until ale production rises by one unit. The net change in ale production is zero, and the net change in bread production is

$$\frac{MP_L^b}{MP_L^a} - \frac{MP_K^b}{MP_K^a}$$

(The first term is the bread gained when labour is brought into the bread industry, and the second term is the bread lost when capital is taken out of the bread industry.)

- Move capital from the ale industry to the bread industry until ale production falls by one unit; and then move labour from the bread industry to the ale industry until ale production rises by one unit. The net change in ale production is zero, and the net change in bread production is

$$\frac{MP_K^b}{MP_K^a} - \frac{MP_L^b}{MP_L^a}$$

The first kind of reallocation raises bread production (while ale production remains fixed) if

$$\frac{MP_L^b}{MP_L^a} > \frac{MP_K^b}{MP_K^a}$$

The second kind of reallocation raises bread production if

$$\frac{MP_L^b}{MP_L^a} < \frac{MP_K^b}{MP_K^a}$$

---

[6] Moving both factors into the ale industry would raise ale production, and moving both factors out of the ale industry would reduce ale production, so ale production can be held constant only if the factors are moved in opposite directions.

Thus, if either of these conditions holds, there *is* a way of reallocating factors so that bread production rises while ale production remains constant. It follows that the economy is operating inside the production possibility frontier, and that the current allocation is not production efficient.

However, neither kind of reallocation raises bread production if

$$\frac{MP_L^b}{MP_L^a} = \frac{MP_K^b}{MP_K^a} \tag{4.6}$$

Since there is no factor reallocation that raises bread production while holding ale production fixed if (4.6) holds, this condition characterizes production efficiency.

The negative of the slope of the production possibility frontier is the **marginal rate of transformation** (MRT), the quantity of bread that can be obtained by sacrificing one unit of ale production (see Figure 4.1). The marginal rate of transformation is MP_K^b/MP_K^a if the extra bread is obtained by transferring capital between the industries; and it is MP_L^b/MP_L^a if the extra bread is obtained by transferring labour between the industries. Since these two values are equal at every point along the production possibility frontier, it does not matter which ratio is used to calculate the marginal rate of transformation.

The appendix to this chapter contains an example of production efficiency that employs Cobb–Douglas production functions. It characterizes the production efficient allocations, and shows that the production function is either linear or (more commonly) bowed away from the origin.

4.1.3 Match Efficiency

Production efficiency ensures that the economy produces a combination of goods that lies on the production possibility frontier, and exchange efficiency ensures that these goods are allocated efficiently. But *which* combination of goods should be produced? This is the issue addressed by match efficiency.

An economy is **match efficient** if it is producing at the "right place" on the production possibility frontier. Only allocations that are both production efficient and exchange efficient are tested for match efficiency. The test involves moving a small distance along the frontier. This movement alters the total quantity of ale and bread available in the economy, forcing a change in someone's commodity bundle. If movement along the frontier, in one direction or the other, raises that person's welfare, the initial allocation is not match efficient. However, if there is no movement along the frontier that raises that person's welfare, the initial allocation is match efficient.[7]

The assumption that the allocation is production efficient implies that MRT can be evaluated. The assumption that it is exchange efficient implies that MRS_G and MRS_H

---

[7] We could also imagine that *both* commodity bundles change as a result of the movement along the frontier, but it is not necessary to do so. The assumption that the allocation is exchange efficient implies that there is no way of raising both people's utilities if there is no way of raising just one person's utility.

take the same value: call this value MRS. Remember what these terms mean:

> MRT is the number of units of bread that can be obtained by sacrificing one unit of ale. Equivalently, one unit of ale is obtained by sacrificing MRT units of bread.

> MRS is the number of units of bread needed to exactly compensate either person for the loss of one unit of ale. Equivalently, one unit of ale is needed to exactly compensate either person for the loss of MRS units of bread.

The numerical values of MRT and MRS under the initial allocation can be calculated and used to evaluate the consequences (for the person whose commodity bundle is changing) of a movement along the frontier. If MRT and MRS are not equal, there is a movement along the frontier that would raise welfare.

- Suppose that MRT is greater than MRS. Each person is willing to give up one unit of ale for MRS units of bread, but if ale production is reduced by one unit, MRT additional units of bread are produced. The person whose commodity bundle is adjusted is made better off, because that person got a better deal (MRT bread for one ale) than the worst acceptable deal (MRS bread for one ale).
- Now suppose that MRT is less than MRS. If MRT units of bread are given up, allowing one additional unit of ale to be produced, the person whose commodity bundle is adjusted is made better off. That person would have been willing to giving up MRS units of bread to get another ale, but only had to give up MRT units of bread. Once again, the deal actually received is better than the worst acceptable deal.

Thus, if MRS and MRT are not equal, there is a small movement along the production possibility that raises welfare, indicating that that the initial allocation is not match efficient. By contrast, the economy *is* match efficient if

$$MRS = MRT \tag{4.7}$$

so that the rate at which the people are *willing* to trade ale for bread is also the rate at which they are *able* to trade ale for bread. Any small movement along the frontier would leave them no better off and no worse off.

4.1.4 A Formal Statement

Each person's marginal rate of substitution is determined by his or her commodity bundle, and the marginal products in each industry are determined by that industry's use of the factors of production. It follows that the conditions for Pareto optimality constitute an equation system whose unknowns are the components of the allocation. This system can be solved to find the Pareto optimal allocations:

> A **Pareto optimal allocation** is a list $(a_G, b_G, a_H, b_H, K_a, L_a, K_b, L_b)$ such that equations (4.1)–(4.7) are satisfied.

As there are only seven equations to determine eight unknowns, this equation system has an infinite number of solutions, as it should.

4.2 COMPETITIVE EQUILIBRIUM

In a competitive economy, George and Harriet and the firms are both buyers and sellers:

- The firms buy factors of production from George and Harriet, use these factors to produce ale and bread, and sell these commodities to George and Harriet. Part of each firm's revenue is used to pay George and Harriet for the factors of production purchased from them, and the rest is profit. The profits are paid to the firm's owners, who are George and Harriet.
- George and Harriet sell factors of production to the firms. They use the income from this sale, and their shares of the firms' profits, to purchase ale and bread.

The markets are competitive if each person and firm believes that it cannot influence the prices at which factors and commodities are traded. Instead, each of them observes the prevailing prices, and attempts to make the best possible trade.

A complete set of markets for this economy includes markets for ale, bread, capital, and labour. The idea of competitive equilibrium can again be used to describe trade in these markets, and its basic characteristics are the same as in the exchange economy. The economy is in a competitive equilibrium if each market is clearing when every participant, having observed the market prices, attempts to make the trades that would make him as well off as possible. More exactly, competitive equilibrium consists of an allocation and a set of prices such that

1) Each person, having observed the prices at which he or she can sell factors of production and buy commodities, chooses the best attainable commodity bundle.
2) Each firm, having observed the prices at which factors of production can be purchased and output (which is either ale or bread) can be sold, chooses the profit-maximizing combination of factors.
3) These choices are consistent with market-clearing. The quantity of each factor of production that the firms, taken together, wish to buy is equal to the amount that George and Harriet wish to sell. The quantity of ale that George and Harriet wish to purchase is equal to the quantity that ale-producing firms wish to sell, and the quantity of bread that they wish to purchase is equal to the quantity that bread-producing firms wish to sell.

Since competitive equilibrium determines only relative prices, one good must serve as the numeraire. Let this good be bread, so that the prices to be determined are the prices of ale (p), capital (r), and labour (w).[8]

---

[8] The "price of capital" is the price at which the services of machines and equipment can be rented for a specified period of time. It is generally known as the **rental rate of capital.**

Each of the three requirements stated above will be examined in turn. Each requirement restricts the nature of competitive equilibrium, and these restrictions will be stated as equations. These equations collectively determine prices, profits, and the components of the allocation.

4.2.1 Consumer Behaviour

George is assumed to care only about his consumption of ale and bread, so he will spend his entire income on these commodities. The commodity bundles (a_G, b_G) that George can afford to purchase satisfy the budget constraint

$$pa_G + b_G = r\overline{K}_G + w\overline{L}_G + \alpha\pi_a + \beta\pi_b \qquad (4.8)$$

The left-hand side of this equation is the market value of George's commodity bundle, measured in bread, and the right-hand side is his income, also measured in bread. His income consists of the market value of his endowment of factors of production, and the profits that accrue to him as a result of his ownership of firms. These profits are $\alpha\pi_a + \beta\pi_b$, where π_a and π_b are the profits of the ale and bread industries, respectively.

George's problem here is essentially the same as it was in the exchange economy. He knows that he can buy both ale and bread in the marketplace, but he must forgo p loaves of bread for every pint of ale that he buys. Given these constraints, his best attainable commodity bundle satisfies the condition

$$MRS_G = p \qquad (4.9)$$

That is, he is correctly dividing his income between ale and bread purchases when the rate at which he is *willing* to trade ale for bread is just equal to the rate at which he is *able* to trade ale for bread. Since MRS_G is a function of a_G and b_G, (4.8) and (4.9) can be solved to obtain George's best attainable commodity bundle for given prices and profits.

Similarly, Harriet is assumed to care only about her consumption of ale and bread. She can afford to buy any commodity bundle (a_H, b_H) that satisfies her budget constraint

$$pa_H + b_H = r\overline{K}_H + w\overline{L}_H + (1 - \alpha)\pi_a + (1 - \beta)\pi_b \qquad (4.10)$$

Of these commodity bundles, the best bundle satisfies the condition

$$MRS_H = p \qquad (4.11)$$

Since MRS_H is a function of a_H and b_H, (4.10) and (4.11) can be solved to obtain Harriet's best attainable commodity bundle under given prices and profits.

4.2.2 Firm Behaviour

A competitive industry is generally imagined to be one in which there are many firms, each of which believes that it cannot influence the prices of the goods that it buys or sells. Each firm chooses its purchases of inputs (and therefore its level of output) so as to maximize its own profits. Summing the firms' demands for an input gives the industry demand for that input, and summing the firms' supplies of a produced good gives the industry supply of that good. However, under competition, the industry supplies and demands can be obtained more simply by maximizing the industry's profits.

Profits in the ale industry are equal to the difference between the market value of the goods that it produces and the market value of the factors of production that it buys[9]:

$$\pi_a = pf(K_a, L_a) - rK_a - wL_a \qquad (4.12)$$

The firms in the ale industry will hire the quantities of capital and labour that maximize industry profits. These quantities satisfy the conditions

$$pMP_K^a = r \qquad (4.13)$$

$$pMP_L^a = w \qquad (4.14)$$

To understand these conditions, consider (4.14). Using one more unit of labour raises ale production by MP_L^a pints. Each pint can be sold for p loaves of bread, so hiring one more unit of labour raises an ale producer's revenue by pMP_L^a loaves of bread. Hiring one more unit of labour also raises the ale producer's costs by w loaves of bread. The cost of hiring additional units of labour is fixed, but the assumption of diminishing marginal productivity implies that the revenue from hiring additional units of labour falls as the use of labour rises (see Figure 4.2).

An adjustment in the firm's use of labour will raise profits if it causes revenues to rise faster than costs, or if it causes revenues to fall more slowly than costs. If pMP_L^a is greater w, hiring another unit of labour raises revenues more than it raises costs, so that hiring another unit of labour is profitable. Firms respond to this situation by hiring more labour. If pMP_L^a is less than w, laying off a unit of labour reduces revenue by less than it reduces costs, so that laying off workers is profitable. Firms respond to this situation by laying off labour. These adjustments drive the level of employment to the point where pMP_L^a is just equal to w, as required by (4.14). Condition (4.13) is interpreted in an analogous fashion.

The profits in the bread industry are

$$\pi_b = g(K_b, L_b) - rK_b - wL_b \qquad (4.15)$$

---

[9] Economists distinguish between **economic profits** and **normal profits.** Normal profits represent the return that an entrepreneur must earn to remain in an industry. They are equal to the entrepreneur's "opportunity cost," that is, his earnings under his best alternate employment. The entrepreneur's total return less his normal profits constitutes his economic profits. These are the profits that influence the entrepreneur's behaviour: he wants to locate in industries in which his economic profits are positive, and he does not want to remain in industries in which his economic profits are negative.

All references to profits in this text are to economic profits. Perhaps the easiest way to understand an equation like (4.12) is to imagine that the entrepreneur provides labour to his own firm and pays himself the market wage. The difference between revenue and total factor payments is then economic profits.

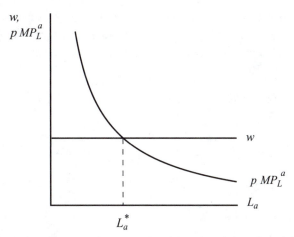

Figure 4.2: A Competitive Labour Market. Firms hire labour until the value of the goods produced by another unit of labour is equal to the cost of another unit of labour.

Profits are maximized when

$$MP^b_K = r \tag{4.16}$$

$$MP^b_L = w \tag{4.17}$$

Again, firms adjust their employment of each factor until the market value of the goods produced by one more unit of the factor is just equal to that factor's cost.

The marginal products in each industry are determined by the quantities of capital and labour used in that industry. It follows that (4.13) and (4.14) can be solved to determine the quantities of capital and labour demanded by the ale industry at any given set of prices, while (4.16) and (4.17) can be solved to determine the quantities of capital and labour demanded by the bread industry.

4.2.3 Market-Clearing

The "adding-up" conditions (4.1)–(4.4) also serve as market-clearing conditions. The first condition states the ale and bread industries buy all of the capital that George and Harriet offer for sale, and the second condition makes the same claim for labour. The third and fourth conditions state that George and Harriet buy all of the ale produced by the ale industry and all of the bread produced by the bread industry.

4.2.4 Equilibrium

A competitive equilibrium satisfies conditions 1–3 set out in Section 4.2. Equivalently,

> A **competitive equilibrium** consists of a list of prices and profits (p, r, w, π_a, π_b) and an allocation $(a_G, b_G, a_H, b_H, K_a, L_a, K_b, L_b)$ such that equations (4.1)–(4.4) and (4.8)–(4.17) are satisfied.

There are fourteen equations in the system but only thirteen unknowns to be determined. If the equations in the system are independent – if each equation adds a new restriction – there will be no solution. But they are not independent. Combining the two budget constraints gives

$$p(a_G + a_H) + (b_G + b_H) = r\left(\overline{K}_G + \overline{K}_H\right) + w\left(\overline{L}_G + \overline{L}_H\right) + \pi_a + \pi_b$$

Then, by (4.1) and (4.2),

$$p(a_G + a_H) + (b_G + b_H) = r(K_a + K_b) + w(L_a + L_b) + \pi_a + \pi_b$$

and by (4.12) and (4.15),

$$p(a_G + a_H) + (b_G + b_H) = pf(K_a, L_a) + g(K_b, L_b)$$

But if this equation holds, one of (4.3) and (4.4) is satisfied if the other is. Either one of them can be dropped from the system. This leaves thirteen equations to determine thirteen unknowns. The following example shows how such a system can be solved to determine the competitive equilibrium.

4.3 AN EXAMPLE OF COMPETITIVE EQUILIBRIUM

Imagine that George and Harriet have the following Cobb–Douglas preferences:

$$U_G = (a_G)^{1/4} (b_G)^{3/4}$$

$$U_H = (a_H)^{1/2} (b_H)^{1/2}$$

The economy is endowed with one unit of labour and one unit of capital. These resources are evenly split between George and Harriet, as is the ownership of each firm. The production functions are

$$a = 2\left[(K_a)^{1/2} + (L_a)^{1/2}\right]$$

$$b = 2\left[(K_b)^{1/2} + (L_b)^{1/2}\right]$$

What will be the competitive equilibrium in this economy?

There is one respect in which it is easier to find the competitive equilibrium in the production economy than in the exchange economy. In the latter economy, the identities of the buyer and seller could not be identified in advance, so we were forced to use excess demand schedules instead of the more familiar supply and demand schedules. In the production economy, however, every unit of both commodities and both factors of production is traded. George and Harriet sell factors of production and buy ale and bread. The ale industry buys factors and sells ale, and of course, the bread industry buys factors and sells bread. Since we know who is on which side of each market, supply and demand schedules are easily formulated.

A market supply schedule shows the total quantity of a good offered for sale, as a function of the prices prevailing in the economy. A market demand curve shows the total quantity of a good that the market participants wish to buy, as a function of the prevailing prices.

4.3.1 Factor Markets

The supplies of the factors are easily identified. The more factors of production that George and Harriet sell, the greater will be their incomes and the more commodities they will be able to purchase. They will therefore offer to sell all of their capital and labour under every set of prices.

The demands for capital and labour in the ale industry are given by (4.13) and (4.14). Evaluating the marginal products in these equations and then re-arranging the equations gives

$$K_a = \left(\frac{p}{r}\right)^2$$

$$L_a = \left(\frac{p}{w}\right)^2$$

A higher price for ale induces firms to produce more ale, using more capital and more labour. A higher price for either factor causes the firms to use less of that factor, and to produce less ale as a consequence. Similarly, evaluating the marginal products in (4.16) and (4.17) and re-arranging these equations gives the demands for capital and labour in the bread industry:

$$K_b = \left(\frac{1}{r}\right)^2$$

$$L_b = \left(\frac{1}{w}\right)^2$$

The market demand for each factor is found by summing the demands of the ale and bread industries. The market-clearing conditions for capital and labour equate market supply to market demand:

$$1 = \left(\frac{1}{r}\right)^2 \left(1 + p^2\right)$$

$$1 = \left(\frac{1}{w}\right)^2 \left(1 + p^2\right)$$

Given any price for ale, these conditions determine the factor prices that clear the factor markets.

4.3.2 Commodity Markets

Since firms buy capital and labour only so that they can produce goods, the firms' demands for factors of production imply an offer to sell ale and bread. These offers are found by substituting the factor demands into the production functions. If S_a and S_b are the quantities of ale and bread offered for sale,

$$S_a = 2p \left(\frac{1}{r} + \frac{1}{w} \right)$$

$$S_b = 2 \left(\frac{1}{r} + \frac{1}{w} \right)$$

To find the market demands for these commodities, note that George and Harriet will have equal incomes because they have equal endowments. Let this income be y, and replace the expressions on the right-hand side of the budget constraints with y. Evaluating the marginal rate of substitution in (4.9), and then solving (4.8) and (4.9), gives George's demands for ale and bread:

$$a_G = \frac{y}{4p}$$

$$b_G = \frac{3y}{4}$$

Harriet's demands are obtained similarly from (4.10) and (4.11):

$$a_H = \frac{y}{2p}$$

$$b_H = \frac{y}{2}$$

Now note that, in any equilibrium, the ale and bread industries sell goods that have a market value (measured in bread) of $pS_a + S_b$. Each industry spends some of its earnings on factors of production, and George and Harriet each receive half of this expenditure. The rest of the earnings are distributed as profits, and George and Harriet each receive half of this distribution. It follows that George and Harriet each receive an income equal to half of the market value of the goods produced:

$$y = (pS_a + S_b)/2 = (1 + p^2) \left(\frac{1}{r} + \frac{1}{w} \right)$$

The market demand for each good is equal to the sum of George's and Harriet's demands. If D_a and D_b are the quantities of ale and bread demanded,

$$D_a = \left(\frac{3y}{4p} \right) = \left(\frac{3}{4p} \right) (1 + p^2) \left(\frac{1}{r} + \frac{1}{w} \right)$$

$$D_b = \left(\frac{5y}{4} \right) = \left(\frac{5}{4} \right) (1 + p^2) \left(\frac{1}{r} + \frac{1}{w} \right)$$

The market-clearing condition for each commodity equates market demand to market supply. As noted above, only one of these conditions is needed.

HOMOGENEITY AND PROFITS

Suppose that the production function for cheese is

$$c = F(K, L)$$

The production function is said to be **homogeneous of degree _r_** if, for every pair (K, L) and every positive λ,

$$F(\lambda K, \lambda L) = \lambda^r F(K, L)$$

For example, if the production function is homeogeneous of degree 1/2, using four times as much of each input will yield only twice as much output. There is a close correspondence between the mathematician's concept of homogeneity and the economist's idea of returns to scale. A production function that is homogeneous of degree 1 displays constant returns to scale, and one that is homogeneous of a degree less than 1 displays decreasing returns to scale.

Euler's rule describes an important characteristic of homogeneous equations. To obtain it, differentiate the above equation with respect to λ:

$$\frac{\partial F}{\partial K} K + \frac{\partial F}{\partial L} L = r\lambda^{r-1} F(K, L)$$

Now evaluate λ at 1:

$$\frac{\partial F}{\partial K} K + \frac{\partial F}{\partial L} L = r F(K, L)$$

This is Euler's rule, and it has an immediate economic interpretation. If the use of each factor is extended until the value of its marginal product is just equal to that factor's price, as occurs under competition, the cost of the factors of production will be equal to the fraction r of the goods produced. Everything else is profit, so profits are equal to the fraction $1 - r$ of the goods produced. There are no profits under constant returns to scale, and there are positive profits under decreasing returns to scale.

4.3.3 Equilibrium

The ale market-clearing condition reduces to

$$3\left(1 + p^2\right) = 8p^2$$

This condition determines the market-clearing price of ale:

$$p = \sqrt{3/5}$$

Substituting this price into the market-clearing conditions for capital and labour yields the factor prices:

$$r = w = \sqrt{8/5}$$

The components of the allocation are determined by substituting these prices into the individual factor and commodity demands. The ale industry employs 3/8 of the capital and 3/8 of the labour, and the bread industry employs the remainder. The economy is then able to produce $\sqrt{6}$ units of ale and $\sqrt{10}$ units of bread. George consumes $\sqrt{2/3}$ units of ale and $6/\sqrt{10}$ units of bread, and Harriet consumes $\sqrt{8/3}$ units of ale and $4/\sqrt{10}$ units of bread. Lastly, the profits are determined by substituting into (4.12) and (4.15). By Euler's rule (see the box on page 71), half of each industry's output is profit.

4.4 THE TWO THEOREMS

The claim of the first theorem is that, under certain conditions, the allocation attained under competitive equilibrium is Pareto optimal. The production economy satisfies the conditions under which the theorem holds. To show this, recall that a Pareto optimal allocation is described by (4.1)–(4.7), and that a competitive equilibrium is described by (4.1)–(4.4) and (4.8)–(4.17). If every restriction contained in the first set of equations is also contained in the second set of equations, so that the restrictions on the competitive allocation are at least as confining as the restrictions on the Pareto optimal allocation, the theorem holds.

Note that the first four equations in each system are the same, so it need only be shown that the equation system describing competitive equilibrium contains the restrictions (4.5), (4.6), and (4.7). Consider these three equations in turn.

- Combining (4.9) and (4.11) to eliminate p yields (4.5). If George and Harriet choose commodity bundles at which their marginal rates of substitution are equal to the relative price p, they choose commodity bundles at which their marginal rates of substitution are equal. The condition for exchange efficiency is satisfied under competitive equilibrium.
- Combining (4.13) and (4.16) to eliminate r gives

$$pMP_K^a = MP_K^b$$

Each industry employs more capital until the value of the goods (measured in bread) produced by the last unit of capital is driven down to the cost of an additional unit of capital (also measured in bread). Consequently, the value of the goods produced by the last unit of capital is the same in each industry. Similarly, combining (4.14) and (4.17) to eliminate w shows that the value of the goods produced by the last unit of labour is the same in each industry:

$$pMP_L^a = MP_L^b$$

Combining these two conditions to eliminate p gives (4.6), so that competitive equilibrium is production efficient.

- Since competitive equilibrium is production efficient, there is a well-defined marginal rate of transformation. Re-arranging either of the last two equations shows that, under competitive equilibrium,

$$MRT = p$$

Competitive equilibrium also implies that the marginal rates of substitution are equal to each other and equal to the relative price:

$$MRS = p$$

But if both of these conditions are satisfied, the marginal rate of transformation is equal to the marginal rate of substitution, so that (4.7), the condition for match efficiency, is also satisfied.

Thus, competitive equilibrium satisfies all of the conditions for Pareto optimality. The first theorem holds in the production economy.

The second theorem also holds in the production economy. Each Pareto optimal allocation stipulates a commodity bundle for George and a commodity bundle for Harriet. They will be able to purchase these bundles in a competitive equilibrium if they have enough purchasing power. Their bidding for commodities will induce firms to supply the correct quantities of ale and bread, and it will also generate the desired division of the commodities between them. Competitive bidding for factors by the firms will ensure that factors are allocated efficiently.

Since George's purchasing power rises relative to Harriet's when he is endowed with a greater share of the factors of production (or, under decreasing returns to scale, a greater share of the ownership of firms), a particular Pareto optimum is reached simply by engineering an appropriate distribution of endowments.

4.5 CONCLUSIONS

The observation that market outcomes in competitive economies can have desirable properties – can be Pareto optimal – causes economists to be wary of market intervention. Some forms of market invention are described in the next chapter, and the loss of welfare resulting from them are measured.

APPENDIX: AN EXAMPLE OF PRODUCTION EFFICIENCY

Let the production functions for the ale and bread industries be

$$a = (K_a)^\alpha (L_a)^{1-\alpha} \qquad 0 < \alpha < 1$$
$$b = (K_b)^{1/2} (L_b)^{1/2}$$

Both of these production functions display constant returns to scale.[10] The marginal products of the factors are

$$MP_K^a = \alpha \left(\frac{K_a}{L_a}\right)^{\alpha-1}, \qquad MP_L^a = (1-\alpha)\left(\frac{K_a}{L_a}\right)^{\alpha}$$

$$MP_K^b = (1/2)\left(\frac{K_b}{L_b}\right)^{-1/2}, \qquad MP_L^b = (1/2)\left(\frac{K_b}{L_b}\right)^{1/2}$$

The importance of the parameter α can best be understood by examining the ratio of the factors' marginal products in each industry:

$$\frac{MP_L^a}{MP_K^a} = \left(\frac{1-\alpha}{\alpha}\right)\left(\frac{K_a}{L_a}\right) \tag{4.18}$$

$$\frac{MP_L^b}{MP_K^b} = \frac{K_b}{L_b} \tag{4.19}$$

Suppose that the ratio of capital to labour is the same in both industries. Then

- If α is less than $1/2$, the first ratio of marginal products is greater than the second. Labour is relatively productive in the ale industry, and capital is relatively productive in the bread industry.
- If α is greater than $1/2$, the second ratio of marginal products is greater than the first. Labour is relatively productive in the bread industry, and capital is relatively productive in the ale industry.
- If α is equal to $1/2$, the two ratios of marginal products are equal. The relative productivities of the two factors are the same in both industries.

Assume also that the economy is endowed with one unit of capital and one unit of labour, so that any allocation of factors between the two industries must satisfy the

---

[10] Returns to scale are easily determined when the production function is Cobb–Douglas. Suppose that the production function is

$$q = K^m L^n$$

where m and n are constants. If K_0 units of capital and L_0 units of labour are used in the production of the good, q_0 units of the good are produced, where

$$q_0 = (K_0)^m (L_0)^n$$

If $2K_0$ units of capital and $2L_0$ units of labour are used, the output q_1 satisfies the condition

$$q_1 = (2K_0)^m (2L_0)^n = 2^{m+n}(K_0)^m(L_0)^n = 2^{m+n}q_0$$

If the sum $m + n$ is equal to one, doubling the inputs leads to a doubling of output, so the production function displays constant returns to scale. If the sum of the exponents is less than one, doubling the inputs leads to less than a doubling of output, implying decreasing returns to scale. Finally, if the sum of the exponents is greater than one, doubling the inputs more than doubles output, implying increasing returns to scale.

conditions

$$K_a + K_b = 1 \qquad (4.20)$$

$$L_a + L_b = 1 \qquad (4.21)$$

Production Efficiency

An efficient allocation of factors satisfies (4.6), which can be also be written as[11]

$$\frac{MP_L^a}{MP_K^a} = \frac{MP_L^b}{MP_K^b}$$

Substituting (4.18) and (4.19) into this condition yields

$$\left(\frac{1-\alpha}{\alpha}\right)\left(\frac{K_a}{L_a}\right) = \frac{K_b}{L_b} \qquad (4.22)$$

An allocation of factors (K_a, L_a, K_b, L_b) is production efficient if it satisfies (4.20)–(4.22).

Since there are only three equations to determine the values of four variables, there are an infinite number of efficient allocations. These allocations can be "indexed" by L_a. That is, there is an efficient allocation in which L_a takes each value from 0 to 1. The components of these allocations can be found by recursive substitution. Substituting (4.20) and (4.21) into (4.22) to eliminate K_b and L_b yields

$$K_a = \frac{\alpha L_a}{(1-\alpha)(1-L_a) + \alpha L_a}$$

---

[11] The interpretation of this condition is similar to that of (4.6). Moving one unit of labour out of the ale industry reduces ale production by MP_L^a units, and each unit of capital moved into the ale industry raises ale production by MP_K^a units. It follows that ale production would remain unchanged if one unit of labour were moved out of the ale industry and MP_L^a/MP_K^a units of capital were moved into that industry. Similarly, bread production would remain unchanged if one unit of labour were moved out of the bread industry and MP_L^b/MP_K^b units of capital were moved into that industry.

Production efficiency requires these two quantities to be the same. To see why, imagine that MP_L^a/MP_K^a is equal to 3 and that MP_L^b/MP_K^b is equal to 5 under some initial allocation of factors. This allocation is not efficient because it is possible to raise the production of one good without reducing production of the other. If one unit of labour is moved from the ale industry to the bread industry, 5 units of capital can be moved out of the bread industry without causing a fall in bread production. Three of these units of capital must be moved into the ale industry to keep ale production from falling (remember that this industry has lost a unit of labour), but that leaves 2 units of capital unemployed. If these units of capital are moved into the ale industry, ale production will rise without bread production falling. If they are moved back to the bread industry, bread production will rise without ale production falling.

A reallocation of factors that raises the output of one good without reducing the output of the other is always possible if the two ratios are not equal. No such reallocation is possible – implying production efficiency – if the two ratios are equal.

Also,

$$L_b = 1 - L_a$$

$$K_b = 1 - K_a = \frac{(1-\alpha)(1-L_a)}{(1-\alpha)(1-L_a) + \alpha L_a}$$

A movement along the production possibility frontier implies a switch from one of these efficient allocations to another. Since L_a and K_a rise together, a movement along the frontier is associated with a shift of *both* factors from one industry to the other.

The nature of this shift is most readily understood by examining the **capital–labour ratio** in each industry:

$$k_a \equiv \frac{K_a}{L_a} = \frac{\alpha}{(1-\alpha)(1-L_a) + \alpha L_a} = \frac{\alpha}{(1-\alpha) + (2\alpha - 1)L_a}$$

$$k_b \equiv \frac{K_b}{L_b} = \frac{1-\alpha}{(1-\alpha)(1-L_a) + \alpha L_a} = \frac{1-\alpha}{(1-\alpha) + (2\alpha - 1)L_a}$$

Note that, by (4.22), the economy is production efficient if

$$\left(\frac{1-\alpha}{\alpha}\right) k_a = k_b$$

There are three cases:

- If α is equal to $1/2$, so that both industries have the same production function, there is no advantage to having different capital–labour ratios in the two industries. Consequently, k_a and k_b are always equal to the economy-wide capital–labour ratio, which is 1.
- If α is less than $1/2$, so that labour is relatively productive in the ale industry and capital is relatively productive in the bread industry, $k_a \leq 1 \leq k_b$. The efficient values of k_a and k_b depend upon the sizes of the two industries. If L_a is near 1, so that almost all of the factors of production are allocated to the ale industry, k_a must be near 1. If L_a is near 0, so that almost all of the factors of production are allocated to the bread industry, k_b must be near 1.[12] Consequently, as L_a rises from 0 to 1, k_a rises from $\alpha/(1-\alpha)$ to 1 and k_b rises from 1 to $(1-\alpha)/\alpha$.[13]
- If α is greater than $1/2$, so that labour is relatively productive in the bread industry and capital is relatively productive in the ale industry, $k_b \leq 1 \leq k_a$. As L_a rises from 0 to 1, k_a falls from $\alpha/(1-\alpha)$ to 1 and k_b falls from 1 to $(1-\alpha)/\alpha$.

---

[12] Recall that the economy is endowed with one unit of capital and one unit of labour, so that the capital–labour ratio in the whole economy is 1. If all of these factors are allocated to ale production, k_a is 1; and if all of the factors are allocated to bread production, k_b is 1.

[13] If the quantities of capital and labour in the economy are fixed, how is it possible for both k_a and k_b to rise simultaneously? To answer this riddle, you might wish to consider Professor X, whose move from university A to university B raised the average intellect in both places.

The Curvature of the Production Possibility Frontier

The production possibility frontier is generally imagined to be bowed away from the origin, as it is in Figure 4.1. That is, rightward movements along the frontier cause the marginal rate of transformation to rise. The example above almost always generates just such a frontier. The marginal rate of transformation is

$$MRT \equiv \frac{MP_L^b}{MP_L^a} = H\left[(1 - \alpha) + J L_a\right]^{J/2}$$

Here, H is a positive constant and J is defined to be $2\alpha - 1$. As resources are transferred from the bread industry to the ale industry (generating a rightward movement along the frontier), L_a rises. If α is equal to $1/2$, the marginal rate of transformation does not change; but if α is either greater or less than $1/2$, the marginal rate of transformation rises.[14]

The reason for this result is that, when production of one of the goods is very small, there is very little flexibility in the way in which factors are allocated between the industries. Suppose, for example, that α is less than $1/2$, so that labour is relatively productive in the ale industry and capital is relatively productive in the bread industry. Ideally, k_a should be below 1 and k_b should be above 1, but

- If very little bread is to be produced, almost all of the factors are in the ale industry, so k_a cannot be pushed very far below 1.
- If very little ale is to be produced, almost all of the factors are in the bread industry, so k_b cannot be pushed very far above 1.

That is, approaching either end of the production possibility frontier limits the choice of industry capital–labour ratios, and these limitations alter the marginal rate of transformation. The greater the quantity of ale produced, the more bread must be given up to get another unit of ale. The greater the quantity of bread produced, the more ale must be given up to get another unit of bread.

Of course, if α is equal to $1/2$, efficiency requires that k_a and k_b be equal to 1. These capital–labour ratios are easily maintained, even at the ends of the frontier, so the marginal rate of transformation is constant and the frontier is linear.

QUESTIONS

1. Assume that the production functions in the ale and bread industry are

$$q_A = (K_A)^{1/2}(L_A)^{1/2}$$

$$q_B = (K_B)^{1/3}(L_B)^{2/3}$$

---

[14] Consider the effects of increasing L_a. If J is positive, the base rises, and since the exponent is also positive, MRT rises. If J is negative, the base falls, but the exponent is negative, so the decline in the base causes MRT to rise.

a) Find the four marginal products, and show that each marginal product can be written as a function of the *ratio* of factor inputs.

b) Assume that there are fixed quantities of capital and labour in the economy, and that they are allocated so that

$$L_A/K_A = 4$$

$$L_B/K_B = 27$$

Calculate the numerical values of the four marginal products. Using *only these numerical values,* fill in the blanks below.

i) Moving one unit of capital out of the ale industry reduces ale production by _____ units, so moving ____ units of capital out of the ale industry reduces ale production by one unit. This amount of capital, put to work in the bread industry, increases bread production by ____ units.

ii) Moving one unit of labour out of the ale industry reduces ale production by _____ units, so moving ____ units of labour out of the ale industry reduces ale production by one unit. This amount of labour, put to work in the bread industry, increases bread production by ____ units.

iii) If bread production is to be increased without any accompanying reduction in ale production, _____ should be moved out of the ale industry and into the bread industry, and _____ should be moved out of the bread industry and into the ale industry. Moving ____ units of ____ from the ale industry to the bread industry and _____ units of ____ from the bread industry to the ale industry leaves ale production unchanged, because the first transfer reduces ale production by one unit and the second transfer raises ale production by one unit. The same pair of transfers increases bread production by _____ units.

c) Assume that there are fixed quantities of capital and labour in the economy, and that they are allocated so that

$$L_A/K_A = 1/2$$

$$L_B/K_B = 1$$

Calculate the numerical values of the four marginal products. Using *only these numerical values,* show that this allocation corresponds to a point on the production possibility frontier.

2. This question deals with an economy in which the issue of production efficiency does not arise, perhaps because there is only one factor of production. The requirement that a Pareto optimal allocation be production efficient is then replaced with the simpler requirement that a combination of goods lying on the production possibility frontier be produced.

Consider an economy inhabited by George and Harriet, whose utility functions are

$$U_G = (a_G)^{1/2} (b_G)^{1/2}$$

$$U_H = a_H + 2b_H$$

The total quantities of ale and bread that can be produced by the economy are a and b, and they are constrained by the production function

$$b = 2(10 - a)^{1/2}$$

There are infinitely many Pareto optimal allocations. In one of them, Harriet's utility is 8.

a) An allocation in this economy is described by a list of four variables. What are these variables?

b) What four equations describe the Pareto optimal allocation in which Harriet's utility is 8?

c) Find this Pareto optimal allocation.

3. This question also deals with an economy in which the issue of production efficiency does not arise.

Consider an economy inhabited by George and Harriet, whose utility functions are

$$U_G = (a_G)^{1/3} (b_G)^{2/3}$$

$$U_H = (a_H)^{1/5} (b_H)^{4/5}$$

The total quantities of ale and bread that can be produced by the economy are a and b, and they are constrained by the production function

$$b = 10 - a$$

There is a Pareto optimal allocation in which George receives $\tilde{a}$ units of ale, where $\tilde{a}$ is any number between 0 and $6\frac{2}{3}$.

a) What list of four variables describes an optimal allocation for this economy?

b) What four equations describe the Pareto optimal allocation in which George receives $\tilde{a}$ units of ale?

c) Find this allocation.

5

Consumer and Producer Surplus

If simple competitive economies are efficient, we should be able to characterize the loss experienced when some unwarranted intervention changes the allocation of resources. Economists use consumer surplus and producer surplus for this purpose. These concepts are reviewed here.[1]

A useful graphical relationship is established in the next section. Consumer and producer surplus are then introduced, and used to describe the welfare effects of some forms of intervention.

5.1 MARGINS AND TOTALS

We will frequently encounter curves that describe marginal *something* – cost, benefit, revenue, damage – and we will often want to know the change in the total when quantity changes. A simple rule applies to all of these situations:

> **The change in the total is equal to the area under the curve showing the corresponding margin, between the old and new quantities.**

For example, suppose that a firm's total costs are represented by the equation

$$C(q) = q^2$$

The increase in the firm's total costs when its output rises from q_0 to q_1 is easily calculated from this equation: it is $(q_1)^2 - (q_0)^2$. Now suppose that the firm's total cost schedule is not known to us, but that its marginal cost schedule is known:

$$MC(q) = \frac{dC}{dq} = 2q$$

Although the marginal cost schedule shows only the cost of raising output by one (arbitrarily small) unit, we can use it to find the required change in total cost. The above

---

[1] The aim of this chapter is to examine the essential ideas underlying consumer and producer surplus. A more rigorous discussion of surplus is contained in Chapter 17, which develops these concepts within a small general equilibrium model.

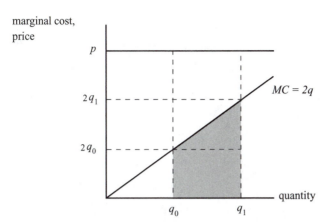

Figure 5.1: An Example. The increase in total cost when output rises is equal to the area under the marginal cost curve, between the initial and final levels of output.

rule tells us that the change in total cost as output rises from q_0 to q_1 is equal to the area under the marginal cost curve, between q_0 and q_1 (see Figure 5.1). As this area is the sum of the areas of two simple figures, a rectangle and a triangle, it is readily calculated:

$$\text{area} = (2q_0)(q_1 - q_0) + \tfrac{1}{2}(2q_1 - 2q_0)(q_1 - q_0) = (q_1)^2 - (q_0)^2$$

Clearly, knowing the marginal cost schedule is as good as knowing the total cost schedule itself. The appendix continues this example to show why the rule works.

The following rule is a simple extension of the first rule.

> **If the margin is represented by the vertical distance between two marginal curves, the change in the corresponding total is equal to the area between these two marginal curves, between the old and new quantities.**

Suppose, for example, that the firm depicted in Figure 5.1 sells its output as price p, and that we wish to calculate the increase in the firm's profits as it raises its output from q_0 to q_1. The increase in the firm's profits is equal to the difference between the increase in its revenues and the increase in its costs, so the increase in profits can be calculated by applying the original rule twice:

> **Since every unit of goods is sold at the same price, the price line is also the marginal revenue curve. The original rule tells us that the increase in revenue is the area under the price line, between q_0 and q_1. That rule also told us that the increase in costs is the area under the marginal cost curve, between the same two quantities. The increase in profits is the difference between these two areas. That is, it is the area between these two curves, between q_0 and q_1.**

The new rule provides a short cut for making the same calculation. The increase in the firm's profits when it produces another unit of goods – its marginal profits – is the difference between its marginal revenue and its marginal cost. Thus, marginal profits are equal to the vertical distance between the marginal revenue (i.e., price) and marginal

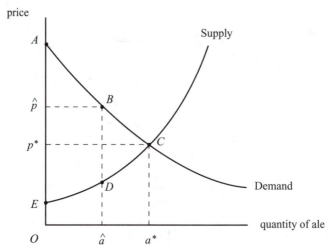

Figure 5.2: Two Equilibria. In the absence of intervention, a^* pints of ale are traded at the price p^*. If the government restricts the sale of ale to $\hat{a}$ pints by placing a limit on each firm's sales, the price rises to $\hat{p}$.

cost curves. The new rule allows us to directly calculate the increase in profits as the area between the two curves, between q_0 and q_1.

5.2 SURPLUS

Trading in organized markets is beneficial to both the buyer and the seller, and these benefits are measured by consumer surplus and producer surplus, respectively. This section defines both concepts and then describes the way in which they are calculated.[2]

Surplus and prices are measured in the same units. If prices are expressed in units of a numeraire, surplus will also be measured in the numeraire. If the prices are currency prices, surplus will be measured in the same currency. In this chapter, prices and surplus will be measured in dollars.

The **consumer surplus** in each market is the difference between the dollar value to the buyers of the goods traded in that market, and the amount that the buyers actually paid for these goods. The latter amount is easily calculated, but what is the former amount?

The height of the demand curve at any level of output represents the value of the last unit of output to the purchaser of that unit. Suppose, for example, that ale is infinitely divisible – can be sold drop by drop – and that its demand is described by the demand curve in Figure 5.2. One drop less than $\hat{a}$ pints of ale can be sold at a price just above $\hat{p}$ dollars per pint, but the full $\hat{a}$ pints can't be sold unless the price per pint falls to $\hat{p}$ dollars. The person who demanded that last drop of ale thinks that, although it isn't worth anything *more* than $\hat{p}$ dollars per pint, it *is* worth $\hat{p}$ dollars. Since $\hat{p}$ is the height of

---

[2] The notion of surplus presented here corresponds to the original formulation by Marshall [43]. Much attention was subsequently given to refining this concept, notably by Hicks [32, 33]. The concept is most familiar to North Americans through the work of Harberger [31].

the demand curve at $\widehat{a}$, we can conclude that the height of the demand curve represents the value to the purchaser of the last (arbitrarily small) unit.[3, 4]

At any level of output, the last unit of goods purchased is called the **marginal unit.** Thus, we could also say that, at each level of output, the height of the demand curve represents the value to the buyer of the marginal unit of goods. Equivalently, the height of the demand curve represents the marginal value of the good to the buyers in the market.

Note that the demand curve, interpreted in this fashion, is one of those marginal *something* – marginal value to the buyer – curves mentioned above. If a^* pints of ale are sold at a price of p^* dollars per pint, the value of the goods to the buyers is the area under the demand curve between 0 and a^*. This is the area $OACa^*$ in Figure 5.2. The amount actually paid is p^*a^* dollars, which is equal to area Op^*Ca^*. The difference between these values, consumer surplus, is area ACp^*.

Analogously, **producer surplus** is the difference between the amount received by the sellers for these goods and the minimum amount that the sellers would have been willing to accept. The first of these amounts is p^*a^* dollars, equal to area Op^*Ca^* in Figure 5.2. The second amount is the increase in the sellers' costs when they increase output from 0 to a^*. Since the supply curve is the industry's marginal cost curve, found by aggregating the marginal cost curves of the individual firms, the increase in the sellers' costs is equal to the area under the aggregated marginal cost curve between 0 and a^*. That is, it is the area $OECa^*$. Producer surplus is therefore equal to the area Ep^*C.

The sum of consumer surplus and producer surplus in the initial equilibrium is represented by the area EAC in Figure 5.2.

Each firm's marginal cost is equal to the market value of the resources needed to produce another unit of that firm's output; but in a system of competitive markets, the price of each resource is determined by competitive pressures. Other firms could use the same resources to produce other goods, and they will continue to bid for them until the resource prices have been driven up so much that further production is unprofitable. It follows that *each firm's marginal cost is equal to the maximum value of the goods that other firms could have produced with the same resources.* This observation leads to an alternative interpretation of surplus (i.e., the sum of consumer and producer surplus).

> **Surplus is the difference between the value to the buyers of the goods actually produced, and the value of the goods that would have been produced if the same resources had been used in the best alternative way.**

---

[3] Note that the price is always the price of some standard unit, even though we are imagining that the good can be sold in arbitrarily small amounts. In the present case, the price is always the price of one pint of ale, even when that ale is being sold drop by drop. For example, if I am willing to pay 1/100 of a cent for one more drop of ale, and if there are 50,000 drops in a pint, my marginal valuation of ale is $5 per pint.

[4] This height is often referred to as the consumer's **willingness to pay.** Welfare measures based upon willingness to pay are frequently used in environmental economics and in other types of empirical work, although other measures (based on the Hicksian demand curve rather than the Marshallian demand curve) are generally used in theoretical work. See Willig [67] for a defence of the Marshallian approach.

The efficiency of a system of competitive markets follows from the fact that competition maximizes surplus. Consider Figure 5.2 once more. In equilibrium, the value to the buyer of the last unit of ale produced is just equal to the value of the goods that could have been produced in its place. Its production adds nothing to surplus. However, each preceding unit of ale was worth more to consumers than the goods that could have been produced in its place, so its production added to surplus.[5] If production were pushed beyond a^*, the additional units of ale would reduce surplus: the additional ale would be worth less to the consumer than the goods that could have been produced with the same resources.

5.3 THE WELFARE COST OF INTERVENTION

Surplus is maximized under a system of free markets because every agent in the economy is responding to price signals. Each consumer observes an array of commodity prices. If a good's price is relatively high, the consumer knows that he must give up significant quantities of other goods to obtain it, and will be sparing in his consumption of that good. On the other hand, if a good's price is relatively low, the consumer knows that he can consume it without significantly curtailing his consumption of other goods, and will be inclined to consume more of it. This behaviour benefits society as a whole because every commodity's price is equal to the resource cost of producing it. The price signal indicates not just what a consumer must give up to acquire a unit of a particular good, but what society as a whole must give up. The consumer's response to such price signals raises society's welfare as well as his own.

Firms respond to price signals in two ways:

- They are aware that there a number of ways to produce any given good, and that each way uses different quantities of scarce resources. Their pursuit of profits causes them to produce each good in the least costly way. This behaviour benefits society because resource prices indicate the relative scarcity of the factors of production. The price of titanium is higher than the price of iron because there is less of it. The price of skilled labour in western countries is higher than the price of unskilled labour because there are more uses for skilled labour than for unskilled labour.
- Firms compare the prices of commodities with the minimum cost of producing them, and produce more of the goods for which the difference between price and marginal cost is positive. Again, this behaviour benefits society. The price of a good is a signal of the value that consumers place on another unit of that good, while its marginal cost is a signal of the value that they place on the goods that could have been produced in its place. Output adjustments of this kind cause goods on which consumers place a high value to be produced in place of goods on which they place a low value.

---

[5] That is, at every lower level of output, the height of the demand curve is greater than the height of the supply curve, indicating that each of these units of ale is worth more to consumers than the goods that could have been produced with the resources used in its production.

Competition among the firms ultimately drives down each commodity's price until it is just equal to its marginal cost of production. That is, the price signals both the good's value to the consumer and the value of the goods that could have been produced in its place. The economy's resources are then being used to produce the goods that are most valuable to consumers.

This price signalling mechanism works less well under certain sorts of intervention. Specifically, it works less well if commodity prices no longer represent the resource cost of producing goods, or if the prices of resources no longer indicate their relative scarcity. It also works less well if agents are prevented from responding to price signals. Some interventions of this kind, namely taxes, subsidies, and quantity constraints, are examined in this section.

Note that some kinds of interventions do *not* impair the price signalling mechanism. The essence of the second theorem is that the redistribution of endowments is one such intervention. Redistribution, away from the rich and toward the poor, *would* affect the prices and quantities of various goods. The price of yachts would fall and fewer of them would be produced. The price of low-quality urban housing would fall and the price of better quality housing would rise, stimulating urban renewal. But the price of every good would continue to be equal to the market value of the goods that could have been produced in its place. Surplus would still be as large as it can possibly be.

5.3.1 Quantity Constraints

Imagine that the government intervenes to limit the quantity of ale made available to the public. Specifically, imagine that it issues permits for the production and sale of $\widehat{a}$ units of ale to the firms that can produce these units at the lowest cost. Since firms are unable to sell as much as they would like at the initial price, they will raise the price until they are selling $\widehat{a}$ pints at the highest possible price (denoted $\widehat{p}$). This equilibrium is shown in Figure 5.2.

In this equilibrium, the value to the buyers of the $\widehat{a}$ pints of ale exchanged is the area $OAB\widehat{a}$ and the amount that they actually pay is area $O\widehat{p}B\widehat{a}$, so consumer surplus is area $\widehat{p}AB$. The minimum amount that sellers would have accepted for these units is $OED\widehat{a}$, and the amount that they actually receive is $O\widehat{p}B\widehat{a}$, so producer surplus is $E\widehat{p}BD$. The sum of consumer and producer surplus falls to $EABD$.

In the presence of the quantity constraint, the market participants lose surplus equal to the area BCD. This lost surplus is the **welfare cost** of the rationing. What exactly is the welfare cost measuring?

In the original equilibrium, trade continues until all of the mutually beneficial trades have been carried out. When the quantity constraint is imposed, some of these mutually beneficial trades no longer take place. The welfare cost is the value of the benefits forgone because some mutually beneficial trades no longer take place.

To see this, note that a^* units are exchanged in the original equilibrium and that only $\widehat{a}$ units are exchanged in the rationing equilibrium. That is, $a^* - \widehat{a}$ units are no longer being exchanged. The people who bought these units in the original equilibrium

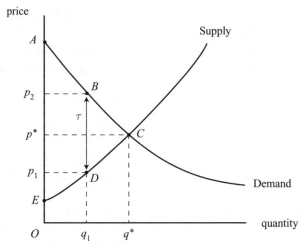

Figure 5.3: The Effects of a Tax. When the government imposes a tax on each unit sold, the price paid by the buyer exceeds the price received by the seller.

did so willingly, so each of these units was worth at least p^* dollars to its buyer. The people who sold them in the original equilibrium were willing sellers, so each of these units was worth no more than p^* dollars to its sellers. Thus, *each* of these buyers places a higher value on a unit of the good than do *any* of these sellers. Every pair consisting of one of these buyers and one of these sellers could reach a deal that makes them both better off, but the rationing prevents them from trading.

The value of the benefits lost because a buyer and a seller are prevented from making a deal is easily discovered. Suppose, for example, that the buyer is willing to pay $2 for a pint of ale and that the seller is willing to give up a pint of ale for $1.50. At any price which is agreeable to both parties (i.e., any price P between $1.50 and $2), the trade is mutually beneficial. The buyer gets something worth $2 (to him) at the price P, and therefore believes himself to be ahead on the deal by $(2 - P)$. The seller gets P for something that he only values at $1.50, and therefore gains $(P - 1.50)$. The benefits generated by this trade are $[(2 - P) + (P - 1.50)]$, or $.50. That is, the benefits generated by a trade are simply the difference between the value of the ale to the buyer and its value to the seller. These benefits are lost if the trade does not occur.

The welfare cost of the constraint is the value of *all* of the benefits forgone because some mutually beneficial trades no longer occur. It is equal to the total value of the goods (i.e., of the units between $\widehat{a}$ and a^*) to the potential buyers less the total value of the goods to the sellers. Since the first value is the area under the demand curve between $\widehat{a}$ and a^*, and the second value is the area under the supply curve between $\widehat{a}$ and a^*, we again conclude that the welfare cost is given by the area BCD.

5.3.2 Taxes

The effects of a tax are illustrated in Figure 5.3, which shows the demand and supply curves for some commodity. The quantity demanded, q_d, falls as the price paid by the buyer, p_d, rises. The quantity supplied, q_s, rises as the price received by the seller, p_s, rises. Write these relationships as

$$q_d = D(p_d) \tag{5.1}$$

$$q_s = S(p_s) \tag{5.2}$$

The market is clearing if the prices are such that

$$q_d = q_s$$

or equivalently:

$$D(p_d) = S(p_s) \tag{5.3}$$

The relationship between p_d and p_s is determined by the tax structure. If there is no tax, the money paid by the buyer goes entirely to the seller, so that p_s is equal to p_d. The market clears when the common value of these prices, p, satisfies the condition

$$D(p) = S(p)$$

The market-clearing price and quantity in the absence of taxes are shown as p^* and q^* in Figure 5.3.

Now suppose that the government imposes a tax of τ dollars on each unit of goods exchanged. The seller no longer receives the entire amount paid by the buyer, because some of the purchase price is taken away by the government in the form of taxes:[6]

$$p_d = p_s + \tau \tag{5.4}$$

Substituting this expression into (5.3) yields

$$D(p_s + \tau) = S(p_s)$$

which can be solved for p_s. Substituting p_s into (5.4) gives p_d, and substituting p_s into (5.2) gives the quantity exchanged. Graphically, the equilibrium occurs at the quantity (labelled q_1 in Figure 5.3) at which the vertical distance between the demand and supply curves is equal to the tax τ. The prices paid by the buyer and received by the seller are p_2 and p_1, respectively.

---

[6] This approach abstracts from the regulations that determine which person (the buyer or the seller) is responsible for collecting the tax and forwarding the revenue to the government. If the seller collects the tax, p_d is the market price. A part τ of this payment is forwarded to the government, leaving the seller with $p_d - \tau$. This amount is p_s. If the buyer pays the tax to the government, the market price is p_s. The buyer's total payments for each unit (that is, p_d) are equal to the market price p_s plus the tax τ. Equation (5.4) holds in either case.

The identity of the person who actually pays the tax (in the sense that he forgoes his own spending so that the government can spend in his place) is determined by market forces rather than government regulations. If the imposition of a tax of size τ causes p_s to fall by $(1/3)\tau$ and p_d to rise by $(2/3)\tau$, one-third of the tax is paid by the seller and two-thirds is paid by the buyer.

The imposition of the tax causes consumer surplus to fall from area ACp^* to area ABp_2, and causes producer surplus to fall from area p^*CE to area p_1DE. The sum of consumer and producer surplus falls by p_2BCDp_1, but some of the "lost" surplus is actually a transfer to the government in the form of tax revenues. The government's tax revenues are τq_1, and they are represented by the area p_2BDp_1. The value of the surplus actually lost is therefore equal to area BCD. This area is the welfare cost of the tax. It occurs because the imposition of the tax reduces the quantity of the good exchanged, so that some mutually beneficial trades no longer take place. The welfare cost is the value of the benefits forgone because these trades do not occur.

A similar argument applies when an ad valorem tax (i.e., a tax expressed as a percentage of the sale price) is imposed. The relationship between the price paid by the buyer and the price received by the seller is then

$$p_d = p_s(1 + t) \tag{5.5}$$

where t is the tax rate. The market-clearing value of p_s satisfies the condition

$$D(p_s(1 + t)) = S(p_s)$$

and this value is then used to find the values of p_d and q. Imposition of the tax transfers surplus to the government in the form of tax revenues (whose value is tp_sq). It also prevents some surplus from being realized, by stopping exchange before all mutually beneficial trades have been made.

5.3.3 Subsidies

A subsidy is the opposite of a tax: the government gives money to people who trade units of the good, rather than taking it away from them. Nevertheless, the framework set out above can be used to discover the effects of subsidies, because both taxes and subsidies are situations in which the price paid by the buyer differs from the price received by the seller.

Specifically, if the value of τ in (5.4) is negative, the price received by the buyer is *lower* than the price received by the seller. This outcome occurs when the government pays a subsidy of $-\tau$ dollars to everyone who buys a unit of the good. The equilibrium quantity exchanged is q_2, at which the vertical distance between the supply curve and the demand curve is $-\tau$ (see Figure 5.4). The buyer's and seller's prices are p_3 and p_4, respectively. The subsidy raises producer surplus by an amount equal to the area p^*BAp_4, and it raises consumer surplus by an amount equal to the area p^*BCp_3. Unfortunately, this gain in surplus is financed by an even larger transfer from the government (represented by the area p_4ACp_3), so the subsidy reduces surplus by an amount equal to the area BAC. This area is the welfare cost of the subsidy.

The welfare cost in this case occurs because the subsidy encourages trades that are *not* mutually beneficial. The subsidy raises output by $q_2 - q^*$ units. Each of these units was sold by someone who placed a value of at least p^* on the unit, and purchased by someone who placed a value of no more than p^* on it. Every one of these trades

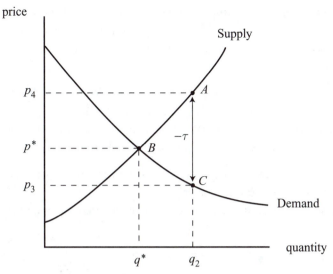

Figure 5.4: The Effects of a Subsidy. When the government subsidizes the sale of a good, the price received by the seller is greater than the price paid by the buyer.

transferred a unit of goods from someone who placed a relatively high value on it, to someone who placed a relatively low value on it.

A similar outcome occurs if the subsidy is expressed as a percentage of the seller's price. The relationship between the buyer's and seller's prices would be given by (5.5) with t negative,[7] and equilibrium output would again be raised by the subsidy. The gains in consumer and producer surplus would again be outweighed by the government's loss of surplus, generating a welfare cost.

5.4 MARKET INTERACTIONS

Surplus is maximized if the value to the consumer of the last unit of goods produced in each market is equal to the value of the goods that could have been produced with the same resources. These values will be equal if the firms behave competitively and if p_s is equal to p_d in every market. The interventions described in the previous section create a gap between the price paid by the buyer and the price received by the seller, so that the second of these two conditions is not satisfied. The surplus lost as a result of the intervention is its welfare cost.

The calculation of welfare cost described in the previous section is correct only if there is only one market in which p_s and p_d are not equalized. The calculation is more complicated if there is a gap between the two prices in several markets. This issue is central to the discussion of taxation. It is introduced here and discussed in detail in Chapter 17.

---

[7] The subsidy on each unit would be $-tp_s$ dollars.

Imagine that taxes are to be imposed on two goods, X and Y, and that these taxes are the only interventions that impair the price mechanism. Let x and y be the quantities of these goods, and let p_x and p_y be their tax-inclusive prices.

Assume that

- Firms are willing to offer each good for sale at a price equal to its marginal cost of production, and each good's marginal cost is fixed at 1.
- The government returns all of its tax revenue to the consumers as "lump-sum" transfers, that is, transfers that are not conditioned upon any action of the recipient.

These assumptions imply that neither the firms nor the government earn any surplus, so that *all* surplus accrues to the consumers.

Finally, assume that the demand for each good depends only upon the two purchase prices:[8]

$$x = D_x(p_x, p_y)$$

$$y = D_y(p_y, p_x)$$

The demand curve for each good is downward sloping:

$$\frac{\partial D_x}{\partial p_x} < 0 \qquad \frac{\partial D_y}{\partial p_y} < 0$$

Each good's demand curve is shifted by a change in the other good's purchase price, but the direction of the shift depends upon the nature of the goods.

- If the goods are **complements,** an increase in one good's price shifts the other good's demand curve to the left:

$$\frac{\partial D_x}{\partial p_y} < 0 \qquad \frac{\partial D_y}{\partial p_x} < 0$$

For example, X might be ski equipment and Y might be day passes at ski resorts. An increase in the price of day passes reduces the number of passes sold, but it also discourages some people from becoming skiers, so that less equipment is sold. A rise in the price of ski equipment also discourages some people from becoming skiers, so that fewer passes are sold.

- If the goods are **substitutes,** an increase in one good's price shifts the other good's demand curve to the right:

$$\frac{\partial D_x}{\partial p_y} > 0 \qquad \frac{\partial D_y}{\partial p_x} > 0$$

For example, X and Y might be plane and train tickets for trips between two cities. A rise in the price of one ticket causes some people to switch to the other mode of travel.

---

[8] The assumption that the government returns all tax revenues to the consumers implies that these demands are compensated demands rather than Marshallian demands.

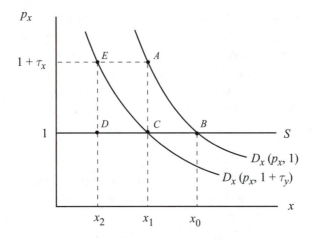

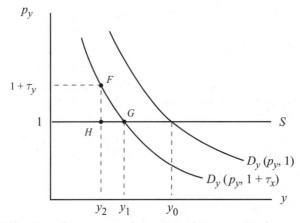

Figure 5.5: The Welfare Cost of Taxes Imposed upon Complementary Goods. A tax imposed on either good shifts the other good's demand curve to the left.

The relationship between the two goods influences the size of the welfare cost, so each case will be considered in turn.

5.4.1 Complements

Imagine that a tax τ_x is imposed on each unit of X sold. The welfare cost of this tax is shown in the top panel of Figure 5.5. The market-clearing price rises from 1 to $1 + \tau_x$, causing output to fall from x_0 to x_1. Scarce resources are shifted out of the production of X and into the production of other goods. The value to the consumer of each unit of good X given up is represented by the height of the demand curve, and the value of the goods produced in its place is represented by the height of the supply curve. The tax generates a welfare cost because the goods given up are more valuable to the consumer than the goods that replace them. The welfare cost is equal to the area ABC.

The bottom panel shows the effect of the tax on the market for Y. The rise in the price of X causes the demand curve for Y to shift to the left. The quantity of Y produced falls, from y_0 to y_1, and other goods are produced with the resources which are no longer being used in the production of Y. There is *no* welfare cost associated with this decline in consumption of good Y. The value of each unit of Y given up, *at the time that it was given up,* was equal to its marginal cost of production.[9] Since the value of the units of Y given up is equal to the value of the goods produced in their place, there is no loss of surplus.

Now imagine that, with the tax on X in place, a tax τ_y is imposed on each unit of Y sold. The welfare cost calculation for this tax differs from the calculation for the first tax, because it is a tax imposed in the presence of another tax. It will have two components, the X market component and the Y market component. The Y market component is shown in the bottom panel of Figure 5.5. The price of Y rises from 1 to $1 + \tau_y$, causing output to fall from y_1 to y_2. The value to the consumer of each of these units is greater than the value of the goods produced in its place, generating the welfare cost component FGH. The X market component is shown in the top panel of Figure 5.5. The rise in the price of Y shifts the demand curve for X to the left, causing output to fall from x_1 to x_2. Each of these units, *at the time that it was given up,* had a value to the consumer equal to the price of X, which is $1 + \tau_x$. The value of the goods produced in place of each of these units was 1. Thus, each one-unit reduction in X caused surplus to fall by τ_x. Since $x_2 - x_1$ fewer units of good X are produced, the total loss is $\tau_x(x_2 - x_1)$. This is the X market component of the tax on Y, and it is represented by the area $ACDE$. The welfare cost of the tax on Y is the sum of the two components, so it is area FGH plus area $ACDE$.

5.4.2 Substitutes

Now imagine that X and Y are substitutes. As before, a unit tax τ_x is imposed upon X, and a unit tax τ_y is subsequently imposed on Y. The effects of this sequence of taxes is shown in Figure 5.6.

The effects of the first tax are essentially the same as before. The imposition of the tax on X raises the price of X from 1 to $1 + \tau_x$, causing production of X to fall from x_3 to x_4 and freeing resources for the production of other goods. The value of the units of X given up is greater than the value of the goods produced in their place, so the tax on X generates a welfare cost equal to area JKL. The rise in the price of X also causes the demand curve for Y to shift – to the right this time – but this shift does not change total surplus. Although production of Y rises from y_3 to y_4, the value of the additional units of Y is exactly equal to the value of the goods that had to be given up to allow their production.

---

[9] Imagine the demand curve for Y shifting slowly to the left as the price of X rises from 1 to $1 + \tau_x$, so that units of Y are given up one at a time. The unit of Y given up always has the property that, when it was last purchased, its value to the purchaser was just equal to the market price. (That's why it was the last: if further units had been purchased, their value to the consumer would have been below market price.) The market price of the good is in turn equal to its marginal cost.

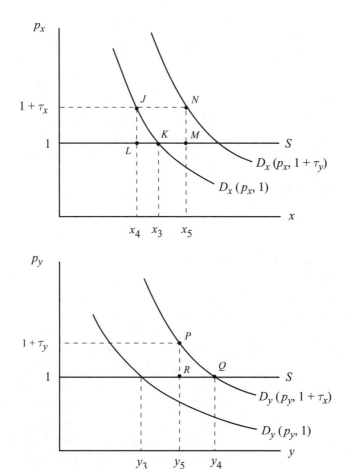

Figure 5.6: The Welfare Cost of Taxes Imposed upon Two Substitutes. A tax imposed on either good shifts the other good's demand curve to the right.

The subsequent tax on Y has two components, the Y market component and the X component. The Y component is routine. The price of Y rises from 1 to $1 + \tau_y$. The production of Y falls from y_4 to y_5, so that resources are shifted out of the production of Y and into the production of other goods. The value to the consumers of the units of Y given up exceeds the value of the goods produced in their place, generating a welfare cost equal to PQR. This cost is the Y market component of the welfare cost of the tax on Y.

The increase in the price of Y also shifts the demand curve for X to the right, causing output to rise from x_4 to x_5. Each of these units had a value to the consumer, *at the time at which it was acquired,* equal to the market price $1 + \tau_x$. The production of each unit required resources to be shifted out of the production of other goods, but the value to the consumer of the goods given up was only 1. Thus, the production of each additional unit of X *increases* total surplus by τ_x. There are $x_5 - x_4$ additional units, so total surplus *rises* by $\tau_x (x_5 - x_4)$. Thus, the X market component of the welfare cost of the tax on Y is an *increase* in welfare equal to the area $JLMN$.

The welfare cost of the tax on Y is the difference between these two components. That is, it is area PQR less area $JLMN$. The welfare cost might be positive, but it might be negative (i.e., welfare might rise rather than fall). The tax on X causes too little of that good to be produced. The tax on Y causes too little of good Y to be produced, but it also pushes up the production of X, undoing some of the damage done by the tax on X. The welfare cost of the tax on Y is negative if it undoes more damage than it creates, and is positive otherwise.

How large can the area $J L M N$ be? The graphical analysis can't tell us, because we don't know how far the demand curve for X shifts. However, we do know (from our earlier discussion of surplus, and from our discussion of the first theorem) that surplus is maximized in the absence of any distortions. It follows that area $J L M N$ cannot be bigger than the sum of area $J K L$ and area $P Q R$.

5.4.3 Devil or Angel?

Economists tend to be wary of interventions that alter the efficiency of the market system. This attitude often puts them at odds with the general population. For example, economists tend to oppose rent controls as a mechanism for ensuring affordable housing, and they tend to oppose tariffs (i.e., taxes on imported goods) as a way of protecting domestic industries. They fear that these policies will reduce surplus; and they argue that a policy objective should be achieved through other means, or that it should not be achieved at all. Rent controls are intended to protect people of low or moderate means, and this might well be a worthy objective. It can be met by redistributing income toward these people. The extra purchasing power will allow landlords to charge relatively high rents, encouraging the production of more housing units and stabilizing rents. Rent controls do the opposite: they push down the landlord's return, discouraging the production of new units and leading to a growing shortage of housing units. Similarly, protecting domestic industry from foreign competition is generally regarded as an unwise policy. This policy harms consumers by raising the price of the goods (both foreign and domestic) that they buy. It probably harms the people working in the protected industries as well. The tariff will allow the domestic producers to survive but not to thrive. Wage growth will be slow and there will be little security of employment. The long-term prospects of the workers would be better if they moved to more successful industries, but the tariff discourages them from doing so.

The validity of this attitude is put into doubt by the analysis contained in this section. The price mechanism is already impaired, both by interventions of the type described in this chapter and by the market failures that have yet to be described. If the mechanism is already impaired, an additional intervention might either lower welfare or raise it. It might be the devil that economists imagine it to be, or it might be an angel. How can economists justify their arguments?

First, economists recognize that additional interventions can either raise or lower welfare, and they argue in favour of interventions if their net effect is to raise welfare. The description of welfare-improving interventions is the subject of the "theory of the second best," which is discussed in Chapter 18.

Second, the welfare effects of any intervention can be divided into two parts, that associated with the market in which the intervention occurs and that associated with other markets. The "own market" effect certainly reduces welfare, while the "other market" effect can either raise or lower welfare. Economists argue that the "own market" effect of an intervention cannot be ignored unless there is very solid evidence that the "other market" effect strongly opposes it. Generally, we have little evidence about the size and direction of the "other market" effect, and must base decisions on the "own market" effect alone. This necessity biases economists towards non-intervention.

5.5 CONCLUSIONS

If competitive markets generate a Pareto optimal allocation, they also maximize surplus. If competitive markets do not generate a Pareto optimal allocation, they do not maximize surplus, and the surplus lost is a measure of the *degree* to which the competitive allocation diverges from a Pareto optimal allocation.

APPENDIX: MARGINS AND TOTALS

Assume that the marginal cost schedule is

$$MC(q) = 2q$$

and consider the problem of calculating the increase in total cost when output rises from q_0 to q_1. Let this increase be ΔC. To construct an approximation of ΔC, divide the interval between q_0 and q_1 into n smaller intervals of length δ. Clearly, the value of δ is determined by n:

$$\delta = \frac{q_1 - q_0}{n}$$

The increase in cost as output rises from q_0 to $q_0 + \delta$ is approximately equal to $MC(q_0)\delta$. Each one-unit increase in output from q_0 raises cost by $MC(q_0)$, and output is being raised by δ units, so the increase in cost is approximately $MC(q_0)\delta$. Similarly, the increase in cost as output rises from $q_0 + \delta$ to $q_0 + 2\delta$ is approximately $MC(q_0 + \delta)\delta$, the increase in cost as output rises from $q_0 + 2\delta$ to $q_0 + 3\delta$ is approximately $MC(q_0 + 2\delta)\delta$, and so on. The increase in cost as output rises from q_0 to q_1 is approximately equal to the sum of the increases in total cost over each of the smaller intervals:

$$\Delta C \approx MC(q_0)\delta + MC(q_0 + \delta)\delta + \cdots + MC(q_0 + (n-1)\delta)\delta \qquad (5.6)$$

This expression can also be written in a somewhat more compact form:

$$\Delta C \approx \delta \sum_{i=0}^{n-1} MC(q_0 + i\delta)$$

This approximation can be represented as an area under the marginal cost curve (see Figure 5.7). The product $MC(q_0)\delta$ is equal to the area of a rectangle with height $MC(q_0)$ and width δ, and this rectangle is the first of the n columns shown in Figure 5.7. Each of the remaining terms of (5.6) is also equal to the area of one of the columns

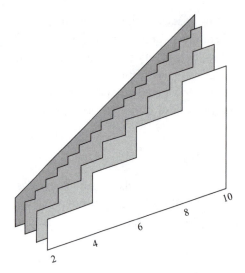

Figure 5.7: Approximations of the Increase in Total Cost when Output Rises from 2 to 10. The first three panels approximate the increase by setting n equal to 4, 8, and 16. The last panel assumes that n is infinitely large, so that the approximation is equal to the area under the marginal cost curve.

in the figure. Our approximation of $C(q_1) - C(q_0)$ is therefore equal to the sum of the areas of n columns. This sum includes much of the area under the marginal cost curve between q_0 and q_1.

The error in the approximation occurs because we are assuming that the marginal cost is constant within each of the n intervals, whereas marginal cost in fact changes continuously.[10] These errors can be reduced by increasing n, which automatically reduces δ (this being the interval over which marginal cost is held constant). Figure 5.7 shows that doubling n also means that the areas of twice as many columns, each half as wide, must be added together to obtain the same cost increase. This sum is greater than before, including more of the area under the marginal cost curve between q_0 and q_1.

Letting n become infinitely large (and δ become infinitely small) reduces the error in our approximation to zero. That is,[11]

$$\Delta C = \lim_{n \to \infty} \left[\frac{q_1 - q_0}{n} \right] \sum_{i=0}^{n-1} MC \left(q_0 + i \left[\frac{q_1 - q_0}{n} \right] \right)$$

At this limit, when ΔC is represented by the sum of the areas of an infinite number of infinitely thin rectangles, the rectangles precisely fill the area below the MC curve.

You might recall that this limit is also *defined to be* the integral of $MC(q)$ between q_0 and q_1. Formally,

$$\Delta C = \int_{q_0}^{q_1} MC(q)dq$$

---

[10] In our example, MC rises continuously, so that our approximation always understates the true MC, and our estimate of the change in total cost will always be too small.

[11] Here's a rough and ready reminder: $\lim_{n \to \infty} f(n)$ is the value that $f(n)$ approaches as n approaches infinity. For example, $\lim_{n \to \infty} (1/n) = 0$ because, no matter how close to zero we choose to make the number z, there is an n^* such that $1/n$ lies between 0 and z for all $n \geq n^*$.

Just as a derivative can always be visualized as the slope of a curve, an integral can always be visualized as an area. Indeed, we can read the right-hand side of this equation as "the area under the function $MC(q)$ between q_0 and q_1."

QUESTIONS

1. Draw a demand-and-supply diagram for the market for life jackets. Identify the areas representing consumer and producer surplus when the price is set competitively. Now imagine that the government, desiring to promote maritime safety, sets a ceiling on the price at which life jackets can be sold. Specifically, it decrees that the price cannot exceed $\widehat{p}$, where $\widehat{p}$ is *below* the initial market-clearing price. In a second diagram, show the quantity of life jackets bought and sold. Show the areas corresponding to consumer and producer surplus. Show the welfare cost of the price ceiling.

2. Consider a market in which the demand and supply curves are
$$q^D = 120 - 2p^D$$
$$q^S = 4p^S$$
where q^D and q^S are the quantities demanded and supplied, and p^D and p^S are the prices paid by the buyer and received by the seller, measured in dollars.

   a) Find the equilibrium in the absence of government intervention. Find consumer and producer surplus.

   b) Suppose that the government levies of tax of $6 on each unit of the good exchanged. Find the new equilibrium. Find the *changes* in consumer surplus, producer surplus, and the surplus collected by government. Find the welfare cost of the tax.

   c) Suppose that the government instead places a subsidy of $3 on each unit of the good exchanged. Find the new equilibrium. Find the *changes* in consumer surplus, producer surplus, and the surplus collected by government. Find the welfare cost of the subsidy.

Externalities

An **externality** is a situation in which the behaviour of a person or firm affects the welfare of another person, or the profitability of another firm, without appropriate monetary compensation occurring.[1] An externality is **positive** if some agent's behaviour makes another agent better off, and it is **negative** if that behaviour makes another agent worse off. Once you start looking, externalities are everywhere:

- Smokers like their nicotine "hit" but nearby non-smokers would prefer that they didn't get it.
- Someone playing music on a beach is emitting an externality – positive if you like the music and negative if you don't.
- Industrial emissions lower air and water quality, damaging our health and that of other species, and imposing additional costs on other firms who need clean air and water as part of their production processes.
- You would be happier if your neighbours were avid gardeners than you would be if they put their old clunkers up on blocks on their front lawns.
- You are better off if you are literate, but so are all the other people who have to deal with you, because they can communicate with you in writing.
- Inoculation protects you against communicable diseases. However, many diseases require a large, dense population of susceptible people before they can establish themselves. Since each inoculation reduces the population of susceptible people, it also protects (to some degree) people who choose not to be inoculated.
- Trails opened to mountain bikers typically widen and turn to mud, and tree falls become more numerous because of damage to their root systems. The mountain biker is just looking for a thrilling ride, but leaves behind imperceptible damage which is devastating in its cumulative impact.
- Each car entering the freeway system at rush hour slows the others down (again, almost imperceptibly) with the result that the same trip can take several times longer during rush hour than it would during slack times.

---

[1] Buchanan and Stubblebine [13] thoroughly discuss the nature of externalities.

- Flying is often the most convenient way to travel, but no one wants to live under the airport's flight path.
- It's easier to throw away than to recycle, but no one want to live near a land fill site.
- Doctors often prescribe antibiotics in cases where there is little probability that they will do any good. This practise makes the doctor look good (he's doing something) and reassures the patient. However, excessive use of an antibiotic increases the probability that bacteria will evolve in ways that make them resistant to the antibiotic, reducing the antibiotic's future usefulness.

If externalities are present, the kind of self-interested behaviour that underlies the market system becomes a handicap. The conclusion of the first welfare theorem – that competitive markets will generate a Pareto optimal outcome – is no longer valid.

Why do privately optimal decisions no longer lead to a socially optimal outcome? Consider the following scenario, which involves decision-making in the presence of an externality. A power plant draws water from a lake to cool its generators. The water returned to the lake is warmer than the water drawn from the lake, so the temperature of the lake rises and the growth of weeds is stimulated. The weedier lake is less valuable to people who use the lake for recreational purposes: swimmers are forced to go elsewhere, sailors find that their centerboards are constantly fouled, and fishermen lose their lures.

The plant could build cooling towers or cooling ponds to reduce the temperature of the water before returning it to the lake. These measures would prevent or at least moderate the growth of weeds, but they are costly. They will not be undertaken if the plant is allowed to relentlessly pursues its own profits. This outcome is unlikely to be socially optimal, because some cooling of the water is likely to be less costly to society than the loss of recreational opportunities than would occur in its absence.

Allowing the recreational users of the lake to dictate the power plant's operating procedures is also unlikely to be socially optimal. They are harmed by any increase in the temperature of the lake, so they will require the power plant to implement a very complete, and very expensive, cooling process. The power plant will recover the cost of this process by raising the price at which it sells electrical power. Thus, the recreational users' self-interested behaviour is harmful to other members of society.

A poor decision will be made if the decision-makers only take their own interests into account – no matter who the decision-makers are. What is needed is an incentive for the decision-makers to take other people's interests into account. Such an incentive is present if a person or a firm is compensated for making decisions that benefit other parties, or is forced to compensate other parties if they are harmed by its decisions – that is, if "appropriate compensation" is given.

In many cases, the simplest way of ensuring that compensation is given is to have direct negotiations between the interested parties. If the above example, the recreational users of the lake could compensate the power plant for the cost of cooling the water, or the firm could compensate the recreational users for the loss that they incur when the water temperature rises. In other instances, however, direct negotiation does not result in an agreement. (Negotiations are most likely to fail – or not to occur at all – if there are many parties involved, because the costs of negotiating are higher and because there is greater scope for strategic behaviour.) In these instances, the government can introduce policies that mimic appropriate compensation. The government could control pollution, for example, by imposing a tax on polluters or by instituting tradable emissions permits.

Our study of externalities begins with a discussion of "appropriate compensation" and the likelihood that it will occur, and examines government policies that substitute for appropriate compensation. Two situations in which externalities are important, common property exploitation and co-ordinated behaviour, are examined in detail.

6

Externalities and Negotiation

Every externality involves people or firms interacting in ways that don't involve the market – perhaps they breathe the same air or drive on the same highways. However, not every non-market interaction results in an externality. An externality only arises when people or firms pursue their own interests so relentlessly that they fail to consider the effects that their actions have on others.

An agent – that is, a person or firm – can be persuaded to recognize the interests of others by compensating him for his beneficial acts and forcing him to compensate others for his harmful acts. When this kind of compensation occurs, every agent will recognize the interests of other agents because doing so advances his own interests.

Much of the economic study of externalities centers on the role of explicit monetary compensation in the control of externalities. Our discussion of this issue will proceed in three steps. First, we will examine the meaning of "appropriate compensation" and its impact upon market transactions. Second, we will consider some of the reasons why compensation might not occur. Lastly, we will consider the role of the government in controlling externalities in the absence of appropriate compensation.

6.1 NEGOTIATED COMPENSATION

When one person's actions affect another's welfare, someone will be searching for a compromise. That person might be the initiator of the action, or the person whose welfare is affected by the action. One form of compromise is an agreement with two elements: a change in the extent of the initiator's activities, and a cash transfer that compensates the person adversely affected by the change.

Who pays whom is largely a matter of **property rights.** The agent (person or firm) who has the property rights is the one who gets to decide what happens in the absence of a negotiated agreement. The assignment of property rights is partly a matter of social custom and partly a matter of law, and can change over time. Attitudes toward smoking are an example of evolving property rights. Turn on the late-night movie and you'll find that Humphrey Bogart smokes in restaurants, taxi cabs, other people's homes, everywhere. If there is a lady present, he will politely ask "Mind if I smoke?" to which the answer will inevitably be "No, not at all." She knows that smokers have the property rights, and she knows the difference between a sincere question and a social nicety. By contrast, smokers today do not even bother to ask – they know the answer. Non-smokers now have the property rights, and in many places, this assignment of property rights is reinforced by increasingly stringent by-laws.

Let's examine the role of negotiated settlements in the control of externalities by imagining that a firm's production activities generate a negative externality for its neighbours. Perhaps the firm emits smoke or dust or noise. Two cases will be considered: one in which the firm has the property rights and one in which the neighbours have the property rights. Certain elements of the analysis are common to both cases.

- Producing one more unit of goods is costly to the firm. More labour must be hired, more raw materials must be purchased, and there is additional depreciation on machinery. These costs constitute the **private marginal cost** of production, PMC. The adjective "private" is used here to emphasize that these costs are borne by the firm itself. It is assumed that PMC rises with the firm's output, q.
- An increase in output also generates costs that are not borne by the firm. Additional output generates additional pollution (such as smoke, dust, or noise) which harms the firm's neighbours. Minimally, additional pollution means that the neighbours live in a less pleasant environment, but pollution might also adversely affect their health. Whatever the form of the harm, it is assumed that the neighbours can place a dollar value on the harm done to them by the firm's activities. The increase in the dollar value of harm caused by a one unit increase in output is called **marginal damage,** MD.
- The cost to society of an increase in the firm's output is simply the sum of the additional costs borne by the firm itself and the additional costs not borne by the firm. This cost is called the **social marginal cost,** SMC. By definition,

$$SMC = PMC + MD$$

- Producing another unit of the good also generates a benefit for the firm, the revenue obtained from its sale. This benefit is called the **private marginal benefit,** PMB. In the absence of taxes, PMB will be equal to the good's market price, p. It is assumed that the firm is sufficiently small that its actions do not significantly affect this price.
- The benefit received by society when an additional unit of the good is produced and consumed is called the **social marginal benefit** of production, SMB. It is assumed that the market price reflects the value placed on the good by the ultimate consumer, and that the consumption of the good does not generate any significant externalities – the good is not cigarettes or gasoline or fireworks. Then SMB and PMB are equal.

Figure 6.1 shows these curves.

The vertical distance between the PMB and PMC curves is **incremental profit,** the increase in the firm's profits associated with a small increase in output. The vertical

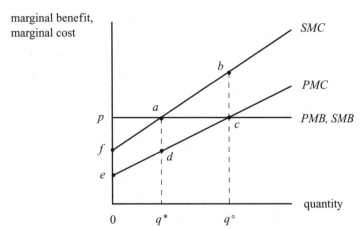

Figure 6.1: Externalities and Property Rights. In the absence of an agreement, the firm produces $q°$ units of output if it has the property rights and nothing if the neighbours have the property rights.

distance between the SMC and PMC curves is marginal damage, the increase in damage associated with a small increase in output.

The optimal level of output is q^*. At lower levels of output, the value of an additional unit of goods to consumers (SMB) is greater than sum of the value of the scarce resources used in its production and the value of the damage generated by its production (SMC). Society as a whole would therefore be better off if more of the good were produced. At higher levels of output, the opposite is true (SMC exceeds SMB) so society as a whole would be better off if fewer units of the good were produced.

6.1.1 The Firm Has the Property Rights

In this case, in the absence of an agreement with its neighbours, the firm would maximize its profits by choosing the level of output at which p is equal to PMC. This output level is $q°$ in Figure 6.1. At all lower levels of output, incremental profit is positive, so the firm can increase its total profits by raising output. At all higher levels of output, incremental profit is negative. An increase in output *reduces* profit, but a decrease in output raises profit. The drive for higher profit will therefore push the firm to $q°$.

The firm chooses an output level which exceeds the socially optimal level because it is not forced to take into consideration the costs that it imposes on others. The production of each unit of goods between q^* and $q°$ results in a net loss to society, because the social cost of producing the unit exceeds the social benefit. The marginal loss to society is represented by the vertical distance between SMC and SMB, so the second rule in Section 5.1 can be used to calculate the total loss. This loss – the welfare cost of the externality – is the area abc.

However, output would not remain at $q°$ if the firm and its neighbours are able to negotiate. At $q°$, a mutually advantageous deal between the firm and its neighbours is possible. The firm earned no profit on its last unit of output, but producing that unit of output imposed damages on the neighbours. The value of these damages is equal to MD evaluated at q° – call this amount MD°. A small decrease in output would therefore cost the firm nothing (in terms of forgone profit) but would allow the neighbours to escape damages valued at MD°. The firm and its neighbours could negotiate an agreement whereby the firm agrees to reduce output by one unit in exchange for a payment of some amount between 0 and MD°. The firm would be better off by the amount of the payment. The neighbours would have to make the payment, but would escape damages valued at MD°, and so would be better off by an amount equal to the difference between MD° and the payment.

This agreement would push the firm's output slightly below q°, but at every output between q^* and q°, similar mutually advantageous deals remain possible. The firm's profit on the last unit of output (its incremental profit) is equal to the vertical distance between PMB and PMC. The damage caused by the last unit of output (marginal damage) is equal to the vertical distance between SMC and PMC. Incremental profit is smaller than marginal damage at every output level between q^* and q°, so there are mutually advantageous bargains that push output lower. Each of these bargains requires the firm to reduce output by one more unit, in exchange for a payment of some amount between incremental profit and marginal damage. Each bargain leaves the firm better off by the difference between the payment and incremental profit, and the neighbours better off by the difference between marginal damage and the payment.

Negotiations between the firm and its neighbours would occur at every level of output greater than q^*, because mutually advantageous deals would remain. These negotiations would result in agreements that push down the firm's output. However, when output has been reduced to q^*, there is no longer any possibility of a mutually advantageous deal. Marginal damage and incremental profit are equal, so the neighbours cannot compensate the firm for its lost profit and still make themselves better off. Output falls to q^* but no farther. That is, *negotiation leads to the socially optimal level of output*.

The size of the (total) payment made by the neighbours depends upon the negotiating skills of the parties involved, but the second rule of Section 5.1 can be used to calculate the smallest and largest possible payments.

- The smallest payment that the firm would accept is compensation for lost profits. Since incremental profits are equal to the vertical distance between PMB and PMC, the profits lost when output is reduced from q° to q^* are equal to area acd. Under this agreement, the firm would be neither better nor worse off. The neighbours would experience a reduction in damages equal to area $abcd$, so their net benefit would be area abc.

- The largest payment that the neighbours would be willing to offer is the reduction in damages afforded by the output reduction. Since marginal damage is equal to the vertical distance between SMC and PMC, the reduction in damages when output is reduced to q^* from q° is equal to area $abcd$. This agreement would have no effect on the neighbours' welfare. The firm would have lost profits equal to area acd, so its net gain would be area abc.

Thus, the negotiations determine the *division* between the firm and its neighbours of the benefit represented by area abc – which is the gain to society generated by the output reduction.

6.1.2 The Neighbours Have the Property Rights

In this case, in the absence of negotiations, the neighbours would avoid all damages by not allowing the firm to produce. This outcome is also inefficient. At sufficiently low levels of output, the value of a unit of goods to the consumer is greater than the sum of the value of the scarce resources used to produce it and the value of the damage that its production entails (that is, SMB is greater than SMC). While the neighbours would be worse off if the firm were allowed to produce, society as a whole (encompassing the neighbours, the firm, and the consumers of the good) would be better off.

Prohibiting the firm from producing lowers society's welfare by an amount equal to the area bounded by SMB and SMC and by the output levels 0 and q^* (area afp in Figure 6.1). Nevertheless, the neighbours would prohibit production if it were unable to negotiate with the firm. When they have the property rights, they have no incentive to consider anyone's interests but their own.

However, this situation is also one in which mutually advantageous deals are possible. The damage inflicted by the first unit of output is positive, but it is smaller than the firm's incremental profit. (Recall that marginal damage is the vertical distance between SMC and PMC, and that incremental profit is the vertical distance between PMB and PMC.) The firm and its neighbours can make a deal allowing the firm to increase output by one unit in exchange for some payment. So long as the payment is bigger than marginal damage and smaller than incremental profit, both parties to the deal will be made better off.

Similarly, there are mutually advantageous deals at every output level between 0 and q^*, and the firm and its neighbours will continue to negotiate increases in output. When output reaches q^* (where marginal damage is just equal to incremental profit), there are no further mutually advantageous deals and negotiations stop. Once again, *negotiation leads to the socially optimal level of output.*

As before, the actual payment made by the firm cannot be predicted, but the smallest and largest payments are known. The neighbours will not accept anything less than compensation for the damages caused by the firm, and these damages are represented by the area $adef$. The firm will not pay anything more than the profits that can be earned at q^*, and these profits are represented by the area $adep$. The difference between these payments is area afp, the welfare gain that occurs when output rises from 0 to q^*. The negotiations are again determining the division of the welfare gain between the firm and its neighbours.

The role of property rights in the control of externalities was first described by Coase [17]. In the presence of an externality, Coase argued,

- A clear assignment of property rights facilitates negotiation among the interested parties.
- Negotiation leads to an efficient outcome under either assignment of property rights.
- The negotiated outcomes under alternative assignments of property rights differ only in the way in which income is distributed.

These observations are known as the **Coase Theorem,** and are illustrated by the example set out above. The optimal level of output is reached under both assignments of the property rights, but the neighbours make payments when they do not have the property rights and receive payments when they do.

6.2 WHY DOESN'T NEGOTIATION OCCUR?

To summarize the argument so far, non-market interactions between people could lead to inefficient outcomes. If someone's actions have negative consequences for others, he will be too active if he has the property rights and not active enough if the affected party has the property rights.[1] These inefficiencies would be eliminated if the agents met and negotiated a settlement.

In the absence of government involvement, external effects *could* give rise to inefficiencies but *do not necessarily do so.* Yet, we are accustomed to believing that external effects need to be controlled through government action. Why does the kind of negotiation described above so often fail to occur? Why must the government so often intervene? There are several reasons.

Negotiation Costs
The negotiations above would be time consuming and expensive. It might well be the case that the costs of reaching a settlement exceed the social gains from the settlement. This outcome is particularly likely when there are diffused costs or benefits. For example, consider a firm whose smoke stack emits pollutants that are carried hundreds of miles downwind. Even though the cost to each individual (perhaps a marginally increased risk of cancer) is quite small, the total cost borne by the thousands of affected people could be sufficient to warrant a reduction in the firm's emissions. The costs of forming these thousands of people into a coalition capable of negotiating with the firm might nevertheless be so great that negotiation does not occur. The same total cost, if borne by a small group of people, might result in negotiations.

Free Riders
Suppose that many people are adversely affected by a firm's activities, and that the firm has the property rights. The neighbours must band together to bribe the firm to lower

---

[1] There will be similar inefficiencies when the agent's actions have positive external effects.

its output. Each neighbour will benefit from an agreement reached by the coalition, but only those neighbours who join the coalition will bear a share of the costs. Each neighbour chooses between joining the coalition and paying part of the costs, or not joining the coalition and not paying part of the costs (i.e., becoming a "free rider"). The latter looks like the better deal, but if enough of the neighbours decide to be free riders, no coalition is formed and no negotiations occur.

Delay Increases Bargaining Power

Suppose again that many people are adversely affected by a firm's activities, but now imagine the affected people have the property rights. The firm will attempt to reach agreements with all of these people. As more people settle with the firm, the number of people with whom the firm must settle before beginning to produce falls until only one remains. The situation is then one of bilateral monopoly: the firm's potential profits will be split between the firm and the last person to settle. The last person to settle is therefore in a powerful position, able to extract an exceptionally large payment from the firm. The bargaining power of the last few people to settle is similarly enhanced. If everyone realizes that the last people to settle have more bargaining power, everyone will try to delay their own settlements in the hope that others will settle before them. The firm is then unable to reach a settlement with anyone.[2]

6.3 GOVERNMENT INTERVENTION

Government regulation of externalities, even if imperfectly done, can raise social welfare in cases where negotiations do not occur. Indeed, government regulation might raise social welfare even in those cases where negotiations would have occurred had the government not acted pre-emptively, because regulations that cover a wide variety of cases might result in a substantial savings in negotiation costs. The government can intervene in several ways.[3]

Prohibition

The control of externalities is often a matter of balancing competing interests, and in such cases, prohibition is not likely to be a good solution. However, there are cases in which the external effects of an activity are so important that the best response is an outright prohibition of the activity. Examples of prohibited activities include whaling, hunting within national parks or out of season, and fishing in areas where stocks have

---

[2] A similar problem arises whenever a firm is attempting to assemble a large block of land for some industrial activity. The firm can circumvent it by entering into an agreement with each landowner which specifies a provisional price for the land, but which guarantees the landowner a price as high as that specified in any of the agreements subsequently signed with other landowners. (The contract price is really a price floor.) Since waiting will not raise the price that a landowner ultimately receives, landowners will not delay in the hopes of increasing their bargaining power.

[3] Blinder [9] provides a thoughtful and entertaining discussion of the government's role in the control of externalities.

been depleted. Some chemicals are so toxic to the environment that their use has been prohibited. The chemical DDT was once used to control mosquitoes, but it proved to be extremely toxic to many forms of wildlife. The peregrine falcon, for example, was driven to the brink of extinction by DDT poisoning. DDT has now been banned. The chemical freon was once commonly used in air conditioners, but it was linked to the destruction of earth's ozone layer and has been banned.

Specifying Technologies

A government could control pollution by specifying the technology that must be used to reduce emissions. For example, noise pollution is controlled by requiring all motor vehicles to have an effective muffler. Sulphur dioxide emissions from coal-burning power plants are controlled by requiring the plants to install "scrubbers" in their smoke stacks.

A presumed advantage of this kind of policy is that it removes the need to monitor emissions, but experience suggests that monitoring might still be necessary. Machinery must be kept in working order if it is to effective, but maintenance and repair are costly. If compliance is not actively monitored, some firms will allow installed pollution control equipment to quietly decay. For example, new automobiles are sold with extensive pollution control equipment, but some governments require every car's emissions to be tested every few years to ensure that this equipment is kept in working order.

This kind of regulation also discourages research into pollution control. Firms have no incentive to search for cheaper ways of controlling emissions because they are told that there is just one way to comply with the law – and that is to install existing equipment. Even if a new and better way were found, it might take a long time for the relevant laws to be amended to allow its use. Consequently, this kind of regulation might, over the longer term, lead to less effective pollution control than more flexible kinds of regulation.

Quantity Constraints

The regulations that govern automobile emissions are of this sort: the manufacturers are told what standards they must meet, and it is up to them to decide how to do it. Indeed, the success of automobile manufacturers in meeting ever tighter environmental standards is a good example of how important new research can be, and how unwise specifying particular technologies can be.

Nevertheless, quantity constraints – laws that specify only the level of emissions of particular pollutants – are an imperfect instrument. The cost of reducing emissions varies drastically from firm to firm and from industry to industry. Consequently, a policy that requires every firm to reduce its emissions by the same proportion is a very expensive way of cleaning up the environment. The same reduction in total emissions could be obtained at a lower cost by concentrating the clean-up at the firms that can reduce their emissions at the lowest cost. A government that attempts to regulate the quantity of each firm's emissions is therefore confronted with a dilemma. It can im-pose proportional reductions in emissions, that is, it can implement an unnecessarily

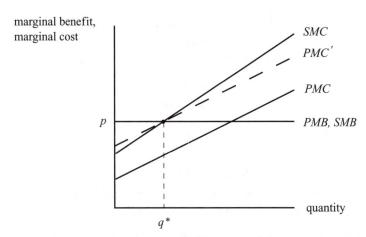

Figure 6.2: The Pigouvian Tax. The unit tax is equal to marginal damage evaluated at the optimal level of output.

expensive environmental policy. Or it can implement non-proportional reductions, violating the expectation that the government will deal with private firms in an even-handed manner.

Taxes and Subsidies

The government could use taxes to deter activities that have negative externalities, and subsidies to encourage activities that have positive externalities. The tax deductibility of educational expenses is one example of the latter. Taxes on cigarettes and gasoline are examples of the former, although governments imposing these taxes are probably more interested in generating revenue than in controlling externalities.

Taxes that control externalities are called **Pigouvian taxes,** after the economist Pigou who first suggested them. Consider the case of a firm which generates a negative externality when it produces goods, and which has the relevant property rights (see Figure 6.2). The government imposes a tax on each unit of output produced by the firm. The tax is set equal to MD^*, marginal damage evaluated at the optimal level of output q^*. This new tax becomes part of the firm's private marginal cost, so the PMC curve is shifted upwards by the amount MD^*. (The new PMC curve is labelled PMC' in Figure 6.2.) The tax does not change social marginal costs because it is simply a transfer from one part of society, the firm, to another part of society, the government. The firm will maximize its profits by choosing the output at which PMC' is equal to PMB. That is, the firm will choose the output level q^*.

This tax forces the firm to "internalize" the damage done to others, that is, to act as if the external costs are borne by the firm itself. In the presence of the tax, the firm's self-interested behaviour leads to the socially optimal outcome.

The tax is a substitute for appropriate compensation. When an agent generates a negative externality, it is important that he pay compensation, because the necessity of doing so induces him to modify his behaviour. The tax forces him to recognize the costs that he imposes on others, causing him to modify his behaviour in the same way. The difference between the tax and negotiation is the identity of the agent that gets the money (the neighbours under negotiation, the government under a tax).

QUESTIONS

A firm's total costs c are

$$c = 4q^2$$

where q is the level of output. It can sell any number of units of output at a price of 64. However, production inflicts damage on the firm's neighbours. The total damage D inflicted depends on the firm's output:

$$D = 4q + q^2$$

a) Assume that the firm has the property rights. In the absence of an agreement with its neighbours, what would its level of output be? Suppose that the neighbours negotiate with the firm. To what level of output would the negotiations lead? What is the minimum payment that the neighbours must make to the firm to achieve this change in output? What is the maximum payment?

b) Assume that the neighbours have the property rights. In the absence of an agreement between the firm and its neighbours, what would the level of output be? If an agreement between the firm and its neighbours is negotiated, what are the smallest and largest payments that the firm would have to pay?

c) Assume that the firm has the property rights. If the government wishes to control the externality by imposing a tax, what should the tax be? How much revenue does it collect?

7

Permit Trading

Suppose that firms are emitting excessive quantities of environmental pollutants, and that the government wants to reduce their emissions. The government's policy options include taxation, direct emissions controls, and laws that require the use of specific pollution control technologies. Another policy, involving tradable emissions permits, has recently been tried. Although our experience with tradable permits is limited, some economists believe that their use avoids some serious problems associated with the other instruments:

- Taxing emissions certainly reduces pollution, but policy-makers can only predict the effects of a given tax if they have detailed information about the costs of individual firms. Lacking this information, they must proceed by trial and error.
- The government could require all firms to reduce their emissions proportionally. However, the costs of reducing emissions can vary quite dramatically across firms, so this approach does not reduce emissions at the least cost. Appropriate non-proportional reductions could only be implemented if the government had detailed information about the firms, and in any case, would become a "political football."
- Specifying the control technologies to be used by firms prevents the firms from adopting better technologies as they become available: they must wait for government regulations to catch up with technology. The producers of abatement technologies, knowing that new technologies will be adopted only slowly, are deterred from investigating cheaper and more effective methods of pollution control.

The shortcoming of each of these policies is the need for the government to possess, understand, and act upon detailed information about individual firms and the current state of technology. The tradable permits approach sidesteps this difficulty by employing the price system. Individual firms make decisions about their own behaviour, and the price system ensures that their decisions are consistent with the government's objectives. A simple example of a permit trading system is developed in this chapter, and compared with proportional emissions reductions.

7.1 ENVIRONMENTAL POLLUTION AND ABATEMENT

Suppose that there are two firms, firm 1 and firm 2, producing fixed quantities of goods. In the absence of any attempt to control its emissions, each firm will emit $\overline{x}$ units of pollution. However, each firm can implement abatement measures that reduce these emissions. If firm i (where i is either 1 or 2) chooses the level of abatement a_i, its emissions x_i are

$$x_i = \overline{x} - a_i$$

Abatement is costly to the firm, and to society, because it requires the use of scarce resources. Firm i's cost of implementing the abatement level a_i is

$$c_i = (m_i/2)(a_i)^2$$

where m_i is a constant. A firm's **marginal cost of abatement** is the cost of increasing its abatement by one unit, or equivalently, reducing its emissions by one unit. The marginal cost of abatement is equal to the derivative of c_i with respect to a_i:

$$\frac{dc_i}{da_i} = m_i a_i$$

It is assumed henceforth that m_1 is less than m_2, so that firm 2's marginal cost of abatement is higher than firm 1's marginal cost at every level of abatement. This situation could arise because firm 2's plant is older and incorporates less efficient technologies. Alternatively, firms 1 and 2 could be producing different goods, with firm 2's good being produced under conditions that make emissions more difficult to control.

In the absence of controls, each firm will minimize its costs by doing no abatement and each firm's emissions will be $\overline{x}$. Let's consider two ways in which the government could control the firms' emissions: direct controls and permit trading. It will be seen that the social cost of reducing emissions is lower under permit trading than under direct controls.

7.2 DIRECT EMISSIONS CONTROLS

Suppose that the government simply instructs each firm to reduce its emissions to $\widehat{x}$, where $0 \le \widehat{x} \le \overline{x}$. Compliance with this ruling reduces overall emissions to $2\widehat{x}$. The firms' cost of compliance is

$$c_1 + c_2 = \left(\frac{m_1 + m_2}{2}\right)(\overline{x} - \widehat{x})^2$$

This policy does not minimize the resource cost of reducing emissions by the required amount. Transferring one unit of abatement from firm 2 to firm 1 reduces firm 2's abatement cost by $m_2(\overline{x} - \widehat{x})$ and increases firm 1's abatement cost by $m_1(\overline{x} - \widehat{x})$. The net saving of scarce resources is $(m_2 - m_1)(\overline{x} - \widehat{x})$, which is positive by assumption.

Further transfers of abatement from firm 2 to firm 1 reduce the total cost of compliance as long as firm 1's marginal cost of abatement remains below firm 2's marginal cost.

The resource cost of reducing total emissions by any specified amount is minimized when the abatement activity is allocated between the two firms in a way that equalizes their marginal costs of abatement. It is difficult to imagine practical non-market policies that achieve this end. The policy would have to be based upon detailed information about each firm's abatement costs, and would have to be responsive to changes in this information. The policy would have to identify specific firms, and would impose a different demand on each of them. This kind of policy would also contravene an ingrained social norm, that governments should deal with competitive firms in an even-handed manner.

Permit trading is a market-based policy that achieves this end without imposing different demands on each firm.[1] Profit-maximizing behaviour on the part of the firms will ensure that each unit of abatement is allocated to the firm with the lowest marginal cost.

7.3 PERMIT TRADING

A tradable permits program has the following characteristics:

1) Each firm is required to possess a permit for each unit of pollution that it emits.
2) The government issues $\widehat{x}$ permits to each firm.
3) The firms are allowed to trade the permits on a competitive market.

Total emissions under this program, as under direct controls, will be $2\widehat{x}$, but the cost of reducing emissions to this level will be as low as it can possibly be.

A firm participating in a tradable permits program could simply reduce its emissions to $\widehat{x}$ and retain all of the permits issued to it. However, it need not do so.

- The firm could purchase additional permits, so that it can reduce its level of abatement and emit more than $\widehat{x}$ units of pollution. If the firm's abatement costs fall by more than the cost of the additional permits, its profits rise.
- The firm could increase its level of abatement, reducing its emissions below $\widehat{x}$, and sell its surplus permits. If the revenue from the sale of the permits is greater than the additional abatement costs, the firm's profits rise.

---

[1] There is a Pigouvian tax that would allocate resources in the same way as a permit trading system. These two policies primarily differ in their informational requirements. Permit trading gives the government direct control over the level of emissions. The Pigouvian tax that leads to a particular level of emissions would have to be found by trial and error. They also lead to different outcomes when the demand for the goods produced by polluting firms grows (perhaps because the population grows). Permit trading automatically keeps total emissions fixed. By contrast, emissions under a fixed Pigouvian tax will grow. The higher demand could induce new firms to enter the industry, so that there are more polluters. If new firms do not enter the industry, the prices of the goods will rise, so that the existing firms can profitably raise their output and their emissions despite the tax. In either case, the tax would have to be raised to reduce emissions to their old level.

The firms will generally discover that trading in the permit market increases their profits.

Note that there must be a seller for every buyer. If one firm is buying permits so that it can reduce its abatement, the other firm must be increasing its abatement so that it can sell permits. Trading in the permit market has no effect on total emissions.

7.3.1 Cost Minimization

The permit market is like any other competitive market, in that the price of permits adjusts to clear the market. To find the market-clearing price, we must first find each firm's excess demand for permits. We can do this by examining the behaviour of a firm facing a fixed price for permits.

Each abatement level is associated with a particular purchase or sale of permits. A firm that reduces its emissions by a units, for example, emits $\bar{x} - a$ units of pollution. Since the firm must possess a permit for each unit of emissions, it requires $\bar{x} - a$ permits. It must purchase $(\bar{x} - a) - \hat{x}$ permits if $\bar{x} - a$ is greater than $\hat{x}$, and it is able to sell $\hat{x} - (\bar{x} - a)$ permits if $\bar{x} - a$ is less than $\hat{x}$.

Each firm minimizes the cost of complying with the pollution control program. Firm i's compliance cost C_i is

$$C_i = \left(\frac{m_i}{2}\right)(a_i)^2 + p(\bar{x} - a_i - \hat{x}) \tag{7.1}$$

where p is the market price of permits. The first term is the firm's abatement cost. The second term shows how the firm's permit trades affect its compliance costs. If $\bar{x} - a$ is greater than $\hat{x}$, so that the firm must buy permits, the second term is positive and represents the cost of the additional permits. If $\bar{x} - a$ is less than $\hat{x}$, so that the firm sells permits, the second term is negative. The second term then represents the revenue from the sale of permits. Revenue from this source partially offsets the abatement cost, reducing the compliance cost.

Firm i must also satisfy the restriction

$$a_i \leq \bar{x} \tag{7.2}$$

This restriction states that there is a limit to the amount of abatement that a firm can do. Specifically, the firm can emit air which is *as clean* as the air that it takes in, but it cannot emit air which is *cleaner* than the air that it takes in.

Firm i's problem is a "constrained minimization" problem. It chooses a_i to minimize its compliance cost (7.1), but it must obey the constraint (7.2). The firm's choice will depend upon the value of p.

- If p is relatively low, the firm will want to reduce, but not eliminate its emissions. Since the constraint is not binding,[2] the firm's optimal abatement level is found in

---

[2] A constraint upon an agent (i.e., a firm or a person) is not binding if the agent acts in the same way in the presence of the constraint as it would in the absence of the constraint. In the case at hand, the

the usual manner:[3]

$$\frac{dC_i}{da_i} = m_i a_i - p = 0$$

Re-arranging this equation yields the cost-minimizing level of abatement:

$$a_i = p/m_i \qquad (7.3)$$

- If p is sufficiently high, the firm will want to sell as many permits as it can. The constraint is then binding: the firm eliminates all of its emissions ($a_i = \overline{x}$) and sells every permit.

At what price does the firm switch from one behaviour to the other? Inspection of (7.3) shows that the firm sets a_i below $\overline{x}$ at all prices lower than $\overline{x}m_i$. At all higher prices, the firm completely eliminates its emissions so that it can sell all of its permits. Combining these results gives the firm's cost-minimizing level of abatement a_i^* at each price p:

$$a_i^* = \begin{cases} p/m_i & \text{if} \quad p < \overline{x}m_i \\ \overline{x} & \text{otherwise} \end{cases}$$

Firm i's excess demand schedule for permits specifies the number of permits that it would like to buy at any given price. It is the difference between the number of permits that the firm wants to have and the number that it already has:

$$ED_i = (\overline{x} - a_i^*) - \widehat{x} = \begin{cases} \overline{x} - \widehat{x} - p/m_i & \text{if} \quad p < \overline{x}m_i \\ -\widehat{x} & \text{otherwise} \end{cases}$$

The excess demand can be either positive or negative, with a negative excess demand indicating a desire to sell rather than a desire to buy.

The excess demand schedules of firms 1 and 2 are shown in Figure 7.1. At prices near zero, each firm does little abatement, preferring to purchase additional permits to cover its emissions. This strategy becomes increasingly costly as the price of permits rises, inducing each firm to increase its abatement level and buy fewer permits. Firm i's purchases of permits are reduced to zero at the price $(\overline{x} - \widehat{x})m_i$, and further price increases will induce it to sell permits. As the price rises, the firm increases both its abatement and its sale of permits until (at the price $\overline{x}m_i$) it completely eliminates its own emissions and sells all of its permits.

---

constraint (7.2) states that the firm cannot have an abatement level greater than $\overline{x}$. If the firm does not want to eliminate its emissions, it wants an abatement level *below* $\overline{x}$, and hence is not bothered by the constraint.

[3] The cost C_i first falls and then rises as a_i rises. The observation that dC_i/da_i is negative means that further increases in a_i will cause C_i to fall. That is, a_i is still below its cost-minimizing value. Similarly, the observation that dC_i/da_i is positive implies that a_i is already too large. Reducing a_i will reduce C_i. The cost-minimizing value of a_i is characterized by the condition $dC_i/da_i = 0$. When this condition is satisfied, neither increases nor decreases in a_i will decrease C_i, so C_i is at its minimum value.

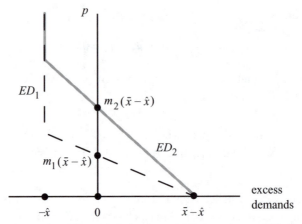

Figure 7.1: The Permit Market. The market-clearing price is the price at which the sum of the excess demands is equal to zero.

7.3.2 The Equilibrium Price of Permits

The excess demand schedules tell us what each firm *would like to do* at any given price, but we won't know what the firms *actually do* until we discover the equilibrium price. This price is, of course, the price that clears the permit market. It is found by solving the equation

$$ED_1 + ED_2 = 0$$

There are two types of equilibria, and in each of them, the firm with the lower marginal cost of abatement (firm 1) sells permits to the firm with the higher marginal cost (firm 2):

- When $\widehat{x}$ is large, the equilibrium price of permits is relatively low. Firm 1 is then unwilling to sell all of its permits, as doing so would drive its marginal cost of abatement above the permit price.
- When $\widehat{x}$ is sufficiently small, the equilibrium price is so high that firm 1 is induced to sell all of its permits.

These cases are examined in turn.

Firm 1 Retains Some of Its Permits
If both firms are on the downward sloping portion of their excess demand schedules, the market clears when

$$2(\bar{x} - \widehat{x}) - p\left(\frac{1}{m_1} + \frac{1}{m_2}\right) = 0$$

so the equilibrium price of permits is

$$p = 2(\bar{x} - \widehat{x})\left(\frac{1}{m_1} + \frac{1}{m_2}\right)^{-1} \tag{7.4}$$

But by (7.3), both firms are on the downward sloping portion of their excess demand schedules only when

$$p < \overline{x}m_1$$

Substituting the equilibrium price (7.4) into the left-hand side of this inequality and re-arranging shows that both firms are on the downward sloping portions of their excess demand schedules when

$$\widehat{x} > \overline{x}\left(\frac{m_2 - m_1}{2m_2}\right)$$

Thus, for sufficiently large values of $\widehat{x}$, (7.4) describes the equilibrium price; and with this price known, the firms' abatement levels, costs of abatement, and permit trades can be determined. The total cost of abatement is

$$c_1 + c_2 = 2(\overline{x} - \widehat{x})^2 \left(\frac{1}{m_1} + \frac{1}{m_2}\right)^{-1}$$

which is readily shown to be smaller than the abatement costs under direct controls.

Firm 1 Sells All of Its Permits
If firm 1 offers to sell all of its permits, the market clears when

$$\overline{x} - 2\widehat{x} - p\left(\frac{1}{m_2}\right) = 0$$

so that the equilibrium price is

$$p = m_2(\overline{x} - 2\widehat{x}) \tag{7.5}$$

But firm 1 will only offer to sell all of its permits if

$$p \geq \overline{x}m_1$$

Substituting the equilibrium price (7.5) into this inequality shows that the inequality is satisfied when

$$\widehat{x} \leq \overline{x}\left(\frac{m_2 - m_1}{2m_2}\right)$$

If $\widehat{x}$ satisfies this condition, firm 1 sells all of its permits to firm 2, implying $a_1 = \overline{x}$ and $a_2 = \overline{x} - 2\widehat{x}$. Total abatement costs are

$$c_1 + c_2 = \left(\frac{m_1}{2}\right)\overline{x}^2 + \left(\frac{m_2}{2}\right)(\overline{x} - 2\widehat{x})^2$$

which is again smaller than total abatement costs under direct controls.

A Numerical Example
Suppose that $m_1 = 1/4$, $m_2 = 1/2$, and $\overline{x} = 10$. If $\widehat{x}$ is greater than or equal to 2.5, firm 1 does not sell all of its permits to firm 2, and the marginal cost of abatement is equalized across firms. Total abatement costs are one-ninth (or 11%) lower under

permit trading than under proportional reductions. If $\hat{x}$ is less than 2.5, firm 1 sells every one of its permits to firm 2. The scarcity of permits forces firm 2 to undertake considerable abatement, forcing its marginal cost of abatement above firm 1's marginal cost, and eroding the cost advantage of permit trading. The difference in costs disappears when emissions are totally eliminated.

7.4 DISCUSSION

Direct emissions controls do not equalize marginal abatement costs across firms. This outcome is not efficient because the *same* reduction in emissions can be achieved at *lower* cost. Permit trading is one way to realize this cost saving. The pursuit of profit leads firms to equate their own marginal abatement costs to the market price of permits. Since each firm faces the same permit price, this behaviour equalizes the marginal cost of abatement across firms.

Further reductions in emissions can always be achieved by reducing the number of available permits. The equilibrium price of permits rises, and firms respond by pushing their abatement activities farther, until once again their marginal costs are equal to the permit price.

The benefits from permit trading could be very large. Carlson et al. [15] have recently examined the market in which American electric utilities trade permits for the right to emit sulphur dioxide. They estimate that this system would save as much as 800 million U.S. dollars annually if the alternative were a uniform emission standard leading to the same overall emissions level. The potential saving would be twice as large if the alternative were forced "scrubbing" of emissions as they leave the smokestack.

Of course, these potential savings are not realized if the permit market does not function efficiently. One potential source of inefficiency is transactions costs. If the act of trading permits is itself costly, trading might end before the marginal costs of abatement are equalized across firms. The government can minimize this efficiency loss by changing the way in which it initially distributes the permits. The closer the initial distribution of permits is to the distribution that equalizes marginal abatement costs, the smaller is the efficiency loss caused by limited trading. However, an unequal distribution of permits can give rise to a new problem. One of the assumptions underlying permit trading is that each firm is a "price taker," believing that its own actions will not significantly alter the market price of permits. If there are few firms in the market, or if there are many firms in the market but the initial distribution of permits is very unequal (so that one firm is buying or selling a large fraction of the permits), this assumption is unlikely to be satisfied. The firms would behave strategically,[4] so that again trading would not equalize the marginal costs of abatement across firms.

---

[4] Sellers would reduce the number of permits that they offer for sale to drive up the price of permits. Buyers would reduce the number of permits that they offer to buy to push the price in the opposite direction.

Another concern is that a permit system might prevent new firms from entering the industry. A new firm must buy enough permits from the existing firms to cover its intended emissions, and the cost of purchasing these permits might be so large that new firms choose not to enter the industry. Since new firms tend to install more modern – and cleaner – technologies, restricted entry would cause the resource cost of controlling emissions to decline more slowly than it otherwise would. This concern is justified only if the market for loans does not function properly.[5] If the loan market is efficient, new firms will be able to cover the cost of the permits by borrowing. They will choose to enter an industry if their anticipated revenues are at least as great as their anticipated costs, and will not enter otherwise. This decision rule maximizes society's welfare. The cost of acquiring permits is a proxy for the damages that the firm's activities impose on others, so it enters only if the value of the goods produced exceeds the *social* cost of these goods. However, if the loan market is inefficient, a firm might be unable to obtain loans to cover the cost of the permits. It would be prevented from entering the market, even if the anticipated social value of its output exceeds the anticipated social cost of its production.

QUESTIONS

1. Let $\bar{x}$ be given. Prove that, for every $\hat{x}$, the total cost of compliance $c_1 + c_2$ is smaller under permit trading than under direct emissions controls.

2. Two firms produce the same good. Each firm earns a profit θ on each unit of goods produced and sold. (That is, θ is the difference between market price and marginal cost.) The firms emit pollutants when they produce, and the only way of reducing these emissions is to reduce production. The relationship between the emissions of the first firm, e_1, and its production, q_1, is

$$e_1 = \frac{1}{2}(q_1)^2$$

The second firm uses a more modern technology, and consequently has lower emissions at every level of output. The relationship between its emissions and its production is

$$e_2 = \frac{1}{4}(q_2)^2$$

The government, in an effort to control these emissions, introduces a permit program. The essential features of this program are that each firm must hold a permit for each unit of emissions that it generates, and that these permits can be traded in a competitive market. Each firm is initially issued $\hat{x}$ permits.

   a) If firm 1 produces q_1 units of output, how many permits must it purchase?

---

[5] Firms often finance their projects by borrowing. The firms know more about these projects than do the lenders, so there is an asymmetry of information of the type described in Section 1.2.4. This asymmetry can cause the market for loans to function badly, in the sense that the volume of lending is smaller than is socially desirable. See Section 22.2 for a detailed discussion of this problem.

b) Let π_1 be firm 1's profits and let p be the price of a permit. What are firm 1's profits when it produces q_1 units of output and purchases the necessary permits on the market (or sells them there, if it has excess permits)?

c) Firm 1's optimal level of output satisfies the condition

$$\frac{d\pi_1}{dq_1} = 0$$

Find the optimal level of output for any permit price p. Find the number of permits that firm 1 would like to buy at any price p – that is, find its excess demand for permits. Show that its excess demand is positive when p is sufficiently low and negative when p is sufficiently high.

d) Following the same procedure, find firm 2's excess demand for permits.

e) Find the range of prices at which firm 1 wants to sell permits and firm 2 wants to buy them. Show that there are no prices at which firm 2 wants to sell and firm 1 wants to buy.

f) Find the market-clearing price of permits. Find the number of permits traded at this price. Calculate the number of permits possessed by each firm after the trading, and calculate each firm's output.

8

Renewable Common Property Resources

A common property resource is a consumption good or factor of production whose ownership has not yet been decided. Ownership is established simply by taking the good. Individuals quite rationally believe that if they do not quickly appropriate the good themselves, someone else will and their own chance will be gone. (Rarely does anyone who finds a $10 bill lying on the street leave it where it is, on the grounds that he can always come back for it when he needs it.) This belief, if acted upon by everyone in a society, leads to an undesirable erosion of the resource. One example of this erosion is the exhaustion of fisheries that cannot be brought under the control of a single nation. The Grand Banks off Canada's east coast is one such case; the west coast salmon fishery is another. A similar erosion results from the poaching of elephants (for their tusks) and rhinoceroses (for their horns), which proceeds at such a pace that these species might not survive. Extinction is more than a theoretical possibility – as any dodo can tell you.

8.1 THE STATIC COMMON PROPERTY PROBLEM

For concreteness, consider the case of a fishery.[1] The annual catch from the fishery, y, depends upon both the stock of fish, s, and the number of active fishing boats, b. (Non-integer values of b imply that at least one boat fishes for only part of the season.) The catch rises with the stock of fish: the more fish there are, the more readily they can be caught. As well, the catch rises with the number of boats, but each successive boat sent to the fishery increases the total catch by a smaller amount.[2] These relationships are captured by a function of the following form:

$$y = \widehat{y}(s, b) \qquad \frac{\partial y}{\partial s} > 0, \quad \frac{\partial y}{\partial b} > 0, \quad \frac{\partial^2 y}{\partial b^2} < 0$$

---

[1] Gordon's paper [28] is an early contribution to the literature on common property resources. It is non-technical and easy to read.

[2] Boats are a factor of production with positive but diminishing marginal product.

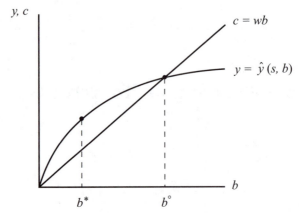

Figure 8.1: The Static Problem. The optimal number of active boats is b^*, and the number of active boats under competition is $b°$.

Recall that the partial derivative $\partial y/\partial s$ measures the change in y caused by a small increase in s, holding all of the other determinants of y constant – in this case, holding b constant.[3] Similarly, $\partial y/\partial b$ measures the change in y caused by a small increase in b, holding s constant. The positive signs of these derivatives imply that y rises when either s or b rises. Recall also that

$$\frac{\partial^2 y}{\partial b^2} \equiv \frac{\partial}{\partial b}\left[\frac{\partial y}{\partial b}\right]$$

A negative sign for this derivative indicates that the amount by which y rises when b rises (i.e., $\partial y/\partial b$) falls as b rises.

The fish caught do not come free, as scarce resources must be used up to crew and provision each boat sent to the fishery. If w is the cost of sending out a single boat, the total cost of fishing, c, is described by the equation[4]

$$c = wb$$

In Figure 8.1, y and c are graphed against b for an arbitrary value of s.

8.1.1 An Unregulated Fishery

Imagine that there are a large number of boats, and that the owner of each boat independently decides whether or not to fish. Each owner makes the choice between fishing and not fishing by applying the decision rule:

> **Go fishing if the estimated profits from fishing are positive. Don't go fishing if the estimated profits are negative.**

---

[3] If the value of this derivative is 5, for example, the change in y is 5 times as great as the change in s that caused it.

[4] The cost w is a relative price: it is the cost of fishing measured in terms of fish. That is, w fish must be caught to cover the cost of sending out a boat.

An owner can estimate profits by observing the success of the boats that are currently fishing. If each owner believes that he would be neither more nor less successful than the average owner, his estimate of his potential catch is the average catch y/b. The cost of obtaining that catch is w, so his estimated profits from fishing are $y/b - w$. Thus, the decision rule above can be restated as follows:

Go fishing if $y > wb$. Don't go fishing if $y < wb$.

Under this decision rule the equilibrium number of boats $b°$ is the number at which profits are exactly equal to zero:

$$\widehat{y}(s, b°) = wb°$$

When this condition is satisfied, no owner has an incentive to change his mind: active boats continue to be active and inactive boats continue to be inactive. This equilibrium is stable.[5] If there are fewer than $b°$ active boats, the active boats earn positive profits. Observing these profits, some of the owners of inactive boats will decide to begin fishing, so that b rises toward $b°$. Similarly, if there are more than $b°$ active boats, the active boats incur losses. Some of these boats stop fishing, so that b falls toward $b°$. Whatever the initial number of active boats, the profit motive moves their number to the equilibrium number $b°$.

Profits are zero in equilibrium. In other words, society gains nothing from the presence of the fishery: the value of the fish obtained is exactly equal to the value of the resources used up in obtaining them. There is overfishing under competition, since society would have gained from the fishery (i.e., the value of the fish would have exceeded the value of the resources used up in obtaining them) if the number of active boats had been smaller than $b°$.[6] The extent of the overfishing can only be determined if we have some notion of proper management, and to this subject we now turn.

8.1.2 A Regulated Fishery

Suppose that the fishery is placed under the control of an agency that seeks to maximize the net benefits from the fishery, or equivalently, the profits from the fishery. These profits are

$$\pi = \widehat{y}(s, b) - wb$$

The agency can only affect profits by adjusting the number of active boats b.

---

[5] An equilibrium is stable if there are pressures that push the economy toward the equilibrium when it is not currently at the equilibrium. Similarly, it is unstable if there are pressures that push the economy away from the equilibrium when it is not currently at the equilibrium.

[6] Profits and total surplus are equal in this model because it has been assumed (implicitly) that the price of fish is independent of the size of the catch, so that there is no consumer surplus. If this assumption were relaxed – if there were a downward sloping demand curve for the fish caught in this fishery – the unregulated fishery would generate zero profits but positive total surplus. The overfishing problem would still remain, however, because total surplus would be even bigger if the fishery were better managed.

The profit-maximizing value of b can be found graphically (see Figure 8.1). Profits at any b are represented by the vertical distance between y and c. As b rises from zero, this distance rises from zero, reaches a maximum, and falls back to zero (at b°). Profits are maximized at the value of b (denoted b^*) at which this vertical distance is maximized.

The profit-maximizing value of b can also be found algebraically. Profits are maximized when the derivative $\partial\pi/\partial b$ is equal to zero[7]:

$$\frac{\partial y}{\partial b} - w = 0$$

Note that $\partial y/\partial b$ is the slope of the graph of y in Figure 8.1, and that w is the slope of the graph of c in that figure. Thus, the equation above states that the vertical distance between the two curves is greatest when the two curves have the same slope – that is, when they are neither converging or diverging.

Profits at b^* are positive while those at b° are zero. More fish are caught at b°, but more resources are used up catching the fish. The extra fish caught are worth less than the resources used to catch them. This situation arises because the exploitation of the fishery, and of any other common property resource, involves a negative externality.

8.1.3 The Nature of the Externality

Recall that a negative externality occurs if the actions of one firm adversely affect the profits of other firms without appropriate compensation being paid. The activity that generates a negative externality is carried out to a greater degree than is socially desirable. The unregulated fishery has precisely these properties.

Each fishing boat in the unregulated fishery constitutes a separate firm. The profits of an active boat, if it is neither more nor less successful than other boats, are $\hat{y}(s, b)/b - w$. Since b is the total number of active boats, the profits of each active boat fall when another boat decides to become active.[8] A boat that decides to become active is not required to pay compensation to the other boats, so it has no incentive to recognize the impact that this decision has upon the other boats' profits. Consequently, too many boats become active.

In a regulated fishery, all of the boats are under the control of one agent who seeks to maximize the total profits of the fishery. There is only one "firm" so there can be no externality.

Placing the fishery under the management of one agent would be one way of correcting the externality, but it is not the only way. A negative externality can also be corrected

---

[7] If this derivative were positive, profits could be increased by raising b. If it were negative, profits could be increased by reducing b. When it is equal to zero, profits cannot be increased by either raising or lowering b, indicating that profits are maximized at the current value of b.

[8] Recall that successive fishing boats increase the total catch by smaller and smaller amounts:

$$\frac{\partial^2 y}{\partial b^2} < 0$$

Consequently, the average catch y/b falls as b rises.

by imposing a Pigouvian tax that forces firms to recognize the adverse consequences of their actions. In the current instance, the Pigouvian tax could be implemented by requiring boats to pay a fee when they become active. The fee would be equal to the damage inflicted upon the other active boats when one more boat becomes active. To calculate this fee, note that the increase in one boat's catch when another boat becomes active is:

$$\frac{\partial}{\partial b}\left(\frac{\widehat{y}(s,b)}{b}\right) = \frac{1}{b}\left(\frac{\partial y}{\partial b} - \frac{y}{b}\right) < 0$$

The *decrease* in one boat's catch when another boat becomes active is the negative of this amount; and the decrease in the catch of the b active boats – which is marginal damage – is b times the negative of this amount[9]:

$$MD = \frac{y}{b} - \frac{\partial y}{\partial b}$$

The Pigouvian tax is marginal damage evaluated when the optimal number of boats are active[10]:

$$MD^* = \left(\frac{y}{b} - \frac{\partial y}{\partial b}\right)\Bigg|_{b=b^*}$$

To see that this tax would control the externality, imagine that there are b^* active boats. If another boat were to become active, its catch would be $\widehat{y}(s,b^*)/b^*$. Since it would have to pay the fee MD^* and bear the operating cost w, it would earn zero profits:

$$\pi = \widehat{y}(s,b^*)/b^* - \left(\frac{y}{b} - \frac{\partial y}{\partial b}\right)\Bigg|_{b=b^*} - w = \frac{\partial y}{\partial b}\Bigg|_{b=b^*} - w = 0$$

Since an inactive boat would have no incentive to become active, the number of active boats would not rise above the socially optimal number b^*.

8.2 THE DYNAMIC COMMON PROPERTY PROBLEM

The static discussion of the common property problem demonstrates that the rate of exploitation of a common property resource is too great. It does not, however, demonstrate the consequences of this over-exploitation. These consequences are seen only when the fishery is observed year after year after year.

We know, of course, that the regulated fishery will earn profits (or net social benefits) while the unregulated fishery will not. This conclusion, derived for a single year, continues to hold when the analysis is extended through time. The same is not necessarily true of another of the results derived above – that the unregulated fishery catches more

---

[9] This expression has a simple interpretation. When one more boat becomes active, the total catch rises by $\partial y/\partial b$. Of this amount, the boat that becomes active takes away the average catch y/b (because it is neither more nor less successful than the other boats), leaving the remaining boats with an "increased" catch of $\partial y/\partial b - y/b$. This number is negative, indicating that the other boats' collective catch actually falls by $y/b - \partial y/\partial b$.

[10] The notated bar indicates the value of b at which this expression is to be evaluated.

fish. Imagine that there are two fisheries, initially of equal size, and that one is regulated while the other is not. For simplicity, also imagine that each group of fishermen catches the same fraction of its fish stock in every year, but that the fraction caught by the regulated fishermen is smaller than the fraction caught by the unregulated fishermen. In the first year, more fish are taken from the unregulated fishery than from the regulated fishery. Since more fish were left alive in the regulated fishery, and since these fish bred more fish, the regulated fish stock will be larger than the unregulated fish stock in the second year. In that year, the unregulated fishermen again take a bigger share of their stock of fish than the regulated fishermen do, even though their stock of fish is smaller. The unregulated fish stock again shrinks in size relative to the regulated stock of fish, and this process continues year after year. Eventually, the unregulated stock of fish is so much smaller than the regulated stock that the unregulated fishermen, taking a bigger share of a much smaller stock, catch fewer fish than do the regulated fishermen.

The dynamic model of the common property gives a much clearer picture of the consequences of over-exploitation than does the static model.

8.2.1 A Dynamic Model of the Fishery

If the fishery is to be followed through time, we must be able to distinguish between values of s and b associated with different years. We can do this by subscripting the variables: s_{2003}, for example, is the stock of fish in 2003 and s_{2004} is the stock in 2004. More generally, s_t is the stock in year t, s_{t+1} is the stock in the following year, and so on. With the addition of subscripts, our original model is characterized by the equations

$$y_t = \widehat{y}(s_t, b_t) \tag{8.1}$$

$$c_t = wb_t$$

To these equations we add another, the **equation of motion,** which states that next year's stock of fish is this year's stock of fish adjusted by two factors, the fish gained through net natural additions and the fish lost through fishing:

$$s_{t+1} = s_t + g_t - y_t \tag{8.2}$$

Here, g_t is the net natural additions to the stock of fish. These net additions are the difference between births and natural deaths (those caused by things like old age and disease – indeed, anything other than fishing). Current net natural additions are determined by the current stock of fish:

$$g_t = \widehat{g}(s_t) \qquad \frac{dg}{ds} > 0, \frac{d^2g}{ds^2} < 0 \tag{8.3}$$

The restriction on the first derivative states that net additions rise with the stock (because the number of births rises with the number of breeding fish). The restriction on the second derivative implies that the growth rate of the stock (g/s) declines as s rises. A greater fish stock implies more competition for food and easier transmission of diseases and parasites, so that the rate of natural death rises (and hence the growth rate falls) as the stock rises.

Steady States

An evolving fishery will (generally) approach a steady state, and we will want to compare the steady states reached under alternative organizations of the fishery. A steady state is defined as follows:

A **steady-state equilibrium** is a pair (b', s') such that two conditions hold:

(a) There are b' active boats when the stock of fish is s'.
(b) If $b_t = b'$ and $s_t = s'$, then $s_{t+1} = s'$.

A steady-state equilibrium is a situation that replicates itself year after year. Suppose, for example, that the stock of fish in the current year (call it year 0) is s': $s_0 = s'$. Then (a) tells us that b_0 is equal to b', and (b) tells us that s_1 is equal to s'. Applying (a) again tells us that b_1 is equal to b'. That is, the fish stock and the number of active boats are the same in year 1 as they were in year 0. Repeatedly applying (b) and (a) in turn shows that the same situation will occur in every subsequent year. Nothing ever changes – the fishery is in a steady state.

What do we have to do to find a steady state? The definition tells us that we are looking for the values of two unknowns, b and s, and we know that two independent equations can be solved to find two unknowns. So what we really need are two equations. The definition also tells us that a steady state must satisfy two conditions, so our strategy will be to turn each of these conditions into an equation, and to solve them to obtain the two unknowns.

The Locus of Possible Steady States

The equation that corresponds to condition (a) shows the number of boats that will be active for any given fish stock. The form of this equation will depend upon the way in which the fishery is organized; for example, the answer is different for a regulated fishery than it is for an unregulated fishery. Let's defer this part of the puzzle until Section 8.2.2 and start with something a little easier. Condition (b) depends upon purely technical factors, and we can easily turn it into an equation.

Equation (8.2) shows that s_{t+1} is equal to s_t if and only if the catch exactly offsets the net natural additions to the stock:

$$g_t = y_t$$

Substituting from (8.1) and (8.3) gives

$$\widehat{g}(s) = \widehat{y}(s, b) \tag{8.4}$$

where s and b are contemporaneous values (i.e., they are evaluated in the same year). Any pair (b', s') that satisfies (8.4) also satisfies condition (b) above. There are infinitely many pairs with this property, and the locus consisting of all such pairs will be called the **locus of possible steady states.**[11]

---

[11] Any pair (b, s) not lying on the locus of possible steady states does not satisfy (b) and therefore cannot be a steady-state equilibrium. A pair lying on the locus is a steady-state equilibrium only if it also satisfies (a).

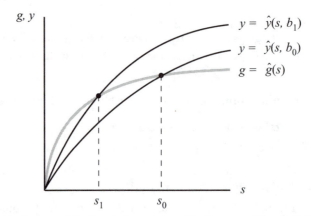

Figure 8.2: The Derivation of the Steady-State Locus. The locus consists of all the pairs (b, s) for which catch and net natural additions are equal. Two such pairs are (b_0, s_0) and (b_1, s_1).

The slope of this locus is derived in Figure 8.2. Here, b_0 and b_1 are two arbitrary values of b, with $b_0 < b_1$. If there are b_0 active boats, net natural additions and the catch are equal when the stock is s_0. If there are b_1 active boats, net natural additions and the catch are equal when the stock is s_1. It follows that (b_0, s_0) and (b_1, s_1) are two points on the locus of possible steady states. Plotting these points shows at once that the locus is downward sloping (see Figure 8.3, where this locus is labelled ss).

Figure 8.2 also shows what it means to be off the locus of possible steady states. Suppose that the number of active boats is fixed at b_0. We already know that the stock of fish is neither rising nor falling when the stock is s_0. If the stock is smaller than s_0, net natural additions to the stock exceed the catch, causing next year's stock of fish to be greater than this year's stock. That is, the stock is growing. Figure 8.2 also shows that, if the stock is greater than s_0, net natural additions are smaller than the catch, so that the stock is shrinking. The arrows in Figure 8.3 reflect these findings: s is falling through time whenever the current situation is represented by a point above the locus of possible steady states, and s is rising through time whenever the current situation is represented by a point below it.

You might have noticed that the claims of the last paragraph hinge upon the manner in which Figure 8.2 is drawn, and in particular, upon the assumption that the graph of y cuts the graph of g from below. What happens when this assumption is violated is a matter of keen interest to the intelligent elephant or rhinoceros. It is touched upon in the final section.

The Iso-Profit Map

We have yet to figure out the relationship between the number of active boats and the size of the fish stock. However, we do know that the agents who make this decision respond to profits, so we won't be able to say much about their behaviour unless we know what profits follow from any given decision. There is a bit of apparatus that tells us exactly that.

An **iso-profit curve** shows all of the pairs (b, s) that yield a specified level of profits. There is one for every level of profits, and taken together, they constitute the **iso-profit**

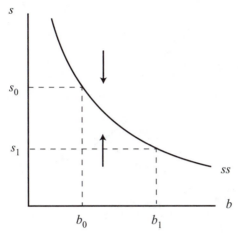

Figure 8.3: The Steady-State Locus. At points above the locus, the catch exceeds net natural addtions, causing the stock to fall. At points below the locus, net natural additions exceed the catch, causing the stock to rise.

map. The iso-profit map completely fills the (b, s) quadrant, in the sense that every point in that quadrant lies on some iso-profit curve.

The iso-profit map is shown in Figure 8.4. The heavy line shows all of the pairs (b, s) at which profits are zero. Stacked above it are the iso-profit curves associated with positive levels of profits. Each iso-profit curve is U-shaped, and profits rise as we move from one iso-profit curve to any other that lies above it.

To understand why the iso-profit map must look like the one in Figure 8.4, recall that profits are the difference between catch and cost:

$$\pi = \widehat{y}(s, b) - wb$$

As the stock of fish rises, so do the catch and the profits. In Figure 8.4, an increase in s is represented by upward movement, so one property of the map is that a move upwards always leads to higher profits. The map is Figure 8.4 has this property. Now consider the effects of changing b. As the number of active boats rises, profits will rise if

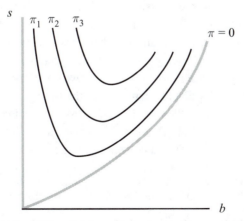

Figure 8.4: The Iso-Profit Map. Points on higher iso-profit curves yield greater profits.

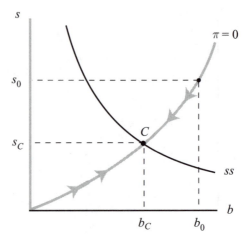

Figure 8.5: The Steady State under Competition. The steady state is approached along the zero-profit curve.

$\partial y/\partial b - w > 0$ and fall if $\partial y/\partial b - w < 0$. Since we have assumed that $\partial y/\partial b$ falls as b rises, profits will first rise and then fall as b rises from 0.[12] In Figure 8.4, an increase in b is represented by rightward movement. Consequently, another property of an iso-profit map is that, starting from any point on the vertical axis, a movement to the right first leads to higher profits and then to lower profits. The iso-profit map in Figure 8.4 has this property.

8.2.2 Fishery Dynamics under Alternative Management Regimes

Now we can return to the missing part of the puzzle, the relationship between the number of active boats and the fish stock. This relationship will allow us to determine the steady-state equilibrium that the fishery eventual reaches and, in some cases, the path taken to reach the steady state. Several ways of organizing the fishery are considered.

An Unregulated Fishery

Consider again the market organization described in Section 8.1.1: there are a large number of independent boat owners, and each owner fishes (does not fish) if the average catch, y/b, exceeds (falls short of) the cost of fishing, w. The number of active boats under this regime will be the number that drives profits to zero. It follows that the upward sloping branch of the iso-profit curve associated with zero profits is also a plot of the relationship between the number of active boats and the stock of fish. This observation allows us to describe the dynamics of the fishery.

Suppose, for example, that the initial stock of fish is s_0 in Figure 8.5. The number of active boats will be b_0, so that the fishery's position in the initial year lies above the locus of possible steady states. The catch will exceed net natural additions (remember

---

[12] In a fishery that cannot be economically exploited, no profits would be earned when there are no active boats, and profits would fall from zero as the number of active boats rose from zero. We will ignore this case.

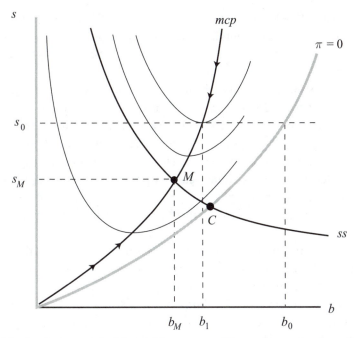

Figure 8.6: The Steady State under Myopic Management. The steady state is approached along the mcp locus.

the meaning of the arrows in Figure 8.3), so the stock of fish in the second year will be smaller than s_0. The number of active boats in the second year will be adjusted so that the fishery's position again lies on the zero-profit curve, still above the locus of possible steady states. Since the position is again above the locus of possible steady states, the stock will be smaller in the third year than in the second. The number of boats is adjusted to return the fishery's position to the zero-profit curve, still closer to the locus of possible steady states. This process is repeated year after year, driving the fishery toward the point C (for "competitive"), which has the co-ordinates (b_C, s_C). This point is the steady-state equilibrium for the unregulated fishery.

If the initial stock of fish is greater than s_C, the steady-state equilibrium is approached by "sliding down" the zero-profit curve. The opposite occurs if the initial stock is below s_C: the steady state is approached by "climbing up" the zero-profit curve.

Myopic Management

Suppose instead that the fishery is managed by an agency which always maximizes the current year's profits. What relationship between the number of boats and the stock of fish would such management imply?

Consider Figure 8.6, and imagine that the current stock of fish is s_0. Choosing the number of boats is equivalent to choosing among the points on a horizontal line at height s_0. Profits are zero when b is equal to zero, and they initially rise as b rises (since points farther to the right lie on higher iso-profit curves). Profits reach a maximum at b_1, where the horizontal line just touches the highest attainable iso-profit curve. Further increases in b would cause profits to fall (since points farther to the right now lie on lower iso-profit curves) until profits are again equal to zero when b is equal to b_0. Thus, the manager who seeks to maximize current profits will choose to have b_1 active boats when the stock is s_0.

What distinguishes b_1 from all of the other possibilities is that it lies on the highest reachable iso-profit curve. More specifically, it is the minimum point – the bottom of the trough – on that iso-profit curve. This observation is going to be true no matter what the current stock of fish is: the profit-seeking manager will always choose a point that lies at the bottom of some iso-profit curve. This is an observation that we can exploit. The locus labelled mcp (for maximum current profits) in Figure 8.6 consists of the minimum points of all of the iso-profit curves.[13] This locus is a plot of the relationship between the number of active boats and the stock of fish when the manager maximizes current profits.

The fishery dynamics now proceeds in much the same way as it did in the unregulated fishery, except that the role played by the zero-profit curve is now played by mcp. The eventual steady-state equilibrium occurs at the point M (for "myopic"), which has co-ordinates (b_M, s_M). Suppose that the initial stock of fish exceeds s_M. The number of active boats is that which maximizes current profits, which means that the initial state of the fishery is represented by a point on the mcp. Since the stock is greater than s_M, this point will be above ss, implying that the stock in the second year will be smaller than in the first. After the number of active boats is adjusted in the second year (so that current profits are again being maximized), the state of the fishery is once again represented by a point on mcp, but one that is closer to the steady state. The stock of fish declines year after year as the steady state is approached. A similar process occurs if the initial stock is smaller than s_M, except that the steady state is approached by "climbing up" mcp rather than "sliding down" it.

A comparison of the points M and C shows that the steady-state fishery under myopic management has a larger stock of fish, a smaller number of active boats, and greater profits than the unregulated fishery.

The managed fishery out-performs the competitive fishery, but the fishery could do still better. The management described here really is myopic (near-sighted): its focus on current profits means that it does not consider the effects of its own actions on future profits. It does not recognize that fishing today diminishes tomorrow's profits. Let's consider an alternative to this kind of management.

Far-Sighted Management

Suppose that the manager, having given some thought to his problem, realizes that the fishery will ultimately reach a steady state, and that he decides that the best way to

---

[13] The mcp curve will be upward sloping if an increase in the stock of fish increases the marginal product of fishing boats – that is, if

$$\frac{\partial}{\partial s}\left(\frac{\partial y}{\partial b}\right) \equiv \frac{\partial^2 y}{\partial s \partial b} > 0$$

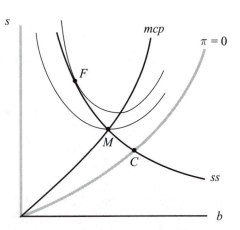

Figure 8.7: The Steady State under Far-Sighted Management. No other steady state has greater profits.

manage the fishery is to maximize the (annual) profits that will be earned in that steady state. The locus of possible steady states is a "menu" for this manager. He will direct his actions to reaching a particular point on this locus, namely the one with the greatest profits. The iso-profit map allows us to identify this point (see Figure 8.7). There is a point F at which an iso-profit curve is just tangent to the locus of possible steady states. This point corresponds to the highest attainable steady-state profits, because every higher iso-profit curve lies everywhere above and to the right of the "menu" of steady states.

We do not know how the far-sighted manager will approach this steady state, but F is the steady state he will choose. The steady-state fishery under far-sighted management has a higher fish stock, fewer active boats, and greater profits than under myopic management.

Even this outcome is not optimal. The myopic manager focusses on current profits at the expense of future profits; the far-sighted manager focusses on future profits at the expense of current profits. Optimal management would seek the best possible trade-off between current and future profits.

Optimal Management

Optimal management would recognize that both future and current profits matter, but that they do not matter equally. If the real interest rate is r, a unit of goods produced today is worth $1 + r$ units of goods in one year, and a unit of resources used up today is worth $1 + r$ units of resources used up in one year. The manager should maximize the present discounted value[14] of the profits from the fishery, always bearing in mind that the stock of fish will evolve from year to year according to the rule (8.2). He does so by choosing the number of active boats in the current year and each future year.

More formally, the manager chooses b_t for $t = 0, 1, 2, \ldots$, where year 0 is the current year. These numbers are chosen to maximize the present discounted value of profits:

$$PDV = \sum_{t=0}^{\infty} (1 + r)^{-t} \{\widehat{y}(s_t, b_t) - w b_t\}$$

[14] See the box on page 136 for a review of present discounted values.

PRESENT DISCOUNTED VALUES

A dollar received today and a dollar received t years from today are not equally valuable. If a dollar received today is invested at the interest rate r, the value of this investment will be $1 + r$ dollars after one year. It will be $(1 + r)^2$ dollars after the second year, $(1 + r)^3$ dollars after the third, and so on. The value of that investment will grow to $(1 + r)^t$ dollars after t years, and hence a dollar received today is as valuable as $(1 + r)^t$ dollars received in t years. Equivalently, one dollar received in t years is worth $(1 + r)^{-t}$ dollars received today.

If a project yields a stream of dollar payments spread through time, its value cannot be found by simply adding together the individual payments. Instead, the dollars that constitute the various payments are converted into dollars of equal value, and then the adjusted payments are added together.

The most common way of doing this is to measure the value of every future payment in terms of today's dollars. The payments are said to be "discounted back to the present," and hence payments adjusted in this fashion are said to be **present discounted values.** Suppose, for example, that a project yields x_0 dollars today, x_1 dollars in one year, and x_2 dollars in two years. The first payment is measured in today's dollars, so no adjustment is necessary. The second payment is measured in next year's dollars, and each of these dollars is worth only $(1 + r)^{-1}$ of today's dollars. The present discounted value of the second payment is therefore $x_1(1 + r)^{-1}$ dollars. The third payment is measured in dollars received in two years, and hence each of these dollars is worth only $(1 + r)^{-2}$ of today's dollars. The present discounted value of this payment is $x_2(1 + r)^{-2}$ dollars. The present discounted value of the entire project – its value in today's dollars – is therefore

$$PDV = x_0 + x_1(1 + r)^{-1} + x_2(1 + r)^{-2}$$

This procedure can be applied even when there is an arbitrarily large number of payments. It can also be used when some of the "payments" are negative, that is, costs rather than revenues.

subject to a set of constraints (one for each of the infinitely many years) which link together the fish stocks in successive years:

$$s_{t+1} = s_t + \widehat{g}(s_t) - \widehat{y}(s_t, b_t) \qquad t = 0, 1, 2, \ldots$$

This problem is complicated, but well defined and solvable.

The manager's optimal plan will lead the fishery to a steady-state equilibrium that lies on the locus of possible steady states somewhere between the points F and M. The higher the interest rate, the closer the steady state will be to M and the farther it will be from F. To see why this is so, consider the limiting cases:

- If the interest rate r is infinitely large, anything that happens in the current year is infinitely more important than anything that happens in the next year, which is in turn infinitely more important than anything that happens in the year after, and so on. The manager under these circumstances will focus almost exclusively on what happens to the fishery in the current year, whatever year that happens to be – he will focus on year 0's profits in year 0, on year 1's profits in year 1, and so on. That is, he will behave in essentially the same fashion as the myopic manager, and will reach a steady state arbitrarily close to that reached by the myopic manager.

- If the interest rate is arbitrarily close to zero, the profits received in each year are viewed as being almost equally important. The manager's plan will involve a transition from the initial fish stock to the steady-state stock which will be (nearly) reached in finite time.[15] Since the transition to the steady state is (virtually) complete in finite time, and since an infinite amount of time is then spent at the steady state, anything that happens in the steady state will be far more important than anything that happens on the way to the steady state. Under these conditions the manager will essentially seek to maximize steady-state profits, and will reach a steady state arbitrarily close to that reached by the far-sighted manager.

8.3 EXTINCTION

The claim made above that all of the steady states lie on the locus of possible steady states is, in fact, not quite true. There is an additional steady state that we have not talked about – that in which the stock falls to zero forever. This steady state does not appear to be particularly important to fisheries. The Grand Banks cod fishery, for example, might be near economic exhaustion but the fish are still out there. Fishing in the North Atlantic is a tough business and it appears that fishermen, faced with declining economic rewards, tire of it more quickly than the cod tire of breeding. The dodo was not quite so lucky. Nineteenth-century seamen found that harvesting these docile birds was an easy way to reprovision their ships in the middle of a long voyage. Knocking birds over the head with a stick on a green tropical isle is much less taxing work than fishing in the wild North Atlantic, and the seamen did not tire of it until the last bird was gone. Although we have the dodo's example in front of us, the economic incentives to harvest wildlife are such that the African elephant, the rhinoceros, and the sea turtle might yet follow it into extinction.

Biology has much to do with whether a harvested species slides into extinction. Fish breed in large numbers; and the cod-fish, finding itself in a favourable habitat and temporarily protected from human predation, might quickly regenerate. They are at one end of a spectrum observed by biologists: some creatures breed rapidly and invest little or nothing in the care of their offspring, while others invest much time and effort into the nurturing of the offspring – so much effort that these offspring are necessarily few in number. The large mammals tend to be at the latter end of the spectrum. The elephant and rhinoceros reproduce sufficiently slowly that the few poachers who elude the conservation authorities could extinguish them.

---

[15] If the initial state is not the steady state, the steady state is never actually reached. However, no matter how finely you define the idea of being "near the steady state," the fishery will get that near to the steady state in finite time and will get even closer as time passes. We might as well think of the fishery as reaching the steady state in finite time.

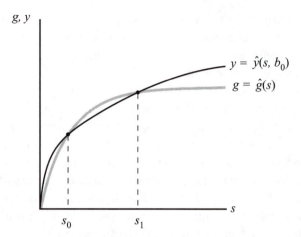

Figure 8.8: Growth and Net Natural Additions. There might be more than one steady-state stock associated with some levels of fishing activity.

The critical interaction between the speed at which animal populations grow and the incentives for human harvest is the one that we have summarized in the steady-state equation

$$\widehat{g}(s) = \widehat{y}(s, b)$$

Our earlier discussion was premised on the assumption that the graph of y cuts the graph of g from below, so that any steady state with a positive population was stable (i.e., the population was moving toward the steady state if it wasn't already at the steady state). Figure 8.8 shows another possibility: the two curves intersect twice, with y cutting g once from above and once from below. There are two steady-state stocks (s_0 and s_1) when b is equal to b_0, and there will be two steady states at other values of b near b_0. The locus of possible steady states might then look like that depicted in Figure 8.9.

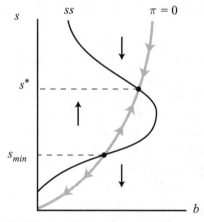

Figure 8.9: The Possibility of Extinction. The configuration of curves in the previous figure gives rise to a backward-bending ss locus. There is then the possibility that the fishery will be driven to extinction.

This doubling of the locus of possible steady states has important implications for population dynamics. Suppose, for example, that the population is being harvested by a group of independent agents who (like the independent fishermen described above) extend their harvest until profits are driven to zero. The relationship between the intensity of the harvest (b) and the population (s) is then given by the zero-profit curve shown in Figure 8.9. The steady-state equilibrium will be approached by either sliding down this curve (if the population is falling over time) or climbing up it (if the population is rising over time). It is evident that s_{min} is a critical value. If the initial stock is above that value, the population will reach the steady state value s^*. If the initial stock is below that value, the population will be driven to extinction.

APPENDIX: AN ALGEBRAIC EXAMPLE

Consider a fishery in which the catch, total cost, and growth functions are

$$y_t = .01s_t (b_t)^{1/2}$$

$$c_t = .125b_t$$

$$g_t = .01[s_t - .01(s_t)^2]$$

and the equation of motion is

$$s_{t+1} = s_t + g_t - y_t$$

The locus of possible steady states (ss) satisfies the condition $g_t = y_t$. Using the above equations, this condition reduces to

$$s_t = 100 \left(1 - (b_t)^{1/2}\right) \qquad (8.5)$$

This equation will be satisfied by every steady state.

Competitive Fishing

Competitive fishing drives profits to zero:

$$y_t = c_t$$

$$.01s_t (b_t)^{1/2} = .125b_t$$

$$b_t = (.08s_t)^2 \qquad (8.6)$$

This is the equation for the right-hand branch of the zero-profit locus.

The steady state in the competitive fishery satisfies (8.5) and (8.6). Solving these equations yields the steady state:

$$b^C = \frac{64}{81}, \quad s^C = \frac{100}{9}$$

Substituting into the catch equation gives the steady-state catch under competition:

$$y^C = .01 \left(\frac{100}{9}\right)\left(\frac{8}{9}\right) = \frac{8}{81}$$

Myopic Management

The myopic manager chooses b_t to maximize current profits π_t, where

$$\pi_t = y_t - c_t$$

or equivalently

$$\pi_t = .01 s_t \, (b_t)^{1/2} - .125 b_t$$

The profit-maximizing value of b_t is characterized by

$$\frac{\partial \pi_t}{\partial b_t} = .005 s_t \, (b_t)^{-1/2} - .125 = 0$$

which reduces to

$$b_t = (.04 s_t)^2 \tag{8.7}$$

This is the equation for the mcp curve.

The steady state under myopic management satisfies (8.5) and (8.7). Solving these equations yields

$$b^M = \frac{16}{25}, \qquad s^M = 20$$

Substituting into the catch equation gives the steady-state catch:

$$y^M = .01 \, (20) \left(\frac{4}{5}\right) = \frac{4}{25}$$

Even though there is less fishing in the myopic steady state than in the competitive steady state, more fish are caught.

Dynamics

The path to the steady state can also be characterized. Substituting the expressions for g_t and y_t into the equation of motion gives

$$s_{t+1} = 1.01 s_t - .01 s_t \left\{.01 s_t + (b_t)^{1/2}\right\} \tag{8.8}$$

Here, s_{t+1} is expressed in terms of s_t and b_t. Under competition, b_t satisfies (8.6). Using this condition to eliminate b_t from (8.8) yields

$$s_{t+1} = 1.01 s_t - .0009 \, (s_t)^2$$

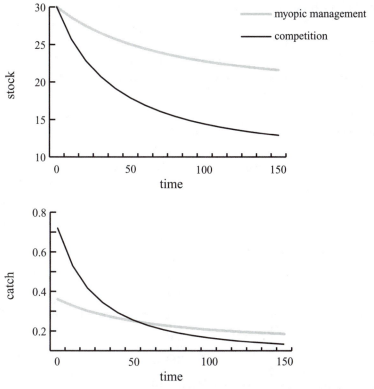

Figure 8.10: The Evolution of Stock and Catch under Alternative Regimes.

Under myopic management, b_t satisfies (8.7). Using this condition to eliminate b_t from (8.8) yields

$$s_{t+1} = 1.01s_t - .0005\,(s_t)^2$$

If the initial fish stock is known, applying one of these equations repeatedly shows the way that the fish stock would evolve under the corresponding regime. That is, s_1 can be calculated from s_0, s_2 can be calculated from s_1, and so forth, as far into the future as you like.

Figure 8.10 shows the time path of the fish stock and the catch (using an arbitrarily chosen initial stock) under these two regimes.

Far-Sighted Management

The far-sighted manager wishes to maximize steady-state profits. Since every steady state satisfies (8.5), he chooses from among the pairs (b, s) satisfying this equation the one that yields the greatest profits. Formally, he wishes to maximize profits:

$$\pi = .01s\,(b)^{1/2} - .125b$$

subject to the constraint

$$s = 100 \left(1 - (b)^{1/2}\right)$$

The simplest way to solve this problem is to eliminate one of the variables by substituting the constraint into the profit function. Using the constraint to eliminate s yields

$$\pi = b^{1/2} - 1.125b$$

The profit-maximizing value of b is characterized by

$$\frac{d\pi}{db} = .5b^{-1/2} - 1.125 = 0$$

or:

$$b^F = \frac{16}{81}$$

Substituting this value into the ss locus gives

$$s^F = \frac{500}{9}$$

This stock is larger than the steady-state stock under either of the previous two regimes.

QUESTIONS

1. A fishery is under the control of a far-sighted manager and has reached its steady state. Alas, the manager consumes far too much navy rum. Attempting to drive home in the early morning hours, he strikes a lamp-post at high speed and instantly attains his personal steady state. He is replaced by a myopic manager.
    a) In a diagram, show how the number of active boats b_t and the stock of fish s_t adjust as the fishery moves to its new steady state.
    b) Show how the profits of the fishery change through time as the fishery adjusts to its new steady state.

2. A herd of mammoths has size s_t and net natural growth g_t, where

$$g_t = .02 \left(s_t - .02(s_t)^2\right)$$

    a) Find the steady-state size of the herd.
    b) Suppose that a tribe of cavemen led by the mighty Alley Oop discovers the herd. Alley Oop is a powerful leader who can unilaterally determine the amount of mammoth hunting done by the tribe. Being a graduate of MIT (Mesolithic Institute of Technology), Alley Oop always maximizes current profits. The catch y_t associated with a hunt of size h_t is

$$y_t = .02s_t h_t$$

    and the cost of the hunt is

$$c_t = .2(h_t)^2$$

    Find the steady-state size of the herd under Alley Oop's leadership.

c) Alley Oop lives long and happily, but at the age of 28, his reflexes slowed by old age, Alley Oop is impaled on the tusk of an angry mammoth. The leaderless tribe falls into anarchy, with each tribesman deciding whether or not he will hunt. Find the steady-state size of the herd under this regime.

3. A group of hunters has discovered a colony of aardvarks. It happens that aardvarks, pan-fried with butter and a little garlic, are quite tasty, so the hunters spend all of their time hunting aardvarks. They kill 10% of the stock of aardvarks each year:

$$y_t = .1s_t$$

Here, s_t is the number of aardvarks in year t and y_t is the number killed in year t.

Aardvarks have peculiar breeding habits, behaving in quite different ways as their population changes. Each year's net natural additions are given by the equation:

$$g_t = \begin{cases} 0 & \text{if} \quad s_t \le 200 \\ .2(s_t - 200) & \text{if} \quad 200 < s_t < 450 \\ 50 & \text{if} \quad s_t \ge 450 \end{cases}$$

That is, net natural additions are equal to 0 if the stock is sufficiently small, and they are equal to 50 if the stock is sufficiently large. For moderate stocks, net natural additions rise with the stock.

a) In a diagram, draw the graphs of y_t and g_t.
b) Under what condition is the stock of aardvarks the same from year to year (i.e., $s_{t+1} = s_t$)?
c) There are two positive values of s that satisfy this steady-state condition. Find them.
d) Show that there is a critical aardvark population, $\hat{s}$, with these properties:

   If the aardvark population is less than $\hat{s}$ when the hunters arrive, they eventually become extinct. If the aardvark population is $\hat{s}$ or greater when the hunters arrive, they do not become extinct.

9

Co-ordination Failures

Competitive markets work well, when they do work well, because everything that a buyer or seller needs to know about other buyers and sellers is summarized by the market price. A buyer or a seller does not need to know why a particular price is low: all that he needs to know is that it *is* low. Knowing only prices, the buyers and sellers make self-interested decisions that lead to desirable outcomes.

Competitive markets do not work well in the presence of externalities because some important information is not summarized by prices. The people who buy the goods produced by a polluting factory only care about the market price of those goods, but the firm's neighbours care about the firm's volume of production and the cleanliness of its technology – information that is not neatly encapsulated in prices.

Alternatively, consider the nightclub to which no one ever goes because no one ever goes. Its location and prices and decor are appealing, but people believe it to be as quiet as a graveyard, so they don't go – making it as quiet as a graveyard. If everyone had expected it to be crowded and noisy and exciting, they would all go, making it just the sort of place that they expected it to be. The nightclub is an example of a **participation externality.** A common characteristic of markets with participation externalities is that there is more than one equilibrium, and that everyone prefers one equilibrium to another. There is an equilibrium in which the nightclub is quiet and another in which the nightclub is crowded, and everyone prefers a crowded nightclub to a quiet one.

A participation externality (sometimes called a **trading externality**) underlies the Keynesian view of the economy. Keynes argued that the economy could fall into an equilibrium in which output is low. Each firm would like to produce and sell more goods at the current prices, but does not increase its production because it believes that any additional goods would go unsold. The firms therefore produce few goods and employ relatively small numbers of workers. Many workers are unemployed and aggregate incomes are low, making people reluctant to spend. Each firm's belief that it is unable to sell more goods is therefore correct.

In this equilibrium, no producer is individually prepared to hire more workers. The new incomes generated by one firm's new hirings would have an insubstantial impact

144

on the demand for its own goods (as well as an insubstantial impact on the demand for all of the other firms' goods), so the goods produced by the newly hired workers would largely go unsold. Nevertheless, there is a multilateral deal that would take the economy to a new equilibrium in which everyone is better off. If all employers were to hire workers at the same time, there would be a substantial increase in incomes and a substantial increase in the demands for all goods. If the newly hired workers were correctly allocated across the firms, all of the additional goods would find willing buyers. An act which no producer is willing to undertake alone would make everyone better off if undertaken by all producers together.

This chapter presents a simple example of a trading externality, based on the work of Diamond [21]. It involves two firms which must independently decide whether to participate in a market. Each firm participates only if it is profitable to do so. Each firm's participation is more profitable when the other firm participates, so the two firms' participation decisions are linked.[1]

9.1 A CO-ORDINATION GAME

Imagine that two firms (call them firm 1 and firm 2) must *independently* decide whether or not to produce. A firm bears no costs and earns no revenue if it chooses not to produce. Its profits are then equal to zero. A firm that chooses to produce, on the other hand, incurs a positive cost c and produces one unit of a good. That good has no value to the firm that produced it, but it has a value x (where x is greater than c) to the other firm. A firm which has produced will take its good to the marketplace in the hope of finding the other firm there. If both firms bring goods to the marketplace, the goods are swapped so that each firm receives a good on which it places the value x. If a firm finds itself alone in the marketplace, no exchange is possible and the firm is stuck with a good that it considers to be worthless. Thus, the profits of a firm that produces are equal to $x - c$ if the other firm produces and $-c$ if the other firm does not produce.

The situation that confronts the firms is described by the matrix in Figure 9.1. Firm 1's choices are shown along the side of the matrix: it either produces (P) or does not produce (NP). Firm 2's choices are the same, and they are shown along the top of the matrix. Each pair in the matrix corresponds to a particular choice for firm 1 (the choice to the left of the pair) and a particular choice for firm 2 (the choice above the pair). The first and second numbers in each pair are the first and second firm's profits under this combination of choices. The bottom left entry, for example, corresponds to the action NP for the first firm and the action P for the second firm. The first firm's profits are zero because it incurs no cost and receives no benefit. The second firm's profits are $-c$ because it incurs a cost to produce but is then unable to swap goods with the first firm (because the first firm does not produce).

---

[1] Cooper [18] provides an extensive review of games in which co-ordination is beneficial, and discusses the experimental evidence relating to such games.

Firm 2's Choice

		P	NP
Firm 1's Choice	P	$x-c, x-c$	$-c, 0$
	NP	$0, -c$	$0, 0$

Figure 9.1: The Co-ordination Game. Each firm either produces (P) or does not produce (NP). The pair in each box shows each firm's pay-off under a particular combination of choices. The first number in each pair is firm 1's profits, and the second number is firm 2's profits.

This scenario constitutes a static **strategic game.** A static game is completely described by three things:

- A list of the **players** involved.
- A list of the **actions** that each player can take.
- A **pay-off function** for each player that shows how his pay-off changes as the action taken by any player in the game changes. Each player tries to maximize his own pay-off.

In the scenario above, the players are the two firms. Each of the two firms chooses between two actions, producing and not producing. The pay-off that each firm is trying to maximize is its profits, and Figure 9.1 shows how each firm's profits vary with the actions taken by the two firms.

Games are studied to discover the behaviour of the players, that is, to determine the action that each player will actually take. The players are generally imagined to make choices that constitute a Nash equilibrium:

> **A Nash equilibrium in a static game is a list of actions, one for each player, such that no player can increase his own pay-off by unilaterally changing his own action.**

The matrix in Figure 9.1 shows that there are four possible pairs of actions, and hence four potential Nash equilibria. Each pair must be checked to determine whether or not it is a Nash equilibrium.

In two of these pairs, one firm chooses to produce and the other firm chooses not to produce. Neither of these pairs is a Nash equilibrium. In each of these pairs, the firm that is not producing could increase its profits (from 0 to $x - c$) by switching from NP to P. Since at least one of the firms *can* make itself better off by unilaterally changing its behaviour, the pair is not a Nash equilibrium.[2]

The remaining two pairs are Nash equilibria. When each firm chooses to produce, neither firm can raise its profits by unilaterally changing its behaviour. If one of the firms were to switch from P to NP, its profits would drop from $x - c$ to 0. Unilateral action would make it worse off, not better off. Similarly, when each firm chooses not to

---

[2] The firm that is producing could also make itself better off through unilateral action: switching from P to NP raises its profits from $-c$ to 0. Because the definition of Nash equilibrium requires that both firms be content with their current actions, either of these arguments is sufficient to show that the original pair is not a Nash equilibrium.

produce, neither firm can raise its profits by unilaterally changing its behaviour. If one of the firms were to switch from NP to P, it would incur the costs of production but would find no trading partner, so its profits would fall from 0 to $-c$.

The firms want to co-ordinate their behaviour. There are two equilibria, one in which each firm does not produce because the other firm is not producing, and one in which each firm produces because the other firm produces. You can think of the first as being a low-output equilibrium (indeed, a zero output equilibrium) and the other as being a high-output equilibrium. The firms would rather be in the high-output equilibrium, but if they are not – if they are in the low-output equilibrium – neither firm has any incentive to change its behaviour.

The low-output equilibrium is clearly not efficient, because both firms are better off at the high-output equilibrium. The latter equilibrium is efficient – but only because the model is so simple! There is no efficient equilibrium when the game is made even slightly more complicated.

9.2 A CO-ORDINATION GAME WITH UNCERTAINTY

Let's consider an alternative game in which firms base their participation decision on their circumstances: they produce if the circumstances are favourable and they don't produce if the circumstances are unfavourable. This game is obtained by modifying the original game in two ways.

First, assume that each firm places a positive value on its own good as well as on the other firm's good. Specifically, the value that a firm places on its own good is y and the value that it places on the other firm's good is x, where $0 < y < x < 1$. Each firm that produces a unit of goods will go to the marketplace. If the two firms meet in the marketplace, they will swap goods so that each obtains a benefit of x. If only one firm goes to the marketplace, there will be no trade and the producing firm will retain its own good. Its benefit will then be y. Each firm's profits are the difference between its benefit and its cost.

Second, assume that each firm's production cost is influenced by random events, such as machinery breakdowns or delivery delays. This idea can be represented formally by assuming that there is a probability distribution of costs from which the firm's actual cost is drawn. For concreteness, let this probability distribution have the following properties:

- The cost c always lies between 0 and 1.
- The probability that c will be smaller than some value γ (where $0 \leq \gamma \leq 1$) is equal to γ.

A statistician would say that c is **uniformly distributed on the interval [0, 1].** The cost c is "distributed on the interval [0, 1]" because it can only take values between 0 and 1. It is "uniformly distributed" because c is just as likely to be taken from one part of the interval as it is to be taken from any other equally wide part of the interval.[3]

---

[3] More formally, let γ and δ be parameters such that $0 \leq \gamma < \gamma + \delta \leq 1$. Then the probability that c lies between γ and $\gamma + \delta$ is the probability that c is smaller than $\gamma + \delta$, less the probability that c

When the firms operate in an uncertain environment, we must be careful about what they know and what they don't know. Assume that

- Each firm knows that its production cost is determined by random events, and knows the probability distribution of its cost.
- Each firm knows that the other firm's production cost is determined by random events, and it knows that the probability distribution of the other firm's costs is the same as the distribution of its own cost.
- Each firm knows that it will discover its own actual cost before it makes its own production decision.
- Each firm knows that it will *not* know the other firm's cost or production decision at the time that it makes its own production decision.
- Each firm knows that its own actual cost provides no information about the other firm's actual cost. That is, each firm's cost is an "independent draw" from the distribution.[4]

Under these circumstances, each firm chooses to produce only if its own cost is sufficiently low. Each firm knows that there is a chance that the other firm will not produce, making a swap of goods impossible. If its own cost is high, the firm will compare the high and certain cost of production to its uncertain benefits, and decide not to produce. However, if its own cost is low, production is a good gamble and the firm will choose to produce. The problem facing each firm is to choose the break point that separates costs low enough to justify production from costs high enough to make production an unwise gamble.

Let $\widehat{c}_i$ be the break point for firm i. That is, imagine that firm 1 produces if and only if its production cost is below $\widehat{c}_1$ and that firm 2 produces if and only if its production cost is below $\widehat{c}_2$. Each firm chooses its break point, but to what end will the firms make this choice?

9.2.1 Expected Profits

Firms operating in an environment of complete certainty maximize their profits, but firms operating in an uncertain environment maximize their **expected profits.** Expected profits are simply the statistician's best guess of the firm's profits, based upon all available information.

---

is less than γ. The second property of the distribution implies that this probability is $\gamma + \delta$ less γ, which is δ. The distribution is uniform because the probability that c lies between γ and $\gamma + \delta$ is the same for every γ.

[4] This assumption means that the random events that determine costs are things like machinery break-downs: knowing that there is a break-down in one firm's plant provides no information about whether there has been a break-down in the other firm's plant. The random events are not things like changes in the cost of raw materials, which would affect the two firms equally.

Let $P(E)$ be the probability with which some event E occurs, and let firm i's expected profits be π_i. Then[5]:

$$\pi_i = (\text{firm } i\text{'s expected profits if it produces}) \times P(\text{firm } i \text{ produces})$$

$$+(\text{firm } i\text{'s expected profits if it does not produce}) \times P(\text{firm } i \text{ does not produce})$$

A firm has no profits if it does not produce, so the second term on the right-hand side is equal to zero. Also, the probability that firm i produces is the probability that its costs are below $\widehat{c}_i$, and our assumptions about the probability distribution imply that this probability is $\widehat{c}_i$. Consequently,

$$\pi_i = (\text{firm } i\text{'s expected profits if it produces}) \times \widehat{c}_i$$

All that remains is to calculate firm i's expected profits when its production cost is low enough to warrant production.

Imagine that firm 1 discovers its production cost and decides to produce. Its expected profits, given that it has decided to produce, are calculated in three steps:

1) If firm 2 produces, the two firms will swap goods and firm 1 will obtain the benefit x. If firm 2 does not produce, firm 1 will be alone in the marketplace and will receive the smaller benefit y. Firm 1's expected benefit is therefore x times the probability that firm 2 produces, plus y times the probability that firm 2 does not produce. The former probability is $\widehat{c}_2$ and the latter probability is $1 - \widehat{c}_2$.
2) Firm 1's decision to produce implies that its cost lies within the interval $[0, \widehat{c}_1]$. Since every cost in this interval is equally likely, the best guess of firm 1's production cost is the mid-point of the interval, $\widehat{c}_1/2$.
3) Firm 1's expected profits, given that it has chosen to produce, are the difference between the expected benefit found in 1) and the expected cost found in 2).

Thus, firm 1's expected profits are

$$\pi_1 = \left(\widehat{c}_2 x + (1 - \widehat{c}_2)y - \frac{\widehat{c}_1}{2} \right) \times \widehat{c}_1$$

By analogous reasoning, firm 2's expected profits are

$$\pi_2 = \left(\widehat{c}_1 x + (1 - \widehat{c}_1)y - \frac{\widehat{c}_2}{2} \right) \times \widehat{c}_2$$

Note that these expressions measure each firm's expected profits *before* the firms' actual production costs are revealed, and that each firm's expected profits depend upon *both* break points.

[5] This expression assumes that firm i produces if its cost is less than $\widehat{c}_i$ and does not produce otherwise. Hence, the observation that the firm is producing, or not producing, provides information about the firm's production cost. This information is used in calculating the terms on the right-hand side of the expression.

9.2.2 Nash Equilibrium

Production in this economy is a gamble. A firm that chooses to produce will incur known costs, but will receive uncertain benefits. By contrast, a firm that chooses not to produce incurs no costs and receives no benefits. Each firm must decide whether it will accept the gamble or sit safely on the sidelines. Each firm resolves this dilemma by producing at all costs below some break point and not producing at any costs above the break point. Since each firm's expected profits depend upon both break points, the best break point for one firm depends upon the break point chosen by the other.

A Nash equilibrium in this environment is a pair of break points, one for each firm, such that neither firm can increase its expected profits by unilaterally changing its own break point.

In a Nash equilibrium, each firm chooses the break point that maximizes its own expected profits given the break point chosen by the other. Firm 1 chooses the value of $\widehat{c}_1$ that maximizes π_1 given firm 2's choice of $\widehat{c}_2$. This break point satisfies the condition

$$\frac{\partial \pi_1}{\partial \widehat{c}_1} = \widehat{c}_2 x + (1 - \widehat{c}_2)y - \widehat{c}_1 = 0 \tag{9.1}$$

(We really didn't need to do the algebra to get this result. Firm 1 knows that it is profitable to produce so long as its production cost is no greater than its expected benefit of production, $\widehat{c}_2 x + (1 - \widehat{c}_2)y$. Its breakpoint is therefore equal to the expected benefit.) Similarly, firm 2 chooses the value of $\widehat{c}_2$ that maximizes π_2 given firm 1's choice of $\widehat{c}_1$:

$$\frac{\partial \pi_2}{\partial \widehat{c}_2} = \widehat{c}_1 x (1 - \widehat{c}_1)y - \widehat{c}_2 = 0 \tag{9.2}$$

A Nash equilibrium is a solution to (9.1) and (9.2). Solving these equations yields

$$\widehat{c}_1 = \widehat{c}_2 = \frac{y}{1 - (x - y)}$$

The break point chosen by each firm is between y and x. A firm would certainly want to produce if its costs are below the smaller benefit y, and it would certainly not want to produce when its costs are above the larger benefit x.

There is only one Nash equilibrium because the underlying probability distribution is so simple. Examples in which there are several equilibria could easily be constructed by assuming a different probability distribution of costs.

9.2.3 The Efficiency of Equilibrium

Our expectation ought to be that the Nash equilibrium is inefficient. Each firm's decision to produce raises the other firm's expected profits. If each firm makes its production decision in its own self-interest, neglecting the impact of that decision on the other firm, it will be too likely to choose not to produce.

The environment in which these firms operate is analogous to a neighbourhood in which each home-owner is an avid gardener, taking pleasure in the appearance of his own home and in the appearance of his neighbours' homes. Each of them continues to garden until the benefit that he gets from an additional hour of gardening (presumably pleasure from the act of gardening itself plus pleasure from the improved appearance of his home) is just offset by the costs of another hour of gardening (back ache and the cost of supplies). Nevertheless, from the viewpoint of the group, each home-owner is doing too little gardening. If each of them did a little more gardening, each would be a little better off. Each home-owner would find that there is a rough balance between the benefits and costs of his own additional gardening, but each of them benefits from the additional efforts of all of the other gardeners. Thus, an act that no neighbour wishes to undertake on his own would, if undertaken by all, benefit each neighbour.

The same situation arises in the current game. In the Nash equilibrium, each firm chooses to produce if and only if its cost is lower than the expected benefit from production. If each firm could commit itself to raising its break point by just a little, the expected profits of both firms would be higher. Each firm would find that the increase in its own break point has a negligible impact on its own expected profits, but that the increase in the other firm's break point raises its expected profits significantly.

How high should their break points be? Imagine that both firms choose the same break point, as they do in the Nash equilibrium, and let this break point be $\widehat{c}$. Each firm's expected profits are π, where

$$\pi = \widehat{c}\left\{\widehat{c}x + (1 - \widehat{c})y - \frac{\widehat{c}}{2}\right\}$$

If $x - y > 1/2$, expected profits rise with $\widehat{c}$, so they are maximized when $\widehat{c}$ takes its maximum value, which is 1. That is, each firm's expected profits are maximized when both firms always produce. If $x - y < 1/2$, expected profits are maximized when

$$\widehat{c} = \frac{y}{1 - 2(x - y)}$$

In either case the value of $\widehat{c}$ that maximizes π is greater than the Nash break point. That is, *each* firm would have higher expected profits if *both* firms would choose higher break points.

9.3 CONCLUSIONS

Competitive markets are not likely to be efficient if a participation externality is present. This externality can give rise to two different problems. First, there might be multiple equilibria. If this occurs, it is quite possible that everyone will agree as to which equilibrium is the best one. Nevertheless, the economy could get stuck in one of the less desirable equilibria: once an equilibrium has been reached, no one benefits by unilaterally moving away from it. Second, it is likely that no equilibrium is efficient. Participation generates a positive externality, and people generally do too little of any activity that has positive external effects.

QUESTIONS

1. The residents of a neighbourhood are considering the establishment of a communal garden. Everyone will be allowed to decide whether or not they will participate. The costs of the garden will be divided evenly among the participants, as will the harvest. The participants will also do all of the work, and although all of the residents recognize that participation will reduce their grocery costs, some are less enthusiastic gardeners than others.

   Most residents would want to participate if the number of participants were large enough. (The benefits would then be divided among many people, but so would the work, and it is the work that concerns most of them.) Specifically, the fraction of the residents that want to participate, n, varies with the fraction that does participate, m, in accordance with the following rule:

$$n = \min\left[1, \frac{1}{8} + \left(\frac{3}{2}\right) m^2\right]$$

   Here, $\min[a, b]$ means "the smaller of the numbers a and b." This construct is used to prevent n from exceeding 1.

   If n is greater than m, the number of willing participants is greater than the number of actual participants. If n is less than m, the number of willing participants is less than the actual number of participants. Finally, if n and m are equal, the number of willing participants is just equal to the number of actual participants: everyone who is participating wants to participate, and no one who is not participating wants to participate.

   An equilibrium group size is a value of m such that m is equal to n. Show that there are three equilibrium group sizes.

2. Some of the inhabitants of Long Beach meet every second Wednesday in the cafe of the local truck stop to swap novels. Literary tastes differ, so each inhabitant finds that the benefit of attending, B, increases with the number of people who attend, n. Specifically,

$$B = 9n^{1/2}$$

   Long Beach is very long, and the cottages of its inhabitants are quite far apart, so the cost of attending is not the same for everyone. If the inhabitants are ordered according to their costs (with person 1 having the lowest cost, person 2 the second lowest cost, and so on), the cost for person n is C_n, where

$$C_n = \begin{cases} 3n & n = 1, 2, \ldots, 10 \\ 20 + n & n = 11, 12, \ldots \end{cases}$$

   Each person chooses to attend if and only if the benefit is at least as high as the cost, so in equilibrium, the number of people who attend, n, satisfies the conditions

$$B \geq C_n$$

$$B < C_{n+1}$$

Show that two values of n satisfy these conditions. Show that the equilibrium in which more people attend is better than the equilibrium in which fewer people attend, in the sense that some of the inhabitants of Long Beach are better off and none are worse off.

Public Goods

Many of the goods in our economy are **rivalrous in consumption,** meaning that consumption of a unit of the good by one person precludes consumption of that same unit by another person. Shoes have this property: if I am wearing a particular pair of shoes, you cannot wear the same pair. The goods ale and bread, discussed at such great length earlier, are both rivalrous in consumption.

Other goods are **non-rivalrous in consumption,** but these goods are much rarer than rivalrous goods. Consumption of a unit of a non-rivalrous good by one person does not preclude its consumption by other people. The classic example of a non-rivalrous good is the lighthouse, whose beam of light warns vessels away from hazardous rocks. If the lighthouse signal can be seen by one boat, it can be seen by all other boats in the vicinity. Knowledge is another non-rivalrous good. Once something has been discovered, one person's use of that knowledge does not preclude others from applying the same knowledge.

Rivalry and non-rivalry are extremes, and there are many goods that lie somewhere between these extremes. Often the degree of rivalry depends upon the number of people using the good. Suppose, for example, that one person is viewing a film in a theatre that seats one hundred people. The good that is being consumed by that person has several dimensions: there is the film itself, the choice of seat, the absence of annoyances and distractions. Nevertheless, it is very likely that when two people are allowed into the theatre, each of the two people are as happy with their viewing as they would have been had they been alone in the theatre. The same is likely to be true if three or four or five people are admitted to the theatre, so it would seem that viewing films is initially non-rivalrous. However, as the number of people admitted rises, there comes a point where the happiness of some of the viewers is diminished by the presence of other viewers – perhaps they don't get the seats that they want, or they are distracted by noisy patrons. They still see the film, but they are less happy than they would have been had there been fewer people in the theatre. Rivalry has set in, and becomes a more and more important factor as the number of people in the theatre rises. If one hundred people are admitted, the last person to enter the theatre has no choice of seats, and might well end up peering around the edges of a basketball player (who himself has his knees pressed against the

155

seat in front of him and wishes he had been able to get an aisle seat). Film viewing now switches from being a good with some degree of rivalry to a completely rivalrous good: with all of the seats filled, another person can see the film only if he displaces one of the hundred people who are already in the theatre.

There are many goods that are partially rivalrous, and many of these have the property that the degree of rivalry rises with the number of people using the good (a phenomenon known as **congestion**). Police and fire protection, parks and recreational facilities, roads and bridges, and national defense are all members of this group. Goods that are non-rivalrous or partially rivalrous are called **public goods.**

The market system generally fails to provide adequate quantities of these goods. The clearest demonstration of the problem arises with Samuelson's **pure public good,** which combines non-rivalrousness with **non-excludability.** A non-excludable public good is one whose use cannot be controlled by the provider. Conventional (air-borne) radio and television signals are pure public goods. One person's decision to listen to a particular radio program does not impair anyone else's enjoyment of that program, so the signal is non-rivalrous. The provider of the signal cannot allow some people to listen to the program and prevent others from hearing it, so the signal is non-excludable.

Non-excludability implies that the users of a pure public good cannot be charged for its use. They can enjoy the benefits of the good and pay for it, or enjoy the benefits and not pay for it. They will generally prefer not to pay for it, or to pay too little for it. Consequently, private firms find that the provision of pure public goods is an unprofitable venture. Pure public goods are more easily provided by the government, which can fund them from its general tax revenues.

Other kinds of public goods – **impure public goods** – have different kinds of problems associated with them. Freeways, for example, are a congestible public good whose access can be controlled. If access is not controlled, how extensive should the freeway system be? Increasing the capacity of the system to ease congestion encourages people to drive more often, so that the congestion returns. Building a freeway system with enough capacity to eliminate congestion cannot be the government's goal. And if access is controlled, what price should people pay to drive the freeways? That price is critical, because it gives the government a tool with which to control congestion.

This part of the book examines several kinds of public goods. It begins with a discussion of pure public goods, and then examines two kinds of impure public goods, the club good and the variable-use public good.

10

Pure Public Goods

The private sector's inability to provide efficient quantities of public goods is most easily understood by examining Samuelson's [53, 54] concept of a **pure public good.** Samuelson defined a pure public good to be one that is both non-rivalrous and non-excludable. Private provision of a pure public good is inefficient because people are able to "free ride," that is, use the good without paying for it.

Section 10.1 examines optimal provision of a public good and Section 10.2 examines its provision by a private firm. It will be shown that the two do not match – that the first welfare theorem does not hold – so that there is a role for government as a provider of public goods.

10.1 OPTIMAL PROVISION OF A PUBLIC GOOD

Consider an economy populated by just two people, George and Harriet. They gain utility from the consumption of a private good, bread, and a public good, parks. Their utility functions are:

$$U_G = u_G(z, b_G)$$

$$U_H = u_H(z, b_H)$$

Here, b_G and b_H are the quantities of bread (measured in loaves) consumed by George and Harriet, respectively, and z is the quantity of parkland (measured in acres). Parks are assumed to be non-excludable, so that George and Harriet have access to the same quantity of parkland. The utility functions u_G and u_H are assumed to be increasing and concave. It is also assumed that the marginal utility of each good becomes arbitrarily large when consumption of that good nears zero.

The economy is endowed with $\bar{s}$ acres of land. Each acre of land can be farmed or used as parkland. An acre of land allocated to farming will grow enough wheat to make k loaves of bread, so the economy's production possibility frontier (ppf) is

$$b = k(\bar{s} - z)$$

157

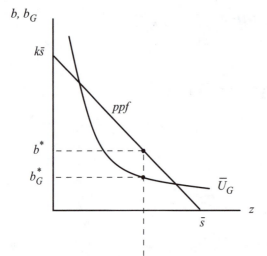

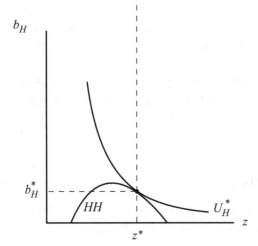

Figure 10.1: A Pareto Optimal Allocation. The allocation (b_G^*, b_H^*, z^*) makes Harriet as well off as is possible, given that George attains the utility $\overline{U}_G$.

where b is the total amount of bread produced. All of the bread produced in the economy is consumed by either George or Harriet:

$$b = b_G + b_H$$

An **allocation** for this economy describes the quantities of bread and parkland available in the economy, and the way in which the bread is divided between George and Harriet. Thus, each allocation is a triplet (b_G, b_H, z). As before, we want to know which allocations are desirable and which are not, and our criterion for deciding what is desirable will be Pareto optimality.

10.1.1 The Samuelson Condition

Samuelson used the simple graphical technique shown in Figure 10.1 to describe Pareto optimal allocations in an economy containing a public good. In a two-person economy, an allocation is Pareto optimal if there is no alternative allocation at which one person is better off and neither person is worse off. One way of finding such an allocation is to look for the allocation that makes one person as well off as possible given that the other person attains some predetermined utility level. This is precisely what is done in Figure 10.1: George's utility is fixed at $\overline{U}_G$, and Harriet is made as as well off as possible.

The top half of the diagram shows the production possibility frontier. For each z the vertical distance to the frontier is the total amount of bread available for consumption, b. One of George's indifference curves is also shown in this part of the diagram. For each z the vertical distance to this curve is the amount of bread that must be given to George if he is to attain the utility level $\overline{U}_G$. The amount of bread remaining for Harriet at each z is the difference between the amount of bread available and the amount that must be given to George. That is, it is the vertical distance between the frontier and George's indifference curve. This quantity is plotted in the bottom half of the diagram.

The resulting locus (labelled HH) contains all of the commodity bundles that could be given to Harriet if George is to attain the utility level $\overline{U}_G$. We must choose the one that makes Harriet as well off as possible. To do this, note that Harriet's indifference curves can be drawn in the (z, b_H) quadrant. Harriet is made as well off as possible by choosing from HH the commodity bundle that lies on Harriet's highest attainable indifference curve. In Figure 10.1 this indifference curve is U_H^*. Harriet attains this utility when she consumes the commodity bundle (z^*, b_H^*); and with z^* units of public good produced, George reaches the utility level $\overline{U}_G$ by consuming the commodity bundle (z^*, b_G^*). Thus, (b_G^*, b_H^*, z^*) is a Pareto optimal allocation.

There are infinitely many Pareto optimal allocations. There is one associated with every possible value of George's utility, and there are infinitely many of these. What we would really like to get out of this diagram is a way of *describing* the Pareto optimal allocations, and to do this, we will need some of our old terminology:

- The **marginal rate of substitution** (MRS) is the quantity of bread needed to exactly compensate a person for the loss of one acre of parkland. The marginal rate of substitution varies from person to person; and for each person, it changes as that person's commodity bundle changes. The marginal rate of substitution at any commodity bundle is measured by the negative of the slope of the indifference curve passing through that commodity bundle.
- The **marginal rate of transformation** (MRT) is the amount of bread that must be given up to obtain one more unit of the public good. The marginal rate of transformation is measured by the negative of the slope of the production possibility frontier. In our example, the marginal rate of transformation is always equal to k.

The slope of any of Harriet's indifference curves is $-MRS_H$. Since HH is a plot of the vertical distance between the production possibility frontier and George's indifference curve $\overline{U}_G$, its slope is the difference between the slope of these two curves. That is, the slope of HH is $(-MRT) - (-MRS_G)$, or more simply, $MRS_G - MRT$.

Now recall that the Pareto optimal allocation in Figure 10.1 occurs where one of Harriet's indifference curves is tangent to the HH locus. Since curves that are tangent to each other have the same slope at the point of tangency, the Pareto optimal allocation satisfies the condition

$$MRS_G - MRT = -MRS_H$$

or equivalently

$$MRS_G + MRS_H = MRT$$

This equation is called the **Samuelson condition:** every Pareto optimal allocation satisfies it.

The Samuelson condition has a relatively direct interpretation. Each person's marginal rate of substitution is the amount of bread that he or she is *willing to give up* to have one more acre of parkland provided. The left-hand side of the Samuelson condition is therefore the total amount of bread that people in this economy would be willing to give up to obtain another acre of parkland. By contrast, the marginal rate of transformation is the amount of bread that *must be given up* if another acre of parkland is to be provided. The Samuelson condition states that, at an efficient allocation, the amount of bread that people in an economy are collectively willing to give up for another acre of parkland is the same as the amount that they have to give up.

More simply, the left- and right-hand sides of this equation represent, respectively, the total benefit and the cost of increasing the quantity of parkland by one acre, with both the cost and the benefit measured in bread. If the total benefit were larger than the cost, George and Harriet could be made better off by increasing the quantity of parkland and appropriately redistributing the remaining bread. Similarly, if the total benefit were smaller than the cost, both people could be made better off by reducing the quantity of parkland and appropriately redistributing bread. When the two are equal, there is no way of changing the allocation so that at least one person is better off and neither person is worse off.

The Samuelson condition is easily generalized to economies containing more than two people. The left-hand side is the total benefit arising from a one-unit increase in the quantity of the public good. It is calculated by adding together the benefits accruing to every individual. If there are n people, indexed by the integers $1, \ldots, n$, the Samuelson condition is

$$MRS_1 + MRS_2 + \cdots + MRS_n = MRT$$

where MRS_i is the marginal rate of substitution of person i.

10.1.2 Example

Let George and Harriet's utility functions be

$$u_G = b_G + 10z$$

$$u_H = (b_H)^{1/2} z^{1/2}$$

Assume that the economy is endowed with one acre of land, and that one acre of land allocated to farming produces 50 loaves of bread. What is the Pareto optimal allocation in which George's utility is $\bar{u}$ (where $\bar{u}$ is less than 50)?

There are actually two ways in which this problem can be solved. The first method replicates algebraically the graphical procedure described above. The second method assumes that the Samuelson condition is known to us and need not be derived again, so it is much simpler.

Method 1

The HH locus shows the amount of bread that is left for Harriet when z units of public goods are produced, given that George must reach his specified utility level. Since all of the bread is given to George or given to Harriet or used in the production of public goods,

$$b_H = 50(1 - z) - b_G \tag{10.1}$$

But George's utility is fixed at $\bar{u}$, so

$$\bar{u} = b_G + 10z \tag{10.2}$$

Using this condition to eliminate b_G from (10.1) gives the HH locus:

$$b_H = 50(1 - z) - (\bar{u} - 10z) = 50 - \bar{u} - 40z \tag{10.3}$$

This locus does not quite have the shape shown in Figure 10.1 (it's downward sloping everywhere, instead of hill-shaped) because George's indifference curves are straight instead of curved, but its interpretation is the same.

We must now find the commodity bundle (z, b_H) that makes Harriet as well off as possible, subject to the constraint that (10.3) is satisfied. The simplest way of finding it is to substitute (10.3) into Harriet's utility function to eliminate one of the variables (i.e., either b_H or z). If b_H is eliminated, Harriet's utility is

$$u_H = (50 - \bar{u} - 40z)^{1/2} z^{1/2}$$

She is as well off as she can possibly be if z is chosen so that

$$\frac{du_H}{dz} = 0$$

Evaluating this derivative and simplifying gives

$$z^* = \frac{50 - \bar{u}}{80}$$

Substituting this value into (10.3) gives

$$b_H^* = \frac{50 - \bar{u}}{2}$$

Since George gets the bread that is not given to Harriet,

$$b_G^* = 50(1 - z^*) - b_H^* = \frac{9\overline{u} - 50}{8}$$

These three values describe the Pareto optimal allocation associated with any given $\overline{u}$. Varying $\overline{u}$ between 0 and 50 yields all of the (infinitely many) Pareto optimal allocations.

Method 2

The Pareto optimal allocation that we are looking for satisfies three conditions. First, it lies on the production possibility frontier. (The economy cannot produce any combination of goods lying outside the frontier, and it would be wasteful to produce any combination lying inside the frontier.) Second, George's utility is exactly equal to $\overline{u}$. Third, the public good is optimally provided, so the Samuelson condition is satisfied.

Expressing each of these conditions as an equation gives us a system of three equations, and this system can be solved to find the three values that constitute an allocation. The first two conditions have already been expressed algebraically – they are equations (10.1) and (10.2) – so the only task remaining is to re-write the Samuelson condition. We can make the following substitutions:

$$MRS_G = \frac{\partial u_G}{\partial z} \div \frac{\partial u_G}{\partial b_G} = 10$$

$$MRS_H = \frac{\partial u_H}{\partial z} \div \frac{\partial u_H}{\partial b_H} = \frac{b_H}{z}$$

$$MRT = 50$$

so that the Samuelson condition reads (after a little rearrangement):

$$b_H = 40z \qquad\qquad (10.4)$$

Solving (10.1), (10.2), and (10.4) yields the allocation.

10.2 VOLUNTARY PROVISION OF THE PUBLIC GOOD

New firms are created in the expectation that they will earn profits for their owners. These firms undertake an initial capital investment (to set up a production facility, open an office, or acquire necessary tools and equipment), after which they offer a good or a service to the public in return for some fee. A firm will be set up only if the firm's revenues are expected to be high enough to allow the firm to recover both its variable costs of production and (slowly, over time) its initial capital outlay.

Under these "rules of the game," private firms would *never* provide pure public goods. Access to a public good cannot be restricted or blocked, so people cannot be charged for access.[1] A firm offering access to public goods would earn no revenue, and therefore would be unable to recover its initial capital outlay or cover its variable costs.

There are, however, other "rules" under which a firm would be willing to provide a public good. Suppose, for example, that the firm solicits contributions for the provision of a public good, and uses the money raised to construct the public good. The size of the public good is determined by the amount of money raised.[2] These "rules" constitute the **voluntary contributions model** of public good provision. Some quantity of the public good will be provided through voluntary contributions, but the amount will not be optimal – that is, public goods provision will not satisfy the Samuelson condition.

Consider an economy populated by n people, and let the people be identified by the integers 1 through n. Each person is endowed with s° acres of land, which is either used to grow grain (which is subsequently made into bread) or converted into parkland. Bread is the only private good in the economy, and parks are the only public good. Person i has the utility function

$$u_i = z^\alpha (b_i)^\beta \tag{10.5}$$

where u_i is his utility, b_i is his consumption of bread, z is the quantity of parkland, and α and β are constants lying between 0 and 1. The assumption that α and β are both smaller than 1 implies that the marginal utility of consumption of each good falls as consumption of that good rises.

Person i chooses to use c_i acres of his land as public parks, reducing his bread consumption to

$$b_i = k(s^\circ - c_i) \tag{10.6}$$

where k is again the marginal rate of transformation. The total amount of parkland is equal to the sum of the contributions:

$$z = c_1 + c_2 + \cdots + c_n \tag{10.7}$$

We want to know what each person's contribution will be, but it is not immediately evident how people make their choices. Do they think only of themselves, or do they display some sort of "fellow feeling" which induces them to contribute more than they otherwise would? How does each person imagine that the contributions of the others would change if he were to change his own contribution? Are they allowed to discuss their contributions, and can they make binding commitments?

---

[1] Their choice would be between receiving the benefits of the public good and paying for them, and receiving the benefits and not paying for them. People would rationally choose to keep their money in their pockets.

[2] If there are no variable costs associated with operating the public good, all of the contributions are spent on the set-up costs of the public good. If there are variable costs, the contributions must be divided between the set-up costs and a fund out of which the operating costs are paid for some period of time.

Game theory studies the behaviour of people whose actions directly affect one another. One of the fundamental concepts of game theory is **Nash equilibrium,** which provides one way of resolving these questions. Applied to the problem at hand, a Nash equilibrium would be a list of contributions (one for each person) such that no one could make himself better off by unilaterally deviating from the list – that is, by changing his own contribution while everyone else continues to make the contributions prescribed by the list. This condition would be met if each person's contribution maximizes his own utility when all of the other people are making the contributions dictated by the list. Suppose, for example, that there are only two people ($n = 2$). The list

$$c_1 = 5, \qquad c_2 = 8$$

constitutes a Nash equilibrium if these two conditions hold:

- When person 2 contributes 8, person 1 maximizes his utility by contributing 5.
- When person 1 contributes 5, person 2 maximizes his utility by contributing 8.

Neither person, knowing the other's contribution, would choose to change his own contribution.

10.2.1 The Two-Person Game

Let's continue the example of a two-person economy. The first step in finding a Nash equilibrium is to find each person's **best response function.** Person 1's best response function shows, for each possible contribution by person 2, the contribution of person 1 that maximizes person 1's utility. Similarly, person 2's best response function shows his utility-maximizing contribution for each possible contribution by person 1.

Substituting (10.6) and (10.7) into (10.5) shows that person 1's utility is

$$u_1 = (c_1 + c_2)^\alpha \, k^\beta \, (s^\circ - c_1)^\beta$$

The utility-maximizing value of person 1's contribution can be found by calculating the derivative du_1/dc_1 and setting it equal to zero:

$$\frac{du_1}{dc_1} = u_1 \left\{ \frac{\alpha}{c_1 + c_2} - \beta \left(\frac{1}{s^\circ - c_1} \right) \right\} = 0$$

Simplifying this expression gives

$$\alpha(s^\circ - c_1) - \beta(c_1 + c_2) = 0$$

For each c_2 the value of c_1 that satisfies this equation is person 1's utility-maximizing contribution. Re-writing the equation in explicit form yields

$$c_1 = (\alpha s^\circ - \beta c_2)/(\alpha + \beta)$$

This equation is person 1's best response function. An analogous procedure shows that person 2's best response function is

$$c_2 = (\alpha s^\circ - \beta c_1)/(\alpha + \beta)$$

A Nash equilibrium is simply a pair (c_1, c_2) that satisfies both best response functions, so that each person is making himself as well off as possible given the contribution of the other person. Solving these two equations shows that there is only one pair of contributions with this property:

$$c_1 = c_2 = \frac{\alpha s^\circ}{\alpha + 2\beta}$$

These are the Nash equilibrium contributions. The associated quantity of public good is

$$z = \frac{2\alpha s^\circ}{\alpha + 2\beta}$$

10.2.2 The n-Person Game

Note that in the above game, two people who have the same preferences and the same endowment behave the same way. An equilibrium with this property is said to be **symmetric.**[3] We can use symmetry to find the equilibrium in an economy with n people, where n is any positive integer.

In this case, person i's utility function is

$$u_i = (c_i + \overline{c}_i)^\alpha \, k^\beta \, (s^\circ - c_i)^\beta$$

where $\overline{c}_i$ is the *total* of the contributions made by everyone other than person i. Proceeding as above, person i's best response function turns out to be

$$c_i = (\alpha s^\circ - \beta \overline{c}_i)/(\alpha + \beta) \tag{10.8}$$

Since everyone has the same preferences, everyone has the same best response function. Each person's utility-maximizing contribution depends only upon the total contributions made by the other $n - 1$ people. In a symmetric equilibrium, everyone makes the same contribution, so $\overline{c}_i$ is equal to $(n - 1)c_i$. Substituting this expression into (10.8) and solving for c_i yields

$$c_i = \frac{\alpha s^\circ}{\alpha + n\beta}$$

---

[3] Not all problems involving people who are identical in every way have symmetric equilibria. Suppose, for example, that two people are playing the following game. Each must choose either A or B. If they make different choices, a judge sends them to Cozumel for an extended vacation. If they make the same choice, the judge sentences them to a year of hard labour in a coal mine. Assuming that these people do not have very twisted preferences, there are only two Nash equilibria and neither is symmetrical. In one equilibrium, person 1 chooses A and person 2 chooses B. In the other equilibrium, their choices are reversed.

Call this value c°. If $n-1$ people contribute c°, the remaining person cannot do better than to contribute c°. Thus, a situation in which each person contributes c° is a (symmetric) Nash equilibrium: no one can make himself better off by unilaterally changing his contribution. The quantity of public good is then

$$z^\circ = \frac{n\alpha s^\circ}{\alpha + n\beta} \tag{10.9}$$

It can be shown that the symmetric Nash equilibrium is the only Nash equilibrium.

10.2.3 Is the Optimal Amount of the Public Good Provided?

The optimal quantity of the public good is determined by the Samuelson condition:

$$\sum_{i=1}^{n} MRS_i = MRT$$

We already know that the marginal rate of transformation is always k. The marginal rate of substitution of person i is[4]

$$MRS_i = \frac{\alpha}{\beta}\left(\frac{b_i}{z}\right)$$

Substituting these expressions into the Samuelson condition and re-arranging gives

$$\alpha \sum_{i=1}^{n} b_i = k\beta z \tag{10.10}$$

If everyone is to end up with the same consumption bundle (as they do in the symmetric Nash equilibrium), everyone must give up the same amount of land to be used as parks. That is, each person i's contribution of land is

$$c_i = z/n$$

Then, by (10.6),

$$b_i = k\left[s^\circ - (z/n)\right]$$

Substituting this expression into the Samuelson condition (10.10) gives

$$n\alpha k\left[s^\circ - (z/n)\right] = k\beta z$$

---

[4] Here, the MRS is the amount of bread needed to exactly compensate an individual for the loss of a unit of public goods, so

$$MRS_i = \frac{\partial u_i}{\partial z} \div \frac{\partial u_i}{\partial b_i}$$

Evaluating the partial derivatives yields the marginal rate of substitution.

or

$$z^* = \frac{n\alpha s^{\circ}}{\alpha + \beta} \tag{10.11}$$

This is the optimal quantity of public goods when every person consumes the same commodity bundle, as they do in the symmetric Nash equilibrium.

If the public good is financed through voluntary contributions, z° units will be provided. The optimal level of public goods provision is z^*. Combining (10.9) and (10.11) gives

$$\frac{z^{\circ}}{z^*} = \frac{\alpha + \beta}{\alpha + n\beta}$$

Thus, the optimal quantity of public good is provided only if there is just one person living in this economy. For every n other than 1, the quantity of public good provided is too small. Both z° and z^* increase as n rises, but z^* rises faster than z°, so that voluntary contributions become an increasingly poor method of financing the public good as the population rises.

One could imagine scenarios under which the optimal quantity of the public good would be provided. For example, suppose that the n individuals in this economy knew that each person would be *required* to make the same contribution, and that they only had to decide what that contribution should be. They would choose to provide z^* units of the public good and set each individual's contribution at z^*/n.

But this agreement would have to be rigidly policed. As long as the contributions are truly voluntary, there is underprovision of the public good. People might get together and agree that the ideal contribution is z^*/n, but at the end of the day, each person will renege on the deal and contribute a smaller amount. Each person reasons in this fashion: "If everyone else makes a large contribution, I will enjoy a relatively high level of public goods provision even if I don't make a large contribution. I would therefore be better off if I made only a small contribution – perhaps no contribution – so that I can consume lots and lots of bread." But everyone argues in this fashion, so everyone pushes their contributions below z^*/n. There is then a downward spiral of contributions that pushes the economy toward the Nash equilibrium described above. This phenomenon is called the **free rider problem:** everyone knows that he will benefit from the public good provided by everyone else, and therefore chooses to make a relatively small contribution.

10.3 IS NON-EXCLUDABILITY THE SOURCE OF THE PROBLEM?

Pure public goods are interesting because they give rise to free riding, and free riding clearly illustrates the difficulty of efficiently providing public goods through competitive markets. However, the problem of under-provision of public goods is not limited to pure public goods. The problem remains with other types of public goods: only the details are different.

Consider, for example, a public good which is non-rivalrous but excludable. Specifically, imagine that a theatre which seats 250 people is located in a town with a population of only 200. A film shown in this theatre is a non-rivalrous good: if it is shown to one person, it can be shown to the other 199 people in the town without additional cost. It is, however, an excludable good because the owner can stand at the door and let in whomever he wants. We can presume that he is willing to let in anyone who pays the price of a ticket, and that he can stay in business if he sets his ticket price appropriately.

Here, a non-rivalrous good is provided by a private firm, but it is not efficiently provided. Efficient provision would require the owner to admit anyone who has any interest, no matter how slight, in seeing the movie offered. Efficiency requires the maximization of net benefits, that is, the difference between total benefits and total costs. Admitting one more person, no matter how small his interest, raises total benefits without raising total costs and therefore raises net benefits. However, a private provider of the good must charge an admission fee (so that he can cover his costs). Any given admission fee will result in the exclusion of people who, although they have some interest in the movie, aren't interested enough to pay the fee. That is, private provision results in the exclusion of some people, and that is not efficient.

10.4 CONCLUSIONS

The tendency for public goods to be underprovided suggests a role for governments as suppliers of these goods, and it is certainly a role that governments have embraced. They deliver a wide range of pure and congestible public goods, including roads and bridges, parks and some recreational facilities, fire and police protection, defence, and in ever smaller numbers, lighthouses.

Governments are not, however, the only provider of public goods. Roads and bridges, which are excludable but to some degree non-rivalrous, are sometimes provided by private firms that recover their costs through tolls.[5] Conventional radio and television signals are provided in several different ways. The most common solution has been to sell these services, not to their ultimate consumers, but to the advertisers who want access to these consumers. Other broadcasters survive on minimal government grants and voluntary contributions. Finally, some broadcasters (particularly in Europe) are completely funded by governments.

---

[5] Levying tolls will discourage some users and might lead to sub-optimal use, but there are two reasons why such tolls might nevertheless be the best solution. First, a government can provide public goods only if it raises the required funds through taxation, and as discussed in Chapter 5, taxation leads to resource misallocation. The choice between private and government provision would then be a "second best" problem of the sort discussed later in this book. Second, roads and bridges are congestible goods, and it is sometimes optimal to levy a toll on congestible goods to control the degree of congestion. Tolls discourage use, and discouragement might well be just what is required.

QUESTIONS

1. Consider an economy in which there are 50 people, who consume a private good (bread) and a public good (circuses). There are, however, two types of people (type 1 and type 2). Each type 1 person's marginal rate of substitution is

$$MRS_1 = 20 - z$$

where z is the number of circuses. Each type 2 person's marginal rate of substitution is

$$MRS_2 = 30 - 2z$$

There are 20 type 1 people and 30 type 2 people. The economy's marginal rate of transformation is

$$MRT = 340 + 40z$$

Find the optimal number of circuses.

2. Consider an economy populated by three agents: Tom, Dick, and Harry. Let MRS be exact compensation (measured in some numeraire) for the loss of one unit of a public good (say, football fields). Each person's MRS depends only upon the quantity of football fields, G.

$$MRS^T = \max[0, 20 - 4G]$$
$$MRS^D = \max[0, 90 - 6G]$$
$$MRS^H = \max[0, 120 - 10G]$$

Here, $\max[0, x]$ means "the greater of the numbers x and 0." Find the optimal quantity of football fields when the marginal rate of transformation between football fields and the numeraire is 150. Also, find the optimal quantity when the marginal rate of transformation is 50.

3. The next question differs in one important respect from the example in the text. In the example, the economy was endowed with units of public good which could be converted into a private good. In this question, the economy is endowed with private good which can be converted into a public good. How does this difference alter the equations that characterize the solutions?

   Consider an economy composed of two people, George and Harriet, who have the utility functions

$$U_G = z^{1/3}(b_G)^{2/3}$$
$$U_H = z^{1/3}(b_H)^{2/3}$$

Here, z is the quantity of public goods, and b_G and b_H are, respectively, George's and Harriet's consumption of bread. The economy is endowed with 120 loaves of bread, and 20 loaves of bread are needed to produce each unit of public good.

a) Find the Pareto optimal allocation in which George and Harriet have the same utility.

b) Suppose that 70 loaves of the economy's endowment are initially held by George, and that 50 loaves are initially held by Harriet. Find the allocation attained when the public good is funded through voluntary contributions.

4. Consider an economy consisting of two people. The utility of person i (where i is either 1 or 2) is

$$u_i = s - (1/2)(c_i)^2$$

where s is the quantity of public good, and c_i is person i's contribution to the provision of the public good (measured in private goods). In this economy, one unit of private goods can always be transformed into one unit of public goods, so s must satisfy the "adding-up condition":

$$c_1 + c_2 = s$$

a) Define the marginal rate of substitution as the amount of private goods which exactly compensates an individual for the loss of one unit of public good. Then

$$MRS_i = - \left[\frac{\partial u_i}{\partial s} \div \frac{\partial u_i}{\partial c_i} \right]$$

Find each person's marginal rate of substitution.

b) Find the Samuelson condition for this economy.

c) An efficient allocation in this economy is a triplet (s, c_1, c_2) which satisfies both the adding-up condition and the Samuelson condition. Show that there are two efficient allocations associated with every s greater than 4.

d) Show that, if s is greater than 4, the two people's contributions are not equal. Show also that the contributions made by the agents become more inequitable as s rises.

11

Two Examples of Pure Public Goods

Even if there were very few pure public goods of any importance, their properties would be worth investigating. Actual goods vary in the degree to which they are excludable and rivalrous. The private good (excludable and completely rivalrous) and the pure public good (non-excludable and completely non-rivalrous) mark the limits of this variation, and for that reason alone, pure public goods would be worth studying. But there are pure public goods that are of far greater consequence than lighthouses. This chapter examines two of them.

11.1 KNOWLEDGE

Knowledge is a pure public good: once something is known, that knowledge can be used by anyone, and its use by any one person does not preclude its use by others.[1] As an example, our use of calculus to study economics does not prevent millions of other people from simultaneously applying calculus to entirely different problems in industry and science. Or consider penicillin. Each unit of penicillin is a private good, requiring scarce resources to produce and available for the treatment of just one patient, but the knowledge of penicillin's antibiotic properties, and of the methods of producing it cheaply, is a public good. Possession of this knowledge means that an infected scratch need no longer lead to death.

Public goods are generally divided into two categories, public consumption goods and public factors of production. These categories are not mutually exclusive. The classic public good is the lighthouse, whose beam of light warns of dangerous rocks. A recreational sailor would regard its signal as a consumption good that makes his voyage less stressful. The captain of a tanker or container ship would regard the same signal as a factor in the safe delivery of his cargo. Knowledge is likewise a good that spans both

---

[1] The classic discussion of knowledge as a public good is that of Arrow [4]. The implications of the patent system have subsequently been discussed extensively in the industrial organization literature, but most of these studies involve games with difficult structures.

categories. Certainly, the sum of all past investigations of the earth and our existence on it has changed our perceptions of ourselves, and to this extent at least, knowledge is a consumption good. But perhaps the role of knowledge as a factor of production is more evident. Knowledge has both pushed out the production possibility frontier and raised its dimensionality. It has pushed out the frontier because it has reduced the inputs required to produce any given good. The desirable qualities of steel were known for thousands of years before it came into general use, because steel's production costs were prohibitively high. These costs were driven down (and the quality of the good improved) through the slow accumulation of knowledge. Perhaps more importantly, knowledge increases the dimensionality of the frontier. In 1900, the only "digital technology" was the telegraph.

It would be difficult to understate the economic importance of knowledge. The simplest economic models argue that aggregate output is determined by the available quantities of labour (adjusted for quality) and physical capital. Such models have a considerable degree of explanatory power. They can be used to show, for example, that the spectacular recent growth of such countries as Singapore and Malaysia is largely explained by changes in the labour force participation rate, the quality of the labour force (as measured by educational attainment), and the savings rate. They do not, however, explain the consistent growth in per capita output in the western economies over the past several centuries. Only models that incorporate the accumulation of knowledge can do that.

Lipsey ([40], pp. 11–12) suggests the following "thought experiment" as a way of comprehending the economic importance of the accumulation of knowledge:

> Imagine freezing technological knowledge at the levels existing in, say, 1900, while continuing to accumulate more 1900-vintage machines and factories and using them to produce more 1900-vintage goods and services and while training more people longer and more thoroughly in the technological knowledge that was available in 1900. It is obvious that today we would then have vastly lower living standards than we now enjoy (and pollution would be a massive problem). The contrast is even more striking if the same thought experiment compares the knowledge and the product and process technologies of today with those that existed at earlier times – say in 1750 at the beginning of the First Industrial Revolution, in 1500 at the beginning of the age of European global expansion, in 1000 when the water wheel was mechanizing European manufacturing for the first time, in 1200 BC at the beginning of the iron age, and in 2700 BC at the beginning of the bronze age.

Newton, working with little more than pen and paper in his drafty Cambridge rooms, set out the principles of mathematical physics. Three hundred years later, Crick and Watson (working in an equally drafty Cambridge laboratory) discovered the double helix structure of DNA with the assistance of what amounts to a Tinkertoy set. Such tales suggest that knowledge is like the fish in the sea: one need only cast in one's line and draw it forth. But these tales are misleading, because knowledge does not come for free. The talents of these people could have been used in other ways; their decision to engage in research meant that they were not able to carry out other important work. All received the best education available in their times. Most importantly, all benefited from the cumulative efforts of their contemporaries and their predecessors. Newton's starting point was Kepler's three laws of motion, the product of a lifetime of work. Kepler's work was in turn based upon the patient astrological observations of his predecessors, including those made by Brahe (and an army of students and collaborators) over the course of his life. The framework within which Kepler organized this data was the heliocentric view of the solar system, the lifetime work of Copernicus. Similarly, the Tinkertoy approach worked for Crick and Watson because a vast body of chemical and physical research had placed so many restrictions on the structure of DNA that they only had to puzzle out the way in which the disparate pieces could be fitted together. The cumulative amount of scarce resources, both human and physical, embodied in each of these discoveries is substantial. Research might be an investment in which the pay-off is potentially spectacular, but it is still an investment.

Knowledge is a public good whose creation requires the expenditure of scarce resources, and which has profound implications for economic welfare. The question of whether a competitive system would allocate sufficient resources to its production is then of crucial importance. The answer is that it will not. Innovators are driven by many things – curiosity, altruism, desire for fame or fortune – but they must still put food on their tables and equipment in their laboratories. Their willingness to engage in research depends at least in part on the economic incentives that confront them. The free-rider problem implies that these incentives would be too small under competition, and that too few resources would be allocated to research.

The optimal amount of resources is allocated to research if the social cost of additional research is just equal to the (expected) social benefit of the research results. An independent research institution, for example, bears the full resource costs of its research (the cost of hiring scientists and equipping the laboratories). The institution would devote the socially optimal amount of resources to research only if it were able to collect the full social benefit of its research. That is, the correct decision would be made only if it could charge every user of its research a price equal to the value of that research to the user. There are a number of reasons why this would not occur:

- The researcher would lose control of the information as soon as it had been sold to one person. That person would be able to sell it or give it away, reducing the researcher's revenue from additional sales. (Bootleg software is a case in point.)
- Even if purchasers of research could be prevented from revealing the information to others, the use of the information would at least partially reveal it to interested parties. Reverse engineering, in which a product is taken apart to discover the principles by which it operates, is the ultimate example of this problem.
- If the researcher sets a fixed price for his product (as is the case, for example, with books and software), he does not extract a price equal to the full value of the information from those who do buy, and he deters some people from buying at all.

The researcher's alternative would be to price discriminate.[2] Incomplete price discrimination would increase the researcher's revenues, but he would still not receive the full social value of his research. Complete price discrimination would allow the researcher to earn the full social value of his research, but is (as always) an unlikely outcome.

- A buyer cannot establish the value of information to him until he knows the information – and once he knows it, he has no reason to pay for it.
- Not all buyers are present at the time that the information is sold. Newton and Leibnitz aren't going to get a dime from you, even though you have been using their invention, differential calculus.

The innovator's inability to obtain adequate compensation for his efforts would, under a competitive system, cause too few resources to be allocated to research. Knowledge, like any other public good, would be underprovided.

There have been essentially two responses to this public goods problem: a combination of subsidization and government provision, and the patent system.

Some research is carried out by the government in its own research organizations. Other research organizations are directly subsidized by the government, or indirectly subsidized through the practice of making some types of private donations tax deductible. Universities and university-based research institutions, for example, are directly subsidized, whereas research into such illnesses as cancer, heart disease, and diabetes is in large part funded through charitable donations.

Basic research is research into the underlying structure of the world. Its full implications are often not immediately evident. (For example, a half century of research separates Watson and Crick's discovery from the cloning of sheep and the treatment of disease through gene therapy.) It is therefore likely to be greatly under-valued in a competitive marketplace. The government's response has generally been to produce or subsidize research of this type. The results of the research are then made available with the fewest possible restrictions on its use.

Research with more immediate commercial applications tends to be protected by the patent system. This system assigns the rights to a particular discovery to a person or firm (usually the discoverer, or the agency that funded the discoverer) for a specified period of time. The holder of the patent can either retain the use of that discovery for himself, or he can assign the use of it to others (who would, of course, pay for that privilege). When the patent expires, anyone can use the discovery without paying any

---

[2] A firm price discriminates when it charges different prices to different customers. Complete price discrimination, in which the firm charges each customer an amount equal to that customer's valuation of the good, is unlikely. The customers know that revealing how much they want the good will only raise the price that they have to pay for it, so they will conceal their true valuations. Incomplete price discrimination, however, is common. Airlines, for example, charge much higher prices for tickets purchased within a week of a flight than for tickets purchased well in advance. They know that people who fly on short notice are predominantly business travellers, who are willing to pay high prices, and that people who plan months in advance are predominantly vacationers, who are much more likely to be deterred by high prices.

fee. The life of the patent is fixed by the laws which govern patents: it is not decided on a case-by-case basis. The ideal choice of patent life trades off the benefits of patent protection against its costs.

A patent holder is essentially a monopolist – the sole seller of a well-defined product – and as such, is able to earn monopoly profits. A researcher will undertake further research so long as the cost of the research is less than the monopoly profits that he expects to earn from the resulting patents. For any given period of patent protection, there will be some research projects for which the expected monopoly profits exceed the research costs and others for which they do not. The former projects will be undertaken and the latter will not. Lengthening the patent life raises the potential monopoly profits on all projects, moving some research projects from the latter group to the former. Thus, a longer patent life gives rise to more research.

Lengthening the patent life delays the full exploitation of all of the knowledge that would have been produced under the shorter patent life. Much of the value of knowledge lies in the fact that, once discovered, it can be used by any number of people. However, the patent holder only benefits from his discovery by controlling and limiting access to it, so that its full social benefits are *not* exploited. Longer patent protection increases the benefits of any particular discovery to the patent holder, but reduces the benefits of that discovery to society.

The essential trade-off involved in choosing the patent life is that a longer patent life raises the rate at which discoveries occurs, but reduces the social benefits of each discovery.

Patents might have additional adverse consequences if innovators compete with one another. Since possession of a patent gives rise to monopoly profits, innovators might engage in a "patent race" which wastes scarce resources. The first innovator to produce a particular technology is rewarded with a patent and the accompanying monopoly profits, while the remaining firms receive no rewards. The innovators' attempts to be first imply that they are, to a great degree, duplicating each other's efforts and squandering scarce resources in the process. A similar duplication of effort might occur after an innovator has acquired a patent. Other innovators are aware that the patent is profitable, and might attempt to steal away a share of those profits by producing a second patentable device that performs essentially the same function as the first. This device would be similar to the first, but not similar enough to infringe upon the initial patent. The pursuit of profits again wastes resources to the degree that the two research programs duplicate each other.

It seems quite certain that the patent system raises economic welfare by encouraging research, but it does have costs as well as benefits. Even under the best possible patent system, resources in the research sector will not be optimally allocated.

11.2 INCOME REDISTRIBUTION

People do care about the welfare of others. They care about the welfare of their immediate family, and to lesser degrees, the welfare of their friends and extended family, their

neighbours, and fellow workers. They care about the welfare of people who are completely unknown to them, as evidenced by the out-pouring of donations that follows a natural disaster or civil strife, whether at home or in some country far away.

Economists often neglect the fact that each person's well-being is contingent upon the well-being of other people. This neglect is justified neglect in many cases. The problems that confront economists always involve a web of relationships; and the first step to understanding any of these problems is to identify the pivotal relationships. An individual's concern for other people is often not pivotal.[3] In other cases the pivotal relationships involve only the family unit. (Decisions related to labour supply and housing are generally of this type.) An economist who wishes to understand these problems would ignore the dependence of the individual's welfare, or the family's welfare, on the welfare of others.

There are, however, problems for which this interdependence is crucial. In particular, the design of social programs hinges not only on what we *can* do for economically disadvantaged people, but also on what we *are willing* to do for them.

This chapter examines a simple problem of this sort. It shows that, when people care about the welfare of others, some income distributions are Pareto optimal and some are not. If the initial distribution is not Pareto optimal, some redistribution of incomes will be needed to reach a Pareto optimal distribution. Moreover, it will be shown that charity has the properties of a public good; and in particular, that charity gives rise to the free-rider problem. A purely voluntary redistribution of incomes is therefore too small to take the economy to a Pareto optimal distribution of income. Forced redistribution can make everyone better off – including those who are required to give up income.[4]

11.2.1 A Framework for the Study of Income Distributions

Imagine a simple economy in which there is only one consumption good. The economy is endowed with $2\overline{y}$ units of this good, and these goods are divided among the four people who live in the economy. These people are split into two pairs, pair A and pair B. Each person in pair A has y_A units of goods and each person in pair B has y_B units of goods. All of the goods belong to someone, so

$$y_A + y_B = \overline{y}$$

The pair (y_A, y_B) describes the distribution of income in the economy. If y_A and y_B are not equal, one pair is rich and the other pair poor.

Each person's welfare depends upon his own consumption and the consumption of the poor. To keep track of each individual's welfare, let one person in each pair be called

---

[3] Let me emphasize that I am arguing that our relationships with others are often not pivotal, but I am *not* arguing that they are often irrelevant. I choose my own lunch from the menu, but if I want to eat that lunch with someone else, that person's tastes influence the choice of venue. I choose my own shirts, but I know that my choice will affect the way that others perceive me.

[4] Pareto optimal income distributions were originally discussed by Hochman and Rodgers [34]; the model in this chapter is based upon Warr's presentation [65].

person 1 and let the other be called person 2. Let c_{Ai} be the consumption of person i (where i is either 1 or 2) in pair A, and let c_{Bi} be the consumption of person i in pair B. Let c_P be the consumption of each person in the poor pair.[5] Then the utility of person i in pair A is

$$U_{Ai} = (c_{Ai})^\alpha (c_P)^{1-\alpha}$$

and the utility of person i in pair B is

$$U_{Bi} = (c_{Bi})^\alpha (c_P)^{1-\alpha}$$

The bigger the value of the exponent α, the more importance individuals place on their own consumption and the less importance they place on the consumption of the poor. It is assumed that α is between $1/2$ and 1, so that individuals consider their own consumption to be more important than that of the poor.

This form of the utility function restricts the motives of the individual in some ways but not in others. Since each individual's utility rises as the consumption of the poor rises, there is no enmity between the rich and the poor. However, it does not follow that the rich empathize with the poor. They might believe that too much income inequality leads to higher crime rates and a less orderly society, and therefore a less pleasant life for themselves. They might simply consider squeegee kids and bag ladies to be aesthetically unpleasant.

11.2.2 Pareto Optimal Income Distributions

If people consume the goods that are allocated to them – no more and no less – which pairs (y_A, y_B) are "good" allocations and which are not? If a "good" allocation is one that satisfies the Pareto criterion, the characteristic of a "good" allocation is that there is no other allocation at which someone is better off and no one is worse off.

The Pareto optimal allocations can easily be found by graphing the utilities associated with any pair (y_A, y_B). Since each person consumes the goods that he is allocated, and since $y_B = \bar{y} - y_A$, the utilities can be written as follows:

$$U_A = \begin{cases} (y_A)^\alpha (\bar{y} - y_A)^{1-\alpha} & \text{if} \quad y_A \geq \bar{y}/2 \\ y_A & \text{otherwise} \end{cases}$$

$$U_B = \begin{cases} \bar{y} - y_A & \text{if} \quad y_A \geq \bar{y}/2 \\ (\bar{y} - y_A)^\alpha (y_A)^{1-\alpha} & \text{otherwise} \end{cases}$$

The people in each pair care about their own consumption and that of the poor when they are rich, but care only about their own consumption when they are poor.

---

[5] For reasons that will soon be apparent, the *possibility* that the people in a particular pair will have different consumption levels must be encompassed. However, the people in each pair will ultimately consume the same amounts, so that the value of c_P will be unambiguous.

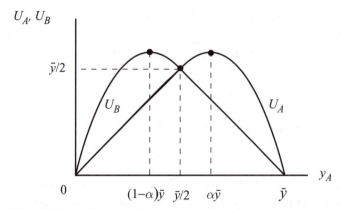

Figure 11.1: Utility and the Distribution of Income. The utility of a poor person rises with his income, while the utility of a rich person first rises and then falls as his income rises. Pair A is rich when y_A is greater than $\bar{y}/2$, and pair B is rich when y_A is less than $\bar{y}/2$.

Figure 11.1 graphs U_A and U_B against y_A. The utility U_A first rises and then falls as y_A rises. When y_A is less than $\bar{y}/2$, the people in pair A are poor and care only about their own consumption: their utilities rise as y_A rises. When y_A exceeds $\bar{y}/2$, the now-rich people in pair A begin to care about the consumption of the now-poor people in pair B as well as their own consumption. Their utilities initially continue to rise with y_A (the people in pair B aren't yet *that* poor), but eventually they become so rich and the people in pair B become so poor that their utilities fall as y_A rises. Their utilities are highest when they are allocated the fraction α of the available goods. The graph of U_B is the same as the graph of U_A except that it is flipped over, because the people in pair B are rich when y_A is small and poor when it is large. Their utilities are also highest when they receive the fraction α of the available goods, or equivalently, when the people in the other pair receive the fraction $1 - \alpha$ of the available goods.

Figure 11.2 presents the same information in a different form. Each point on the loop plots the pair (U_A, U_B) associated with some y_A. Both utilities are zero when y_A is zero. As y_A grows from zero, both utilities rise but U_B rises faster than U_A, so that the top half of the loop is traced out. The highest point on the loop (i.e., the highest value of U_B) occurs when the people in pair A receive the fraction $1 - \alpha$ of the available goods; transferring still more goods to this pair causes U_B to fall while U_A continues to rise. The utilities are equal when y_A is $\bar{y}/2$. Now, as y_A rises, U_A rises toward its maximum and then falls toward zero, and U_B falls steadily toward zero. The resulting loop is symmetrical about the 45° line.

The Pareto optimal allocations are evident from Figure 11.2. No allocation in which y_A is less than $(1 - \alpha)\bar{y}$ is Pareto optimal, because both utilities could be increased by raising y_A. No allocation in which y_A is greater than $\alpha\bar{y}$ is Pareto optimal, because both utilities could be increased by reducing y_A. Every intermediate value of y_A corresponds to a Pareto optimal allocation. From any of these allocations, each pair's welfare can only be raised by reducing the welfare of the other pair.

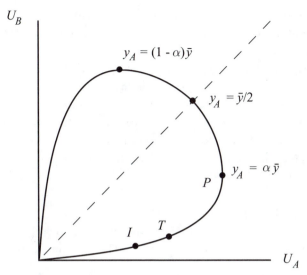

Figure 11.2: The Utility Possibility Frontier. Each point on the loop represents the utilities associated with a particular distribution of income.

11.2.3 Charitable Donations

We have seen that income distributions that are too unequal are not Pareto optimal. If the actual income distribution were of this kind, and if the government could transfer income between the pairs, it could raise everyone's welfare by transferring income from the rich to the poor. But suppose that the government did not act. Would the rich people *voluntarily* transfer income to the poor? Would they voluntarily transfer *enough* income to move the economy to a Pareto optimal distribution? These are the questions that we must answer.

It is worth remembering that these same questions are being asked in the "real world" economies in which we live. Many western countries sought to bring their budget deficits and national debts under control during the last decade of the last century. Government spending was reduced, largely by trimming social programs. These reductions were justified in part by arguing that the programs were too generous, and that their generosity created severe misallocations of resources that could not be sustained. But the reductions were also justified by arguing that private and corporate donations would rise to offset the fall in government spending. Our abstract model is a "virtual laboratory" in which this latter argument can be tested.

Our approach will be as follows. It will be assumed that

- The initial income distribution is not Pareto optimal.
- Each person in the rich pair is allowed to donate some of his goods to the poor, and the donated goods are divided equally between the people in the poor pair.
- Each rich person chooses his donations to maximize his own utility.

We will look for the Nash equilibrium donations, that is, the pair of donations (one for each rich person) such that neither rich person can make himself better off by unilaterally changing his donation. The properties of the post-transfer distribution of income will then be studied.

The Nash equilibrium will be found by deriving each rich person's best response function. Person 1's best response function indicates, for each donation by person 2, the donation that person 1 would have to make to maximize his own utility. Person 2's best response function is similarly defined. A pair of donations that satisfies both best response functions is a Nash equilibrium because each person's donation maximizes his own utility given the donation of the other person. Anyone who deviated from the equilibrium would lower his own utility.

The Best Response Functions

For concreteness, assume that $y_A > \alpha \bar{y}$, so that pair A is rich. Let v_1 and v_2 be the donations of person 1 and person 2, respectively. Then person 1's utility is

$$U_{A1} = (y_A - v_1)^\alpha \left(\bar{y} - y_A + \frac{v_1 + v_2}{2} \right)^{1-\alpha}$$

and person 2's utility is

$$U_{A2} = (y_A - v_2)^\alpha \left(\bar{y} - y_A + \frac{v_1 + v_2}{2} \right)^{1-\alpha}$$

The best response functions must be derived with a modicum of care, because a donation can be positive or zero but not negative. Let's start with person 1. For him,

$$\frac{dU_{A1}}{dv_1} = U_{A1} \left\{ -\frac{\alpha}{y_A - v_1} + \frac{(1 - \alpha)}{2(\bar{y} - y_A) + (v_1 + v_2)} \right\}$$

There are two possibilities:

- If $\alpha v_2 \geq (1 + \alpha) y_A - 2\alpha \bar{y}$, the derivative is negative whenever v_1 is positive. That is, person 1's utility rises as his donations fall. His utility-maximizing donation is therefore zero.
- If $\alpha v_2 < (1 + \alpha) y_A - 2\alpha \bar{y}$, the derivative is positive when v_1 is small and negative when v_1 is large. Person 1's utility is maximized when the derivative dU_{A1}/dv_1 is equal to zero. The utility-maximizing donation is $(1 + \alpha) y_A - 2\alpha \bar{y} - \alpha v_2$.

Combining these observations gives person 1's best response function:

$$v_1^* = \begin{cases} 0 & \text{if} \quad v_2 \geq (1 + \alpha) G / \alpha \\ (1 + \alpha) G - \alpha v_2 & \text{if} \quad v_2 < (1 + \alpha) G / \alpha \end{cases}$$

where

$$G \equiv y_A - \left(\frac{2}{1 + \alpha} \right) \alpha \bar{y}$$

The constant G is the gap between the *actual income* of a rich person and his *target income*. Our maintained assumption that the initial distribution of incomes is too unequal to be Pareto optimal implies that actual income is greater than $\alpha \bar{y}$. Since $1 + \alpha$ is less than 2, the target income is also greater than $\alpha \bar{y}$. Consequently, the gap could be either positive or negative.

Person 2's best response function is derived in a similar fashion:

$$v_2^* = \begin{cases} 0 & \text{if} \quad v_1 \geq (1+\alpha)G/\alpha \\ (1+\alpha)G - \alpha v_1 & \text{if} \quad v_1 < (1+\alpha)G/\alpha \end{cases}$$

Since these two people are alike in every way, it is not surprising that person 2's best response function is the same as that for person 1, but with all of the subscripts switched.

Nash Equilibrium

The two best response functions are shown in Figure 11.3. The top graph assumes that $G > 0$. The Nash equilibrium is in the interior of the quadrant, with both rich people contributing G. The bottom graph assumes that $G \leq 0$. The Nash equilibrium in this case is at the origin: both rich people contribute nothing. In light of our interpretation of the constant G, the Nash equilibrium can be described as follows:

- If the actual income of a rich person is less than or equal to his target income, rich people do not make charitable donations.
- If the actual income of a rich person exceeds his target income, each rich person contributes just enough to reduce his own income to the target income. The increase in each poor person's income is, of course, equal to the decrease in each rich person's income.

A Pareto optimal income distribution is not reached. If the economy is sufficiently close to a Pareto optimal distribution, there is no voluntary redistribution whatsoever. If the economy is sufficiently far from a Pareto optimal distribution, voluntary redistribution takes the economy closer to, but not to, a Pareto optimal distribution.

These results are illustrated in Figure 11.2. The utilities corresponding to the target income distribution correspond to a point on the lower part of the loop. This point is labelled T. The Pareto optimal distribution that is most favourable to the rich people is labelled P. If the initial income distribution corresponds to a point on the loop between T and P, each rich person's income is less than his target income (i.e., G is negative). There is no redistribution and the economy ends up where it began. If the initial distribution corresponds to a point between T and the origin, each rich person's income is greater than his target income (i.e., G is positive). Voluntary redistribution takes the economy to T but no farther. In either case, *both* the rich and the poor are worse off than they would be at P.

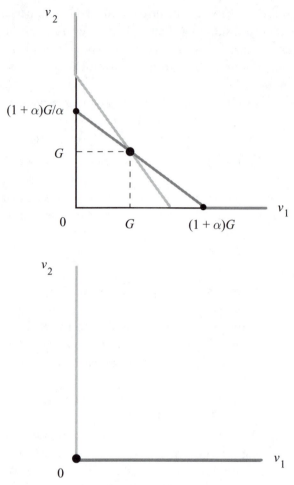

Figure 11.3: Best Response Functions and Nash Equilibrium. Person 1's best response functions are light gray, and person 2's best response functions are dark gray. If G is positive, as in the top panel, the Nash equilibrium is (G, G). If G is negative or zero, as in the bottom panel, the Nash equilibrium is $(0, 0)$.

11.2.4 Government-Mandated and Voluntary Redistribution

Let's now return to the policy issue raised above. Imagine that the government can also engage in redistributive policies, taking from the rich and giving to the poor. To what degree do charitable donations supplement the government's redistributive policies? How would these donations change if the government's redistributive policies were scaled back?

Imagine that the initial distribution corresponds to point I in Figure 11.2, and that the government mandates transfers that take the economy toward, or to, P. People then decide whether they wish to supplement the government's efforts by making voluntary donations. How large would these donations be?

The answer follows immediately from our previous results. If the government-mandated transfers were large enough to carry the economy to a point between T and

P, the rich would make no voluntary donations. If these transfers were on a smaller scale, moving the economy to a point between I and T, the rich would make donations that move the economy to T itself.

The effects of reduced government-mandated redistribution are then evident.

- If the government's original policies had moved the economy to a point somewhere between I and T, the subsequent voluntary redistribution would have carried the economy to T. Any reduction in the scale of the government's redistributive policy would be accompanied by an offsetting increase in voluntary donations, so that the economy would remain at T.
- If the government's original polices had moved the economy to a point between T and P, there would have been no voluntary contributions at all. A scaling-back of the government's policies would elicit no new donations so long as the scaled-back policies also left the economy between T and P. Voluntary donations would be elicited only if the government policies were reduced by so much that the economy were moved to a point between I and T – and then these donations would only take the economy as far as T itself.

In short, a reduction in the scope of the government's redistributive policies would lead to offsetting increases in private donations only if the scope of these policies was initially far too small.

11.2.5 Charity as a Public Good

The act of giving charity is a public good in this economy. Both of the rich people care about the welfare of the poor, so giving by one of them increases the welfare of both. The observation that voluntary donations fail to take the economy to a Pareto optimal income distribution is therefore unsurprising: it is simply another manifestation of the free-rider problem.

In light of this observation, we ought to be able to find the optimal size of the charitable donations. The Samuelson condition in this case states that

$$MRS_1 + MRS_2 = MRT$$

Here, MRS_i is the number of units of his own consumption that person i (in pair A) is willing to sacrifice to raise c_P by one unit, and MRT is the total amount of consumption that the rich must sacrifice to raise c_P by one unit.

The marginal rate of transformation is always 2: the rich must collectively give up two units of their own consumption to raise each poor person's consumption by one unit. The marginal rate of substitution is calculated in the usual fashion:

$$MRS_i = \frac{\partial U_{Ai}}{\partial c_B} \div \frac{\partial U_{Ai}}{\partial c_{Ai}} = \frac{1-\alpha}{\alpha}\left(\frac{c_A}{c_B}\right)$$

Substituting into the Samuelson condition shows that the charitable donations of the rich are optimal when

$$\frac{c_A}{c_B} = \frac{\alpha}{1 - \alpha}$$

This condition is satisfied only if the redistribution of income takes the economy to point P in Figure 11.2, this being the Pareto optimal income distribution that most favours the rich. The required donation by each rich person is $y_A - \alpha \bar{y}$, which is greater than G and therefore greater than the donation that a rich person would voluntarily make.

QUESTIONS

1. The following question employs a production function of the form

$$y = \ln x$$

where y is output and x is an input. This function states that y is the "natural logarithm" of x. For the present purpose, the important properties of this function are:

- Its graph, plotted in the (x, y) plane, is positively sloped everywhere and passes through the point $(1, 0)$. The positive slope implies that the input's marginal product is always positive.
- Its derivative is

$$\frac{dy}{dx} = \frac{1}{x}$$

  so the slope of the graph falls toward zero as x rises. That is, the marginal product is diminishing.
- If x is itself a function of a third variable w, the derivative of y with respect to w is found by applying the chain rule:

$$\frac{dy}{dw} = \frac{dy}{dx}\frac{dx}{dw} = \frac{1}{x}\frac{dx}{dw}$$

The only problem with using this function as a production function is that output is negative if too little of the input is used (specifically, if x is less than one). The question below is rigged to ensure that enough of the input is used to generate positive output.

Imagine an economy in which n firms (identified by the integers $1, \ldots, n$) engage in two activities, research and production. Each firm first engages in research, and then produces for two periods.

Research generates knowledge. The dollar cost to firm i of acquiring a stock of knowledge x_i through research is

$$c_i = x_i/2$$

A firm that has more knowledge at its disposal is more productive, but firms are not necessarily allowed to use all of the existing knowledge. Specifically, each firm can use: (*i*) the knowledge that it has acquired, and (*ii*) the knowledge acquired by the other firms, *provided that this knowledge is not protected by a patent*. Consequently, each firm's output is strongly influenced by the patent laws. Three kinds of patent laws will be examined below:

- There are no patents in either period.
- Knowledge is protected by patents in both periods.
- Knowledge is protected by patents in the first period but not the second.

The dollar value of firm i's output in period t (denoted y_{it}) is

$$y_{it} = \begin{cases} \ln(x_1 + x_2 + \cdots + x_n) & \text{if knowledge is not patented in period } t \\ \ln(x_i) & \text{if knowledge is patented in period } t \end{cases}$$

Firm i's profits are equal to the dollar value of total production less the dollar value of its research costs:

$$\pi_i = y_{i1} + y_{i2} - c_i$$

Each firm, taking the other firm's stock of knowledge as given, chooses it own stock of knowledge to maximize its own profits.

a) Assume that there are no patents in either period, and consider the behaviour of some firm i. What are its profits if it chooses to acquire a stock of knowledge x_i and every other firm chooses to acquire a stock of knowledge $\tilde{x}$? Find the stock of knowledge x_i that maximizes firm i's profits when every other firm chooses to acquire the stock of knowledge $\tilde{x}$ – that is, find firm i's best response function. Find the stock of knowledge acquired by each firm in the symmetric Nash equilibrium, and find each firm's profits in that equilibrium.

b) Assume that knowledge is protected by patents in both periods. Find the stock of knowledge acquired by each firm in the symmetric Nash equilibrium, and find each firm's profits in that equilibrium.

c) Assume that knowledge is protected by patents only in the first period. Find the stock of knowledge acquired by each firm in the symmetric Nash equilibrium, and find each firm's profits in that equilibrium.

d) Show that, so long as there is more than one firm in the economy, the economy's stock of knowledge $x_1 + x_2 + \cdots + x_n$ rises with the duration of the patent protection.

e) Show that, so long as there is more than one firm in the economy, profits are lower when knowledge is patented in both periods than when it is patented in neither period.

f) Assume that n is 2. Calculate numerically each firm's profits when there is no patent protection and when there is patent protection only in the first period. Does this kind of patent protection increase profits?

g) Assume that n is 10. Calculate numerically each firm's profits when there is no patent protection and when there is patent protection only in the first period. Does this kind of patent protection increase profits?

2. Tom, Dick, and Harry live in the same apartment building in downtown Los Angeles. Tom and Dick work at local auto parts stores, and each of them has an income of y dollars per week. Harry is less fortunate. He used to have a good job at the LAPD, but his penchant for firing large caliber weapons in crowded public places led to

his dismissal. He currently has no income. Tom and Dick (who are originally from Texas) firmly believe in a man's right to draw his gun in the defence of just about anything, and are happy to financially support Harry. Tom gives Harry z_T dollars each week, and Dick gives Harry z_D dollars each week.

Tom's utility U_T depends upon the dollar value of his own weekly consumption, c_T, and of Harry's weekly consumption, c_H:

$$U_T = 2 \, (c_T)^{1/2} + (c_H)^{1/2}$$

Likewise, Dick's utility U_D depends upon the dollar value of his own weekly consumption, c_D, and of Harry's weekly consumption:

$$U_D = 2 \, (c_D)^{1/2} + (c_H)^{1/2}$$

Harry spends all of the money that he receives from Tom and Dick. Tom and Dick spend all of the money that they have left after giving a little to Harry.

a) Find the Nash equilibrium values of the transfers z_T and z_D.

b) Imagine that Tom and Dick agree to give the same amount, $\widehat{z}$, to Harry, and that they choose this amount to maximize the sum of their utilities. What is $\widehat{z}$?

12

Impure Public Goods

It has been assumed so far that all goods fall into one of two categories. Pure public goods are non-rivalrous in consumption, meaning that one person's consumption of any of these goods does not interfere with any other person's consumption of the same good. The clarity of your radio reception, for example, is independent of the number of other listeners. Private goods are rivalrous in consumption, meaning that only one person can consume each unit of these goods. Food and clothing are examples of goods in this category. But there are many other goods, including parks and recreational facilities, police and fire protection, and roads and bridges, that do not fit into either category. Consumption of one of these goods by another person reduces, but does not eliminate, the benefits that other people receive from their consumption of the same good. These goods are called **impure public goods,** and are said to be **partially rivalrous** or **congestible.**

Impure public goods also differ from pure public goods in that they are often excludable. Access to many recreational facilities is controlled, and toll roads and toll bridges are not unfamiliar. Fire and police protection are more problematic. Controlling access to these services is more difficult, and even if it were feasible, it would raise serious ethical questions.

The possibility of controlling access to impure public goods has two important implications. First, provision by private firms or by governments on a "fee for service" basis becomes possible, because free riding can be eliminated. Second, the provider of the good can influence the degree of congestion by regulating either the number of people who use the good, or the frequency with which they use the good, or both.

The study of impure public goods has centered on two broad classes of goods: the club good, first studied by Buchanan [14], and the variable-use public good, first analyzed by Oakland [47] and Sandmo [56]. **Club goods** include such facilities as swimming pools, fitness clubs, and tennis courts. It is generally assumed that the number of users (or members) of each facility is controlled, but that the frequency of each member's use is not. These goods are assumed to be **replicable,** so that individuals who are excluded from one facility (or club) can become members of another equivalent club. **Variable-use public goods** are goods such as roads, bridges, and public transit systems. They can be either excludable or non-excludable, but if they are excludable, frequency of use rather than number of users is controlled. They are not replicable, so one facility must provide the service to all potential users. These two classes of goods will be examined in turn.

12.1 CLUB GOODS

The benefit received by each club member depends upon the size of the club's facilities and the club's membership. This benefit can be described by the equation

$$B = b(s, m)$$

where B is each member's benefit, s is the size of the facility, and m is membership. This equation contains a general functional form: it asserts that B is determined by s and m, but does not give definite instructions for calculating the benefit. The form of the function b must be restricted so that the relationship between B and its determinants, s and m, is a sensible one. But we can't know what restrictions should be placed on the function unless we know what kind of behaviour we want to depict. Let's imagine a particular kind of club – a tennis club – and consider how the typical member would respond to a change in the club's size and membership.

First, imagine that the membership is fixed, and that a bigger facility means one with more tennis courts. Members meet, find other players with whom they are compatible, and try to book court time. If the club has only a few courts, the most desirable time slots are quickly booked, and the remaining players must either accept inconvenient time slots or cancel their matches. Building another court increases the number of desirable time slots, so more matches are played, and more matches are played in desirable time slots. The benefits associated with the additional court are large. However, if the club has many courts, an additional court yields quite small benefits. The members are already playing as much tennis as they would like, and the additional court simply allows them to obtain bookings in slightly more convenient time slots. Arguably, the benefit associated with each increase in facility size declines as the facility size rises.

Now imagine that the club's size is fixed and that the membership is changing. When the membership is small, each member has difficulty finding fellow players who have roughly equal skills and compatible schedules. Adding members increases the likelihood that any given member will be able to find a satisfactory partner, increasing the benefit that he obtains from club membership. But adding members also increases the competition for time slots, and this congestion reduces the benefit that each member obtains from club membership. The first effect is likely to dominate when the membership is small, because there are few compatible pairs, and therefore little demand for courts. Increasing the membership creates more compatible pairs who readily find court time. The second effect is likely to dominate when the membership is large. A large membership implies that there are already many compatible pairs, and that the courts are highly congested. Increasing the membership does not markedly increase the number of matches that each member would like to play, but the greater congestion

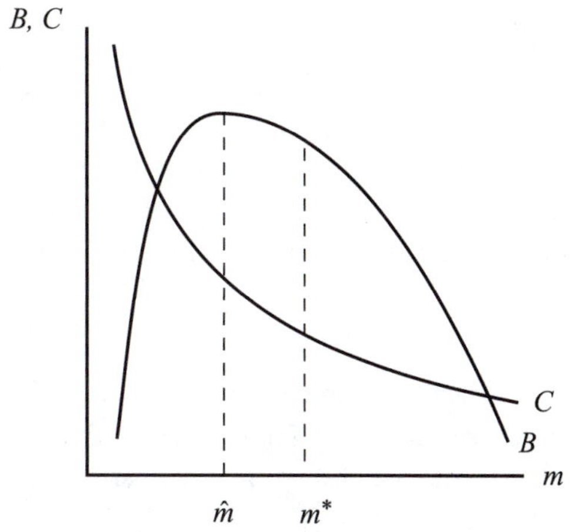

Figure 12.1: Optimal Membership of a Club of Given Size. The assumption that clubs are replicable implies that it is socially optimal to maximize the net benefits of each club member. The optimal membership is m^*.

forces each member to play in less convenient time slots. Thus, the benefit received by each member first rises and then falls as the number of members rises.

Members prefer bigger facilities to smaller facilities, but successive increases in facility size bring smaller and smaller increases in benefits. These aspects of the club are incorporated by assuming that

$$\frac{\partial b}{\partial s} > 0$$

$$\frac{\partial^2 b}{\partial s^2} \equiv \frac{\partial}{\partial s}\left(\frac{\partial b}{\partial s}\right) < 0$$

The idea that each member's benefit first rises and then falls as the membership rises can be expressed by assuming that, for each s, there is a critical membership $\widehat{m}(s)$ such that

$$\frac{\partial b(s, m)}{\partial m} = 0 \qquad \text{when} \qquad m = \widehat{m}(s)$$

and that

$$\frac{\partial^2 b}{\partial m^2} \equiv \frac{\partial}{\partial m}\left(\frac{\partial b}{\partial m}\right) < 0$$

The second condition states that the marginal benefit of an additional member gets smaller as the membership rises. If the marginal benefit of an additional member is zero when there are $\widehat{m}(s)$ members, it must be positive when there are fewer than $\widehat{m}(s)$ members, and negative when there are more than $\widehat{m}(s)$ members.[1] This relationship is shown in Figure 12.1.

Clubs have costs as well as benefits. If the club's total cost is proportional to its size, and if each member bears an equal share of the costs, each member's share of the cost,

---

[1] Note that $\widehat{m}(s)$ could be zero for all s, so that benefits per person always decline as membership rises. This situation might describe swimming pools and libraries, where increased interaction between members yields too few benefits to offset the effects of congestion.

C, is

$$C = \frac{ks}{m}$$

Here, k is the cost of each unit of the club's facilities, and hence ks is the total cost of the club's facilities. This relationship is also shown in Figure 12.1. The net benefit NB of each club member is the difference between the benefit and the cost:

$$NB = b(s, m) - \frac{ks}{m}$$

The assumption that the clubs are replicable implies that the social net benefits of a system of clubs are maximized when an individual member's net benefit is maximized.[2] That is, the socially optimal club size and membership maximize NB and therefore satisfy the conditions

$$\frac{\partial NB}{\partial s} = \frac{\partial b}{\partial s} - \frac{k}{m} = 0 \tag{12.1}$$

$$\frac{\partial NB}{\partial m} = \frac{\partial b}{\partial m} + \frac{ks}{m^2} = 0 \tag{12.2}$$

These conditions have simple interpretations:

- Re-arranging (12.1) gives

$$m\left(\frac{\partial b}{\partial s}\right) = k$$

  which is the Samuelson condition in another guise. The facility is of the optimal size if the sum of the members' marginal benefits from a unit of facilities is equal to its marginal cost.
- The optimal membership maximizes NB, which is the vertical distance between B and C in Figure 12.1. This distance is maximized when the two curves have the same slope, and the slopes are equal when (12.2) is satisfied. Alternatively, re-arranging (12.2) yields

$$m\left(\frac{\partial b}{\partial m}\right) = -\frac{ks}{m} \tag{12.3}$$

  which states that the club has the optimal membership when a small change in membership has no net change in the welfare of the existing members. Adding

---

[2] People excluded from one club are accommodated by building more clubs, so it is socially optimal to design each club to maximize the net benefits of its members. If clubs were not replicable – this case is discussed by Ng [45] – people excluded from the club would not be accommodated elsewhere and hence would receive no benefits. The social net benefits of the club would then be equal to mNB, or equivalently, $mb(s, m) - ks$. The socially optimal membership would trade-off the gain from providing one more person with a membership, $b(s, m)$, against the loss that his membership imposes upon the other members, $m(\partial b/\partial m)$.

another member increases congestion, reducing the benefits of each of the existing m members by an amount $-\partial b/\partial m$. (Note that $\partial b/\partial m$ must be negative for this condition to be satisfied.) Since the new member bears an equal share of the costs, adding a new member reduces the existing members' share of the cost by ks/m. A new member has no net effect on the welfare of the existing members when his impact on their benefits and costs are exactly offsetting.

Since (12.1) and (12.2) constitute a two-equation system in two unknowns, they can be solved to obtain the optimal size and membership.

12.2 VARIABLE-USE PUBLIC GOODS

The variable-use public good is made available to everyone, but each person chooses the frequency with which he uses it. Each person's use creates congestion which adversely affects every other person who uses the facility, and reduces the frequency with which the others use it. Each person's frequency of use therefore depends upon every other person's frequency of use.

Imagine, for example, that the public good is a road connecting a suburb to a city center. Each user believes that trips to the city (for work, or for a night on the town) are rewarding, but that each additional trip has a smaller value than the last. A simple function that reflects these beliefs is

$$B = (2h)t^{1/2}$$

where B is the value that a single user places on t trips to the city, and h is a positive constant.

The *act* of travelling to the city imposes (potentially) two types of costs on the user. There might be a monetary cost; specifically, a toll p might be charged for each use of the road. Travellers might also experience delays, or aggravation, or be exposed to an element of danger when road use is high. These costs are referred to as congestion costs, and are represented by z.

Congestion costs depend upon the capacity of the road system, s, and the number of trips made by the other users. If there are $m - 1$ other users, and if the average number of trips made by these users is v, the total number of trips by other users is $(m - 1)v$. Assume that the congestion costs incurred by a single user are

$$z = \frac{(m - 1)v}{s} \tag{12.4}$$

An increase in use raises each person's congestion costs, while an increase in capacity reduces these costs.[3]

---

[3] This particular function is adopted to simplify the algebra, but it is a little too simple to properly describe congestion costs. It is very unlikely that congestion is *linearly* related to the other drivers'

Constructing the road system uses up scarce resources. Assume, as before, that the flow cost[4] of building a road with capacity s is ks. If the number of users is fixed and equal to m, the capacity cost per user is ks/m.

The social net benefit of the public good, expressed on a per capita basis, is

$$SNB = (2h)t^{1/2} - \left[\frac{(m-1)v}{s}\right]t - \frac{ks}{m}$$

That is, the social net benefit is the value of the trips taken, less the associated congestion costs and the individual's share of the capacity cost. Note that the social net benefit is not reduced by the toll (if one is charged), because the toll is simply a transfer from one member of society, the user, to another member of society, the provider.

Since the users are assumed to be identical, the equilibrium number of trips taken by each user will be the same, implying that v is equal to t. The social net benefit of the public good then depends only upon t and s:

$$SNB = (2h)t^{1/2} - \frac{(m-1)t^2}{s} - \frac{ks}{m} \tag{12.5}$$

Inspection of this equation shows that

- *Capacity can be either too large or too small.* For each value of t, the partial derivative $\partial SNB/\partial s$ is positive when s is sufficiently small, indicating that the social net benefit would be higher if capacity were greater. It is negative when s is sufficiently large, indicating that the social net benefit would be higher if capacity were smaller. Thus, for each t, there is an ideal capacity. At this capacity, a small increase in capacity would reduce the congestion costs encountered by each person by exactly as much as it would raise each person's share of the capacity costs.
- *The number of trips taken by each user can also be too small or too large.* For each value of s, the partial derivative $\partial SNB/\partial t$ is positive when t is small and negative

use of the road. When there are few cars on the road, another can be added without increasing the congestion, but in bumper-to-bumper traffic, each additional car slows down every other car by a significant amount. As well, doubling both use and capacity might, in reality, increase the congestion. If the number of lanes and the flow of traffic were doubled, there would be more than twice as many lane changes, as cars work their way into the flow of traffic near entrances and work their way out of the flow near exits. Traffic would therefore move more slowly near these points, and the congestion costs would be higher.

4   The arguments that follow involve a comparison of the benefits of travel, the congestion costs and the capacity cost. They must therefore be measured in the same units. Suppose, for example, that B is the benefit when a single user takes t trips per month. The comparison can only be made if z is the congestion cost when the average user takes v trips per month, and if the capacity cost is expressed on a monthly basis. The first requirement is satisfied if t and v are measured over the same time period. The second requirement is not so easily satisfied, because most of the capacity costs are borne when the road is built. To turn these costs into monthly costs, it must be imagined that the construction of the road is financed by borrowing money, and that this loan is repaid over the life of the road. Then the monthly capacity cost is the sum of the monthly maintenance cost and the monthly loan payment.

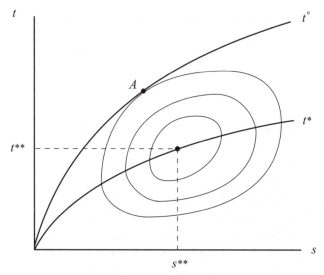

Figure 12.2: Social Indifference Curves. Each curve shows the combinations of s and t that yield the same social net benefits.

when t is large, indicating that the users can take either too few or too many trips. They are taking the ideal number of trips when the benefit of an additional trip is just offset by the added congestion costs.

The combinations of s and t that give rise to the same social net benefit constitute a kind of indifference curve. These indifference curves are shown in Figure 12.2, and have these properties:

- Each indifference curve is a closed ring. The curve slopes downward when the partial derivatives $\partial SNB/\partial s$ and $\partial SNB/\partial t$ have the same sign. This configuration occurs when both s and t are too small, and when both are too large. In either case, the welfare effect of an increase in one of the two variables is offset by a decrease in the other. The curve slopes upward when one of the partial derivatives is positive and the other is negative, so that the welfare effects of an increase in one variable are offset by an increase in the other.
- The indifference curves are concentric. Here, as always, indifference curves that cross would give rise to contradictions; but if they do not cross, they must be concentric.
- In each pair of indifference curves, points lying on the inner curve yield a higher value of SNB than do points on the outer curve. To see this, consider points on the downward sloping segments of an arbitrarily selected indifference curve. If both s and t are too small at this point, increasing either one would raise SNB. If both s and t are too large, reducing either one would raise SNB. That is, moving inside the indifference curve raises welfare.

Nestled inside the tightest indifference curve is the point (s^{**}, t^{**}). This combination of s and t maximizes the social net benefit. It is characterized by the conditions

$$\frac{\partial SNB}{\partial s} = -\frac{1}{m} \left\{ mt \frac{\partial z}{\partial s} + k \right\} = 0 \tag{12.6}$$

$$\frac{\partial SNB}{\partial t} = ht^{-1/2} - \frac{2(m-1)t}{s} = 0 \tag{12.7}$$

because, at the maximum, there is no small adjustment in s or in t that will raise the social net benefit.

The first condition is the Samuelson condition. The benefit that each individual receives from an increase in capacity is a reduction in congestion $(-\partial z/\partial s)$ on each of the t trips taken by that individual. The facility size is optimal when the sum across all users of the benefits from expansion is just equal to the cost of expansion (k).

The second condition states that, if each person takes one more trip, the benefit that each person obtains from his additional trip is exactly offset by the increase in his congestion costs. Each person's congestion costs are higher for two reasons: he travels one more time, and (because every other person also takes an additional trip) the congestion costs are higher on each of the trips that he takes. This condition can be rearranged to obtain the socially optimal number of trips associated with each capacity:

$$t^* = \left[\frac{hs}{2(m-1)} \right]^{2/3}$$

Note that the ideal number of trips rises with capacity. The ideal number of trips is *not* t^{**} if capacity is not s^{**}. Similarly, the ideal capacity varies with the number of trips taken, and is equal to s^{**} only if the number of trips taken is t^{**}.

Although the government sets capacity unilaterally, each person chooses the number of trips that he takes. The government's ability to implement the best possible outcome hinges upon its ability to influence this decision. Let's consider the factors that determine how often each person will travel.

12.2.1 Equilibrium Use

Each person's private net benefit of travel, PNB, is the difference between the benefit of travel and its private costs, which include both tolls and congestion costs:

$$PNB = (2h)t^{1/2} - (p+z)t \tag{12.8}$$

Here, p is the toll. Each person believes that the congestion cost z is beyond his control, and hence chooses the number of trips, t, that satisfies the condition

$$\frac{\partial PNB}{\partial t} = ht^{-1/2} - (p+z) = 0 \tag{12.9}$$

However, z is determined by the average number of trips taken by the other users, and each of these users is applying the same reasoning to determine the number of trips that they will take. Each individual will ultimately choose to make the same number of trips as every other user, implying

$$t = v$$

Substituting (12.4) into (12.9), and setting v equal to t, yields

$$ht^{-1/2} = p + \frac{(m-1)t}{s} \tag{12.10}$$

This condition describes the number of trips taken by each user.

If no toll is charged ($p = 0$), the number of trips taken by each person is

$$t^\circ = \left[\frac{hs}{m-1} \right]^{2/3} \tag{12.11}$$

This number is greater than the socially optimal number

$$t^\circ = 2^{2/3} t^* > t^*$$

Each person's travel increases the congestion experienced by all of the other travellers, so travel is an activity that generates a negative externality. Each person would be better off if every person could be persuaded to travel less.

Tolls are the lever that the government can use to control the degree of congestion. Inspection of (12.10) shows that the number of trips taken by each person falls as the toll rises.[5] Imposing a positive toll pushes the number of trips below t°. The ideal toll behaves like a Pigouvian tax, in the sense that it induces each user to make the socially optimal number of trips.

The ideal toll will cause each person to take t^{**} trips, so that the ideal capacity will be s^{**}. That is, the best possible outcome is achievable if tolls are levied.

12.2.2 The Optimal Toll

The nature of the optimal toll is most easily understood by recasting the problem in terms that are already familiar to us from our study of externalities: private and social marginal costs, and private and social marginal benefits. Private and social marginal benefit are easily evaluated. They are both equal to the value of one more trip:

$$PMB = SMB = ht^{-1/2}$$

The interpretation of the costs, however, must be slightly amended. These concepts were first used to describe the behaviour of a single externality-generating firm. Now we are concerned with a group of m users, and the behaviour of each user impacts every other user. The marginal costs will depend upon the actions of *every* user, and their definition

---

[5] Increasing p raises the right-hand side of (12.10). Increasing t reduces the left-hand side of (12.10) and raises the right-hand side. It follows that a smaller value of t satisfies this equation when p is higher.

must reflect that dependence. Specifically,

- Private marginal cost (PMC) is the cost borne by an individual when he – and he alone – takes one more trip, given that all users are initially taking t trips.
- Marginal damage (MD) is the increase in the congestion costs borne by all other users when one user takes one more trip, given that all users are initially taking t trips.
- Social marginal cost (SMC) is the cost borne by all users when one user takes one more trip, given that all users are initially taking t trips.

Each individual's private marginal cost is the sum of the toll that he must pay and the congestion costs that he must incur when he takes one more trip. If all individuals are initially taking t trips (so that v is equal to t),

$$PMC = p + \frac{(m-1)t}{s}$$

Now consider marginal damage. An extra trip by one person raises the congestion costs faced by *each* of the other $m - 1$ people on *each* of their t trips by $1/s$ units. Since marginal damage is the total increase in congestion costs that one person's additional trip imposes on the other people in the community,

$$MD = \frac{(m-1)t}{s}$$

Finally, the social marginal cost of travel is the sum of two components. The first component is the congestion cost willingly borne by an individual who chooses to take one more trip, and the second component is marginal damage:

$$SMC = z|_{v=t} + MD = \frac{2(m-1)t}{s} \qquad (12.12)$$

These concepts can be used to reinterpret some of the conditions set out above. Equation (12.10) describes the number of trips taken by each person. It can be written as

$$PMB = PMC$$

Each person extends his travels until the private benefit of one more trip is just offset by its private cost. By contrast, (12.7) describes the socially optimal number of trips. It can be written in the familiar form

$$SMB = SMC$$

These relationships are shown in Figure 12.3, which parallels Figure 6.2. Since private marginal benefit and social marginal benefit are equal, each individual will choose the socially optimal number of trips if he correctly perceives the social marginal cost of travel. He will do so if the toll is set equal to marginal damage, evaluated at the socially optimal number of trips t^*. Thus, the optimal toll is the Pigouvian tax.

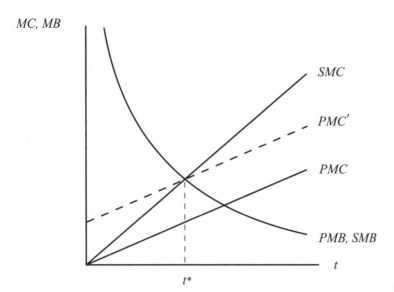

Figure 12.3: The Marginal Costs and Benefits of Travel in a Symmetric Equilibrium. The optimal toll shifts the private marginal cost curve from PMC to PMC'.

12.2.3 Optimal Provision When Tolls Are Not Imposed

The provider of the public good might choose not to impose a toll for any of a number of reasons. The resource cost of collecting the toll might be prohibitive. The act of collecting the toll might create further congestion, frustrating the intent of the toll. And the toll constitutes regressive taxation, in the sense that it falls equally on both the rich and the poor. However, a decision not to impose a toll also adversely affects society's welfare. The number of trips taken, $t°$, will be greater than the socially optimal number, t^*, at every capacity, so the best outcome is not obtainable.

The government's decision not to control use means that it must adopt a different rule to choose capacity. The relationship between $t°$ and s in the absence of tolls is shown by the curve $t°$ in Figure 12.2. The combination (s, t) attained by the economy always lies on this line, and the government determines the combination that is attained through its control of capacity. The combination that maximizes the social net benefit is characterized by a tangency between the curve $t°$ and one of the indifference curves. It is labelled A in Figure 12.2.

This tangency has a simple interpretation. The effect of an increase in capacity on social net benefits is found by totally differentiating SNB with respect to s:

$$\frac{dSNB}{ds} = \frac{\partial SNB}{\partial s} + \frac{\partial SNB}{\partial t}\frac{dt°}{ds} \qquad (12.13)$$

The first term on the right-hand side is the direct effect of added capacity on social net benefits. Given the number of trips taken by each user, an increase in size reduces congestion but expends scarce resources. The social net benefit rises if the reduction in congestion costs is greater than the resource cost. However, each person will respond to the reduced congestion by travelling more. Each person will receive the benefit of extra trips, but will also bear higher congestion costs. The effect of this adjustment is described by the second term on the right-hand side. The socially optimal capacity has been reached when the two effects are exactly offsetting, so that

$$\frac{dSNB}{ds} = 0$$

or equivalently

$$-\frac{\partial SNB}{\partial s} \div \frac{\partial SNB}{\partial t} = \frac{dt^\circ}{ds}$$

The left-hand side of this condition is the slope of the indifference curve and the right-hand side is the slope of the curve t°. The slopes are equal at a point of tangency.

12.3 SUMMARY

The central issue in the discussion of impure public goods is the control of congestion. Congestion of club goods is controlled by limiting the membership of each facility and replicating the facility to accommodate everyone who wants a membership. Congestion of variable use goods is controlled by regulating the frequency of use through tolls, or failing that, through the choice of facility size.

QUESTIONS

1. Consider a club of size s and membership m. The benefits accruing to each member are given by

$$B = (36 - m^2)s^{2/3}$$

and each member's share of the costs is

$$C = \frac{27s}{m}$$

Find the optimal size and membership of the club.

2. Suppose that there are a large number of identical agents. The dollar value of the benefits that each agent would receive from membership in a congestible club is

$$B = s^{1/2}[20m - m^2 + 225]$$

where s is the size of the club and m is the number of agents belonging to the club. Now suppose that the cost per member is

$$C = \gamma s/m$$

where γ is a parameter. Show that the optimal size of the club falls as γ rises, but that the optimal membership remains constant. Find the optimal size of the club when γ is 1000.

3. In the model of variable use public goods described in this chapter, assume that

$$h = 72, \quad k = 30, \quad m = 10$$

Assume that the government initially chooses not to charge a toll.

a) What number of trips is taken by each user under any given capacity s?
b) What is optimal capacity?

    Hint: You might, at some point, find it useful to define a new variable, θ, to be equal to $s^{1/3}$ and to solve for θ as a preliminary to calculating s.
c) Assume that the optimal capacity found in b) has been installed. If the government wishes to reduce the number of trips taken by each user to 16, what toll should it charge?

13

The Link between Public Goods and Externalities

A community league operated in the neighbourhood in which I grew up. It was funded by the families living in the neighbourhood, and had a number of functions. One of them was to operate an outdoor skating rink each winter. Particular time slots were made available to figure skaters, hockey players, and recreational skaters, but if you were prepared to change into your skates outdoors, you could use the rink just about any time. This rink would certainly seem to fit the description of a congestible public good.

Some parents would also construct smaller rinks in their backyards, so that their younger children could skate without having to walk to the community rink. Since skating alone isn't much fun, these children generally had the company of other neighbourhood kids. Arguably, these parents were providing for their own benefit a good which had positive externalities for neighbouring families.[1]

These projects are intrinsically very similar, and yet we do not hesitate to categorize one as a public good and the other as a good with positive externalities. We hope that the distinction between these two goods is a useful one, and indeed our analyses of the two goods have been quite different, but this example suggests that we might be making strong distinctions between quite similar goods.

One might argue that the backyard rink offers distinctly different benefits to the family that builds it than it does to other families, and that it should therefore be categorized as a good with externalities. For instance, its builders can look out the window and know where their children are, while the parents of the visiting children cannot. Its builders decide the nature of its use – figure skating or hockey – and all other users must accept that decision. But there is no presumption that public goods yield the same kind of benefit to every user. Some users of national parks (which are surely public goods) enjoy the view from the comfort of their cars, while others are not truly happy unless they have a trail beneath their feet. Still others might not visit the park at all, but value it as a sanctuary for endangered wildlife.

---

[1] When spring came, and the water running off these rinks had nowhere to go but near-by basements, the externality switched from a positive one to a negative one.

This chapter shows that public goods and goods with externalities are different aspects of a single phenomenon, namely interdependent preferences. Preferences are interdependent when a single action (such as the production or consumption of a good) affects the welfare of more than one person. The chapter is based upon Shibata's [59] graphical presentation of this issue.

13.1 INTERDEPENDENT PREFERENCES

Imagine, as usual, that George and Harriet are the only two people in the economy. Their utility functions are

$$U_G = u_G(z, b_G)$$

$$U_H = u_H(z, b_H)$$

Their utilities depend upon their consumption of bread (b_G and b_H) and upon the consumption of some other good (z). These utility functions are consistent with several possibilities:

1) The first good is a public good, and z is the quantity of the good made available. For example, z might measure the quantity of fire-fighting equipment available for the use of either person. Each person's utility rises with z.
2) The first good is consumed by one person – say, George – but its consumption gives rise to a positive externality. George might be an avid gardener, for example, and z might measure the extent of his flower gardens. Harriet, living across the street, takes pleasure in the sight of these flowers. George's utility rises with z, and so does Harriet's.
3) The first good is consumed by George, but its consumption gives rise to a negative externality. George might enjoy sitting in front of a roaring fire, but the ash from the fire drifts downwind to Harriet's house, leaving her windows grimy. If z measures the amount of time that George's fire burns, George's utility rises and Harriet's utility falls as z increases.

It is initially assumed that the first good has the properties described in either 1) or 2), so that both utilities rise with z. The third possibility is investigated in Section 13.6.

George and Harriet are endowed with $\overline{b}_G$ and $\overline{b}_H$ units of bread, respectively, so the total amount of bread in the economy is

$$\overline{b} = \overline{b}_G + \overline{b}_H$$

This bread can either be consumed or allocated to the production of the first good. The economy's production possibility frontier is

$$\overline{b} = b_G + b_H + kz \tag{13.1}$$

where k is the number of units of bread needed to produce one unit of the first good. The production possibility frontier is shown in Figure 13.1, where z is measured horizontally

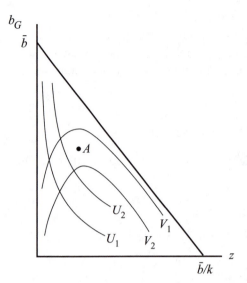

Figure 13.1: Indifference Curves in the Shibata Box. Both sets of indifference curves are plotted against George's commodity bundle.

and quantities of bread are measured vertically. An allocation in this economy is a list (z, b_G, b_H) that satisfies (13.1).

The **Shibata box** is the region in Figure 13.1 bounded by the production possibility frontier and the axes. It has the same basic properties as the Edgeworth box:

- Each point in the box represents a particular allocation. Point A in Figure 13.1, for example, corresponds to this allocation: z is the horizontal distance between the left edge of the box and point A, b_G is the vertical distance between the bottom of the box and point A, and b_H is the vertical distance between the production possibility frontier and point A.
- Each individual's preferences over his or her commodity bundles can be represented by indifference maps drawn in the box.

Getting George and Harriet's indifference curves into the box is, however, a little trickier with the Shibata box than with the Edgeworth box, and it is to this issue that we now turn.

13.2 INDIFFERENCE CURVES

George's commodity bundle is (z, b_G). If George's consumption of the first good is measured horizontally (in Figure 13.1) and his consumption of bread is measured vertically, every point in the quadrant lying on or below the production possibility frontier represents a possible commodity bundle for George. A set of indifference curves representing George's preferences over these commodity bundles can be drawn into the quadrant. They are downward sloping and bowed toward the origin. Two of George's indifference curves (U_1 and U_2) are shown in Figure 13.1.

Harriet's commodity bundle is (z, b_H). Her preferences could be described by a set of indifference curves drawn in the (z, b_H) quadrant, and these curves would also be downward sloping and bowed toward the origin. But her indifference curves don't have to be plotted in this quadrant. Harriet's commodity bundle can be inferred from George's commodity bundle, because bread that is not consumed by George or used to produce the first good must go to Harriet. Specifically, if George's commodity bundle is (z, b_G), Harriet's commodity bundle is $(z, \overline{b} - b_G - kz)$ and her utility is

$$U_H = u_H(z, \overline{b} - b_G - kz) \tag{13.2}$$

It follows that Harriet also has preferences over George's commodity bundles, and these preferences can be represented by indifference curves drawn in the (z, b_G) plane. But what would these preferences look like?

Let's step back from this question, and think about marginal rates of substitution. First, define each person's marginal rate of substitution in the usual manner:

MRS_G **is the amount of bread that exactly compensates George for the loss of one unit of the first good. Alternatively, a one unit reduction in** z **accompanied by an** MRS_G **unit increase in** b_G **leaves George's utility unchanged.**

MRS_H **is the amount of bread that exactly compensates Harriet for the loss of one unit of the first good. Alternatively, a one unit reduction in** z **accompanied by an** MRS_H **unit increase in** b_H **leaves Harriet's utility unchanged.**

Each of these marginal rates of substitution is readily calculated:

$$MRS_G = \frac{\partial u_G}{\partial z} \div \frac{\partial u_G}{\partial b_G}$$

$$MRS_H = \frac{\partial u_H}{\partial z} \div \frac{\partial u_H}{\partial b_H}$$

The first of these is the negative of the slope of George's indifference curve. The second is the negative of the slope of Harriet's indifference curve, when the indifference curves are defined over Harriet's *own* commodity bundles.

We can also define a marginal rate of substitution for Harriet that corresponds to the negative of the slope of her indifference curve, when the indifference curves are defined over *George's* commodity bundles:

MRS_H^* **is the change in George's bread consumption that exactly compensates Harriet for the loss of one unit of the first good, in the sense that a one unit reduction in** z **accompanied by an** MRS_H^* **increase in** b_G **leaves Harriet's utility unchanged.**

The usual rule is used to calculate this marginal rate of substitution: it is the ratio of the marginal utility of the thing taken away to the marginal utility of the thing given in compensation.

$$MRS_H^* = \frac{\partial U_H}{\partial z} \div \frac{\partial U_H}{\partial b_G} \tag{13.3}$$

Differentiating (13.2) gives[2]

$$\frac{\partial U_H}{\partial z} = \frac{\partial u_H}{\partial z} - k\frac{\partial u_H}{\partial b_H}$$

$$\frac{\partial U_H}{\partial b_G} = -\frac{\partial u_H}{\partial b_H}$$

Substituting these expressions into (13.3) and simplifying gives

$$MRS_H^* = k - MRS_H \tag{13.4}$$

This equation has an immediate interpretation. Both MRS_H^* and MRS_H represent increases in bread consumption that exactly compensate Harriet for the loss of a unit of the first good: MRS_H^* is the increase in George's bread consumption and MRS_H is the increase in her own bread consumption. Producing one fewer unit of the first good frees up k units of bread, and these units must be allocated to someone.

- If MRS_H is less than k, not all of the available bread needs be given to Harriet in compensation, and the remaining $k - MRS_H$ units can be given to George. MRS_H^* is then positive.
- If MRS_H is greater than k, there is not enough unallocated bread to compensate Harriet for the loss, so $MRS_H - k$ additional units must be taken from George and given to Harriet. MRS_H^* is negative.

Exact compensation for Harriet can imply either an increase or a decrease in George's consumption of bread, depending upon the relative sizes of MRS_H and k.

MRS_H^* is the negative of the slope of Harriet's indifference curve when this indifference curve is drawn in the (z, b_G) quadrant. How do movements along a single indifference curve change its value? When they are drawn in the (z, b_H) quadrant, Harriet's indifference curves are downward sloping and bowed toward the origin. Movements down a single indifference curve are associated with a decline in MRS_H. As z rises, MRS_H is first greater and then smaller than k. Then (13.4) implies that MRS_H^* is first negative and then positive (again, for rightward movements along a single indifference

---

[2] A one-unit increase in z makes Harriet better off because she values the first good itself. It also makes Harriet worse off because producing another unit of the first good uses up k units of bread, and with George's bread consumption fixed, these units of bread must be taken from Harriet. The change in Harriet's utility is equal to the difference between the value of another unit of the first good and the value of the bread that must be given up to produce it.

An increase in George's bread consumption with z fixed can only be achieved by taking a unit of bread away from Harriet. Harriet's utility falls by an amount equal to the value of this unit of bread.

curve). Thus, Harriet's indifference curves, drawn in the (z, b_G) quadrant, have an inverted U shape. Two of Harriet's indifference curves (labelled V_1 and V_2) are shown in Figure 13.1. Indifference curves that are lower down in the diagram correspond to higher utility levels for Harriet.[3]

13.3 PARETO OPTIMAL ALLOCATIONS

An allocation is Pareto optimal if there is no other allocation such that someone is better off and no one is worse off. Our task is to find the Pareto optimal allocations, and this is an easy task because the rules that applied to the Edgeworth box also apply to the Shibata box:

- If the indifference curves passing through an allocation form a lens-shaped area, that allocation is not Pareto optimal. (Any allocation lying inside the lens is preferred by both people.)
- If the indifference curves passing through an allocation are tangent to each other, that allocation is Pareto optimal. (Any change that places one person on a more preferred indifference curve must push the other onto a less preferred indifference curve.)

Thus, in Figure 13.2, B is not a Pareto optimal allocation and C is Pareto optimal.

As in the Edgeworth box, one of Harriet's indifference curves is tangent to each of George's (infinitely many) indifference curves, so there are infinitely many Pareto optimal allocations. They form an efficiency locus that crosses the box (see Figure 13.2). An upward movement along the efficiency locus makes George better off at Harriet's expense.

Tangent curves have the same slope at the point of tangency, so the characteristic of a Pareto optimal allocation is that

$$MRS_G = MRS_H^*$$

or

$$MRS_G + MRS_H = k$$

where k is the marginal rate of transformation. Thus, the Samuelson condition characterizes optimal provision of the first good.

This finding is independent of the interpretation given to the first good: it holds if that good is a public good, a good with a positive externality, or (as will be shown shortly) a good with a negative externality. The common characteristic of these situations is that the provision of the good for one person has implications for the welfare of all people. The optimal quantity of the good is provided when the social benefit of another unit

---

[3] Given z, a reduction in b_G must be accompanied by an increase in b_H. It follows that moving to an allocation that is lower down in the box makes Harriet better off.

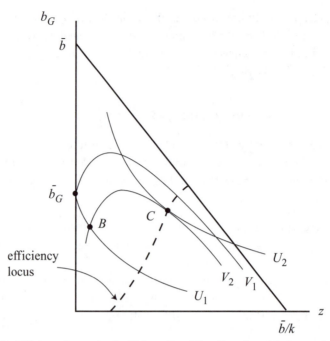

Figure 13.2: The Efficiency Locus in the Shibata Box. The allocation C is Pareto optimal, but the allocation B is not.

of the good is equal to the resource cost of providing another unit. The social benefit is calculated by adding together the individual benefits.[4]

The efficiency locus is almost never a vertical line, and hence the optimal quantity of the public good depends upon the way in which its cost is divided between the two agents. If the efficiency locus is upward sloping, for example, the optimal quantity of the public good rises as Harriet bears a greater and greater share of its cost.

Whether an optimal quantity of the first good is provided depends upon the mechanism for its provision. This issue will be examined under the three possible interpretations of the first good.

13.4 A PUBLIC GOOD

The endowment point in the Shibata box is $(0, \bar{b}_G)$ because neither person is endowed with units of the public good. In Figure 13.2, the indifference curves U_1 and V_1 pass through this point.[5] Since these curves form a lens-shaped area, there are many

---

[4] In the case of a negative externality, some of the individual "benefits" will be negative.

[5] Indifference curves are generally drawn so that they are asymptotic to the axes (i.e., they approach the axes but never touch them). This shape implies that the compensation for the loss of successive units of any good becomes arbitrarily large as consumption of that good falls to zero. Many goods (such as food and water) have this property, but many others do not. The indifference curves in Figure 13.2 have been drawn so that the public good is of the latter type. George and Harriet can be bribed to give up every last bit of the first good – they *can* live by bread alone – and hence their indifference curves strike the vertical axes.

allocations that make both people better off. The allocation to which they move depends upon the nature of the dealings between them.

13.4.1 Voluntary Contributions

Imagine, as before, that George and Harriet contribute to a fund which is then used to provide units of the public good. (One unit of the public good is provided for every k units of bread contributed.) A Nash equilibrium is a list of contributions, one for George and one for Harriet, such that neither person can raise his or her own utility by unilaterally deviating from the list. To find the Nash equilibrium, first consider the individual budget lines in the Shibata box.

If Harriet contributes nothing to the provision of the public good, George's budget line begins at $(0, \overline{b}_G)$ and has a slope of $-k$. That is, there will be no public goods provided if he chooses to consume all of his bread endowment, and he must give up k units of bread to obtain each unit of public goods. However, if Harriet contributes enough bread to produce z' units of public goods, George's budget line begins at $(z', \overline{b}_G)$ and has a slope of $-k$. He enjoys the benefits of z' units of public goods even if he consumes his entire endowment, but he can increase the quantity of public good at a cost of k bread for each additional unit of public goods.

Now consider Harriet's budget line, which will be a little unusual because Harriet's preferences are a little unusual. Harriet's preferences, you will recall, are defined over *George's* commodity bundles rather than her own. The budget line that interests her, therefore, is the one that tells her how George's commodity bundle changes as her contribution to the provision of the public good changes.

If George contributes nothing to the provision of the public goods, his bread consumption is fixed at $\overline{b}_G$, and z varies as Harriet's contribution varies. Thus, the set of George's commodity bundles that can be reached through variations in Harriet's contribution is given by a flat line at the height $\overline{b}_G$.[6] If, however, George contributes enough bread to produce z'' units of the public good, his consumption of bread is fixed at $\overline{b}_G - kz''$, and the quantity of public good provided rises from z'' as Harriet increases her contribution from zero. Harriet's budget line is a flat line running from the point $(z'', \overline{b}_G - kz'')$ to the production possibility frontier.

These results are illustrated in Figure 13.3:

- George's budget line is $E\,G$ when Harriet contributes nothing, and Harriet's budget line is $E\,H$ when George contributes nothing. Call these lines the "initial" budget lines.

> If Harriet were willing to give up the last unit of the public good for less than k units of bread, her indifference curves would be downward sloping everywhere. If George were willing to give up the last unit of the public good for less than k units of bread, his indifference curves would be everywhere flatter than the production possibility curve. For concreteness, these possibilities will not be considered.

[6] Harriet's consumption of bread at any of these allocations is given by the vertical distance between the allocation and the production possibility frontier. It is equal to $\overline{b}_H$ at one end of the budget line and 0 at the other end.

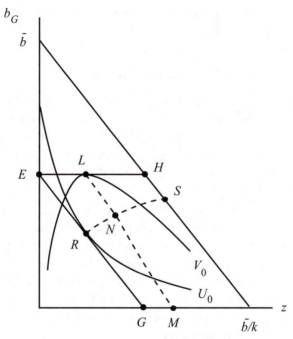

Figure 13.3: Income Expansion Paths. An increase in George's income would cause him to choose a commodity bundle farther out along RS. Similarly, an increase in Harriet's income would cause him to choose a commodity bundle farther down LM.

- As Harriet's contribution rises, George's budget line shifts outward but its slope does not change. George's budget line always begins at Harriet's initial budget line and ends at the bottom of the box.
- As George's contribution rises, Harriet's budget line shifts downward with an unchanged slope. Harriet's budget line always begins at George's initial budget line and ends at the production possibility frontier.

The position of each person's budget line is determined by the other person's contribution.

Each person's budget line shows the commodity bundles that are attainable through variations in that person's contribution. Each person chooses the best commodity bundle from among the set of attainable commodity bundles. The best attainable commodity bundle will, as always, be characterized by a tangency between the budget line and an indifference curve. For example, George's best attainable commodity bundle when Harriet contributes nothing is R; and Harriet's best attainable commodity bundle when George contributes nothing is L.

The way in which each person's best attainable commodity bundle varies with the other person's contribution is described by an **income expansion path.** An increase in Harriet's contribution pushes George's budget line to the right, and for every possible position of his budget line, there is a best attainable commodity bundle. The locus composed of these best attainable bundles is George's income expansion path, denoted RS in Figure 13.3. Similarly, an increase in George's contribution shifts Harriet's budget

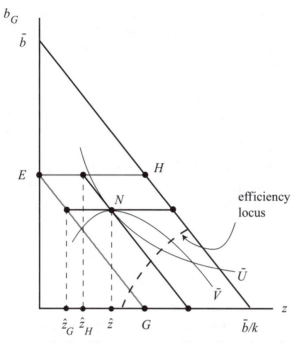

Figure 13.4: Nash Equilibrium. Here, $\widehat{z}$ is the sum of $\widehat{z}_G$ and $\widehat{z}_H$. If Harriet contributes $\widehat{z}_H$ units of public good, George maximizes his utility by contributing $\widehat{z}_G$ units. If George contributes $\widehat{z}_G$ units of public good, Harriet maximizes her utility by contributing $\widehat{z}_H$ units.

line downward, causing Harriet's best attainable commodity bundle to change. The locus composed of these best attainable bundles is Harriet's income expansion path and is denoted LM in Figure 13.3.

The allocation reached under the Nash equilibrium contributions is the one at which the two income expansion paths intersect (N in Figure 13.3).[7]

- Since N lies on George's income expansion path, it is a point at which one of George's budget lines is tangent to one of his indifference curves. The relevant budget line and indifference curve are shown in Figure 13.4. The budget line is the one that would be in effect if Harriet were to contribute $k\widehat{z}_H$ units of bread. Although George could consume his entire endowment of bread and nevertheless obtain the benefits of $\widehat{z}_H$ units of the public good, he would actually prefer to contribute to the provision of the public good. Specifically, he would prefer to contribute enough bread to raise the quantity of the public good to $\widehat{z}$. This quantity is $k\widehat{z}_G$. Thus, George wants to contribute $k\widehat{z}_G$ units of bread when Harriet contributes $k\widehat{z}_H$ units of bread.
- Since N lies on Harriet's income expansion path, it is a point at which one of Harriet's budget lines is tangent to one of her indifference curves. The relevant budget line and indifference curve are shown in Figure 13.4. This budget line would be in effect

---

[7] It is assumed here that the income expansion paths intersect in the region between the two budget lines. The nature of the Nash equilibrium when the intersection occurs outside of this region is explored in the next section.

if George were to contribute $k\widehat{z}_G$ units of bread. Confronted with this budget line, Harriet makes herself as well off as possible by contributing enough bread to raise the quantity of public good from $\widehat{z}_G$ to $\widehat{z}$. That is, she wants to contribute $k\widehat{z}_H$ units of bread when George contributes $k\widehat{z}_G$ units of bread.

When George contributes $k\widehat{z}_G$ units of bread and Harriet contributes $k\widehat{z}_H$ units of bread, George cannot raise his welfare by adjusting his own contribution, and Harriet cannot raise her welfare by adjusting her own contribution. These contributions therefore constitute a Nash equilibrium. The associated allocation is N.

It is clear that both agents are better off at N than they were at the endowment point E, but it is equally clear that they have failed to reach a Pareto optimal allocation. The indifference curves passing through N (denoted $\overline{U}$ and $\overline{V}$) form a lens-shaped area, and a move to any allocation inside this lens-shaped area would make both people better off.

13.4.2 Negotiation

George and Harriet would be better off if they were able to negotiate an agreement that specifies each person's contribution. During these negotiations, either person would be able to put forward a proposal, and the other person would be able to accept it or counter it with an alternative proposal. If the negotiations were successfully concluded – if there were no stalemate – the agreement would take George and Harriet to a Pareto optimal allocation. Any agreement that did not do so could be improved upon, and hence would not be the final agreement.

Negotiation takes George and Harriet to the efficiency locus. The particular allocation chosen cannot be determined, but there are some allocations on the efficiency locus that will *not* be chosen. Neither of them will agree to an allocation that does not make them as well off as they could have been in the absence of an agreement. George can ensure himself of the utility level U_0 (in Figure 13.3) by moving along his initial budget line; and Harriet can ensure herself of the utility level V_0 by moving along her initial budget line. Thus, George will not agree to any allocation at which his utility is lower than U_0, while Harriet will not agree to any allocation at which his utility is lower than V_0. The part of the efficiency locus reached under negotiation is the part bounded by these two indifference curves.

Negotiation leads to an efficient outcome but voluntary contributions do not. The economist's presumption that public goods will be underprovided in the absence of government action stems from a belief that, in larger economies, the barriers to successful negotiation (notably, negotiation costs and the free rider problem) are severe. Actual outcomes might well be better characterized by the Nash equilibrium.

13.5 A GOOD WITH A POSITIVE EXTERNALITY

Imagine that the first good is consumed by George, and that George's consumption of that good raises Harriet's welfare. In the absence of any transfer between the two

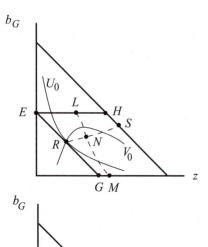

Figure 13.5: Nash Equilibria in the Presence of a Positive Externality. The characteristics of an equilibrium depend upon the shape of the income-expansion paths.

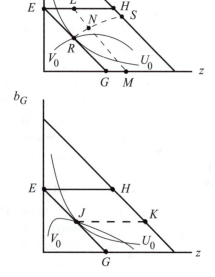

individuals, George's budget line is his initial budget line, and his best attainable commodity bundle is R in the top panel of Figure 13.5. Harriet consumes her entire endowment of bread.

Since MRS_G is equal to k at R, and since MRS_H^* is everywhere smaller than k, Harriet's indifference curve V_0 is flatter than George's indifference curve U_0 at R. These indifference curves form a lens-shaped area, so R is not a Pareto optimal allocation. The efficiency locus must pass through this lens-shaped area, and therefore lies below and to the right of R.

If George and Harriet are able to negotiate, they will make an agreement that specifies both George's consumption of the first good and a transfer of bread from Harriet to George. Their agreement will change the allocation to one of those lying on the efficiency locus, between the indifference curves U_0 and V_0. George's consumption of the first good will be greater than at R, Harriet's bread consumption will be smaller, and George's bread consumption might be either greater or smaller.

Imagine, however, that Harriet cannot tie the size of her transfer to the amount of the first good that George consumes. She could still transfer some of her bread to George, and George could decide how much of his augmented store of bread to allocate to his consumption of the first good.

The interaction between George and Harriet can be described by a game, but the nature of the game depends upon the ordering of their decisions.

- Suppose that Harriet transfers some bread to George, and then George goes home, considers his options, and decides how much of his own bread to add to Harriet's contribution. In effect, Harriet decides first and George decides second. Harriet is in a strong position here, because she can anticipate the way in which George will respond to any given transfer. She will make the transfer that induces George to respond in the way that is most beneficial to herself. Specifically, she knows that an increase in the transfer shifts George's budget line outward, and that George will respond by choosing the commodity bundle at which one of his indifference curves is tangent to the budget line. These choices constitute George's income expansion path. Harriet will choose the transfer that induces George to select, from among the commodity bundles on the income expansion path, the one that is most favourable to her.[8] If the income expansion path lies everywhere above her indifference curve V_0, Harriet will make no transfer; otherwise, she will make a positive transfer.

- Now suppose that George and Harriet make their choices simultaneously. George allocates an amount of bread c_G to acquiring units of the first good, which he will then consume. Harriet transfers an amount of bread c_H to George to allow him to acquire and consume additional units. George's consumption of the first good is therefore $(c_G + c_H)/k$. George, knowing c_H, chooses c_G to make himself as well off as possible; and Harriet, knowing c_G, chooses c_H to make herself as well off as possible. A Nash equilibrium in this game is a pair (c_G^*, c_H^*) such that neither person wishes to unilaterally deviate from the list. This game is analytically equivalent to the voluntary contributions model of public goods provision, so the Nash equilibrium is (generally) characterized by the intersection of the income expansion paths.

The formal difference between these games is in the timing of the choices. However, the difference in timing merely reflects differences in the way that George is assumed to behave. In the first game, George treats the transfer as income that he can allocate to his consumption of either good. In the second game, George understands that the transfer is to be spent only on the first good. Neither game takes George and Harriet to a Pareto optimal allocation.

---

[8] This commodity bundle will be characterized by a tangency between George's income expansion path and one of Harriet's indifference curves.

The panels in Figure 13.5 show three kinds of equilibria in the second game. In the top panel, the Nash equilibrium lies in the lens-shaped area outlined by U_0 and V_0. Both agents prefer the Nash equilibrium to the initial equilibrium in which George individually determines his consumption of the first good. In the second panel, the Nash equilibrium lies outside the lens but between the initial budget constraints. George is better off than he was in the initial equilibrium, but Harriet is worse off. In the third panel, the Nash equilibrium is the initial equilibrium J. George, receiving no contribution from Harriet, is confined to his initial budget constraint and chooses the best attainable commodity bundle (J). Harriet then perceives her budget line to be JK (because she can raise z by making a transfer to George), and maximizes her own utility by making no transfer, leaving George at J. Harriet benefits from George's consumption of the first good, but does not help to finance it.

13.6 A GOOD WITH A NEGATIVE EXTERNALITY

If George's consumption of the first good reduces Harriet's welfare, her indifference curves, drawn in the (z, b_H) plane, would be upward sloping. It is generally assumed that they would become steeper as z rises, indicating an increasing unwillingness to be compensated in bread for the harm done by additional units of z. That is, along any single indifference curve, MRS_H is negative and becomes more negative as z rises.

Now consider Harriet's preferences over *George's* commodity bundles. Her preferences are represented by indifference curves drawn in the (z, b_G) plane, and the negative of the slope of each indifference curve is measured by MRS_H^*. By (13.4), MRS_H^* is a positive number which is always greater than k, so these indifference curves are everywhere downward sloping and steeper than the production possibility frontier. Each indifference curve becomes steeper as z rises. One of these curves is shown in Figure 13.6.

In the absence of any transfer of purchasing power between the two people, George will choose the best commodity bundle (T) from among those lying on his initial budget line. Since MRS_G is equal to k at T, and since MRS_H^* is everywhere greater than k, Harriet's indifference curve V_1 is steeper than George's indifference curve U_1 at T. These indifference curves form a lens-shaped area, so T is not a Pareto optimal allocation. The efficiency locus passes through this lens-shaped area, lying above and to the left of T.

Harriet must bribe George to reduce his consumption of z. These negotiations will take them to an allocation that lies on the part of the efficiency locus bounded by the indifference curves U_1 and V_1. Harriet will obtain a reduction in z, but only by giving up some of her bread consumption so that George can consume more.

Note that this situation is a little unlike the one discussed earlier, in the chapter on externalities. In the earlier model, negotiation led to a well-defined change in the behaviour of the agent generating the externality, but the associated transfer was not precisely determined. In the current model, neither the change in z nor the cash transfer

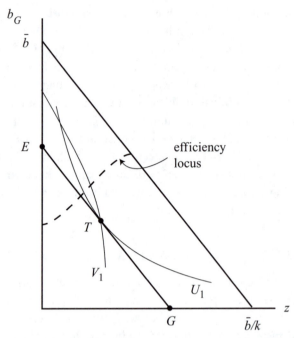

Figure 13.6: A Negative Externality. Both indifference curves are downward sloping everywhere. A Pareto optimal allocation is still characterized by a tangency between two indifference curves.

is exactly determined – but for any given change in z, the associated transfer is exactly known. This outcome follows from the observation that the Pareto optimal value of z cannot be determined independently of its financing.

13.7 SUMMARY

Public goods and goods with externalities are simply goods whose consumption (or production) affect the welfare of more than one person or firm. The optimal quantity of such a good is characterized by the Samuelson condition. The quantity provided in the absence of government intervention depends upon the institutional framework that applies to a particular good.

QUESTIONS

1. Dick, Jane, and their dog, Spot, share an apartment. Their utilities depend upon the cleanliness of the apartment and the hours spent doing housework. Dick and Jane are both averse to housework, though Dick finds it especially troublesome. Their utility functions are

$$U_D = c - (h_D)^2$$

$$U_J = c - \frac{1}{2}(h_J)^2$$

where c is an index of cleanliness and h represents hours of housework. The degree of cleanliness is determined by the "production function"

$$c = h_D + h_J$$

a) Define the marginal rate of substitution MRS_i as the increase in cleanliness that exactly compensates person i for one more hour of housework:

$$MRS_i = -\left(\frac{\partial U_i}{\partial c} \div \frac{\partial U_i}{\partial h_i} \right) \qquad i = D, J$$

and define the marginal rate of transformation as the number of hours of leisure that must must be given up to generate a one unit increase in cleanliness. Find the Samuelson condition for this economy.

b) An allocation is a triplet (h_D, h_J, c). What two conditions must a Pareto optimal allocation satisfy? Show that there are Pareto optimal allocations in which Dick, despite his aversion to housework, does more housework than Jane.

c) Assume that Dick and Jane independently decide how much housework they will do. Find the hours of work done by each of them in the Nash equilibrium, and show that both people would be better off if each of them did a little extra housework.

2. Petunia Potts was born with a green thumb, while Joe Crabgrass can't make dandelions grow. This is their story.

a) Petunia's utility is determined by the size of her gardens, s, and by her consumption of other goods, c_P:

$$U_P = 3s^{1/3} + c_P$$

Her income is y_P dollars, and she spends it on gardening supplies and other goods. The price of each of these items is one dollar, so her budget constraint is

$$s + c_P = y_P$$

Assume that y_P is greater than 1. Find her best attainable commodity bundle, and find her utility.

b) Joe lives next door to Petunia, and despite his horticultural shortcomings, he takes great pleasure in gardens. His utility function is

$$U_J = 3s^{1/3} + c_J$$

where s is again the size of Petunia's gardens and c_J is Joe's consumption of private goods. His income is y_J dollars, and he initially spends it all on his own consumption. Find Joe's utility when Petunia is consuming her best attainable commodity bundle.

c) Imagine that Petunia makes the following proposal to Joe: if he will pay the fraction α of the cost of the gardens, she will allow him to determine the extent of the gardens. Use a Shibata box to show that Joe should accept if α is sufficiently low. Also, show that if α is very low, Petunia is made worse off by the deal.

d) Let $\bar{\alpha}$ be the value of α at which Joe is indifferent between accepting and rejecting the deal. Calculate $\bar{\alpha}$.

Imperfect Competition

By Christmas of 1999, initial public offerings of dotcom companies had netted many of these companies millions of dollars in operating capital. The founders of these companies also acquired personal fortunes, based on the market value of the shares that they had retained. Investors went smug to their beds, while visions of huge profits danced in their heads.

The operating capital was quickly spent. The companies argued that this was an inevitable feature of growth. They would have to rely on advertising for most of their revenues, but only the most popular sites would be able to earn sufficient revenues from this source. The strategy, therefore, was to grow as quickly as possible, elbowing aside their dotcom competitors. Costs would initially be large and revenues small, but the potential for future profit justified these expenditures. Investors seemed not to notice the corollary of this argument, that most of the companies in which they had invested were doomed.

By Christmas of 2000, it had been realized that the potential for profit was much smaller than had originally been believed. A great many dotcom companies had "gone for a walk in the snow," and the market value of the rest had imploded. The resources of these companies had been squandered for no evident gain.

The investors were credulous, but they weren't crazy. The advent of the dotcom companies represented the opening of an industry in which there are enormous economies of scale. Preparing the content of a site involves significant costs, but that content can be made available to additional users at a negligible cost. Consequently, cost per user falls steadily as the number of users rises. If a company's revenues are proportional to the number of users, it will become more profitable as it grows bigger. This cost structure gives rise to a race to grow big, with only one firm ultimately surviving.[1] Industries with this kind of cost structure are said to be **natural monopolies.** Delong [20] has shown

---

[1] It would be more precise to say that *at most* one firm will survive. There might well be huge economies of scales in the production of the good, but so little demand for that good that even a monopoly would not be profitable. This observation has a direct bearing on the failure of most dotcom companies.

that in the past, the opening of industries with large economies of scale has produced enormous wealth for a fortunate (or ruthless) few. He cites as examples the railroads, the early twentieth-century steel and chemical industries, and the computer software industry. The dotcom investors were simply hoping that history would repeat itself.

An industry in which there is only one firm, or very few firms, frequently yields large profits. Firms will expend scarce resources in the pursuit of these profits, just as the dotcom companies did. This expenditure is, from a social perspective, largely useless: it only determines *who* will earn the profits, not *whether* profits will be earned. This use of resources is called **rent seeking.** Since these resources are diverted from more productive uses, rent seeking pushes the economy inside the production possibility frontier.

Imperfect competition results in a loss of economic efficiency even when resources are not squandered in this manner. An imperfectly competitive firm can earn profits by setting its price above marginal cost, whereas the competitive firm sets its price equal to marginal cost and earns no profits. The higher price dissuades consumers from buying the good, resulting in a movement along the production possibility frontier. Consequently, the condition for match efficiency is not satisfied under imperfect competition.

Thus, imperfect competition could result in a loss of economic efficiency for two reasons. Resources could be wasted in the pursuit of profit, pushing the economy inside the production possibility frontier. Prices could be set too high, causing the economy to move to the wrong point on the frontier. Both of these issues are examined in the chapters that follow.

14

Monopoly

The first theorem's claim that every competitive equilibrium is Pareto optimal hinges upon the assumption that perfect competition prevails in the markets for both consumption goods and factors of production. Economists are much less sanguine about the efficiency of free markets when large firms dominate some of the markets.

A firm's domination of a market is most complete when it is the sole seller or sole buyer in a market, that is, when it is a monopolist or a monopsonist. This chapter examines some of the consequences of monopoly.

14.1 NATURAL MONOPOLY

A production process displays **increasing returns to scale** if output more than doubles when the use of every input is doubled. The cost curves of a firm that produces under increasing returns to scale have two important properties[1]:

- Average cost falls as output rises.
- Marginal cost is everywhere below average cost.

A market in which production is characterized by increasing returns to scale is said to be a **natural monopoly** because only one firm can survive in such a market. Initially, a number of competing firms will "race to get big." The larger firms will have lower average costs than their smaller competitors and will be able to charge lower prices. The smaller firms will be unable to earn profits and will be driven from the market. Ultimately, only one firm will remain in the market.

Utilities are often natural monopolies because they deliver services through networks. An electric power company, for example, must have generating stations to

---

[1] Average cost falls because, as output rises, smaller amounts of every input are needed to produce each unit of output. The observation that the margin must be below the average when the average is falling is most easily understood by analogy. Suppose that the average height of a basketball team is 6 feet. If adding another player reduces the average height of the team, the player added – the marginal player – must be shorter than 6 feet, that is, shorter than the average. The average falls (rises) when the margin is below (above) the average.

produce power and trunk lines to distribute it before it can begin operations, but it can then deliver power to large numbers of customers by connecting them to its power grid. The expansion of its customer base allows the power company to spread the fixed costs (of the generating stations and trunk lines) over a greater number of users, so that average cost falls. Similar arguments apply to water and sewage systems, mail delivery, local telephone service, cable TV, and railways.[2]

The behaviour of such a monopolist can be described by a simple model. Suppose that the firm's total costs are

$$C = \gamma + \mu q$$

where C is total cost, q is output, γ is a fixed cost, and μ is the marginal cost. The firm's average and marginal costs are then

$$AC \equiv \frac{C}{q} = \gamma/q + \mu$$

$$MC \equiv \frac{dC}{dq} = \mu$$

Inspection shows that AC declines as output rises, and that AC is everywhere greater than MC. Suppose also that the demand curve for the good sold by the monopolist is

$$p = a - bq$$

The firm's revenue R is equal to pq, and hence its marginal revenue is

$$MR \equiv \frac{dR}{dq} = a - 2bq$$

These equations are graphed in Figure 14.1. The configuration of curves shown here allows the monopolist to earn profits at some levels of output.[3]

14.1.1 What Does the Monopolist Do and Is It Optimal?

The monopolist maximizes its profits by expanding production until marginal cost is equal to marginal revenue. Its quantity and price are $q°$ and $p°$ in Figure 14.1, and its profits are $q°(p° − AC°)$.

These choices do not maximize society's welfare. At any level of output, the value to consumers of one more unit of the monopolist's good is given by the height of the demand curve. The value of the resources needed to produce that unit is given by the height of the marginal cost curve. The difference between the two heights is the increase in society's welfare when one more unit is produced. Inspection of Figure 14.1 shows that additional units of the good raise society's welfare until output reaches q^*,

---

[2] Advances in technology coupled with deregulation have now introduced competition into other markets that were once thought to be natural monopolies, long distance telephone service being one example.

[3] Specifically, the average cost curve lies below the demand curve in some places.

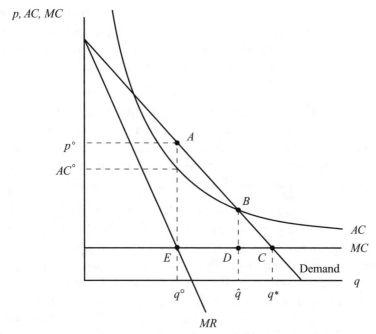

Figure 14.1: Natural Monopoly. Marginal cost is everywhere below average cost, causing average cost to fall as output rises. If the firms in an industry have cost curves of this kind, the largest firm will be able to undercut its competitors' prices and drive the others out of the industry.

after which additional units reduce society's welfare. Social welfare is maximized when output is q^*, where the value to consumers of one more unit of the good is exactly offset by the cost of producing that unit.

The monopolist's decision to limit output causes total surplus to be lower than it otherwise would be. This loss of surplus, the **welfare cost of monopoly,** is measured by the area ACE in Figure 14.1.[4]

14.1.2 Regulation and Public Ownership

There are two ways of increasing the net social benefits of a monopoly. The first is to regulate the monopoly, meaning that the government sets the monopolist's price and output. The second is for the government to purchase and operate the firm.

A regulator would require the monopolist to raise its output from q° so that the welfare cost of the monopoly is reduced. It could not, however, require the monopolist to increase output to q^*. The highest price at which a monopolist can sell q^* units of output is p^*. This price is just equal to its marginal cost, so the firm's revenues p^*q^* would just equal its variable costs μq^*, leaving the firm with a loss equal to its fixed cost γ. In the long run the firm would abandon the market, and net social benefits would ultimately be lower than they were before the regulator's intervention.

---

[4] This measurement is another application of the second rule in Section 5.1.

What is the best outcome that the regulator can achieve? Social welfare rises as output rises from $q°$, but the monopolist's profits fall. The monopolist should be required to raise its output until its profits are driven to zero (since these are the smallest profits consistent with the monopolist's continued participation in the market). This rule would force the monopolist to produce $\widehat{q}$ units of its good:

> **The regulator wants profits to fall to zero at the highest possible output, so it will allow the monopolist to charge the highest price that the market will bear. Then the monopolist's price is equal to the vertical distance to the demand curve and its average cost is equal to the vertical distance to the average cost curve. Its profits are zero when these two distances are equal.**

Raising output from $q°$ to $\widehat{q}$ will reduce the welfare cost of the monopoly by an amount equal to the area $ABDE$. A welfare cost equal to the area BCD would remain.

The alternative to regulation is government ownership. A government-owned firm does not need to earn non-negative profits, because its fixed costs (γ) can be paid out of the government's general revenues. The government-owned firm should therefore operate at the socially optimal output q^* and charge the price p^*. A switch from regulation to government ownership would eliminate the remaining welfare cost of monopoly.

This discussion suggests that social welfare is higher under government ownership than under regulation, but it is somewhat incomplete. The fixed costs of a government-owned monopolist are paid out of tax revenues, so choosing government ownership forces the government to adjust its budget. It has two options:

- *Reduce spending on other programs.* These programs were implemented because they raised social welfare, so reducing the amount spent on them would cause social welfare to fall.
- *Increase tax revenue.* Taxation reduces welfare, and the higher the taxes, the greater the loss of welfare. Thus, this option would also reduce social welfare.

When the full consequences of government ownership are taken into account, regulation might be preferred to government ownership.

Both policies are viable ways of dealing with natural monopoly. Water, sewage, and mail delivery are natural monopolies, and these services are typically provided by government-owned firms. Local telephone service and cable TV are often examples of regulated monopolies.

14.2 RENT-SEEKING BEHAVIOUR

The welfare cost of an entrenched monopolist is generally assumed to arise because the monopolist limits output to push its price above marginal cost. However, monopoly can generate a welfare cost in additional ways.

If being a monopolist is profitable, firms will compete for the opportunity to *become* the monopolist in a particular market. Furthermore, once the monopoly has been established, the monopolist will try to maintain its monopoly profits by deterring potential competitors. This kind of behaviour, which is called **rent seeking,** uses up some of society's scarce resources. From society's perspective, these resources are largely – perhaps entirely – wasted. Rent seeking does not determine whether monopoly profits will be earned; it only determines who earns them, and this issue does not affect social welfare.

The value of the resources wasted in this fashion is a second component of the welfare cost of monopoly. In the most extreme case, the value of these resources is equal to the value of the monopolist's operating profits. The appropriate measure of the welfare cost of monopoly would then be the area ACE plus the operating profits ($p^° - AC^°)q^°$.[5]

The argument that the monopolist's operating profits are a component of the welfare cost of monopoly rests on two basic presumptions. The first is that the resources expended by firms in their attempts to earn monopoly profits are entirely wasted. The second is that the firms, taken together, will expend resources equal to monopoly profits in their attempts to gain control of those profits. Neither of these presumptions appears to be entirely correct.

14.2.1 Is Rent Seeking Wasteful?

The wastefulness of rent seeking depends upon the activities undertaken by those who would become (or remain) monopolists.

Consider, for example, a market in which there are increasing returns to scale, so that a monopoly will ultimately be established.

- In the absence of regulation, the competing firms will "race to become big" and might use advertising to increase their market shares. Informative advertising has some social benefits, but to the extent that advertising is just gloss and glitter, it represents wasted resources.
- If the monopolist is to be selected by a regulator, the competing firms might be required to submit proposals. These submissions might well perform a socially useful function. Perhaps the firms will be forced to examine the environmental impact of their actions, and to develop comprehensive plans for ameliorating that impact, something that they might not otherwise have done.

Another possibility is that a monopolist's ownership of patents prevents other firms from duplicating its production process, and therefore prevents other firms from entering the market. Its monopoly would be lost, however, if some other firm discovers an alternative process that allows it to produce a competing product without violating the monopolist's patents. This prospect might induce the monopolist to investigate and patent alternative processes that it does not intend to use: the monopolist's only objective is to extend the "patent wall" that protects its monopoly. Expending resources on research whose results will never be used is not socially useful, but such research might

---

[5] The argument that the measure of the welfare cost of monopoly should include part or all of monopoly profits was originally put forward by Posner [49], although the concept of rent seeking had previously been advanced by Krueger [37] in another context.

accidentally produce discoveries which are too good to be passed up – in which case the resources are not entirely wasted.

These examples suggest that competition for monopoly profits causes firms to expend resources in ways that are partly, but perhaps not entirely, wasteful.

14.2.2 How Much Do Firms Spend to Become Monopolists?

Let V be the profits that a monopolist could earn in a particular market, and suppose that n firms are competing to become the monopolist. Each of the n firms would be willing to pay V/n for an equal chance (i.e., one chance in n) of becoming the monopolist.[6] If every firm did so, the amount spent by the firms in their efforts to gain monopoly status would be $n \times (V/n)$, which is exactly equal to the monopoly profits.

However, the maximum amount that firms would be willing to pay is not necessarily the amount that they do pay. The competition for monopoly status can be described by a game.[7] Identify the firms by the numbers $1, 2, \ldots, n$; and let s_i be the amount that firm i spends in its attempt to become the monopolist. If firm i becomes the monopolist with probability P_i, the best guess of its profits is π_i, where

$$\pi_i = P_i V - s_i$$

Firm i's own spending increases its probability of becoming the monopolist, while spending by other firms reduce its probability of becoming the monopolist. For simplicity, assume that firm i's probability of becoming the monopolist is equal to its share of the total spending:

$$P_i = \frac{s_i}{s_1 + s_2 + \cdots + s_n}$$

or, if $\bar{s}_i$ is spending by all firms *other than* firm i,

$$P_i = \frac{s_i}{s_i + \bar{s}_i}$$

A Nash equilibrium in this game is a list of expenditures, one for each firm, such that no firm can make itself better off by unilaterally deviating from the list.

The first step to finding the Nash equilibrium is to determine the best response functions. Since every firm is in the same situation, every best response function will have the same form. For firm i (where i can be anything from 1 to n), the best guess of profits is

$$\pi_i = \left(\frac{s_i}{s_i + \bar{s}_i} \right) V - s_i$$

---

[6] The firm would earn V with probability $1/n$ and nothing with probability $(n-1)/n$, so the "best guess" of the gain from participating in this gamble would be V/n. A firm which paid more than this amount for the chance to participate would expect to lose money, and a firm that paid less would expect to make money.

[7] The game described here is a simplified version of one developed by Rogerson [51].

Firm i does not care about the individual amounts spent by its competitors; it only cares about the total amount that they spend $(\bar{s}_i)$. Its best response function will therefore show the profit-maximizing value of s_i for every possible value of $\bar{s}_i$. The profit-maximizing value of s_i satisfies the condition

$$\frac{d\pi_i}{ds_i} = \left(\frac{1}{s_i + \bar{s}_i}\right)^2 \bar{s}_i V - 1 = 0 \qquad (14.1)$$

This equation is the best response function in implicit form: for any $\bar{s}_i$, the profit-maximizing value of s_i is the one that satisfies this equation.

Let's look for a symmetric Nash equilibrium.[8] In the present case, a symmetric Nash equilibrium is one in which every firm spends the same amount s^*. The amount s^* that we are looking for has the property that each firm maximizes its profits by spending s^* when every other firm is spending s^*. Since the best response function tells us what each firm's profit-maximizing expenditures are, this property could also be expressed as follows:

For each firm i, s^* is the value of s_i that satisfies (14.1) when $\bar{s}_i = (n-1)s^*$.

Substituting $s_i = s^*$ and $\bar{s}_i = (n-1)s^*$ into (14.1) yields

$$s^* = \left(\frac{n-1}{n}\right) \frac{V}{n}$$

Let the total expenditures by the n firms be σ. Since $\sigma = ns^*$,

$$\sigma = \left(\frac{n-1}{n}\right) V$$

Inspection shows that firms always choose to spend less than V/n on their attempts to become monopolists. The amount that each firm spends rises as the number of firms rises. As n becomes arbitrarily large, s^* approaches V/n and therefore total expenditures approach V.

14.2.3 Rent Seeking and Resource Misallocation

Competition for monopoly profits will cause scarce resources to be diverted from other, more socially valuable, purposes. The cost to society of this competition might be as large as the value of the monopoly profits themselves. It will, however, generally be smaller. When there are a limited number of competitors, the competitors (taken together) will spend an amount smaller than monopoly profits in their pursuit of these profits. Not all of their expenditures are entirely without social value. Certainly, the competition for monopoly profits generates a welfare loss which is equal to some part of the monopoly profits themselves, but it is difficult to know whether it is a large part or a small part.

---

[8] There is only one Nash equilibrium, and it is symmetric.

14.3 CONCLUSIONS

It has been shown that monopoly leads to two kinds of resource misallocation. First, the monopolist produces fewer units of goods than is socially optimal. Second, the pursuit of monopoly profits squanders scarce resources. Nevertheless, no firm conclusions can be drawn. A complete analysis of the consequences of monopoly must include a discussion of the alternatives. Suppose, for example, that one firm in a competitive industry becomes dominant and ultimately takes over the entire industry. This firm will certainly raise its price above the competitive price, reducing the number of units sold. This price change causes social welfare to fall. But if the monopolization of the industry leads to economies of scale that lower unit costs, the change in the structure of costs will cause social welfare to rise. The net effect of these two changes is something that cannot be estimated without very specific information about the industry.

QUESTIONS

1. A monopolist's total costs are

$$c = 15 + 12q$$

    The monopolist operates in a market in which the demand curve is:

$$p = 20 - q$$

    a) Find the monopolist's profit-maximizing price and output.
    b) Suppose that the government decides to regulate the monopolist so as to maximize the net benefits to society. What price and output should the government set?
    c) Suppose that the government takes over the firm and operates it to maximize net social benefits. What should the price and output be? What will the firm's losses be?

2. Imagine that two firms (named firm 1 and firm 2) are competing for monopoly status. The expected profits of firm i (where i is either 1 or 2) are

$$\pi_i = P_i V_i - s_i$$

    where P_i is the probability that firm i becomes the monopolist, V_i is a measure of its profits if it does become the monopolist, and s_i is the resources expended in the attempt to become the monopolist. It is assumed that firm 1 would be a more successful monopolist (perhaps because it has access to some technology that would allow it to produce at lower cost), in the sense that its profits would be higher:

$$V_1 > V_2 > 0$$

    The probability with which each firm succeeds in becoming the monopolist depends upon the resources that it expends in pursuit of that status:

$$P_i = \frac{s_i}{s_1 + s_2}$$

Show that firm 2 has a chance of becoming the monopolist. More specifically, show that the Nash equilibrium has the property

$$P_i = \frac{V_i}{V_1 + V_2}$$

Show also that, in the Nash equilibrium, both firms have positive expected profits.

15

Pricing Rules under Imperfect Competition

Competitive firms play an important role in ensuring that resources are allocated efficiently, while monopolies behave in ways that lead to resource misallocation. To a large degree, this difference in outcomes follows from the difference in their pricing rules: competitive firms engage in marginal cost pricing while monopolies do not. The efficiency of other market structures will likewise hinge upon the pricing rules that they follow.

This chapter begins with a discussion of the role played by marginal cost pricing in generating efficient outcomes. It then considers some alternative market structures, with an emphasis on the pricing rules. While the results are somewhat mixed, they do show that competition among price-taking firms is the only market structure under which marginal cost pricing is ensured.

15.1 MARGINAL COST PRICING

An economy reaches an efficient allocation if marginal social benefit is equal to marginal social cost in every market. This condition is satisfied if

1) The private marginal benefit of consuming any good is equal to its social marginal benefit, and the private marginal cost of producing any good is equal to its social marginal cost.
2) Production and trade continue until there are no further mutually beneficial trades.

Competitive markets can be the *mechanism* that ensures that 2) is satisfied. Competitive firms engage in **marginal cost pricing** – that is, each competitive firm expands its production until private marginal cost is equal to the market price. Since each consumer will continue to buy goods until private marginal benefit is just equal to the market price, private marginal cost and private marginal benefit are equalized.[1]

---

[1] See the appendix for a more formal discussion of the relationship between marginal cost pricing and economic efficiency.

By contrast, monopoly prevents the economy from reaching an efficient allocation because the monopolist sets its price above marginal cost. Each consumer continues to buy the monopolist's good until his private marginal benefit is equal to the good's market price, so in equilibrium, the private marginal benefit of the monopolist's good exceeds its private marginal cost. Not all mutually beneficial trades are carried out.

It is not competition that carries the economy to an efficient allocation; it is marginal cost pricing. The criterion for judging other industry structures should be whether the firms in the industry adhere to marginal cost pricing.

15.2 UNDIFFERENTIATED GOODS

If there were only one firm selling sugar, the owner of that firm would have a good thing going. He would earn monopoly profits, making himself better off at the expense of consumers. However, the entry of just one more firm might be enough to drive the price down to marginal cost, eliminating the industry's profits.

Imagine that the two firms have no fixed costs, and that their marginal costs are constant and equal. If each firm set its price to maximize its own profits, given the other firm's price, the firms will ultimately set their prices equal to marginal cost – just as perfectly competitive firms would. The key to this result is that one firm's sugar is exactly like the other's, so that consumers will always buy from the seller with the lowest price. If one firm set a price above marginal cost, the second firm would set its price just below the first firm's price. Every customer would buy from the second firm and it would earn unit profits equal to the gap between its price and marginal cost. But the first firm would then have an incentive to undercut the second firm. The incentive to undercut the other firm's price would be eliminated only when each firm's price has been driven down to marginal cost. Each firm would then be earning zero profits but could do no better. It would lose all of its customers if it raised its price; and although it would win all of the customers if it lowered its price, it would be selling goods at less than their cost of production. Thus, marginal cost pricing is the outcome of a price-setting game.

This price-setting game is known as the Bertrand duopoly game, and its Nash equilibrium is known as the Bertrand equilibrium. More generally, if n firms play the game rather than just two, the Bertrand equilibrium has two or more firms setting their prices equal to marginal cost, and the remaining firms setting their prices above marginal cost. Every firm earns zero profits. The high price firms sell no goods. The low price firms do sell goods, but their revenues are just equal to their costs.

15.2.1 Collusion

This outcome is, however, not the only possible one. The firms' owners might meet over brandy and cigars and decide that they'd be better off if they each charged the monopoly price, so that each would get an equal share of the monopoly profits. This agreement would leave the owners with two problems. The first is that the agreement itself constitutes collusion and is illegal. The second is that each firm has an incentive to violate the agreement. Why should a firm settle for a share of the monopoly profits, if it can earn almost all of monopoly profits by setting a price just below the monopoly price?[2]

Tacit collusion, in which the firms do not actually negotiate, but nevertheless ultimately charge prices above marginal cost, is also a possibility. Here, the firms do not engage in aggressive price cutting because each firm is aware that its own price cutting would elicit a price-cutting response from its competitor, to the detriment of both. Tacit collusion avoids the first problem.

The second problem might also be avoidable, even when the collusion is tacit. Friedman [25, 26] has constructed a formal model of tacit collusion between duopolists that are contesting a market today and in the foreseeable future. The firms must take into account their competitor's future price response to any price that they choose today. There is an equilibrium in which each firm always chooses the monopoly price (and earns half of monopoly profits) because it believes that any attempt to undercut its competitor in the current period will lead to cutthroat competition – and no profits – in every future period. A firm that set its price just below the monopoly price in the current period would be able to earn monopoly profits in the current period, but would give up half of monopoly profits in *every* future period. The firms are so discouraged by this prospect that they continue to set their own prices equal to the monopoly price.[3]

15.2.2 Capacity Constraints

The behaviour of duopolists can also be represented by the Cournot game. Here, each of two firms chooses the quantity of goods that it intends to sell in a particular market, and the firms allow the price to adjust to ensure that all of these goods are sold. The equilibrium level of output is higher, and the price lower, than under collusion, but profits are still positive.

The Cournot game has been criticized for imagining that firms behave in a way that differs radically from our casual observations of their behaviour. Firms don't choose

---

[2] A group that engages in collusive price setting is called a **cartel.** One example of a cartel is the Organization of Petroleum Exporting Countries (OPEC), which attempts to regulate the price of crude oil by setting restrictive production quotas. The history of OPEC illustrates the difficulty of enforcing even explicit collusion. OPEC was initially successful at raising the price of oil but has not subsequently been of much consequence. A number of its members are so unwilling to forgo the profits from oil sales that they will not abide by the quotas assigned to them. Indeed, some members have even increased their own production when other members have decreased theirs. The remaining members have become reluctant to set low quotas because the benefits would be small and would accrue largely to the renegades.

[3] The firms charge the monopoly price if the current period's monopoly profits are smaller than the present discounted value of a half share of all future monopoly profits. This condition seems likely to be satisfied, although it will not be if the discount factor is exceptionally high. A firm would have a high discount factor if, for example, it expected other firms to enter the industry, driving down industry profits.

a level of output and passively accept prices; they compete for sales by setting prices. The Bertrand game, in which firms compete through prices, seems to describe the behaviour of duopolists better than the Cournot game. However, the outcome of the Bertrand game – that profits are relentlessly driven to zero – seems less appealing than the outcome of the Cournot game.

Kreps and Scheinkman [36] argue that the Cournot game might be a better description of the behaviour of duopolists. They imagine that an equilibrium is reached in two steps. In the first step, the firms build their production facilities. Each firm must construct one unit of capacity (at a positive cost) for each unit of goods that it expects to ultimately produce and sell. In the second step, the firms compete through prices to attract a share of the market. Thus, the game couples a quantity-setting game to a price-setting game.

Kreps and Scheinkman show that, in the second step, the firms' willingness to cut prices is limited when their installed capacity is relatively low. (Each firm could win more customers through aggressive price cutting, but would then be unable to produce enough goods to satisfy these customers.) Since the firms can foresee the outcome of the price-setting game when they choose their capacities, each firm chooses to install a relatively limited capacity. Prices are not driven down to marginal cost, and profits are not driven to zero. Indeed, the outcome of this game is sometimes exactly the same as the outcome of the simpler Cournot game.

15.3 DIFFERENTIATED GOODS

The range of outcomes would be smaller if the firms were selling shirts rather than sugar. Sugar is an undifferentiated product but shirts are not. Although the shirts produced by the various firms have the same basic characteristics, they are in other ways distinctive – if only because some have alligators embroidered on the pockets and others have polo players. The fact that every producer's shirts are in some way distinctive means that its sales will vary smoothly with the price that it charges. If the manufacturer of alligator shirts raises its price slightly, it will lose some of its customers to the other shirt manufacturers, but will still keep many of its original customers. Similarly, it will capture some, but not all, of the other firms' customers if it lowers its price. The shirt business is a little bit like monopoly in that each firm operates along a downward-sloping demand curve; and it is a little bit like competition in that customers who don't like any one firm's price can buy from other firms. This industry structure is known as **monopolistic competition.**[4]

---

[4] The model of monopolistic competition in this section is a stripped-down version of a model developed by Dixit and Stiglitz [23]. This model assumes that each person buys goods from a number of firms producing slightly different versions of the same good. Another type of model would be needed to describe behaviour when each individual purchases goods from just one or two of the many firms producing slightly different goods. Such a model would describe goods like hotel rooms and cars.

15.3.1 The Commodity Group

The goods produced by the various firms in a monopolistically competitive industry constitute a **commodity group.** The goods within the group are sharply different from the goods outside of the group, and somewhat different from each other. A person's consumption of goods in a particular commodity group is represented by the index

$$C = \left[\sum_{i=1}^{n} (c_i)^{\alpha} \right]^{1/\alpha}$$

where $0 < \alpha < 1$. There are n firms producing goods contained in this commodity group, and these firms are assigned the numbers from 1 to n. The individual's consumption of the good produced by firm i is c_i. The above equation shows how the individual's consumption of the various goods in the group is aggregated to obtain a measure, or an index, of his consumption. Two basic properties of the index are as follows:

- The index displays constant returns to scale, in the sense that doubling the consumption of every good within the index doubles the value of the index.
- The individual likes variety. Additional units of any one good increase aggregate consumption C by progressively smaller amounts. Given the choice between an extra unit of two different goods, the individual would always choose the good of which he currently has the smaller amount.

The parameter α describes the ease with which one good can be substituted for another. Imagine that we take a unit of the first firm's good from an individual, and compensate him with enough units of the second firm's good so that the consumption index C does not fall. How many units of the second firm's good would have to be given in compensation? You will note that this question parallels that asked when we wanted to calculate the marginal rate of substitution, so we can adopt a parallel solution. The number of units of compensation γ is[5]

$$\gamma \equiv - \left. \frac{dc_2}{dc_1} \right|_{C \text{ constant}} = \frac{\partial C}{\partial c_1} \div \frac{\partial C}{\partial c_2} = \left(\frac{c_1}{c_2} \right)^{\alpha - 1}$$

Consider these limiting cases:

- If α is equal to one, aggregate consumption is calculated by adding up the quantities of the individual goods consumed. The goods in the commodity group are perfect substitutes for each other; in other words, the commodity is undifferentiated. One unit of any good would exactly compensate for the loss of one unit of any other good.

---

[5] The notated bar following dc_2/dc_1 is simply a reminder that we are comparing the change in c_2 to the change in c_1 under the assumption that these changes do not alter the value of C.

- Now re-write the above equation:

$$-\left(\frac{dc_2}{c_2} \div \frac{dc_1}{c_1}\right)\bigg|_{C \text{ constant}} = \left(\frac{c_1}{c_2}\right)^{\alpha}$$

As α approaches 0, the value on the right-hand side approaches 1. In this limiting case, the compensation for a given *percentage change* in c_1 is an equal *percentage change* in c_2. As c_1 falls toward zero, the required compensation for the loss of another unit of c_1 becomes infinitely large.

More generally, a lower value of α implies that the goods in the commodity group are poorer substitutes for each other – that is, the goods have fewer similarities and more distinguishing features.

The index C measures an individual's aggregate consumption of goods in a particular commodity group. Units of aggregate consumption can be purchased at a price, but because C is an index, so its price. The appropriate price of aggregate consumption is

$$P \equiv \left[\sum_{i=1}^{n} (p_i)^{\alpha/(\alpha-1)}\right]^{(\alpha-1)/\alpha}$$

where p_i is the price of a unit of the good produced by firm i.

A consumer who intends to spend a certain amount of money on goods in this commodity group, and who knows the price of each of the goods in the group, will purchase the combination of goods that maximizes the value of C. If some of the prices change, the consumer will adjust his purchases – buying less of the goods that have become relatively expensive and more of the goods that have become relatively cheap – so that he is once again maximizing the value of C. The price index P is the appropriate price for units of aggregate consumption because it has these properties:

- Any combination of price changes that leaves P unchanged will also leave the maximal value of C unchanged.
- Any combination of price changes that raises P will reduce the maximal value of C, and any combination that reduces P will raise the maximal value of C.
- A doubling of all prices will double P.

The last property follows from the form of the index, and the first two properties will become evident as the model is developed.

15.3.2 Demand Curves

A utility-maximizing consumer will spend part of his income on the goods contained in a particular commodity group. The amount spent on these goods, E, will depend upon the consumer's income, the prices of goods outside of the commodity group, and upon P. The relationship between expenditure E and the price index P is determined by the price elasticity of demand of aggregate consumption C.[6]

Having decided how much to spend on the goods contained in the commodity group, the consumer must decide how much of each good within the group he will purchase. He wants to maximize his aggregate consumption C, but his purchases must satisfy the budget constraint

$$\sum_{i=1}^{n} p_i c_i = E \qquad (15.1)$$

This decision could be formulated mathematically, as a constrained maximization problem, but it is more easily solved by less formal means. The consumer is going to allocate each of his E dollars to the purchase of one of the goods in the commodity group, and his allocation is optimal if he cannot raise C by spending a dollar more on one good and a dollar less on another. This condition will be satisfied if the last dollar spent on each good raises C by the same amount. Another unit of good i raises C by $\partial C/\partial c_i$ and another dollar spent on good i buys $1/p_i$ units of good i, so spending another dollar on good i raises C by

$$\frac{\partial C}{\partial c_i} \frac{1}{p_i}$$

Evaluating the derivative (and cleaning up a little) gives

$$C^{1-\alpha} \left[\frac{(c_i)^{\alpha-1}}{p_i} \right]$$

Thus, the condition for an optimal allocation is that this expression take the same value for every good i. Since only the expression in square brackets can vary across goods, this condition can be written as

$$\frac{(c_i)^{\alpha-1}}{p_i} = k \qquad \text{for all } i$$

where k is a constant that is yet to be determined. This equation is the demand curve for good i, and can be written in a more conventional form:

$$c_i = \left(\frac{1}{k p_i} \right)^{1/(1-\alpha)} \qquad (15.2)$$

---

[6] The **price elasticity of demand** describes the way in which the quantity of a good demanded varies with the good's own price. It is measured as the negative of the ratio of the percentage change in the quantity demanded to the percentage change in price. If the elasticity is between zero and one, a price increase will induce such a small reduction in the quantity demanded that expenditure on the good will rise with the good's price. Demand is then said to be inelastic. If the elasticity exceeds one, a price increase will cause the quantity demanded to fall by so much that expenditure will fall. Demand is then said to be elastic. If demand is unit elasticity, expenditure does not change with price.

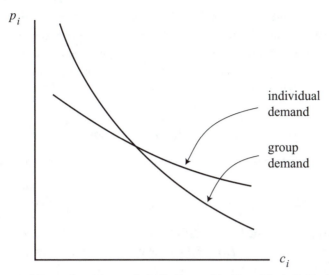

Figure 15.1: Demand Curves for a Monopolistically Competitive Firm. The individual demand curve shows how the demand for a firm's good changes when that firm alone changes its price. The group demand curve shows how the demand for a firm's good changes when every firm in the commodity group changes its price by the same proportion.

What is the right value for k? If k is too large, the consumer would be buying so little of each good that his expenditures would fall short of E; and if k is too small, he would be buying so much of each good that his expenditures would exceed E. The right value of k is the one that at which he spends exactly E. To find it, substitute (15.2) into (15.1) and rearrange the resulting equation:

$$k = \frac{E^{\alpha-1}}{P^{\alpha}}$$

Substituting this value of k into (15.2) gives the final form of the demand for good i:

$$c_i = \left[\frac{E}{P}\right]\left(\frac{p_i}{P}\right)^{1/(\alpha-1)} \tag{15.3}$$

and substituting this equation into the definition of C shows that

$$C = \frac{E}{P}$$

This equation confirms the earlier assertion that any combination of price changes that raises P will lower C, and any combination that reduces P will raise C.

If n is reasonably large, firm i's decision to adjust its price will not have a significant effect on P. Firm i will therefore perceive the demand curve for its good to be (15.2). This demand curve is shown in Figure 15.1. It is downward sloping because a fall in firm i's price will cause consumers to buy more of good i and less of the other goods in the commodity group.

Also shown in Figure 15.1 is a demand curve that shows how the demand for good i varies with the price of good i, when the prices of all other goods in the commodity group change by the same proportion as the price of good i. This "group demand curve" is similar to a market demand curve, and it is negatively sloped because a rise in all prices causes the consumer to shift away from the goods contained within the commodity group and toward the goods outside of the commodity group. This demand curve is steeper than firm i's individual demand curve.[7]

15.3.3 Profit Maximization

Assume that each firm has no fixed costs and a constant marginal cost. Then firm i's profits are

$$\pi_i = (p_i - \mu) \, c_i = k^{1/(\alpha-1)} \left[(p_i)^{\alpha/(\alpha-1)} - \mu \, (p_i)^{1/(\alpha-1)} \right]$$

where μ is the firm's marginal cost. The firm chooses the price that maximizes its profits. Calculating the derivative $d\pi_i/dp_i$ and setting it equal to zero gives

$$p_i = \left(\frac{1}{\alpha} \right) \mu$$

Each firm, aware that it is choosing a point along a downward-sloping demand curve, sets its price above marginal cost. Specifically, the firm "marks up" its marginal cost by the factor $1/\alpha$. The greater the similarities between firm i's good and the other goods in the commodity group, the closer α is to one and the smaller is the mark-up. Only in the limiting case in which the firms' goods are identical (so that α is equal to one) will the firm adopt marginal cost pricing.

Each firm's price depends only upon its marginal cost and the ease with which one good in the commodity group can be substituted for another. The number of firms in the commodity group has *no effect* on the price set by each firm.

15.4 SUMMARY

Marginal cost pricing is a key element in the proof of the first theorem, so it is of some importance to know whether competition among price-taking firms is the only industry structure that gives rise to this rule. The findings of this chapter are mixed. It is possible that the presence of just one other firm in the market will force a firm to engage in marginal cost pricing – but it is also possible that a firm could set its price above marginal cost even though there are many other firms producing similar goods.

---

[7] The market demand curve is steeper when $\varepsilon(1 - \alpha) < 1$, where ε is the price elasticity of demand of aggregate consumption C. This condition is satisfied if aggregate consumption is inelastic, or if it is elastic but not too elastic. However, aggregate consumption should not be highly elastic. A high elasticity would indicate that some goods not contained in the commodity group are close substitutes for goods contained in the commodity group – but if they are close substitutes, they should be included in the commodity group. A high elasticity therefore suggests that the commodity group has been improperly defined.

APPENDIX: MARGINAL COST PRICING
AND ECONOMIC EFFICIENCY

Marginal cost pricing is crucial to the proof of the first theorem. To see this, imagine again an economy in which ale and bread are produced using labour and capital. The bread industry is competitive and engages in marginal cost pricing:

$$r\left(\frac{1}{MP_K^b}\right) = p_b$$

$$w\left(\frac{1}{MP_L^b}\right) = p_b$$

Here, r, w, and p_b are the currency prices of capital, labour, and bread. However, ale is produced by a monopolist which sets its price above marginal cost. For concreteness imagine that the price of ale, p_a, exceeds its marginal cost of production by a factor λ:

$$\lambda r\left(\frac{1}{MP_K^a}\right) = p_a$$

$$\lambda w\left(\frac{1}{MP_L^a}\right) = p_a$$

These equations can be combined to obtain the condition for production efficiency, so a combination of goods lying somewhere on the production possibility frontier will be produced. However, this combination will *not* be match efficient. The factors of production are divided between the industries so that

$$\frac{p_a}{p_b} = \lambda\left(\frac{MP_L^b}{MP_L^a}\right) \equiv \lambda MRT$$

That is, the price ratio is greater than the marginal rate of transformation. Consumers, however, will choose their commodity bundles so that each person's marginal rate of substitution is equal to the same price ratio:

$$\frac{p_a}{p_b} = MRS$$

It follows that

$$MRS = \lambda MRT > MRT$$

In equilibrium, the number of units of bread that each consumer is willing to give up to obtain another unit of ale is greater than the number of units that must be given up to provide that unit. Consumers would be better off if more ale and less bread were produced. Too little of the economy's resources are devoted to ale production and too much of these resources are devoted to bread production.

QUESTIONS

1. Two firms (called firm 1 and firm 2) are the only sellers of a good for which the demand equation is

$$q = 1,000 - 200p$$

Here, q is the total quantity of the good demanded and p is the price of the good measured in dollars. Neither firm has any fixed costs, and each firm's marginal cost of producing a unit of goods is $2. Imagine that each firm produces some quantity of goods, and that these goods are sold to consumers at the highest price at which all of the goods can be sold. A Cournot equilibrium in this environment is a pair of outputs (q_1, q_2) such that, when firm 1 produces q_1 units of goods and firm 2 produces q_2 units of goods, neither firm can raise its profits by unilaterally changing its output. Find the Cournot equilibrium. Determine whether the price at which the goods are sold exceeds marginal cost.

2. Consider again the situation described above, but now imagine that each firm sets a price, selling as many units of the good as it can at that price. Each firm is aware that
   - It will not be able to sell any goods if its price exceeds the other firm's price, because every consumer will prefer to buy from the other firm.
   - If the two prices are the same, total purchases will be determined by the demand equation, and each firm will sell an equal quantity of goods.
   - If its price is lower than the other firm's price, every consumer will prefer to buy from it rather than the other firm, and its total sales will be determined by the demand equation.

   A Bertrand equilibrium in this environment is a pair of prices (p_1, p_2) such that, when firm 1 charges p_1 and firm 2 sells p_2, neither firm can raise its own profits by unilaterally changing its price. What is the Bertrand equilibrium?

3. Now consider a slight variant of the situation described above. Imagine that firm 1's marginal cost is $1, rather than $2, and that every other aspect of the problem is as described in question 2. Also, assume that prices must be expressed in dollars and cents, so that $4.07 is an admissible price but $4.065 is not. What is the Bertrand equilibrium?

Taxation and Efficiency

It is inevitable that people will try to avoid paying taxes. These attempts are, in the aggregate, futile – the government ultimately does raise the revenue that it wants – but they do have important economic implications. The adjustments that people make in their attempts to dodge taxes reduce economic efficiency.

Governments have a role to play in the provision of public goods, and in the regulation of externalities and "increasing returns" industries. In each of these roles, the government's activities have the potential to reduce economic inefficiency. But these activities must be funded through taxation, and taxation generates other inefficiencies. The social benefits of additional government expenditures will at some point fall short of the social costs of the additional taxation required to finance them, so that the intervention reduces welfare instead of raising it. The welfare gains of intervention will be maximized if the government targets its expenditures to generate the greatest social gains, and designs its tax system to minimize the damage done by it. These issues are discussed in the next few chapters.

Governments also, to greater or lesser degrees, attempt to reduce economic disparities by redistributing income. A major element of any redistributive policy is the design of the tax system, and the welfare costs associated with taxation limit the government's ability to redistribute income, or its willingness to do so. The relationship between economic efficiency and income distribution is discussed in the last part of the book.

16

Taxation

The things that people do to avoid paying taxes alter the allocation of resources in ways that reduce economic welfare. To see this, compare the following situations:

1) On the morning of the first of January, you discover that $100 that you had in your pockets is no longer there. You do not know whether it was lost or stolen or spent in the previous night's revelry; all that you know is that you will have $100 less to spend in the coming year than you had expected. You decide that you can trim a little from your budget: it's no big deal.

2) On the morning of the first of January, the government bids you a happy new year and announces that it is imposing a 20% tax on movie tickets. You have been in the habit of spending $750 each year on tickets, so this tax will cost you $150 over the year if you do not change your habits. However, movie-going has suddenly become a relatively expensive pastime, so you decide that you will go to the movies only 2/3 as often as you had in the past. The tickets will cost you $500 and the tax on these tickets will cost you $100, so you will have an additional $150 to spend on other items.

These situations are alike in that your net-of-tax expenditures are reduced by $100. They are different in the way in which you adjust your budget. In the first case, the amounts spent on many different goods and services are reduced by small amounts. In the second case, you are forced to treat a commonplace item as if it were a relatively scarce commodity, like caviar or saffron. You purchase less of that commodity, and instead purchase more of the other goods and services.

The tax both takes $100 out of your pockets and discourages you from buying a particular commodity. The result is that you are worse off than you would have been if $100 had simply been removed from your pockets by a taxman or pickpocket. How much worse off? That depends upon your preferences, but certainly, not as badly off as you would have been if $150 had been lifted from your pockets. After all, you could have responded to the tax by putting $150 in an envelope, and taking money out of the envelope to pay the tax every time that you went to the movies. This would allow you to behave *as if* you were $150 poorer and the price of movie tickets hadn't changed. You didn't exercise this option because there were other ways of adjusting to the tax that made you better off.

So, paying the tax is worse than simply losing $100, but it's not as bad as losing $150. Let's say that it is equivalent to losing $$Z$. The government takes away $100 of this amount as tax revenue. Since this money will be used to provide goods and services, or perhaps transferred to another person, your loss is offset by a benefit accruing to others: there is no social loss.[1] The remaining $$(Z - 100)$ is a loss to you, which is not offset by a benefit accruing to someone else. This loss is the part of the welfare cost of the tax that is borne by you.

The welfare cost of a tax is sometimes referred to as the **deadweight loss** of the tax. It arises because the tax discourages mutually beneficial trades. The tax in 2), for example, causes you to see fewer movies than you otherwise would have.

16.1 IS LUMP-SUM TAXATION POSSIBLE?

An individual who incurs the loss described in 1) finds that his income is less than his planned consumption. He is forced to trim his consumption plans to bring them into balance with his income. This adjustment is the **income effect** of the loss.

An individual who is confronted with the tax described in 2) is also forced to trim his consumption plans. The adjustment needed to equate planned consumption with income at the current (tax inclusive) prices is the income effect of the tax. But the revisions in his consumption plan go beyond those needed to simply balance his budget. The tax raises the price of movie tickets relative to all other goods, inducing him to shift his consumption away from movie tickets and toward other goods. (This adjustment, not coincidentally, also reduces his tax bill.) The adjustment made because the tax changes relative prices is called the **substitution effect** of the tax.

The income effect does not carry with it a deadweight loss, because the income given up by the taxpayer is transferred to some other member of society – the government, or the people to whom the government subsequently transfers the income. However, the substitution effect does generate a deadweight loss, and this loss is incurred by the taxpayer himself. It is *willingly* incurred because the taxpayer prefers it to a greater tax bill (for example, seeing fewer movies is better than paying an extra $50 in ticket taxes). Although this calculation makes sense from each person's point of view, the aggregate effect of each individual acting upon it is not socially desirable. If the government intends to raise a specific amount of revenue, attempts by each individual to evade the tax simply induce the government to set higher tax rates, leading to further evasion and

---

[1] This claim is not exactly true. The government could spend its revenues in ways that yield very large social returns, or in ways that yield very small returns. The established convention, however, is to treat a dollar of surplus transferred to the government as being no less and no more valuable than a dollar of producer or consumer surplus. This assumption allows us to study separately the government's spending and the tax system.

further deadweight losses.[2] Everyone would be better off if no one attempted to evade the tax.

A tax on gasoline is evaded by driving less and a tax on income is evaded by working less. The only tax that cannot be evaded is the **lump-sum tax,** which is not linked to anything within the control of the taxpayer. Instead, the taxman simply taps you on the shoulder and presents you with a demand for, say, $1,000.[3] If all tax revenue were raised in this fashion, there would be no deadweight loss associated with taxation and we would all be better off.

While some revenue could be raised in this manner, the amount of revenue needed to finance a modern government could not. The lump sum levied on each individual would need to be so large that some people could not pay it, and others would be impoverished if they did pay it. The government would be forced to levy different taxes on those with high incomes and those with low incomes – which would make it an income tax. It would be, however, an income tax in which the deadweight loss is particularly high, because anyone who was initially just above the dividing line between high and low incomes would choose to earn less, so that he could pay the lower tax. Attempts to reduce the deadweight loss would lead to an income tax in which the payment varies more smoothly with income, much like the ones now in place.

The observation that a lump-sum tax is both desirable and unworkable has led economists to ask whether there are combinations of contingent taxes that behave like lump-sum taxes.

16.1.1 Good News

The potential for such combinations can be seen by imagining an economy in which people consume only ale and bread. These goods are produced by firms with very simple production processes: a unit of labour can be converted into $1/k$ units of ale or one unit of bread. There are n people in the economy, and they are identified by the numbers 1 through n. Each person is endowed with $\overline{h}$ units of labour. Each person's utility is an increasing and strictly concave function of his consumption of ale and bread. Each person prefers any commodity bundle containing some of both goods to any commodity bundle containing only one of the two goods.

---

[2] Economists sometimes say that people "avoid" a tax if they use legal means to reduce their tax bill, and "evade" a tax if they use illegal means to reduce their tax bill. As this distinction is of no consequence to us, I will use these terms interchangeably.

[3] Note that even an unconditional demand like this is not really lump sum, because it is based upon place of residency. A city that imposed lump-sum taxes would risk having people migrate to the suburbs. A country would risk having people migrate internationally. This consideration might not be of great importance if the government wishes to raise moderate amounts of revenue, because the jurisdictions to which people might move would also be raising revenue, possibly in ways that generate deadweight losses. People would only move if the cost of paying the lump-sum tax were out of line with the cost of paying the taxes of the competing jurisdictions.

Formally, an allocation in this economy is a list showing the commodity bundle assigned to each person and the quantity of labour assigned to each industry. Since the assignment of labour can be inferred from the commodity bundles,[4] let's define an allocation to be simply a list of commodity bundles.

This economy is a very simple production economy, so it is fairly easy to describe the Pareto optimal allocations.[5]

- All of the available labour must be used to produce goods, and these goods must be given either to the people living in the economy or to the government. If a_j and b_j are the quantities of ale and bread consumed by person j, and if R is the revenue required by the government (measured in units of labour), this condition is

$$\sum_{j=1}^{n} \left(ka_j + b_j\right) + R = n\overline{h} \tag{16.1}$$

  The right-hand side of this equation is the quantity of labour available in the economy, and the left-hand side is the quantity of labour required to provide the commodity bundle (a_j, b_j) to each person j and the revenue R to the government.
- Now consider the efficiency conditions. There is only one factor of production, so the issue of production efficiency does not arise. Exchange efficiency requires each person's marginal rate of substitution to be equal to every other person's marginal rate of substitution, and match efficiency requires the marginal rates of substitution to be equal to the marginal rate of transformation.[6] Since the marginal rate of transformation is equal to k, the efficiency conditions are summarized by n conditions of the form

$$MRS_j = k \qquad j = 1, \ldots, n \tag{16.2}$$

These conditions state that the rate at which each person is *willing* to trade ale for bread is equal to the rate at which the economy is *able* to transform ale into bread. Person j's marginal rate of substitution is, of course, determined by his commodity bundle (a_j, b_j).

Thus, a Pareto optimal allocation is a solution to an equation system:

A **Pareto optimal** allocation is a list $(a_1, b_1, a_2, b_2, \ldots, a_n, b_n)$ that satisfies (16.1) and the n equations in (16.2).

---

[4] Specifically, the amount of labour allocated to the bread industry is equal to total bread consumption, and the amount allocated to the ale industry is k times larger than total ale consumption.

[5] The allocation described here is sometimes called the "constrained Pareto efficient" allocation, to emphasize that it is the best possible allocation when some part of production must be given to the government. I have retained the term "Pareto optimal" because its use in this context is unlikely to cause confusion.

[6] As before, MRS_j is the amount of bread needed to exactly compensate person j for the loss of one unit of ale, and MRT is the amount of bread that can be produced if one less unit of ale is produced.

Since the equation system contains $2n$ variables and only $n + 1$ equations, there are infinitely many solutions – and hence infinitely many Pareto optimal allocations.

Now consider the nature of competitive equilibrium in this economy. There are markets for labour, ale, and bread. Firms buy labour at the market-clearing wage. They use the labour to produce goods, which are sold back to the workers at market-clearing prices. The workers pay for these goods with the wages that they earned by selling their labour.

A competitive equilibrium is described by an allocation and a set of market-clearing prices. Ordinarily, the allocation and the prices are determined simultaneously, but production in this economy is so simple that the prices charged by the firms can be determined without reference to the allocation. Let labour be the numeraire, so that the wage is equal to one and the prices of ale and bread are measured in units of labour. If the price of ale were greater than k, the ale producers would earn a profit on every unit of ale that they produced and sold. They would want to produce and sell a huge quantity of ale, so there would be an excess supply of ale. This excess supply would cause the price of ale to be bid downward. Similarly, if the price of ale were less than k, the ale producers would incur a loss on every unit of ale produced and sold, so they would be unwilling to produce any ale. There would be an excess demand for ale, causing the price of ale to be bid upwards. Consequently, the market-clearing price of ale can only be k. The same kind of argument shows that the market-clearing price of bread must be 1. The firms earn no profits; and in the absence of taxes, the aggregate wage earnings of the workers are just sufficient to purchase all of the goods produced by the firms.

All that remains is to determine the competitive allocation. With the market-clearing prices already known, the competitive allocation is found by determining each person's best attainable commodity bundle under these prices. The characteristics of the allocation depend upon the manner in which the government raises revenue.

No Taxation
If the government requires no revenue ($R = 0$), person j's budget constraint is

$$ka_j + b_j = \overline{h} \tag{16.3}$$

His wage income $\overline{h}$ could be used to purchase $\overline{h}$ units of bread, or $\overline{h}/k$ units of ale, or any other combination of ale and bread that satisfies this budget constraint. The best of these bundles occurs at the point of tangency between one of person j's indifference curves and the budget constraint. (It is W in Figure 16.1.) The slope of the indifference curve is $-MRS_j$ and the slope of the budget constraint is $-k$, so this bundle satisfies the condition

$$MRS_j = k \tag{16.4}$$

Since MRS_j is determined by a_j and b_j, (16.3) and (16.4) can be solved to find person

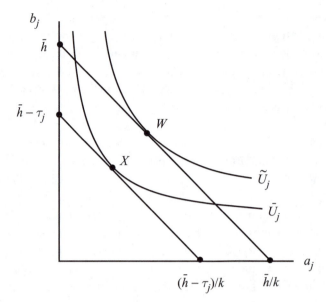

Figure 16.1: Consumer Choice under a Lump-Sum Tax. The tax shifts person j's budget constraint inward. Person j's best attainable commodity bundle changes from W to X.

j's commodity bundle under competition. Thus,

> **If the government does not impose any taxes, the competitive allocation is a list $(a_1, b_1, a_2, b_2, \ldots, a_n, b_n)$ that satisfies (16.3) and (16.4) for every person j.**

This system contains $2n$ variables and $2n$ equations. The restrictions placed on the utility functions ensure that the system has a unique solution.

In the absence of taxes the competitive allocation is Pareto optimal. This result is proved by comparing the equation systems that describe the Pareto optimal allocation and the competitive allocation. Each equation in the former system either appears in the latter system or is implied by equations in the latter system:

> **If (16.4) is satisfied for each person j, the n equations in (16.2) are satisfied. If (16.3) is satisfied for each person j, and if R is equal to zero, (16.1) is satisfied.**

It follows that a solution to the latter system is also a solution to the former system, or equivalently, that the competitive allocation is Pareto optimal.

Lump-Sum Taxation

Suppose that the government has a positive revenue requirement but that it can impose non-contingent taxes. Is the competitive equilibrium still Pareto optimality?

The conditions that characterize the competitive equilibrium are somewhat changed by the introduction of lump-sum taxes. To raise an amount of revenue R, the government must impose a tax τ_j on each person j, where

$$\sum_{i=1}^{n} \tau_i = R \tag{16.5}$$

Person j's budget constraint in the presence of this tax system is:

$$ka_j + b_j = \overline{h} - \tau_j \tag{16.6}$$

His new budget line (shown in Figure 16.1) lies below the old budget line but parallel to it. The vertical distance between the two budget lines is τ_j.[7] Person j will choose, from the bundles lying on his new budget line, a commodity bundle that satisfies (16.4). Then

> Suppose that the government imposes a tax τ_j on each person j, and that these taxes satisfy the condition (16.5) for some positive value of R. The competitive allocation is a list $(a_1, b_1, a_2, b_2, \ldots, a_n, b_n)$ that satisfies (16.6) and (16.4) for every j.

The restrictions placed on the utility functions ensure that this system has a unique solution.

Once again, each equation in the system describing a Pareto optimal allocation either appears in the system describing the competitive allocation or is implied by equations in this system:

> If (16.4) is satisfied for each person j, the n equations in (16.2) are satisfied. Summing the individual budget constraints (16.6), and using (16.5) to eliminate the individual taxes, yield (16.1).

Consequently, the solution to the latter system is also a solution to the former system: the competitive allocation in the presence of lump-sum taxation is Pareto optimal.

Commodity Taxation

Finally, suppose that the government has a positive revenue requirement but cannot impose lump-sum taxes. Is there a set of commodity taxes under which the competitive allocation is Pareto optimal?

The price charged by competitive firms for each good is equal to its marginal cost, which is k for ale and 1 for bread. The price paid by the consumer includes both the payment to the firm and the payment of taxes to the government. That is, the prices paid by the consumer for ale and bread, p_a and p_b, are

$$p_a = (1 + t_a)k \tag{16.7}$$

$$p_b = 1 + t_b \tag{16.8}$$

where t_a is the rate at which ale is taxed and t_b is the rate at which bread is taxed.

---

[7] This distance is revenue measured in bread, but since one unit of bread is produced with one unit of labour, it is also revenue measured in labour.

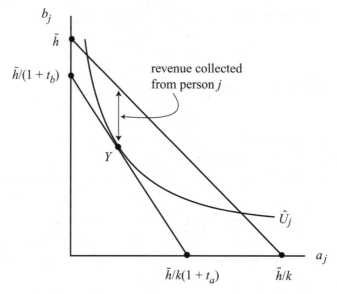

Figure 16.2: Consumer Choice under Commodity Taxes. Person j's budget line is again shifted inward, but if the commodities are not taxed at the same rate, the new budget line is not parallel to the old one. Person j's best attainable commodity bundle is Y.

Person j's budget constraint is now

$$p_a a_j + p_b b_j = \overline{h}$$

Figure 16.2 shows this constraint, along with the original (no tax) constraint. The best of the affordable commodity bundles is characterized by a tangency between an indifference curve and the budget constraint, and this tangency satisfies the condition

$$MRS_j = \frac{p_a}{p_b}$$

Substituting (16.7) and (16.8) into these two equations gives

$$(1 + t_a)k a_j + (1 + t_b)b_j = \overline{h} \tag{16.9}$$

$$MRS_j = \frac{(1 + t_a)k}{1 + t_b} \tag{16.10}$$

Person j's best attainable commodity bundle is found by solving (16.9) and (16.10).

The amount of taxes that person j pays to the government is equal to the vertical distance between the no-tax budget constraint and the new budget constraint, measured at person j's best attainable commodity bundle (see Figure 16.2). The government raises the required revenue if

$$\sum_{i=1}^{n}(t_a a_i + t_b b_i) = R \tag{16.11}$$

Thus,

If the government imposes taxes on ale and bread at the rates t_a and t_b, respectively, the **competitive allocation** is a list $(a_1, b_1, a_2, b_2, \ldots, a_n, b_n)$ that satisfies (16.9) and (16.10) for every j. The government raises the required revenue R if (16.11) is satisfied.

Suppose that both goods are taxed at the same rate. The n conditions of the form (16.10) are equivalent to (16.2). Summing together the individual budget constraints (16.9), and then using (16.11) to eliminate the taxes, yields (16.1). Once again, every restriction imposed upon Pareto optimal allocations is also imposed on competitive allocations, so that the competitive allocation is Pareto optimal. *That is, there is no deadweight loss if the commodity tax rates are equal. Taxes imposed at the same rate on all commodities are equivalent to a lump-sum tax.*

If the taxes are not equal, the two equation systems impose different restrictions on the allocation. Specifically, the n conditions of the form (16.10) are inconsistent with (16.2). The competitive allocation does not match any of the Pareto optimal allocations, so the tax system generates a deadweight loss.

This deadweight loss arises because the tax system changes the relative prices of the two goods. If ale is taxed relatively heavily (as in Figure 16.2), each person chooses a commodity bundle such that his marginal rate of substitution is greater than k. There are gains from further trade in this situation because the price (measured in bread) that people are willing to pay for extra ale is greater than the resource cost of the extra ale. However, these trades do not occur because the price system, distorted by the taxes, does not accurately convey to the buyers the true cost of acquiring ale. A similar sort of situation occurs if bread is taxed relatively heavily.

16.1.2 Bad News

Governments are able to tax goods that are exchanged in organized markets only if there is a paper trail for the taxman to follow. This requirement limits the government's ability to tax either commodities or income. High tax rates would induce some people to trade in the black market, beyond the reach of government.

There is also one important good, leisure, that is not purchased in markets and is therefore inherently untaxable. The inability of governments to tax leisure has far-reaching consequences, for it implies that a lump-sum tax cannot be constructed by combining individual taxes.

Imagine an economy like the one described above, except that people divide their time between leisure and market work. Leisure, like ale and bread, yields positive but diminishing marginal utility. A decision to take an additional hour of leisure is also a decision to work an hour less, and to forgo the ale and bread that could have been purchased with that hour's wages. Each person allocates his time so that the utility yielded by the last hour of leisure is just equal to the utility of the ale and bread forgone.

Taxing ale and bread reduces the amount of these commodities that can be purchased by working an additional hour, causing people to substitute away from them and toward leisure. An appropriate tax imposed upon leisure would undo this effect (i.e., cause people to substitute away from leisure and toward ale and bread), restoring the lump sum nature of the tax system. But non-market activities cannot be taxed, so a lump-sum tax system cannot be constructed.

Governments can, of course, subsidize as well as tax; and a subsidy on market work has the same substitution effect as a tax on leisure. Can taxes and subsidies be combined to generate a system with no deadweight loss? Sandmo [57] has investigated, and rejected, this possibility. Sandmo's reasoning can be illustrated by slightly extending our model.

Let $\overline{h}$ be the number of hours available to each person for work and leisure, and let h_j be the number of hours that person j takes as leisure. A commodity bundle for person j is now a triplet (a_j, b_j, h_j), and an allocation lists each person's commodity bundle.

Let MRS_j^a and MRS_j^h be the amounts of bread that exactly compensate person j for the loss of one unit of ale and one hour of leisure, respectively. The conditions that describe a Pareto optimal allocation in the expanded economy are

$$\sum_{i=1}^{n} (ka_i + b_i) + R = \sum_{i=1}^{n} (\overline{h} - h_i) \tag{16.12}$$

$$MRS_j^a = k \qquad j = 1, \ldots, n \tag{16.13}$$

$$MRS_j^h = 1 \qquad j = 1, \ldots, n \tag{16.14}$$

The first condition is the analogue of (16.1): the right-hand side is the amount of work done in the economy, and the left-hand side is the amount of work that needs to be done to provide each person with his commodity bundle and the government with its required revenue. The next set of conditions states that the rate at which each person is willing to trade ale for bread is equal to the rate at which the economy is able to transform ale into bread. The final set of conditions states that the rate at which each person is willing to trade leisure for bread is equal to the rate at which the economy is able to trade leisure for bread. The latter rate is 1, because one unit of bread is produced with one hour of labour.

Now consider the competitive equilibrium. An equilibrium consists of a set of prices and an allocation. The market-clearing prices in this economy are the same as those in the simpler economy, so only the competitive allocation needs to be described. Each person chooses the number of hours of work that he will do, and then uses his wage income to purchase ale and bread. If the government subsidizes wage earnings at the rate s, person j's choice maximizes his utility subject to the budget constraint

$$p_a a_j + p_b b_j = (1 + s)(\overline{h} - h_j)$$

He works $\overline{h} - h_j$ hours and the subsidy-inclusive wage rate is $1 + s$, so the right-hand side of this equation is his total income. The left-hand side is his expenditures on ale and bread. The budget constraint states that all of his income is spent on ale and bread. Since the competitive prices are (16.7) and (16.8), the budget constraint can also be written as

$$(1 + t_a)ka_j + (1 + t_b)b_j = (1 + s)(\overline{h} - h_j) \tag{16.15}$$

Assume that person j's utility is an increasing and strictly concave function of his consumption of ale, bread, and leisure. Assume also that he prefers any commodity bundle containing some of all three goods to any commodity bundle that does not contain some of all three goods. He will choose a commodity bundle that has these characteristics:

$$MRS_j^a = \frac{p_a}{p_b}$$

$$MRS_j^h = \frac{(1 + s)}{p_b}$$

That is, his best attainable commodity bundle equates the rate at which he is *willing* to trade one commodity for another to the rate at which the price system *allows* him to trade one commodity for another. These conditions reduce to

$$MRS_j^a = \frac{(1 + t_a)k}{1 + t_b} \tag{16.16}$$

$$MRS_j^h = \frac{1 + s}{1 + t_b} \tag{16.17}$$

Since these two marginal rates of substitutions are functions of a_j, b_j, and h_j, person j's commodity bundle under competition is found by solving the three equation system consisting of (16.15), (16.16), and (16.17).

The net revenue of the government is the difference between the tax revenues and the cost of the subsidy:

$$R = \sum_{i=1}^{n} \left[t_a ka_i + t_b b_i - s(\overline{h} - h_i) \right] \tag{16.18}$$

Each term in this sum represents the difference between the amount of tax revenue paid by some person and the amount of the subsidy paid to that person. Thus,

> If the government taxes ale and bread at the rates t_a and t_b and subsidies wages at the rate s, the **competitive allocation** is described by a system of $3n$ equations. This system consists of equations (16.15), (16.16), and (16.17) for each person j. The government raises net revenues R if (16.18) is satisfied.

The usual procedure of matching equation systems shows that the competitive allocation is Pareto optimal if and only if t_a, t_b, and s are equal:

> If these rates are equal, the n conditions of the form (16.16) are the same as (16.13), and the n conditions of the form (16.17) are the same as (16.14). Summing over the n equations of the form (16.15), and using (16.18) to eliminate the tax rates, yields (16.12).

Unfortunately, the requirement that the tax and subsidy rates be equal implies that the government cannot raise any net revenue. If t is the common rate, (16.18) can be written as

$$R = \sum_{i=1}^{n} t\left[ka_i + b_i - (\overline{h} - h_i)\right] \tag{16.19}$$

while (16.15) reduces to

$$ka_j + b_j = \overline{h} - h_j$$

Substituting this condition into (16.19) show that the government's tax revenues are equal to the cost of its subsidy, so its net revenue is equal to zero. *That is, any tax/subsidy system under which the competitive allocation is Pareto optimal doesn't raise a dime.* There is no system of commodity taxes and subsidies that is lump sum, in the sense that it raises revenue without generating an efficiency loss.

Here are two final observations on this exercise:

- An equal tax (or subsidy) on all consumption goods and a flat rate income tax (or subsidy) are equivalent. They impose the same deadweight loss if they raise the same amount of revenue. Anything that can be done with an income tax or subsidy can be done without one, and for this reason, many academic discussions of ideal commodity tax structures assume that labour income is neither taxed nor subsidized.[8]
- Corlett and Hague [19] have argued that leisure can be indirectly taxed by taxing more heavily those goods that are intensively used during leisure time (e.g., beer, beaches, and baseball bats). The higher cost of pursuing leisure activities would induce substitution away from leisure and undo some of the deadweight loss associated with commodity taxation. However, this kind of taxation mimics a tax on leisure imperfectly, so some deadweight loss would always remain.

16.2 THE OPTIMAL SIZE OF GOVERNMENT

Government spending can increase social welfare, but the government must raise revenue through taxes before it can spend it. The social benefit of government spending is at least partially offset by the social cost of raising revenue, which includes both the taxpayers' loss of income and the deadweight loss of the tax system. How far should the government push its spending, and how would a more efficient tax system affect this decision?

[8] Income taxation becomes critically important once differences in earning potential are recognized. Although flat rate income taxes would still have no edge over commodity taxes, variable rate income taxes (in which the tax rate varies with income) can have important efficiency effects in this environment.

The social cost of raising revenue, SC, includes the taxpayers' loss of income and the deadweight loss induced by the tax system:

$$SC = R + DWL$$

Here, R is the revenue raised by the government and DWL is the deadweight loss of the tax system. The **social marginal cost of raising revenue,** SMC, is the increase in social cost when revenue rises by one dollar:

$$SMC \equiv \frac{dSC}{dR} = 1 + \frac{dDWL}{dR}$$

The deadweight loss of taxation generally increases with the government's revenue.[9] Indeed, the deadweight loss associated with collecting another dollar of revenue generally rises as revenue rises.[10] That is,

$$\frac{dDWL}{dR} > 0, \quad \frac{d^2 DWL}{dR^2} > 0$$

The relationship between the social marginal cost of raising revenue and the amount of revenue raised is shown in Figure 16.3.

Also shown in this figure is the **social marginal benefit of spending revenue,** SMB, which is the social benefit of an additional dollar of government spending. This dollar might be spent on public goods, or on the government's regulatory activities, or even on private goods such as health care. The social marginal benefit falls as revenue rises if the government first undertakes the programs which yield the largest social benefits for each dollar spent, and then moves on to programs with successively smaller benefits.

The net social benefits from government action are maximized when revenues and spending are extended until SMB and SMC are equal. Since the deadweight loss associated with the marginal unit of revenue can be quite substantial, the optimal level of spending might fall well short of the point at which a dollar spent on government programs yields a dollar of social benefits (that is, at which SMB is equal to 1).

Reducing the inefficiencies of the tax system shifts the SMC curve downward. This change restores some of the lost surplus at any given level of expenditures. It also raises the optimal level of government expenditure, generating further net benefits for society.

---

[9] An obvious exception is the imposition of a tax on a good which generates a negative externality. The quantity exchanged is too great (i.e., the marginal social costs exceed the marginal social benefits) in the absence of the tax. The tax limits the quantity exchanged, so that welfare initially rises with the government's revenues.

[10] The net social benefit of the marginal trade (measured by the vertical distance between the demand and supply curves at the equilibrium quantity) rises with the tax. People forgo the marginal trades as the tax rises, and in doing so, they give up trades with increasingly large social benefits. This observation accounts for the propensity for the deadweight loss of raising another dollar of revenue to rise as total revenue rises.

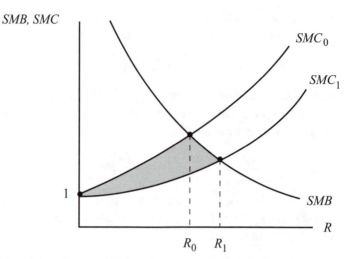

Figure 16.3: The Effects of a More Efficient Tax System. Improved efficiency shifts the SMC curve downward. The optimal size of the government rises, and the net social benefits of the government's programs rise by an amount equal to the shaded area.

16.3 CONCLUSIONS

A system of taxes causes people to change their behaviour. These changes can be separated into income effects and substitution effects. The income effects occur because the government is taking away some of their purchasing power, and the substitution effects arise because people try to limit their exposure to the taxes. It is the latter effects that give rise to the deadweight loss of taxation.

QUESTIONS

1. Robinson Crusoe has been shipwrecked on the shores of an uninhabited island. His only source of food is coconuts, and he finds that he can collect 20 coconuts in an hour. His utility depends only upon the number of coconuts that he consumes each month, c, and the number of hours that he spends collecting coconuts during that month, h.

$$U = c - h^2$$

a) What is Robinson's budget constraint? What pair (c, h) maximizes Robinson's utility in the presence of this constraint? What is Robinson's maximal utility?

b) During his eighth year on the island, Robinson's isolation is broken when a British frigate drops anchor off the coast of the island. Robinson expects to be rescued, but the captain simply declares the island to be a British colony and departs. However, every month thereafter, the frigate stops to collect 32 coconuts from Robinson as his share of the administration costs of the British empire. What is Robinson's new budget constraint? What is his best attainable pair (c, h)? What is his utility?

c) During Robinson's tenth year on the island, the fixed levy of 32 coconuts is replaced with an income tax. The frigate now carries away one-fifth of all the coconuts collected by Robinson. What is Robinson's budget constraint? What is his best attainable commodity bundle, and what is his utility? How much tax does Robinson pay? How many coconuts would have to be given to him to make him as well off as he was under the fixed charge? What is the welfare cost of the income tax, measured in coconuts?

2. Andy is a pensioner who spends exactly $27 on groceries each week. It's not much, so it is fortunate that Andy is a man of humble tastes: he consumes only ale and bread. His utility function is

$$U = a^{1/3} b^{2/3}$$

where a is his weekly consumption of ale in pints and b is his weekly consumption of bread in loaves. The baker sells a loaf of bread for a $1, and the brewer sells a pint of ale for $1.

a) What is Andy's budget constraint, and what is his best attainable commodity bundle?

b) Assume that the government imposes a tax of $3 per week on Andy. What is his budget constraint, and what is his best attainable commodity bundle?

c) Assume that the government abandons the non-contingent tax, and instead imposes a tax of $(1/8)$ on each pint of ale and each loaf of bread purchased. The baker and the brewer are selling their goods at marginal cost, so they do not change the amount that they are willing to accept for their goods. What is Andy's best attainable commodity bundle? How much does he pay in taxes? Explain why Andy is exactly as well off under the tax in c) as he was under the tax in b).

d) Now imagine that the only tax is $(1/5)$ on each loaf of bread purchased. What is Andy's best attainable commodity bundle? How much does he pay in taxes?

e) Finally, imagine that the only tax is $(1/2)$ on each pint of ale purchased. What is Andy's best attainable commodity bundle? How much does he pay in taxes?

f) Show numerically that Andy is worse off under the tax in d) than under the tax in c), and that he worse off under the tax in e) than under the tax in d).

17

The Welfare Cost of Tax Interactions

Society's net benefit from trade in any good is maximized when the good's social marginal benefit is equal to its social marginal cost. This outcome is achieved in a market economy if these two conditions hold:

- The private marginal benefit of consuming each good is equal to its social marginal benefit, and the private marginal cost of producing each good is equal to its social marginal cost.
- Production and trade continue until private marginal benefit and private marginal cost have been equalized.

We have already examined a number of reasons why these conditions might be violated in some markets. The first condition is violated if there are public goods, externalities, or taxes; and the second condition is violated if the good is produced and sold by a monopolist or a monopolistic competitor.

If marginal social benefit and marginal social cost are not equalized in some market, economists say that the market is distorted. The gap between marginal social benefit and marginal social cost is called the **market distortion.** It was shown in Chapter 5 that if only one market is distorted, the welfare cost of that distortion can be discovered by examining only the distorted market. It was also shown that the welfare cost of a new distortion in an already distorted economy is more difficult to measure, because the new distortion can change the welfare cost of the existing distortions.

Taxation is one area in which this kind of interaction between distortions is particularly important, and tax interactions are the focus of this chapter. A model in which two goods are produced and consumed is described. It is imagined that a tax is imposed first on one good and then on both goods. The welfare cost of each tax is calculated.[1]

---

[1] For a more exact and more general discussion of welfare cost in a general equilibrium context, see Boadway and Bruce [11].

17.1 A ROBINSON CRUSOE ECONOMY

Imagine an economy in which there are two goods, ale and bread, and one factor of production, labour. Each good is produced by one firm, and there is just one person living in the economy. That person – Robinson Crusoe – is the sole seller of labour and the sole owner of the two firms. His income is the sum of his wage earnings and a transfer from the government (described below).[2] He uses his income to purchase units of the two commodities, and indeed, he is the only purchaser of these commodities.

Robinson's utility function and the firms' production functions are assumed to take very simple forms – forms that give interesting results with the least fuss. Robinson's utility function is

$$U = a + 2\sqrt{2b}$$

where a and b are Robinson's consumption of ale (measured in pints) and bread (measured in loaves), respectively. This form of the utility function implies that the marginal utility of ale is a positive constant, while the marginal utility of bread is positive but declining. As for production, each pint of ale and each loaf of bread is produced with one hour of labour and no other inputs. The labour is provided only by Robinson, who is able to do $\overline{L}$ hours of work. It follows that the production possibility frontier for this economy consists of all of the pairs (a, b) that satisfy the equation

$$a + b = \overline{L} \tag{17.1}$$

It is assumed henceforth that $\overline{L}$ is greater than or equal to eight.

17.2 PARETO OPTIMALITY

A commodity bundle is Pareto optimal if it makes Robinson as well off as possible.[3] Graphically, the Pareto optimal commodity bundle is characterized by a tangency between one of Robinson's indifference curves and the production possibility frontier (see Figure 17.1). The slopes of the indifference curve and the production possibility frontier are, of course, equal at the point of tangency. This tangency can be described by the condition

$$MRS = MRT$$

---

[2] He would also receive as income the profits of the two firms, if there were any, but the assumptions set out below ensure that the firms' profits are equal to zero.

[3] Formally, we should be looking for a Pareto optimal allocation, where an allocation is a list showing the amount of each good consumed by Robinson and the amount of labour used in each industry. Since the allocation of labour can be inferred from Robinson's commodity bundle (one unit of labour is needed to produce one unit of each good), the search for a Pareto optimal allocation reduces to the search for the best possible commodity bundle.

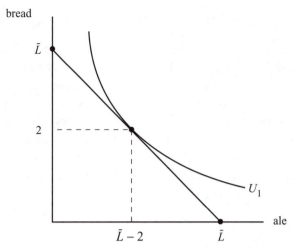

Figure 17.1: The Efficient Allocation. Robinson's attainable commodity bundles lie on the production possibility frontier. The best of these bundles is characterized by a tangency between one of his indifference curves and the frontier.

where

- MRS is Robinson's marginal rate of substitution, defined as the amount of bread required to exactly compensate him for the loss of one pint of ale. It is equal to the negative of the slope of the indifference curve.
- MRT is the marginal rate of transformation, defined as the amount of additional bread that can be produced if ale production is reduced by one pint. It is equal to the negative of the slope of the production possibility frontier.

Evaluating both sides of the tangency condition gives

$$\sqrt{\frac{2}{b}} = 1 \tag{17.2}$$

Since the Pareto optimal commodity bundle lies on the production possibility frontier and satisfies the tangency condition, it is the solution to equations (17.1) and (17.2). The Pareto optimal bundle contains $\bar{L} - 2$ pints of ale and 2 loaves of bread.

17.3 COMPETITIVE EQUILIBRIUM

Our purpose in this section is to characterize competitive equilibrium under any system of commodity taxes, so that the impact of the taxes on Robinson's welfare can be studied.

Any tax will have both an income effect and a substitution effect, but the deadweight loss of the tax is caused only by the substitution effect. That deadweight loss can only be measured if the income effect can be separated from the substitution effect. The easiest way to isolate the substitution effect is to assume that the government simultaneously taxes Robinson and transfers the tax revenue back to him as a lump sum. This procedure eliminates (or **impounds**) the income effect, so that only the substitution effect remains. Any loss of surplus, or any fall in Robinson's utility, is then attributable to the distortionary effects of the tax.

If the tax revenues are transferred back to Robinson, a competitive equilibrium has these properties:

- Robinson, knowing the market prices and his transfer (which might be zero), offers for sale the quantity of labour and demands the quantities of ale and bread that maximize his utility.
- The ale firm, having observed the market prices, demands labour so that it can produce and offer for sale the profit-maximizing quantity of ale. The bread firm, having observed the market prices, demands labour so that it can produce and offer for sale the profit-maximizing quantity of bread.
- These choices clear the markets. Specifically, the quantities of ale and bread demanded by Robinson are equal to the quantities that the firms offer for sale, and the sum of the firms' demands for labour is equal to the quantity of labour that Robinson offers for sale.

Let's examine these requirements in turn.

17.3.1 Robinson's Choices

Robinson offers for sale a quantity of labour L and demands a quantity of ale a and a quantity of bread b. His choices are constrained by his budget constraint

$$p_a a + p_b b = wL + R$$

and by the inequality

$$L \le \overline{L}$$

Here, p_a and p_b are the dollar prices of ale and bread, w is the hourly wage rate (also measured in dollars), and R is a cash transfer received from the government. The budget constraint states that his expenditures on ale and bread are equal to his income, which is the sum of his wage earnings and his government transfer. The inequality simply states that Robinson cannot offer for sale more labour than he has.

Robinson chooses the best of the triplets (a, b, L) that satisfy these constraints. His supply of labour is easy to deduce. The more labour that Robinson sells, the greater will be his income and the greater will be his consumption of ale and bread. He will therefore offer for sale the maximum quantity of labour

$$L^\circ = \overline{L}$$

His demands for ale and bread depend upon income. Specifically, he will buy only bread if he cannot afford to buy more than b° loaves of bread, where

$$b^\circ = 2 \left(\frac{p_a}{p_b} \right)^2 \tag{17.3}$$

If he can afford to buy b° loaves of bread, he will buy exactly this much bread, and spend the rest of his income on ale. His ale consumption will then be

$$a^\circ = \frac{Y}{p_a} - 2\left(\frac{p_a}{p_b}\right) \tag{17.4}$$

Here, Y is Robinson's income:

$$Y \equiv wL^\circ + R$$

To understand Robinson's demands for ale and bread, consider the consequences of spending one more dollar on each good. A dollar spent on ale buys $1/p_a$ pints of ale, each of which increases Robinson's utility by ale's marginal utility, MU_a. Thus, a dollar spent on ale increases Robinson's utility by MU_a/p_a. Likewise, a dollar spent on bread raises Robinson's utility by MU_b/p_b. The marginal utilities correspond to the partial derivatives of the utility function, so

$$\frac{MU_a}{p_a} = \frac{1}{p_a}$$

$$\frac{MU_b}{p_b} = \frac{\sqrt{2/b}}{p_b}$$

The utility gained by spending a dollar on ale is constant. The utility gained by spending a dollar on bread falls as bread consumption rises, and it is equal to the utility gained by spending a dollar on ale when Robinson is consuming b° loaves of bread.

Suppose that Robinson initially chooses to purchase fewer than b° loaves of bread. If he spends a dollar more on bread and a dollar less on ale (so that his total expenditure continues to be equal to his income Y), the increase in his utility is

$$\frac{\sqrt{2/b}}{p_b} - \frac{1}{p_a}$$

which is positive. That is, this adjustment makes Robinson better off. The strategy of spending more of his income on bread and less of his income on ale would continue to raise his utility until either his bread consumption reaches b°, or his entire income is spent on bread. Similarly, if Robinson initially chooses to purchase more than b° loaves of bread, he could raise his utility by spending more of his income on ale and less on bread. Continuing to reallocate his income in this fashion would raise his utility so long as his bread consumption has not fallen to b°. Once his bread consumption reaches b°, no reallocation of his expenditure will raise his utility. Thus, Robinson makes himself as well off as possible by purchasing b° loaves of bread if he can afford to do so, and purchasing only bread if he cannot.

The assumption that $\overline{L}$ is greater than or equal to eight ensures that, in the absence of taxes and in each of the tax regimes examined below, Robinson will demand a° pints of ale and b° loaves of bread.

Equations (17.3) and (17.4) show that the quantity of each good demanded by Robinson falls as its own price rises. Furthermore, an increase in the price of either good causes Robinson to demand more of the other good.

17.3.2 The Firms' Choices

The ale firm can produce a pint of ale with an hour's labour. If the payment that it receives for a pint of ale is greater than the wage rate w, the firm earns a profit on every pint of ale that it sells. It will therefore demand an arbitrarily large amount of labour, so that it can produce and offer for sale an arbitrarily large amount of ale. If the payment is less than the wage rate, the firm incurs a loss on every pint of ale that it sells. It will avoid these losses by demanding no labour and offering no ale for sale. Finally, if the payment is equal to the wage rate, the firm's profits are equal to zero at every level of output. It does not care how many pints of ale it offers for sale, but it must demand an hour of labour for every pint of ale that it does offer for sale.

The bread firm maximizes its profits by behaving in the same way. If the payment that it receives for a loaf of bread is greater than the wage rate, it will offer for sale an unlimited quantity of bread and demand an unlimited quantity of labour. If the payment is less than the wage rate, it will offer for sale no bread and demand no labour. If the payment and the wage rate are equal, the firm does not care how much bread it offers for sale, but it must demand an hour of labour for each unit that it does offer for sale.

17.3.3 Market-Clearing

The economy is in a competitive equilibrium if the market prices are such that the choices made by Robinson and the firms are consistent, in the sense that Robinson demands precisely the quantities of ale and bread that the firms offer for sale, and the firms demand precisely the quantity of labour that Robinson offers for sale. What configuration of prices has this property?

There is one bit of housekeeping to deal with before we address this question. Competitive equilibrium determines relative prices but not dollar prices. Consequently, we must adopt one of two procedures. The first is to pick one good to be the numeraire, and to express all of the other prices in units of that good. The second is to arbitrarily set one of the dollar prices, and then to find the dollar prices of the remaining goods that would be consistent with that choice (in the sense that they give the correct relative prices). Let's adopt the latter option by fixing the wage rate at $\overline{w}$ dollars.

The markets will clear only if the ale firm receives $\overline{w}$ dollars for each pint of ale that it sells and the bread firm receives $\overline{w}$ dollars for each loaf of bread that it sells.

If a firm received more than $\overline{w}$ dollars for a unit of its good, it would want to produce and sell an arbitrarily large amount of that good. However, producing an arbitrarily large amount of a good requires an arbitrarily large amount of labour, and Robinson can only supply $\overline{L}$ hours of labour. There would be an excess demand for labour. If a firm received less than $\overline{w}$ dollars for a unit of its good, it would incur a loss on every unit of the good that it sold. It would choose not to offer for sale any units of its good. However, Robinson demands a positive amount of each good,[4] so there would be an excess demand for any good that is not produced. Thus, markets do not clear if either firm receives anything other than $\overline{w}$ dollars for each unit of its good.

The prices received by the firms are fixed, but the prices paid by Robinson depend upon the taxes imposed by the government. If t_a and t_b are the rates at which ale and bread are taxed, the prices paid by Robinson are

$$p_a = (1 + t_a)\overline{w} \tag{17.5}$$

$$p_b = (1 + t_b)\overline{w} \tag{17.6}$$

When the firms receive $\overline{w}$ dollars for each unit of goods that they sell, they are indifferent to the quantities of ale and bread that they sell, and therefore indifferent as to the quantity of labour that they buy. The labour market will clear when the two firms demand exactly the quantity of labour that Robinson wants to sell, which is $\overline{L}$. Since each firm uses one hour of labour to produce a unit of its own good, the combination of goods that will be produced when the labour market clears satisfies (17.1). The goods markets are also clearing if the combination of goods produced is the one that Robinson actually wants – that is, if it is $(a°, b°)$.

17.3.4 Summary

These results permit a much more concrete description of competitive equilibrium:

Assume that the government taxes ale and bread at the rates t_a and t_b, and that the government transfers the revenue back to Robinson as a cash transfer R. Let L_a and L_b be the quantities of labour used by the ale and bread firms, and let a and b be the quantities of ale and bread that they produce. If the wage rate is fixed at $\overline{w}$, a **competitive equilibrium** is an allocation (a, b, L_a, L_b) and a set of tax-inclusive prices (p_a, p_b) with these characteristics:

1) The price received by the firms for a unit of ale or bread is equal to the wage rate $\overline{w}$. The prices paid by Robinson for units of these commodities are given by (17.5) and (17.6).
2) Robinson sells all of his labour, and the firms acquire all of the labour that they need. That is,

$$L_a = a$$

$$L_b = b$$

$$L_a + L_b = \overline{L}$$

---

[4] Remember that we have assumed that $\overline{L}$ is large enough that $a°$ is positive.

These conditions imply that the pair (a, b) lies on the production possibility frontier (17.1).

3) The commodity bundle (a, b) is Robinson's best attainable commodity bundle. It is characterized by a tangency between one of his indifference curves and the budget constraint that he faces when he sells all of his labour. Algebraically, it is characterized by (17.3) and (17.4), with Y equal to $\overline{w}\overline{L} + R$.

These requirements can be used to find Robinson's commodity bundle under any set of taxes. A key determinant of that commodity bundle is the position of Robinson's budget constraint when he sells all of his labour and buys ale and bread at the equilibrium prices.

Equilibrium without Taxation

If there are no taxes (and therefore no transfer), Robinson's budget constraint coincides with the production possibility frontier. Consequently, Robinson's best attainable commodity bundle is also the Pareto optimal commodity bundle. This bundle contains $\overline{L} - 2$ pints of ale and 2 loaves of bread.

Equilibrium with Taxation

The budget constraint changes in two ways when taxes are imposed:

- Its slope is $-p_a/p_b$, or equivalently, $-(1 + t_a)/(1 + t_b)$. If the tax on ale is greater than the tax on bread, the budget constraint will be steeper than the production possibility frontier; and if the tax on bread is greater than the tax on ale, the budget constraint will be flatter than the production possibility frontier.
- Its distance from the origin is determined by Robinson's income, which is the sum of his wage income and his transfer. Robinson's wage income is always the same, but the size of the transfer depends upon the tax rates.

In a competitive equilibrium, the tangency between one of Robinson's indifference curves and this budget constraint lies on the production possibility frontier, as shown in Figure 17.2.

Robinson's best attainable commodity bundle is characterized by (17.3) and (17.4). Since this bundle lies on the production possibility frontier, his equilibrium income can be found by substituting (17.3) and (17.4) into (17.1):

$$Y = p_a \left[\overline{L} + 2 \left(\frac{p_a}{p_b} \right) - 2 \left(\frac{p_a}{p_b} \right)^2 \right] \tag{17.7}$$

Substituting this income back into (17.3) and (17.4) gives Robinson's commodity bundle. It is easy to verify that his chosen commodity bundle contains fewer than $\overline{L} - 2$ pints of ale and more than two loaves of bread if p_a is greater than p_b, and that it contains more than $\overline{L} - 2$ pints of ale and less than two loaves of bread if p_a is less than p_b.

Table 17.1 shows three competitive equilibria in which $\overline{w}$ is one dollar and $\overline{L}$ is twelve hours. When neither good is taxed, there is no transfer and Robinson's income

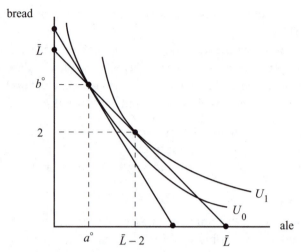

Figure 17.2: Equilibrium in the Presence of Commodity Taxes. Here, the tax rate on ale is greater than the tax rate on bread. Robinson is discouraged from buying ale by its relatively high price, so the new equilibrium is farther to the left along the production possibility frontier. His utility falls from U_1 to U_0.

is equal to the market value of his labour, $12. When a 100% tax is imposed on ale, the transfer raises Robinson's income from $12 to $16. With this income and the new set of prices, Robinson chooses to purchase 4 pints of ale and 8 loaves of bread. The 100% tax on ale therefore raises $4 of revenue for the government, which is exactly the amount of the transfer. Similarly, when a 100% tax is subsequently imposed on bread, the transfer raises Robinson's income from $12 to $24. Robinson uses this income to purchase 10 pints of ale and 2 loaves of bread, so that the two taxes raise $12 of revenue, which is the amount of the transfer.

Robinson consumes the Pareto optimal commodity bundle when there are no taxes. The imposition of a 100% tax on ale makes ale relatively expensive, causing Robinson to substitute away from it and reducing his utility. The subsequent imposition of a 100% tax on bread restores the original relative prices and returns Robinson to his original utility level. *The welfare costs of these taxes must mirror the changes in Robinson's utility.* The welfare cost of the ale tax must be positive, and the welfare cost of the bread tax imposed in the presence of the ale tax must be negative. The manner in which these welfare costs are calculated is the subject of the remainder of this chapter.

Table 17.1: Equilibria under Alternative Tax Regimes

Equilibrium ($w = 1, \bar{L} = 12$)	p_a	p_b	Y	a°	b°	U
Neither good is taxed	1	1	12	10	2	14
Ale is taxed	2	1	16	4	8	12
Both goods are taxed	2	2	24	10	2	14

17.4 WELFARE COST CALCULATIONS

The welfare cost of a commodity tax can be calculated from information about the demand and supply schedules of the taxed commodity if one of these conditions holds in every other market:

1) There is no distortion.
2) The quantity of goods exchanged is not affected by the imposition of the tax.

If there are some markets for which neither of these conditions is satisfied, the calculation of the welfare cost is more elaborate. It will include several components, one for the market in which the tax is imposed, and one for each market in which neither condition is satisfied.

In the present case, there are two welfare costs to be calculated: one for the ale tax alone, and one for the bread tax imposed in the presence of the ale tax. Conditions 1) and 2) determine the number of components in each welfare cost calculation.

- Suppose that only the ale tax is imposed. Since neither the bread market nor the labour market is distorted, at least one of the two conditions holds in each of the remaining markets. The welfare cost of the first tax therefore includes only one component.
- Now suppose that a tax is also imposed upon bread. Since there is still no distortion in the labour market, the welfare cost of the bread tax will not include a labour market component. However, there is a distortion in the ale market, namely the pre-existing ale tax. Furthermore, as the tax-inclusive price of bread rises, Robinson's demand curve for ale shifts to the right, and the quantity of ale that he consumes rises. Thus, the ale market satisfies neither condition 1) nor condition 2). The welfare cost of the bread tax will therefore include an ale market component as well as a bread market component.

There is one other wrinkle to be worked into our welfare cost calculations. The demand curve that is relevant to these calculations is not the ordinary **Marshallian demand curve,** which shows the relationship between the quantity of a good demanded and the good's own price when income and all other prices are held constant. An exact welfare cost calculation would actually be based upon the **general equilibrium (GE) demand curve.** A change in any good's price induces a series of adjustments throughout the economy. Incomes change, and if the production possibility frontier is not linear, the prices of other goods change. The GE demand curve shows how the quantity of a good demanded changes with the good's own price when the effect (on the quantity demanded) of the induced changes in incomes and other prices are included.

In the present case, the production possibility frontier is linear, so there are no induced changes in prices. The only induced change is to income, and (17.7) shows the way in which income is affected by the tax-inclusive prices. Substituting (17.7) into the Marshallian demand function for ale gives the GE demand function for ale:

$$a_{GE} = \overline{L} - 2\left(\frac{p_a}{p_b}\right)^2$$

Since Robinson's demand for bread is independent of his income, his GE demand function is the same as his Marshallian demand function:

$$b_{GE} = 2\left(\frac{p_a}{p_b}\right)^2$$

17.4.1 The Welfare Cost of the Ale Tax

The tax on ale raises the price of ale from \$1 to \$2. Transferring the tax revenue back to Robinson causes his income to rise from \$12 to \$16. Think of these changes in terms of what is happening in each market. The Marshallian demand curve for bread shifts to the right (because p_a rises) but the price of bread remains the same. The Marshallian demand curve for ale shifts to the right (because Y rises) and the price of ale rises. We are interested in the welfare implications of these changes.

Imagine that the tax is imposed in very small steps, so that the price of ale slowly rises from \$1 to \$2. These price increases drive the economy from one short-lived equilibrium to another; and with each price increase, Robinson cuts back on his consumption of ale and increases his consumption of bread. The relationship between Robinson's consumption of ale and the price of ale, as the economy moves from one equilibrium to another, is given by the GE demand curve. It differs from the Marshallian demand curve only in that income is not fixed but rises with the price of ale. Since the price of bread is \$1, the GE demand curve for ale is

$$a_{GE} = 12 - 2(p_a)^2$$

The GE demand curve and the initial and final Marshallian demand curves are shown in the top half of Figure 17.3.

The height of the GE demand curve represents the value placed upon each arbitrarily small unit of ale *at the time that it was given up*. No single Marshallian demand curve has this property. The height of the Marshallian demand curve indicates the value that would be placed upon each unit of ale *if* income remained fixed. However, this condition is never satisfied.[5] The height of the Marshallian demand curve can only indicate the value placed upon the *marginal* unit of ale.

---

[5] Movements along each Marshallian demand curve occur because the good's price is changing, but each price change drives the economy to a new equilibrium with a different income. Thus, movements along the demand curve and shifts of the demand curve are inextricably linked.

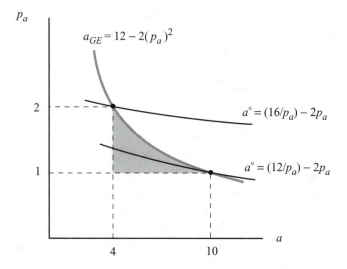

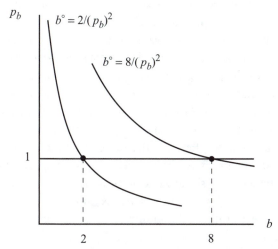

Figure 17.3: The Welfare Cost of the Ale Tax. The tax raises the price of ale from 1 to 2, causing Robinson's consumption of ale to fall. The welfare cost of the tax is the shaded area under Robinson's general equilibrium demand curve for ale.

The tax causes society to give up units of ale, and the welfare cost of the tax is the net social value of the units of ale given up. It can be calculated using either of the rules set out in Section 5.1:

The height of the GE demand curve represents the value placed on each unit of ale and the height of the marginal cost curve represents the value of the resources used to produce it. The difference between these heights is therefore the net value to society of an additional unit of ale. The net value of all of the units given up is represented by the area below the GE demand curve and above the marginal cost curve, between the old and new quantities.

Thus, the welfare cost of the ale tax is the shaded region in the top half of Figure 17.3. The area of the shaded region is readily calculated – it is $(10/3)$. That is, the misallocation of resources caused by the ale tax reduces Robinson's welfare by as much as an outright loss of $(10/3)$.

Of course, the consumption of bread rises as the consumption of ale falls. Why is there no net social benefit from the additional bread consumption? Here are two answers (which are really one answer in two guises):

- As the price of ale slowly rises from $1 to $2, the Marshallian demand curve for bread shifts to the right. The intersection of the current demand curve with the marginal cost line always determines the current equilibrium quantity of bread. (See the bottom half of Figure 17.3.) Each increase in the price of ale raises the quantity of bread by a small amount, but what is the net social benefit of this additional bread? The height of the current Marshallian demand curve gives the value of the marginal unit of bread, and the height of the marginal cost curve gives the value of the resources used up in its production – and these heights are equal. Each of the additional units of bread has *no* net social value.
- The marginal cost of ale is the market value of the resources needed to produce one more unit of ale. Competition ensures that the market value of these resources is equal to the value of the goods that could be produced with them if they are employed elsewhere. That is, the marginal cost of ale is the value of the bread that would have to be given up to produce one more unit of ale. It follows that the vertical distance between the GE demand curve and the marginal cost curve (in the top half of Figure 17.3) is the difference between the value of a unit of ale and the value of the bread that could be produced in its place. The welfare cost of the ale tax is then the difference between the social value of the ale given up and the social value of the bread that is produced in its place. There is no need to consider the bread market directly because the value of the additional bread has already been taken into consideration.

Note that these arguments can only be made because there is no distortion in the bread market.

17.4.2 The Welfare Cost of the Bread Tax

The welfare cost of the bread tax has both a bread market component and an ale market component. The bread market component is calculated in much the same way as the welfare cost of the ale tax.

The new equilibrium price of bread is $2. Suppose, as before, that the tax is imposed in very small increments, so that the price of bread rises from $1 to $2 in very small steps. Each increase in the price of bread will steer the economy to another temporary equilibrium. At each of these equilibria, the price of ale is 2 and income is determined by (17.7). The GE demand curve for bread gives the quantity of bread demanded in the

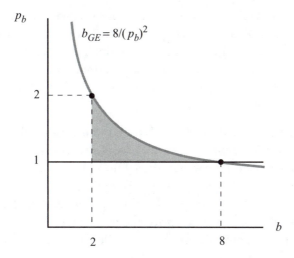

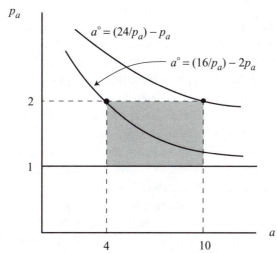

Figure 17.4: The Welfare Cost of a Bread Tax Imposed in the Presence of an Ale Tax. The welfare cost of the bread tax has two components: a positive component represented by the shaded area in the upper panel, and a negative component represented by the shaded area in the lower panel.

equilibrium associated with each price of bread:

$$b_{GE} = \frac{8}{(p_b)^2}$$

The GE demand curve (which happens to be the same as the Marshallian demand curve) is shown in the top half of Figure 17.4.

The net benefit to society of another unit of bread is equal to the vertical distance between the GE demand curve and the marginal cost curve. The bread market component is therefore equal to the area of the shaded region in the top half of Figure 17.4.

Now consider the ale market component. Again imagine that the price of bread rises slowly from \$1 to \$2, steering the economy from one equilibrium to another until the final equilibrium is reached. Income rises with each increase in the price of bread. The Marshallian demand curve for ale shifts slowly to the right. The initial and final Marshallian demand curves are shown in the bottom half of Figure 17.4.

As the price of bread rises, so does ale consumption, and each increase in ale consumption carries with it *positive* net social benefits. The ale market component of the bread tax is the value of these benefits:

> In each of the equilibria through which the economy passes, the social benefit of the marginal unit of ale is given by the price of ale, because this is the amount that was willingly paid for each additional unit of ale. The social cost of the marginal unit of ale is the marginal cost. Since the price is fixed at $2 and the marginal cost is fixed at $1, the net social benefit of additional units of ale is always $1, the difference between price and marginal cost. The value of all of the additional ale is simply the net social benefit of each unit multiplied by the number of additional units.

Since the bread tax has a beneficial impact on the ale market, the ale market component of the welfare cost of the bread tax is *negative*.

The welfare cost of the bread tax is the sum of the two components. Since the bread market component is positive and the ale market component is negative, the welfare cost of the bread tax is the area of the shaded region in the top half of Figure 17.4, less the area of the shaded region in the bottom half. A cursory inspection of the figure shows that the benefit is larger than the cost, so that the second tax actually raises welfare. For the parameter values used in these examples, the welfare gain is $4. That is, the imposition of the bread tax reallocates resources in a manner that raises Robinson's welfare as much as would an additional $4 of income.

There would seem to be a contradiction here. The imposition of the ale tax reduces Robinson's utility, and the subsequent imposition of the bread tax returns Robinson's utility to its original level. Yet, the welfare cost of the ale tax, $(10/3), is smaller than the welfare gain of the bread tax, $4. How can this be?

The welfare cost of the ale tax is the amount of money that would compensate Robinson for the resource misallocation created by the tax, if he could use the money to buy goods at the prevailing market prices.[6] But Robinson is already buying as much bread as he wants, so any additional income would be spent only on ale. Consequently, the welfare cost is the amount of money that would buy Robinson enough ale to compensate him for the resource misallocation. The required compensation is two pints of ale. This compensation is being given to him in small amounts as the price of ale rises slowly from $1 to $2. If he were buying ale only at the lower price, the required compensation would be $2, and if he were buying ale only at the higher price, the required compensation would be $4. But he is buying ale at all the prices between $1 and $2, so the required compensation turns out to be $(10/3).

---

[6] He cannot actually do so, because he is already buying all of the goods that the economy produces. Nevertheless, we can imagine what Robinson would do if he could do it.

Similarly, the welfare gain of the bread tax is the amount of income which, if lost, would undo the increase in welfare generated by the imposition of that tax. Since Robinson already has as much bread as he wants, all of this income would have been spent on ale. The loss of two pints of ale would undo Robinson's welfare gain, and since the price of a pint of ale is now fixed at $2, the equivalent loss of income is $4.

In short, the welfare cost of the ale tax is two pints of ale, and so is the welfare gain associated with the bread tax, but the dollar value of these two pints of ale depends upon the price or prices at which they were bought.

17.5 CONCLUSIONS

If there is more than one distortion in the economy, removing just one distortion could either increase or decrease welfare. For example, in the model developed in this chapter, eliminating the ale tax would raise welfare if there were no bread tax. With the bread tax in place, however, eliminating the ale tax would reduce welfare. This observation has important policy implications, some of which are examined in the next chapter.

QUESTIONS

John Henry provides all of the labour in an economy, selling each month 150 hours of labour to the ale and bread industries. One hour of his labour will produce a loaf of bread, and two hours will produce a pint of ale. John's wage is $1 per hour, and the ale and bread industries are competitive, so the tax-exclusive prices of a pint of ale and a loaf of bread are $2 and $1, respectively. He spends his entire income on two commodities, ale and bread. His utility function is

$$U = a^{1/3}b^{2/3}$$

where a and b are his monthly consumption of ale (measured in pints) and bread (measured in loaves).

a) Let p_a and p_b be the tax-inclusive prices of ale and bread, and let Y be his monthly income. Find his Marshallian demands for ale and bread.

b) Find the economy's production possibility frontier. Show that when John's only source of income is his wage earnings and there are no taxes on ale and bread, John purchases all of the economy's output.

c) A tax on ale raises p_a above $2, and a tax on bread raises p_b above $1. Assume that, whenever taxes are imposed, the government transfers money to John so that he can continue buying all of the economy's output. Find John's income (wage earnings plus government transfer) under any price pair (p_a, p_b). Show that the government transfer is always equal to the government's tax revenue.

d) Find the GE demand curve for ale when p_b is equal to one. Find the GE demand curve for bread when p_a is equal to two.

18

The Theory of the Second Best

The **theory of the second best**[1] states that if *all* of the distortions in the economy cannot be eliminated, all bets are off. Eliminating or reducing another distortion might raise welfare, but can just as easily reduce welfare. For example, Samuelson [55] recognized that the optimal quantity of a public good would not be characterized by the Samuelson condition if the public good were financed through distortionary taxation. This condition assumes that expanded provision of public goods is costly to consumers *only* in that it requires scarce resources to be transferred from the production of other goods. However, if the production of public goods is financed through distortionary taxation, providing more public goods is also costly because it increases the amount of revenue that the government must raise, and hence increases the deadweight loss of the tax system. The optimal quantity of a public good when taxes are distortionary is generally (but not always) smaller than that dictated by the Samuelson condition.

This chapter looks at two important illustrations of the theory of the second best: the design of the tax system, and the pricing of goods produced by a regulated or government-owned monopoly.

18.1 OPTIMAL TAXATION

Every tax system that raises a significant amount of revenue will impose a deadweight loss upon the economy.[2] The system that raises the required revenue with the smallest deadweight loss is said to be "optimal." The nature of the **optimal tax system** was first analyzed by Ramsey [50], whose results continue to form the core of this literature. Much later, Diamond and Mirrlees [22] re-examined the issue using modern general equilibrium methods. Their work reawakened interest in the subject, and there have been numerous subsequent developments. This literature is quite technical, and it is

---

[1] This term was coined by Lipsey and Lancaster [41].
[2] There are instances in which taxation initially raises welfare (a tax imposed upon a negative externality is one example), but the revenue that can be raised from such sources falls well short of the needs of a modern government.

discussed here only in the context of a "rock bottom" model from which most of the complications have been excluded.

One candidate for the optimal tax system is the **proportional tax system,** which taxes every commodity at the same rate.[3] This system raises the price of every commodity, so that fewer goods can be bought with an hour's wages. People are discouraged from working, generating a deadweight loss. However, the proportional tax system does not favour one commodity over another, and so does not distort the consumer's choices in any other way. Since every tax discourages work, a tax that *only* discourages work would seem to impose the least possible disruption upon the economy. Nevertheless, it is never – well, hardly ever – the optimal tax system.

Let's consider a Robinson Crusoe economy with these properties:

- Robinson's utility rises with his consumption of ale, bread, and leisure. Specifically, his utility function is

$$U = u(a) + v(b) - kh$$

where a and b are his consumption of ale and bread, respectively, and h is the amount of market work that he performs. The functions u and v represent the utility obtained from the consumption of ale and bread, respectively. It is assumed that u and v have positive first derivatives and negative second derivatives (so that both goods have positive but diminishing marginal utilities). The last term represents the utility lost by the individual when he forgoes leisure. The constant k is positive and represents the marginal utility of leisure.
- Robinson sells his labour in a competitive marketplace, and uses his wage income to purchase ale and bread in competitive markets.
- Robinson's labour is purchased by firms that produce ale and bread. One hour of labour can be used to produce one pint of ale or one loaf of bread. Firms behave competitively, setting the commodity prices equal to their marginal cost of production. This cost is simply the cost of an hour of labour, w. Thus, in equilibrium, the prices paid by Robinson for units of ale and bread are

$$p_a = (1 + t_a)\, w$$

$$p_b = (1 + t_b)\, w$$

where t_a and t_b are the taxes applied to purchases of the two commodities.

Robinson's budget constraint is

$$p_a a + p_b b = wh$$

The left-hand side of the equation is Robinson's expenditures on ale and bread, and the

---

[3] This tax system is equivalent to a flat rate income tax (i.e., one under which income is taxed at a fixed rate).

right-hand side is his wage earnings.[4] This constraint can also be written as

$$(1 + t_a)a + (1 + t_b)b = h \tag{18.1}$$

Robinson must choose a commodity bundle that satisfies this constraint. The best of these commodity bundles is characterized by the conditions

$$\frac{MU_a}{1 + t_a} = k \tag{18.2}$$

$$\frac{MU_b}{1 + t_b} = k \tag{18.3}$$

where MU_a and MU_b are the marginal utilities of ale and bread. An hour of work always reduces utility by k. An hour's wages buys $1/(1 + t_a)$ units of ale, each of which raises utility by MU_a, so an hour's wages spent on ale raises utility by $MU_a/(1 + t_a)$. Similarly, an hour's wages spent on bread raises utility by $MU_b/(1 + t_b)$. The above conditions state, therefore, that the consumption of each commodity should be extended until the utility of the commodities that can be purchased with another hour's wage earnings is just equal to the disutility of another hour of work.

Of course, the marginal utilities correspond to the partial derivatives of the utility function:

$$MU_a = \frac{\partial U}{\partial a} = \frac{du(a)}{da}$$

$$MU_b = \frac{\partial U}{\partial b} = \frac{dv(b)}{db}$$

Substituting these marginal utilities into (18.2) and (18.3) shows that Robinson's optimal consumption of ale depends only upon t_a, rising as t_a falls, and that his optimal consumption of bread depends only upon the t_b, rising as t_b falls. These observations can be expressed as equations:

$$a^* = A(t_a)$$

$$b^* = B(t_b)$$

where A and B are decreasing functions.[5] Robinson's optimal hours of work, h^*, can then be deduced from (18.1).

---

[4] Robinson also receives all of the firms' profits, but these profits are equal to zero in equilibrium. There is no transfer from the government, as the government is assumed to require the tax revenue for its own purposes. It is this assumption – that the government is actually taking purchasing power away from Robinson – that converts the tax problem into a second-best problem.

[5] For example, (18.2) can be written as

$$\frac{du(a)}{da} = (1 + t_a)k$$

The assumption that the marginal utility of ale is diminishing implies that the left-hand side of this equation falls as a rises. For any given value of t_a, a^* is the value of a that satisfies this equation. If t_a falls, the left-hand side must fall to maintain the equality, and hence a^* must be larger.

18.1.1 The Optimal Tax Rule

The deadweight loss of a proportional tax arises because Robinson, finding the government's hand always in his pocket, chooses to work less. But the proportional tax has an interesting property. For any *given* amount of work h that Robinson chooses to do, his utility from consumption, $u + v$, is as high as it can possibly be. That is, under any other tax system that raises the same amount of revenue, the maximal value of $u + v$ associated with each h would be smaller. You might think that this fact means that a proportional tax system generates the smallest disincentive to work, and that the deadweight loss caused by Robinson's disinclination to work is therefore minimized by this system. Neither of these inferences is correct. There are other tax systems that push Robinson into doing more work, raising his welfare along the way.

The basic rule for designing an optimal tax system is strongly analogous to another rule with which we are already familiar. Robinson allocates his income in the best possible way when

$$\frac{MU_a}{p_a} = \frac{MU_b}{p_b}$$

The left-hand side of this equation is the utility gained by spending another dollar on ale, and the right-hand side is the utility gained by spending another dollar on bread. If this equation were not satisfied, Robinson could increase his utility by spending a dollar less on one commodity (the one for which the utility gain is the smallest) and spending a dollar more on the other. Thus, Robinson follows the rule

Allocate spending so that the last dollar spent on each commodity raises utility by the same amount.

The optimal tax rule imagines that a fixed amount of income is to be taken away from Robinson through the tax system, and that the only issue is the *way* in which it is to be taken away. The rule is

Set the taxes so that the last dollar raised by taxing each commodity reduces utility by the same amount.

Raising a dollar of tax revenue through the ale tax reduces Robinson's utility, and raising a dollar of revenue through the bread tax also reduces Robinson's utility. However, if these two actions reduce Robinson's utility by different amounts, the tax rates can be adjusted to make Robinson better off. Specifically, the rates can be adjusted so that a dollar less is raised through the tax that reduces Robinson's utility the most, and a dollar more is raised through the tax that reduces it the least.

Under the best tax system, the last dollar of revenue raised under each tax reduces Robinson's utility by the same amount. But how large is the change in Robinson's utility when a dollar of revenue is raised through any given tax?

- If increasing a particular tax by one percentage point raises the government's revenue by x dollars, \$1 of additional revenue is raised when that tax is increased by $1/x$

percentage points. It follows that an additional dollar of revenue is raised if the ale tax is raised by the reciprocal of dR/dt_a, or if the bread tax is raised by the reciprocal of dR/dt_b.

- A one percentage point increase in the ale tax changes Robinson's utility by dU/dt_a, so if the ale tax is raised enough to add \$1 to the government's revenue, the change in Robinson's utility is

$$\frac{dU}{dt_a} \div \frac{dR}{dt_a}$$

Similarly, if the bread tax is raised enough to add \$1 to the government's revenue, the change in Robinson's utility is

$$\frac{dU}{dt_b} \div \frac{dR}{dt_b}$$

The characteristic of the optimal tax system is that these two values are equal:

$$\frac{dU}{dt_a} \div \frac{dR}{dt_a} = \frac{dU}{dt_b} \div \frac{dR}{dt_b} \tag{18.4}$$

We can make use of this rule only if we can evaluate each of the four derivatives. Their evaluation is the next step in characterizing the optimal tax system.

18.1.2 Changes in Utility

Robinson makes himself as well off as possible when he consumes a^* pints of ale and b^* loaves of bread, and does as much work as is required to finance these purchases. His utility is then

$$U = u(a^*) + v(b^*) - k\big[(1 + t_a)a^* + (1 + t_b)b^*\big]$$

where a^* and b^* are functions of t_a and t_b, respectively. The effect on utility of a tax rate change is found by differentiating this expression with respect to the tax rate. The effect of a change in the tax rate on ale is[6]

$$\frac{dU}{dt_a} = \frac{du}{da}\bigg|_{a=a^*} \frac{da^*}{dt_a} - k\left[a^* + (1 + t_a)\frac{da^*}{dt_a}\right]$$

Since a^* is the value of a at which (18.2) is satisfied,

$$\frac{du}{da}\bigg|_{a=a^*} = k(1 + t_a)$$

Substituting this equation into the preceding one yields

$$\frac{dU}{dt_a} = -ka^* \tag{18.5}$$

---

[6] The annotated bar behind the derivative du/da indicates that this derivative is evaluated at a^*.

An increase in the tax rate forces Robinson to work longer hours to finance his ale purchases. The decline in Robinson's utility is equal to the disutility of these additional hours of work. A similar procedure shows the effect on Robinson's utility of an increase in the bread tax:

$$\frac{dU}{dt_b} = -kb^* \tag{18.6}$$

18.1.3 Changes in Revenue

The government earns revenue R from taxes on ale and bread:

$$R = t_a a^* + t_b b^*$$

The revenue gained by increasing a tax rate is found by differentiating this equation with respect to the tax rate:

$$\frac{dR}{dt_a} = a^* + t_a \frac{da^*}{dt_a} \tag{18.7}$$

$$\frac{dR}{dt_b} = b^* + t_b \frac{db^*}{dt_b} \tag{18.8}$$

The first terms represent the revenue gained by imposing a higher tax on given purchases of the commodity, and the second terms (which are negative) represent the revenue lost when Robinson responds to the higher price by reducing his consumption of the commodity.

These two terms are tied together by the commodity's **price elasticity of demand.** The price elasticity of demand measures the way in which the demand for any good varies with the good's price. Specifically, it is the negative of the ratio of the percentage change in quantity demanded to the percentage change in price.[7]

These percentage changes can be expressed algebraically by "disassembling" the derivatives da^*/dt_a and db^*/dt_b. Consider the first of these derivatives. Robinson's consumption of ale is determined by the tax rate on ale, so any small change in the tax rate will induce a change in ale consumption. The derivative da^*/dt_a is just the ratio of these two changes. (The letter d in the derivative notation indicates a change in a variable: dt_a is the change in the tax rate, and da^* is the induced change in ale consumption.) These changes appear separately – rather than as a ratio – in the expressions for the percentage changes:

- The percentage change in ale consumption is da^*/a^*.
- The percentage change in the price of ale is dp_a/p_a. Since p_a is equal to $(1 + t_a)\, w$, dp_a is equal to $w \times dt_a$, and hence

$$\frac{dp_a}{p_a} = \frac{dt_a}{1 + t_a}$$

---

[7] The elasticity, defined in this way, will be *positive* for any downward-sloping demand curve.

Letting α be the price elasticity of demand for ale,

$$\alpha \equiv -\left(\frac{da^*}{a^*} \div \frac{dp_a}{p_a}\right) = -\left(\frac{da^*}{a^*} \div \frac{dt_a}{1+t_a}\right)$$

"Reassembling" the derivatives gives

$$\alpha = -\left(\frac{da^*}{dt_a} \times \frac{1+t_a}{a^*}\right) \tag{18.9}$$

An analogous argument shows that, if β is the price elasticity of demand for bread,

$$\beta = -\left(\frac{db^*}{dt_b} \times \frac{1+t_b}{b^*}\right) \tag{18.10}$$

Substituting (18.9) and (18.10) into (18.7) and (18.8) gives

$$\frac{dR}{dt_a} = a^*\left[1 - \alpha\left(\frac{t_a}{1+t_a}\right)\right] \tag{18.11}$$

$$\frac{dR}{dt_b} = b^*\left[1 - \beta\left(\frac{t_b}{1+t_b}\right)\right] \tag{18.12}$$

These derivatives are not necessarily positive. If a tax rate on a good is sufficiently high, and if that good's elasticity is greater than one, the corresponding derivative will be negative. That is, an increase in the tax rate will cause revenue to fall. If this is the case, the tax rate is unambiguously too high. The discussion that follows imagines that Robinson is not so grossly overtaxed that one or both of the derivatives is negative.

18.1.4 Back to the Optimal Tax Rule

Substituting (18.5), (18.6), (18.11), and (18.12) into (18.4), and then simplifying it, yields

$$\alpha\left(\frac{t_a}{1+t_a}\right) = \beta\left(\frac{t_b}{1+t_b}\right)$$

This equation allows us to draw a number of conclusions about the optimal tax system.

The Inverse Elasticity Rule
The bracketed expressions in this equations are a kind of tax rate; specifically, they are the fraction of the tax-inclusive price that goes to the government as taxes. Under the optimal tax system, these tax rates are proportional to the inverse of the elasticities of the goods. That is,

$$\frac{t_a}{1+t_a} = \frac{\theta}{\alpha}$$

$$\frac{t_b}{1+t_b} = \frac{\theta}{\beta}$$

where θ is a parameter chosen by the government. The more revenue that the government must raise, the higher is θ.

To understand this rule, remember that an increase in a tax rate has two opposing effects on revenue: more tax is collected on each unit of the good that Robinson buys, but Robinson buys (and pays tax on) fewer units of the good. The size of the latter effect *relative to* the former effect is jointly determined by the good's elasticity and the tax rate:

1) The greater the price elasticity of the good, the greater is the reduction in Robinson's consumption of the good caused by an increase in the tax rate, and the greater is the resulting revenue loss.
2) The greater the tax rate, the greater is the revenue lost from any given reduction in Robinson's consumption of the good.

These relationships determine the optimal tax structure. Imagine that both commodities are initially taxed at the same rate. Can the tax system be adjusted so that Robinson is better off, even though the same revenue is being raised? The implication of 1) is that a tax on a good with a high elasticity of demand is a relatively ineffective tax, because the latter (revenue-destroying) effect is large relative to the former (revenue-creating) effect. Thus, the government makes Robinson better off by reducing the tax on the good with the higher elasticity and raising the tax on the good with the lower elasticity. But 2) implies that this policy can only be pushed so far, because this adjustment of the tax rates tends to equalize the effectiveness of the two taxes. Eventually, the various taxes will be equally effective tools for raising revenue, in the sense that the relative sizes of their revenue-destroying and revenue-creating effects are equal, and there will be no gain from further tax adjustments.

The inverse elasticity rule does not exactly describe the optimal tax structure under all circumstances. Indeed, the utility function assumed above appears to be the only one for which it does. The inverse elasticity rule is nevertheless a handy rule of thumb, because it approximates the optimal tax structure, and because it offers a concrete and easily understandable policy prescription.

Quantities

Another common rule of thumb is that taxes should be set so that the imposition of the taxes causes the consumption of each good to fall by the same proportion. This rule follows immediately from the inverse elasticity rule.

Recall that the percentage change in the demand for a good and the percentage change in its price are connected by the price elasticity of demand. For ale,

$$\frac{da}{a} = -\alpha \frac{dp_a}{p_a}$$

Imagine that the price of ale changes because a tax has been imposed on ale, raising its price from 1 to $1 + t_a$. The increase in the price of ale, measured as a percentage of the new price, is $t_a/(1 + t_a)$. The resulting percentage change in Robinson's demand for ale is

$$\frac{da}{a} = -\alpha \frac{t_a}{1 + t_a}$$

Similarly, the imposition of a tax on bread raises its price from 1 to $1 + t_b$. The ensuing percentage change in Robinson's demand for ale is

$$\frac{db}{b} = -\beta \frac{t_b}{1 + t_b}$$

If the tax rates are set optimally (i.e., in accordance with the inverse elasticity rule),

$$\frac{da}{a} = \frac{db}{b} = \theta$$

This is an alternative characterization of the optimal tax rule: the optimal tax system causes the consumption of each commodity to decline by the same proportion.

This result is not an exact characterization of the optimal tax system. It is another rule of thumb, and it is sometimes better and sometimes worse than the rule from which it is derived. The inverse elasticity rule describes the optimal way of raising any amount of revenue when the utility function takes the form set out above. By contrast, if appropriate modifications are made in the way that the percentage changes in consumption are measured, the alternative characterization holds for many kinds of utility functions, but only when the amount of revenue being raised is very small.[8]

A Corlett and Hague Rule

A proportional tax on all goods discourages people from working, and this discouragement can give rise to a substantial deadweight loss. Corlett and Hague [19] argue that the deadweight loss can be reduced by abandoning the proportional tax system. Goods that are complimentary with leisure should be taxed at relatively high rates. The high tax rates will discourage consumption of the complimentary goods, and hence discourage people from engaging in leisure activities – leaving them no option but to go back to work. Similarly, the goods that are the most substitutable for leisure should be taxed at the lowest rates.

Acting on intuition alone, we can identify some goods that complement leisure and some that substitute for it. Beer and beach balls would fall into the former category, and cell phones into the latter. But a formal evaluation of Corlett and Hague's hypothesis requires a formal rule for identifying complements and substitutes. This rule can be expressed in terms of **compensated elasticities.**

These elasticities describe the behaviour of an individual who is maximizing his utility subject to the constraint that his expenditures cannot exceed his income. His income is the sum of his wage earnings and a lump-sum transfer (which might be equal

---

[8] Since the changes in price and consumption in any given market are supposed to be small, our derivation is only correct if the no-tax equilibrium and the tax equilibrium are very close together. This condition will only be satisfied if the amount of revenue raised is very small.

to zero). If the price of one of the goods rises, he will change the quantity of labour that he sells and the quantity of each good that he buys, but he will nevertheless be worse off than before:

> If he chooses not to work longer hours (so that his income remains the same), he cannot afford to purchase his original commodity bundle, and must instead purchase a less desirable commodity bundle. If he chooses to purchase a commodity bundle as good as his original one, he must work longer hours to pay for it, and the longer hours of work make him less happy. He will probably choose to compromise, working a little longer and purchasing a slightly less desirable commodity bundle, but even the best compromise leaves him worse off.

Suppose, however, that he is given a lump-sum transfer to compensate for the price increase. As more income is given to him, he adjusts his commodity bundle and his hours of work, and his utility rises toward its original level. He is "exactly compensated" for the price increase when he is just as well off as he was before the changes in the price and the transfer. The compensated elasticity of demand for good x with respect to a price q, denoted $E(x, q)$, is the ratio of the percentage change in the quantity of good x demanded to the percentage change in the price q when the individual is exactly compensated for the price increase. Similarly, the compensated elasticity of the supply of labour with respect to the price q, denoted $E(h, q)$, is the ratio of the percentage change in the quantity of labour supplied to the percentage change in the price q when the individual is exactly compensated for the price increase.

Let p_j be the price of some good j. Good j and leisure are **complements** if an exactly compensated increase in p_j causes an individual to allocate less time to leisure (and more time to work). Good j and leisure are **substitutes** if an exactly compensated increase in p_j causes him to allocate more time to leisure (and less time to work). Equivalently, good j and leisure are complements if $E(h, p_j)$ is positive and substitutes if $E(h, p_j)$ is negative. In any pair of goods, the one with the higher compensated elasticity is more complementary to leisure, or less substitutable for it.

Robinson's utility function is very simple, giving rise to a very simple connection between the regular elasticities of demand and the compensated elasticities. Specifically, if s_a and s_b are the shares of Robinson's income spent on ale and bread, respectively,

$$\alpha = -E(a, p_a) = -\frac{E(h, p_a)}{s_a}$$

$$\beta = -E(b, p_b) = -\frac{E(h, p_b)}{s_b}$$

Both ale and bread are substitutes for leisure.

Substituting these expressions into the optimal tax rule gives

$$-E(h, p_a)\left(\frac{1}{s_a}\right)\left(\frac{t_a}{1 + t_a}\right) = -E(h, p_b)\left(\frac{1}{s_b}\right)\left(\frac{t_b}{1 + t_b}\right)$$

This version of the optimal tax rule illustrates Corlett and Hague's hypothesis. Suppose, for example, that the tax rates are initially set optimally, but that ale subsequently becomes more substitutable for leisure. Then $E(h, p_a)$ becomes a smaller negative number, and $-E(h, p_a)$ becomes a larger positive number. The tax rates must be adjusted; in particular, the tax rate on ale must fall relative to the tax rate on bread. This adjustment is precisely the one suggested by Corlett and Hague.

Note, however, that the tax structure is determined by both the compensated elasticities and the expenditure shares. If the expenditure share of the more substitutable good is substantially greater the expenditure share of the less substitutable good, the more substitutable good could bear the higher – not the lower – tax rate.

18.2 NATURAL MONOPOLY AND THE RAMSEY PRICING RULE

Two rules for pricing the output of a natural monopoly were presented in Section 14.1:

- If the monopoly is owned and operated by the government, and *if lump-sum taxes are possible,* price should be set equal to marginal cost.
- If the monopoly is regulated by the government, and *if the government can neither subsidize an unprofitable monopoly, nor appropriate part of the revenue of a profitable monopoly,* price should be set equal to average cost.

The assumptions that underlie these rules (shown in italics) are quite restrictive. If they are removed – if it is recognized that significant amounts of revenue cannot be raised through lump-sum taxation, and that cash transfers between the government and a regulated monopoly are generally possible – a single pricing rule emerges. Laffont and Tirole [38] call it the **Ramsey pricing rule,** in recognition of Ramsey's [50] early research on departures from marginal cost pricing. This rule, like the optimal tax rule, is motivated by the government's desire to raise a fixed amount of revenue at the smallest cost to society.

As before, let the total cost function of the monopolist be

$$C = \gamma + \mu q$$

where C is total cost and q is output. The parameters γ and μ are positive, and represent the fixed and marginal costs of production. Let the demand curve for the monopolist's output be

$$p = a - bq$$

where p is the price at which each unit of output is sold, and a and b are positive constants. Finally, let η be the elasticity of demand:

$$\eta = -\left(\frac{dq}{dp} \times \frac{p}{q}\right) = -\left(\frac{p}{q} \div \frac{dp}{dq}\right)$$

For concreteness, imagine that the monopoly is owned and operated by the government.

18.2.1 Lump-Sum Taxation

Imagine that the government can raise revenue through lump-sum taxation. The net benefit to society of the monopoly's activities, $W(q)$, is then equal to the total surplus generated in the monopoly's market. Total surplus is the value of q units of goods to the consumer less the cost of producing these goods:

$$W(q) = V(q) - \mu q - \gamma$$

Here, $V(q)$ is the value to consumers of q units of output – that is, it is the area under the demand curve to the left of the output level q. The optimal level of output maximizes $W(q)$, and the optimal price is the highest price at which this quantity of output can be sold.[9]

The level of output that maximizes $W(q)$ satisfies the condition

$$\frac{dW}{dq} = \frac{dV}{dq} - \mu = 0$$

The derivative dV/dq is the amount by which V rises when q rises by one unit, or equivalently, it is the value to the consumers of the last unit of output when q units are produced. The value to the consumers of the marginal unit of goods is simply the amount that some consumer is willing to pay for it, and it is therefore equal to the height of the demand curve, $p(q)$. Making this substitution yields

$$p(q) = \mu$$

which is the marginal cost pricing rule: the monopoly should produce as many units of output as can be sold at a price equal to marginal cost.

Alternatively, total surplus is the sum of the consumer surplus *generated in the monopoly market* and profits:

$$W(q) = [V(q) - p(q)q] + [p(q)q - \mu q - \gamma] \tag{18.13}$$

Profits can be either positive or negative. If profits are positive, the monopoly provides the government with another source of revenue. If profits are negative, additional revenue must be raised elsewhere to cover the monopoly's losses.

Equation (18.13) shows that if lump-sum taxes exist, consumer surplus in the monopoly market and the monopoly's profits are equally valuable to society. They are equally valuable because profits represent the increase in surplus that the monopoly's operation generates in *other* markets. The government wishes to raise a particular amount of revenue, so earning a dollar of monopoly profits allows it to reduce taxes elsewhere by a dollar. Since tax revenue is surplus that has been appropriated by the government, the tax reduction returns a dollar of surplus to the private economy.[10]

---

[9] Charging the highest price at which all of the goods can be sold ensures that the goods are sold to the people who value them most.

[10] Who gets the surplus? The surplus appropriated by the government through taxation could be either consumer surplus or producer surplus. The surplus returned to the private economy when

18.2.2 Distortionary Taxation

When the government collects revenue through distortionary taxes,[11] people adjust their behaviour in an attempt to reduce their tax obligations. These adjustments misallocate resources, destroying consumer surplus. The lost surplus is the welfare cost, or deadweight loss, of the tax.

Raising one more dollar of revenue through distortionary taxes causes $1 of surplus to be transferred from the private economy to the government, and causes some amount of surplus to be destroyed. Assume that z dollars of surplus are destroyed when one more dollar of revenue is raised.

The consumer surplus and profits generated by a government-owned monopoly are not equally valuable in this environment. If the monopoly earns another dollar of profits, the amount of revenue that the government must raise through distortionary taxes is reduced by a dollar. The tax reduction increases the surplus of the private economy by $1 + z$ dollars – $1 as a transfer from the government and z dollars from improved resource allocation. The net social benefits of the monopoly's activities are therefore

$$W(q) = [V(q) - p(q)q] + (1 + z)[p(q)q - \mu q - \gamma] \qquad (18.14)$$

The first term represents the consumer surplus generated in the market in which the monopoly operates. The second term represents the surplus generated elsewhere in the economy when distortionary taxes are reduced by an amount equal to the monopoly profits. If the monopoly does not earn a profit, but instead incurs a loss, the second term represents the reduction in surplus that occurs when the government raises distortionary taxes to cover these losses.

The optimal level of output maximizes net social benefits, and the optimal price is the highest price at which the optimal level of output can be sold. The optimal level of output is characterized by the condition

$$\frac{dW}{dq} = \left[\frac{dV}{dq} - \frac{dp}{dq}q - p\right] + (1 + z)\left[\frac{dp}{dq}q + p - \mu\right] = 0 \qquad (18.15)$$

Simplifying the derivative, and recalling that dV/dq is equal to p, yields

$$(1 + z)(p - \mu) = -z\left(\frac{dp}{dq}q\right)$$

By the definition of the elasticity of demand,

$$(1 + z)(p - \mu) = z\left(\frac{p}{\eta}\right)$$

taxes are reduced could, therefore, go either to firms or to consumers. However, the people living in the economy are both the consumers of the goods and the owners of the firms, and they ultimately collect both consumer and producer surplus.

[11] Contingent taxes are also called "distortionary taxes," because the allocation of resources is distorted when they are imposed.

or

$$\frac{p - \mu}{p} = \frac{z}{1 + z} \frac{1}{\eta}$$

This equation is the Ramsey pricing rule. It states that the price of the monopolist's good should be set above marginal cost if taxation is distortionary. The greater the social cost of raising another dollar through distortionary taxes (i.e., the higher z is), the farther above marginal cost the price should be set.

The monopoly's losses are equal to its fixed cost when price is set equal to marginal cost. If taxation is distortionary, society would be better off if the price were set a little higher. The higher price discourages consumers from buying the monopoly's output, so that some consumer surplus is lost, but it also reduces the monopoly's losses. The government is then able to reduce the amount of revenue raised through distortionary taxes, restoring surplus elsewhere in the economy. The greater the welfare cost of raising a dollar of revenue through distortionary taxes (z), the more important it is to reduce the monopoly's losses, and the higher the price should be set.

If the welfare cost of raising revenue through distortionary taxes is sufficiently high, the price should be set so high that the monopoly earns a profit rather than a loss. This extra source of revenue allows the government to further reduce the amount of revenue raised through taxes.

How high might the optimal price be? As z grows unimaginably large, $z/(1 + z)$ gets arbitrarily close to 1, and the optimal price gets arbitrarily close to p_M, where

$$p_M \equiv \frac{a + \mu}{2}$$

This price is also the price that would be charged by a profit-maximizing monopolist. When taxes are extremely distortionary, reducing the amount of revenue raised through such taxes is more important than anything else. Taxes can be reduced by earning monopoly profits, so the government's best policy is to make these profits as large as possible, in other words, to behave like a privately owned and unregulated monopolist.

Although this pricing rule was derived for a government-owned monopoly, it also applies to a regulated monopoly. Under regulation, the government would cover any loss that the monopoly incurred (so that the monopoly remains in business), and it would appropriate any profits that the monopoly earned (so that distortionary taxes can be reduced). It follows that profits and losses would have the same impact on the level of distortionary taxation as they have when the government owns the monopoly. Net social benefits would be the same for both types of monopoly, and consequently, the optimal pricing rule would be the same.

18.2.3 An Alternate Derivation

The motivation for the Ramsey pricing rule is the same as the motivation for the optimal tax rules, namely the desire to raise a fixed amount of revenue at the lowest cost to society.

Given this conceptual similarity, it might be expected that the rules themselves could be derived in similar ways, and in fact they can.

The optimal tax system has this property:

The social cost of raising another dollar of revenue through each tax is the same.

But raising the price of the monopoly's product is rather like raising a tax. The monopoly's profits take the place of tax revenues, and in both cases, social costs are measured as a loss of consumer surplus. The optimal price has this property:

The social cost of raising another dollar of monopoly profits is the same as the social cost of raising another dollar of revenue through a tax.

The social cost of raising a dollar of revenue through a tax is, by assumption, $1 + z$ dollars. One dollar of this loss is a transfer of surplus from the consumers to the government, and the other z dollars is the welfare cost of raising a dollar of revenue.

The social cost of raising a dollar of monopoly profits is a little more difficult to calculate. Let's begin by examining the effects of an increase in the monopoly's output.

- The consumer surplus $S(q)$ generated by the production of q units of goods is

$$S(q) = V(q) - p(q)q$$

If the monopoly's price is reduced by enough to raise the quantity of output demanded by one unit, the increase in consumer surplus is

$$\frac{dS}{dq} = \frac{dV}{dq} - q\frac{dp}{dq} - p \tag{18.16}$$

- The profits π associated with the output level q are

$$\pi = p(q)q - \gamma - \mu q$$

If the monopoly's price is reduced by enough to raise the quantity of output demanded by one unit, the increase in profits is

$$\frac{d\pi}{dq} = q\frac{dp}{dq} - p - \mu \tag{18.17}$$

A one-unit increase in output raises profits by $d\pi/dq$, so the increase in output needed to raise profits by only \$1 is $1 \div d\pi/dq$. A one-unit increase in output raises social welfare by dS/dq, so an increase in output of $1 \div d\pi/dq$ units raises welfare by $(dS/dq) \times (1 \div d\pi/dq)$.

This change in welfare is the welfare gained when profits rise by a dollar – and therefore the *negative* of this change in welfare is the welfare *lost* when profits rise by a dollar.

Substituting these results into the general rule gives

$$-\frac{dS}{dq} \div \frac{d\pi}{dq} = 1 + z$$

or

$$-\left[\frac{dV}{dq} - q\frac{dp}{dq} - p\right] = (1 + z)\left[q\frac{dp}{dq} - p - \mu\right]$$

This equation is equivalent to (18.15), from which the Ramsey pricing rule was derived.

18.3 CONCLUSIONS

If a Pareto optimal (or "first best") allocation cannot be reached, policy decisions revolve around making appropriate compromises. The best available compromise (the "second best" allocation) sometimes involves actions that can be justified only if *all* of the ramifications of the policy are considered. The best compromise might be to create an additional market distortion, or to forgo an opportunity to eliminate a distortion, as in the case of natural monopoly. There are no simple rules.

QUESTIONS

It has been shown the same methodology can be used to derive the pricing rule for a regulated monopoly and the optimal tax rule. In this question, this methodology will be used to determine the optimal quantity of a public good when the public good must be financed through distortionary taxation. First, however, this problem will be solved using basic mathematical techniques. This solution will be compared with that obtained by applying the "optimal tax" methodology.

Imagine an economy in which there are 400 people, each of whom has the utility function

$$U = 2\left(c^{1/2} + z^{1/2}\right) - h$$

where c is the individual's consumption of private goods, z is the quantity of public good provided by the government, and h is the individual's hours of work. The wage rate in the economy is $1 per hour, and each unit of private consumption goods costs $1. Each unit of public goods costs $900, and this cost is spread equally across the 400 people living in the economy. The public good is financed through an income tax: everyone pays to the government the fraction t of their labour income.

Basic Mathematics:
a) Assume that z units of the public good are provided and that income is taxed at rate t. Find each person's budget constraint, and find his optimal hours of work. Find his maximal utility for arbitrarily selected values of z and t.
b) If the income tax is used only to finance the public good, and if each person chooses his hours of work optimally, what is the relationship between z and t? Use this relationship to express each person's utility as a function of t.
c) Assume that the government chooses t to maximize the typical person's utility. Find the condition that characterizes the utility-maximizing value of t. Show that this condition is satisfied when t is 0.2.

Hint: At some point, you will have to evaluate the derivative of $[t(1-t)]^{1/2}$. There are several ways of doing so, but the rest of this question is more easily solved if you use the chain rule:

$$\frac{d}{dt}[t(1-t)]^{1/2} = \left(\frac{1}{2}\right)[t(1-t)]^{-1/2}(1-2t)$$

"Optimal Tax" Methodology:
Our rule is going to be:

> Set the quantity of public good so that the utility gained by spending one more dollar on the public good is equal to the utility lost by raising one more dollar through distortionary taxation.

We will have to find the required changes in utility, and then put the pieces together to get the rule.

d) Find the utility gained by each person when the government spends one more dollar on the public good.

e) Find the utility lost by each person when the government raises the tax rate marginally. Find the increase in tax revenue when the government raises the tax rate marginally. (Remember that an increase in the tax rate raises the taxes of 400 people.) Find the utility lost by each person when the government raises one more dollar of tax revenue.

f) Equate these changes to obtain an algebraic form of the above rule. Show that it is the same as the utility-maximization condition in c).

Asymmetric Information and Efficiency

The consensus among art experts is that a number of the Van Goghs hanging in prestigious galleries around the world are forgeries. There is less agreement as to which paintings are the forgeries and which are genuine. Some experts question the authenticity of *Garden at Auvers.* The French government had once considered this painting to be so important that, in 1992, it declared the painting to be an historic monument to prevent its sale to a foreigner.[1] When the painting was last offered for sale, in 1996, concerns over its authenticity were so great that it failed to find a buyer. Other experts question *Sunflowers,* which was purchased by a Japanese company in 1987 for $39.9 million (U.S. dollars), at that time the highest price ever paid for a work of art. Also under suspicion are the "self-portraits" hanging in the Gemeentenmuseum in the Hague, the Van Gogh Museum in Amsterdam, and the Metropolitan Museum in New York. The number of possible forgeries is currently estimated to be about 100.

Some of these paintings reached their privileged positions in innocent ways. They are copies of real Van Goghs made by art students, or paintings in the style of Van Gogh done by competent hobbyists. They were incorrectly attributed to Van Gogh at some time, and the attribution stuck.

Others were deliberately forged for financial gain. The art dealer Otto Wacker, for example, sold thirty Van Goghs during the late 1920s. He claimed that these had been sold to him by a Russian who, fearing reprisals against relatives still living in post-revolutionary Russia, could not reveal his identity. But the Russian did not exist, the paintings were forgeries, and Wacker was convicted of fraud and falsifying documents.

Wacker's paintings were sold under asymmetric information: Wacker knew the paintings were forgeries, the prospective buyers did not. Wacker exploited this asymmetry, selling the paintings for much more than the going price of pictures that look a lot like Van Gogh's but aren't.

---

[1] This decision proved to be an expensive one for the French government. The painting had previously been valued at 200 million francs [nearly $30 million (U.S. dollars)], but with the bidding restricted to French citizens, it sold at auction for only 55 million francs. Its previous owner then sued the French government for the 145 million francs that the government's decision had cost him, and won.

Asymmetric information often leads to economic inefficiency, but Wacker's sale of the paintings at high prices does not itself constitute inefficiency. The premium paid by the buyers is simply a transfer from one person to another, and has no evident effect on welfare. The inefficiency arises from the subsequent reallocation of scarce resources. Forgery is an industry. Resources are drawn into it, and out of other industries, if there are profits to be made. People who would not be willing to make their living by selling copies of famous pictures are willing to do so if they can sell those copies as originals.

The presence of art forgery also leads people to take precautions against buying forged art. Scarce resources are devoted to separating the fake from the real. The details of an artist's style, the nature of the canvas that he used, and the types of paint that he favoured are all intensively studied in the hope of distinguishing one from the other. Each painting's provenance (or history) is carefully studied in the hope of tracing the painting's origins back to the painter or some other reputable source. These activities are all carried out by talented people who, were it not for the possibility of forgery, could have been employed in more productive work. As well, the discovery of a forgery often leads to a trial, either a criminal case against the forger himself or a civil case against a previous owner of the forgery. These trials, and the investigations that precede them, also expend scarce resources.

Efforts to detect forgeries are matched by efforts to make forgeries less detectable. The materials used by a particular artist are duplicated as closely as possible, and the paintings are carefully "aged" (their surfaces finely crackled and covered with appropriate amounts of grime). Alternatively, the forger can follow the example of John Drewe. He commissioned cheaply made imitations of the work of famous artists, and sold them as the work of the artists themselves. Had anyone studied these paintings, it would soon have been evident that they were forgeries – but no one did, because Drewe had infiltrated the archives of a number of prestigious museums, creating for each painting a false provenance that seemed to conclusively demonstrate the painting's authenticity. Scarce resources were again wasted, and the integrity of our store of knowledge was brought into doubt.

Fraud is an obvious instance of asymmetric information, but there are many other, and more important, examples in modern economies. Asymmetric information gives rise to two major problems: moral hazard and adverse selection.

Moral hazard means that the asymmetry of information allows people to alter their behaviour in ways that are detrimental to society. Outright fraud is an extreme example, but there are many less dramatic examples. Most people insure their cars against accident and their houses against fire, because the loss of a car or a house could be financially devastating. However, once they have been insured, people are likely to be less careful in their cars and in their homes. This change in behaviour makes sense to the individuals – they are willing to accept a higher probability of a bad outcome because the cost of a bad outcome is smaller – but it is costly to insured people as a group. The replacement of a car or house is financed from the premiums collected by the insurance company. If everyone were a little more careful, everyone's insurance premiums could be reduced by enough to make everyone better off.

Adverse selection occurs when a proposal is made to a group of people who have private knowledge about their own characteristics, and when each person's willingness to accept the proposal depends upon these characteristics. One such example is life insurance, which is more likely to be purchased by unhealthy people than by healthy people. This outcome might not seem to be a bad one – it doesn't seem much different from finding that pianists are more likely to buy pianos – but it does have serious implications for market efficiency. If only relatively unhealthy people are choosing to buy life insurance, relatively healthy people are choosing not to buy it. For them, the price of insurance is simply too large relative to its likely benefits. Consequently, they remain uninsured, even though they would have happily purchased insurance at a price that more closely reflected their own mortality rates.

This part begins by examining moral hazard and adverse selection within the context of simple models. It then applies these concepts to a number of important economic problems. These include the willingness of people to reveal the value that they place on public goods, and the regulation of natural monopoly.

19

Asymmetric Information

People search for relevant information but they can never get it all. A commodity trader's decision to buy or sell grain futures hinges upon his prediction of the size of the grain harvest. The trader could improve his prediction if he knew next month's weather, but he can't get this information today at any cost. His uncertainty about next month's weather won't be resolved until next month, when it will be resolved for every trader.

This kind of uncertainty – uncertainty shared by every market participant – isn't fatal to the efficiency of the marketplace, and indeed there are many market transactions that occur simply because this kind of uncertainty exists. There would, for example, be no insurance markets and no futures markets if there were no shared uncertainty.

By contrast, uncertainty that is not shared by all participants can lead to significant inefficiencies. Situations in which some people know things that others do not are said to involve **asymmetric information,** and these situations give rise to two problems, **adverse selection** and **moral hazard.**

Adverse selection occurs when people must decide whether to accept a contract. Suppose, for example, that a firm employing 200 people must lay off 20 of them. It might do so by announcing a severance package[1] and permitting the first 20 volunteers to take the package. A firm making this kind of offer is hoping for a form of self-selection that will minimize the burden of the lay-offs on its employees. Workers who are less concerned about being jobless (notably young single workers and workers approaching retirement) will accept the offer, leaving those with large fixed obligations (those raising children, or holding mortgages) with their jobs intact. But there will also be a second kind of self-selection which is detrimental to the firm itself. Highly skilled workers can obtain new jobs more readily than less skilled workers, and their new jobs are likely to pay better salaries than those obtained by the less skilled workers. Since the highly skilled workers are hurt less by lay-offs, they are more likely to believe that the severance package provides them with adequate compensation, and are more likely to accept it.

---

[1] The severance package describes the terms on which a worker leaves a firm. It generally includes a one-time cash payment and describes the employee's options with respect to the company pension plan.

The loss of these people causes the average skill level of the firm's workers to fall, reducing the firm's profits. This outcome is the result of adverse selection – selection that works against the interests of the agent offering the contract.

Moral hazard occurs whenever the consequences of a contract are affected by hidden actions or hidden information. A **hidden action** is an action which is not observed by others. The moral hazard associated with hidden actions is the stuff of late-night movies: a man takes out $1,000,000 of life insurance on his wife and disconnects the brakes on her car, the wife goes driving along a steep and winding road, . . . Economists being what they are, they are more interested in the man's insurance company than in his wife. The insurance company is the victim of moral hazard: it was willing to insure the man against an event (his wife's death) because it believed that he could not influence the probability of that event occurring, but he could and he did. **Hidden information** is information that is not available to everyone. The people from whom the information is hidden can observe actions but cannot tell whether the actions are appropriate. They risk being misled by better informed agents. This misleading behaviour is another form of moral hazard, and we might encounter it when we deal with a doctor, dentist, lawyer, or auto mechanic. Do you really need those new brakes? Do you really need that root canal?

19.1 ADVERSE SELECTION

Akerlof's "lemons" model [1] shows that the adverse selection problem can be so extreme that a market breaks down entirely – no goods are bought or sold. He imagines a market for used cars in which there are two groups of people, buyers and sellers. For simplicity, imagine that there are equal numbers of buyers and sellers, and that each seller has one car that he would be willing to part with if the price were right. The sellers' cars differ in their qualities. Each car's quality is determined by an independent draw from the uniform distribution on the interval $[0, 1]$. You will recall from Section 9.2 that this assumption means that

- Each car's quality q is represented by a number lying between 0 and 1.
- The probability that a car's quality is less than $\tilde{q}$ (where $0 \leq \tilde{q} \leq 1$) is $\tilde{q}$.
- The *average quality* of all of the cars that have qualities less than $\tilde{q}$ is $\tilde{q}/2$.

The value that each seller places on his car is equal to the car's quality. The value that each buyer places on a car of quality q is $3q/2$.

The **full information equilibrium** describes the buyers' and sellers' behaviour when the quality of each car is observable to everyone. To find this equilibrium, imagine that each buyer is matched with a seller. In each pair the buyer would place a higher value on the car than would the seller. The sale of a car of quality q at any price between q and $3q/2$ would make both the buyer and the seller better off. Presumably, after some haggling, each pair would agree on a price and the car would change hands.

The social benefit from the sale of a car of quality q is $q/2$, because this is the difference between the value of the car to the buyer and the value of the car to the seller.

ATTITUDES TOWARD RISK

Economists categorize people's attitudes toward risk by their willingness to play **statistically fair** games. A game is statistically fair, or **actuarially fair,** if the statistician's best guess of the winnings is zero. An example would be a game in which a coin is flipped, and in which you lose $1 if it comes up heads and win $1 if it comes up tails. Since the coin is as likely to come up heads as tails, the best guess of your winnings (no matter how many times the game is played) is zero dollars.

A person exhibits **risk-neutral** behaviour if he is neither bothered by nor attracted to risk. He would be willing to play a game which is statistically fair but would not be excited by the prospect. A person exhibits **risk-averse** behaviour if, by contrast, he is bothered by risk and would avoid statistically fair games. Lastly, a person displays **risk-seeking** behaviour if he seeks out risk, readily playing statistically fair games and even playing games in which the odds are somewhat against him.

It is unlikely that any one person responds in the same way to every risk. For example, people who seek risk by visiting casinos or buying lottery tickets often avoid risks by insuring their houses and lives. You might also consider your own behaviour toward risk. How would you respond to the following gambles (both of which are statistically fair)?

1) You must pay $1 to play the first lottery. Anyone who plays it has one chance in 50,000 of winning $50,000.
2) Anyone who plays the second lottery automatically receives $1. However, each player also has one chance in 50,000 of losing $50,000.

Economists generally assume that people are risk-neutral when confronted with gambles in which the potential gains and losses are relatively small, but that they are risk averse when the stakes are high. They almost always assume that firms are risk-neutral.

Since every car is sold, the social benefit from the sale of cars is as great as it can possibly be. That is, the market outcome is efficient.

Akerlof examines the **asymmetric information equilibrium** that arises when only the current owner of a car knows the car's actual quality. Since the buyers cannot observe the quality of particular cars, all of the cars will trade at the same price. The buyers can only choose blindly from the cars offered for sale and hope for the best.

The behaviour of the buyers in this situation depends upon their attitude toward the risk involved.[2] Let's assume that the buyers are risk-neutral, and hence would be willing to pay as much as $3\mu/2$ for a car when the average quality of the cars offered for sale is μ. (The buyer would then be taking a statistically fair gamble, in the sense that he is just as likely to overpay for the car he purchases as to underpay.)

If the market price were p, the sellers would only offer to sell cars that have qualities less than p, and the average quality of the cars offered for sale, μ, would be $p/2$. The

---

[2] See the box on this page for a discussion of behaviour toward risk.

highest price that buyers would be willing to pay for a car would be $3p/4$. That is, the highest price that buyers would willingly pay would be smaller than the market price. There would be an excess supply of cars – some sellers and no buyers – so the market price would fall. Each decline in the market price would cause the sellers to withdraw the best cars from the market, reducing the average quality μ. Each fall in average quality would cause buyers to reduce the amount that they are willing to pay for a car. However much the market price fell, the amount that buyers would be willing to pay would remain below the market price until, at last, the market price reached zero.

When the price of cars is zero, no one wants to sell a car and no one wants to buy a car. The market is clearing in a formal sense, but none of the gains from trading cars are realized. The asymmetric information equilibrium is inefficient because the social benefits of trade are smaller in this equilibrium than in the full information equilibrium.

Adverse selection leads to the collapse of this market, but it does not always do so. Suppose, for example, that the value that buyers place on a car of quality q is $a + (3/2)q$, where a is between 0 and $1/4$. Under full information, every car is traded and the full social benefits of trade are realized. Under asymmetric information, some but not all of the cars are traded. If the market price were $4a$, the average quality of the cars offered for sale would be $2a$, and risk-neutral buyers would just be willing to pay $4a$ – that is, $a + (3/2)(2a)$ – for a randomly selected car. The market clears at this price:

> **The expected value of a randomly selected car is exactly equal to the market price, so each buyer is indifferent as to whether he purchases a car. He will buy a car if one is offered to him, but he won't be unhappy if no car is offered. Sellers who have cars of quality $4a$ or less want to sell their cars and are able to do so. Sellers who have cars of higher qualities don't sell because they prefer not to sell. Since there are no unsatisfied buyers or sellers at this price, the market is clearing.**

The market doesn't collapse under these assumptions, but that doesn't mean that the market is efficient. The quality of the best unsold car is $4a$. Its owner does not care whether it is sold because the market price is just equal to his valuation of the car. However, the car's true value to a buyer is $a + (3/2)(4a)$, which is $7a$. The sale of this car at any price between $4a$ and $7a$ would make both buyer and seller better off.

The full information equilibrium again realizes all of the social benefits of trade: the sale of each car is socially beneficial and every car is sold. The asymmetric information equilibrium yields only some of the social benefits of trade. The sale of each car is still socially beneficial, but not all of the cars are sold. Since the social benefits of trade are smaller in the asymmetric information equilibrium than in the full information equilibrium, the asymmetric information equilibrium is (again) inefficient.

19.2 MORAL HAZARD

Moral hazard has wide-ranging implications for the structure of all kinds of contracts – between a firm and its suppliers, between the management of the firm and the firm's employees, between the firm's owners and its managers. However, to add a little excite-ment to our lives, let's consider its effects on crime and punishment.[3]

Imagine a town that is split down the middle by railroad tracks. On one side of the tracks live G good guys. They don't smoke, drink, or gamble, and they would never ever steal. On the other side of the tracks live B bad guys. They gamble, and will deal from the bottom of the deck if you don't watch them closely. They smoke and drink, buying only from smugglers and bootleggers to avoid paying the excise taxes. And they'll steal if it's worth their while. In spite of their shortcomings, there's honour among these thieves, so they steal only from good guys.

Each good guy has an income of $\overline{y}_G$. If he is successfully robbed, he loses a part z of that income. However, robberies are not necessarily successful. The good guys have banded together, installing detection devices that result in the apprehension of a fraction p of all robbers. Every apprehended robber is convicted and transported to Australia where, after intensive instruction in the finer points of horse racing, they are let loose among the native population. The good guys can increase p by spending more on detection, but there is an increasing marginal cost of detection. In mathematical terms, the cost per good guy of apprehending robbers is $c(p)$, where

$$\frac{dc}{dp} > 0, \qquad \frac{d^2c}{dp^2} > 0$$

Good guys care only about their incomes, net of the expected loss from robbery, and the cost of detection. If a fraction q of all bad guys attempt a robbery, the probability of any given good guy being the object of a robbery attempt is Bq/G (i.e., the ratio of robbers to potential victims). Then the utility of a good guy is

$$u_G = \overline{y}_G - (Bq/G)(1-p)z - c(p)$$

where the middle term is the expected loss from robbery. The good guys will choose p to make themselves as well off as possible.[4]

If A is the loss experienced by a bad guy who is transported to Australia, a bad guy who becomes a robber experiences a gain of b, where

$$b = (1-p)z - pA$$

The first term is the expected income from robbery, and the second term is the expected cost of robbery. Bad guys consider only their own interests when deciding whether to steal.

This environment contains a hidden action. A good guy knows whether he has been robbed, but he does not immediately know who did it. He doesn't know where to go to

---

[3] The crime model in this section is loosely based on the work of Becker [7], who pioneered research into the economics that underlie such diverse activities as crime, discrimination, and family decision-making.

[4] Note that detection is a public good. We are assuming here that p is set through joint action which overcomes the free-rider problem, so that the moral hazard problem can be examined in isolation.

retrieve his stolen goods, and he doesn't know which bad guy should be transported. He has a chance of learning the identity of the perpetrator only if scarce resources are devoted to detection. The social consequences of the hidden action can be discovered by comparing, once again, the asymmetric information equilibrium to the full information equilibrium.

19.2.1 Asymmetric Information Equilibrium

The situation described above involves interaction between people, and we will again use ideas from game theory to describe the equilibrium. We actually have some choice in the way that the game is set up. One approach treats q as the fraction of agents who choose to become robbers. The other treats q as the probability with which any given bad guy chooses to become a robber. He steals if q is equal to 1 and he does not steal if q is equal to 0, while any value of q between 0 and 1 means that he steals with some positive probability. (If q is equal to 1/2, for example, he mentally flips a coin to decide whether to steal.) The latter approach, while somewhat less intuitive than the former, results in a slightly simpler game.

Each individual bad guy cares only about b, which is influenced by the probability of detection p. Given p, he chooses q to make himself as well off as possible. Since all of the bad guys are alike, and therefore choose the same q, the best guess of the fraction of bad guys becoming robbers is also q. Given q, the good guys choose p to maximize u_G. A Nash equilibrium in this game is a pair (p^*, q^*) such that

1) Each bad guy, knowing p^*, cannot do better than to choose q^* as his probability of becoming a robber.
2) The good guys, knowing q^*, cannot do better than to choose p^* as their probability of detection.

Let's look at their behaviour.

A bad guy's behaviour depends upon the sign of b: he will steal if it is positive, he will not steal if it is negative, and he does not care whether he steals if it is zero. Equivalently,

A bad guy does not steal ($q = 0$) if $p > z/(A + z)$. He steals ($q = 1$) if $p < z/(A + z)$. He does not care whether he steals (i.e., he is equally happy with any q) if $p = z/(A + z)$.

The above rule tells us a bad guy's best choice of q under every possible detection probability p. It is shown graphically in Figure 19.1.

The good guys choose p to maximize u_G, so the best choice of p satisfies the condition

$$\frac{\partial u_G}{\partial p} = (Bq/G)z - \frac{dc}{dp} = 0$$

or

$$\frac{dc}{dp} = (Bq/G)z \tag{19.1}$$

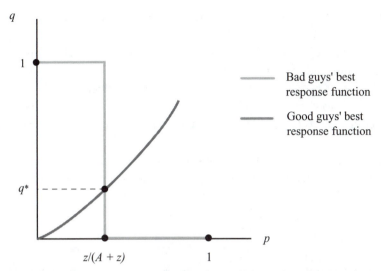

Figure 19.1: Equilibrium in the Robbery Game. The bad guys' best response function shows their best choice of q for any given p, and the good guys' best response function shows their best choice of p for any given q. The Nash equilibrium is the point at which the best response functions intersect.

This condition is an implicit equation that shows the relationship between p and q. The right-hand side of (19.1) rises with q. The left-hand side rises as p rises because

$$\frac{d}{dp}\left[\frac{dc}{dp}\right] \equiv \frac{d^2c}{dp^2} > 0$$

To maintain the equality in (19.1), p must rise when q rises – that is, the good guys spend more on detection as the probability of being robbed rises. The graph of (19.1) is also shown in Figure 19.1.[5]

The Nash equilibrium is the intersection point of the two graphs. In this equilibrium, some but not all of the bad guys try their hand at thievery. The expected gain from a robbery, b, is zero. The good guys devote some scarce resources to catching thieves, but catching them all is prohibitively expensive and some go free. For the good guys, the consequences of the bad guy's ability to make hidden actions appear both as the losses from theft and the cost of detection.

19.2.2 Full Information Equilibrium

Full information implies that the actions of bad guys are not hidden from the good guys. If a robbery occurs, the robber will be transported and the stolen goods returned to their rightful owner. Crime does not pay, so bad guys do not rob. Since the identity

---

[5] Actually, two additional restrictions must be imposed on c to ensure that the graph of (19.1) looks like that shown in Figure 19.1. The best response function passes through $(0, 0)$ if dc/dp, evaluated at $p = 0$, is equal to zero. The best response function becomes arbitarily steep as p approaches 1 if $\lim_{p \to 1}(dc/dp)$ is infinite. These restrictions also ensure that the best response functions intersect in the interior of the quadrant.

of a robber would be known immediately, the good guys need not devote any of their resources to detection.

The bad guys are just as well off under the full information equilibrium as under the asymmetric information equilibrium: the expected return to robbery under asymmetric information was zero, so a switch to an equilibrium in which they do not steal does not change their welfare. The good guys, however, are better off under full information. They never lose goods through theft, and they do not expend any of their resources on detection.

Society is better off under the full information equilibrium than under the asymmetric information equilibrium, leading again to the conclusion that asymmetry of information is damaging to the economy.

QUESTIONS

1. The amount of output produced by each worker at a firm depends upon the worker's ability. Specifically, each worker produces $1 + \theta$ units of goods each day, where θ represents the worker's ability and varies between workers. The abilities of the firm's current workers are uniformly distributed on the interval $[0, 1]$. Workers know their own abilities, but the firm cannot observe an individual worker's ability or his contribution to output.
   a) What is the average daily output of the firm's workers?
   b) The firm reduces its workforce by 20% by offering the workers a "buy-out" (i.e., financial compensation for voluntarily leaving the firm). Workers with higher abilities are more confident of finding equally good employment elsewhere, and hence the 20% of the workforce with the highest ability leave the firm. What is the average daily output of the firm's workers after the buy-out?
   c) Suppose that the firm randomly selects 20% of its workforce to be laid off. What is the average daily output of the firm's workers after the lay-offs?
   d) Suppose that the firm offers a buy-out in order to reduce its workforce by 20%, but that its buy-out is so generous that 40% of the workforce accepts it. The firm reduces its workforce by 20% by giving the buy-out to half of the workers who wanted it and retaining the remainder of the workers. The workers given the buy-out are randomly selected from the workers who asked for it. What is the average daily output of the firm's workers after the buy-out?

2. Imagine an economy in which the only industry is picking apples. An apple picker earns an income of 1 if he can work, but with probability $1 - \theta$ he will fall out of a tree, breaking a leg and rendering himself unfit for further apple picking. His income will then be 0. Each person's utility is

$$U = y^{1/2}$$

where y is his income, so his expected utility – the statistical best guess of his utility – is

$$E U_0 = \theta(1)^{1/2} + (1 - \theta)(0)^{1/2} = \theta$$

Apple pickers can protect themselves by buying falling-out-of-a-tree insurance. The terms of this insurance are that the insurer will provide the apple picker with an income z (where $z \leq 1$) if he falls out of a tree, and in return, the apple picker will pay the insurer a fraction p of his income, whatever that income turns out to be. The expected utility of an insured apple picker is therefore

$$EU_1 = \theta(1 - p)^{1/2} + (1 - \theta)[z(1 - p)]^{1/2} = (1 - p)^{1/2}[\theta + z^{1/2}(1 - \theta)]$$

a) Assume that the insurer offers full insurance (i.e., z is equal to one) and knows the value of θ. Find the largest premium p at which an apple picker will accept insurance – that is, find the largest p at which his expected utility when insured is at least as great as his expected utility when he is not insured. Calculate the expected profits of the insurer on a single insurance contract. Finally, show that if the insurer charges the highest premium that apple pickers will pay, its expected profits are positive.

b) Assume that the insurer offers full insurance, and that there are two kinds of apple pickers, awkward and clumsy. Awkward apple pickers fall out of trees with probability $1/3$, and clumsy apple pickers fall out of trees with probability $2/3$. A fraction α of the apple pickers are awkward, and the rest are clumsy. Each apple picker knows whether he is awkward or clumsy, but an insurer cannot tell the difference between the two. If both kinds of workers buy insurance, an insurer's expected profits on a single insurance contract are

$$E\pi = \alpha E\pi_a + (1 - \alpha)E\pi_c$$

where $E\pi_a$ and $E\pi_c$ are the expected profits on a contract issued to an awkward and a clumsy person, respectively. Show that if an insurer charges the highest premium at which both kinds of workers are willing to purchase insurance, his expected profits will be positive if α is sufficiently large and negative if α is sufficiently large. Find the value of α at which his expected profits are exactly equal to zero.

c) Assume again that there are two kinds of apple pickers and that an insurer cannot distinguish between them, but now assume that the insurer offers only partial insurance. Specifically, assume that z is only $1/4$. Show that if an insurer charges the highest premium at which both kinds of workers are willing to purchase insurance, his expected profits will be positive for any value of α.

3. Life is even tougher for the sugar cane cutters. If a cane cutter is fortunate, he collects an income of y_G, and his utility is

$$U_G = 9(y_G)^{1/2}$$

If he is unfortunate, he is bitten by a snake. His income is y_B, and he experiences a great deal of pain. His utility is

$$U_B = 9(y_B)^{1/2} - 6$$

A cane cutter can reduce the probability of being bitten by a snake to $7/16$ by taking a number of tedious and annoying precautions. These precautions reduce his utility by an amount 3/4. Thus, if a cane cutter takes these precautions – if he is careful – his expected utility is

$$EU_1 = \tfrac{9}{16}U_G + \tfrac{7}{16}U_B - \tfrac{3}{4}$$

If he elects to take no precautions, his probability of a snake bite is 5/9 but he avoids the tedium of the precautions themselves. The expected utility of a careless cane cutter is therefore

$$EU_0 = \tfrac{4}{9}U_G + \tfrac{5}{9}U_B$$

a) Assume that a cane cutter's income is 1 if he is not bitten and 0 if he is bitten, and that the cane cutters cannot obtain insurance. Show that the cane cutters will take precautions against snake bites. Calculate the expected utility of a cane cutter.

b) Now assume that insurance becomes available. An insured cane cutter receives from the insurer an income of 1 if he is bitten, but he pays to the insurer a fraction p of his income whether or not he is bitten. Show that insured cane cutters do not take precautions against snake bite.

c) Assume that the insurers cannot determine whether a cutter takes precautions or not, so the premium cannot depend upon the behaviour of the cutter. Assume also that competition among insurers drives down the premium to the point that an insurer's expected profits on each contract is equal to zero. Calculate the expected utility of an insured cane cutter. Would cane cutters buy insurance?

d) Show that if every cane cutter took precautions against snake bites, and if the premium were again set so that the insurer's expected profits were equal to zero, each cane cutter would be better off than he is when everyone is insured but no one takes precautions.

4. An individual hires an agent to sell an object for him. The object's owner does not know the actual value of the object, but he knows that it is worth nothing with probability 1/2, and worth \$10 with probability 1/2. The agent will sell the object, report its sale price to the owner, and pay the owner part or all of the proceeds from the sale. Specifically,

- If the agent reports that the sale price was \$10, he pays R dollars to the owner.
- If the agent reports that the object was worth nothing and the owner accepts this report, the agent pays nothing to the owner. However, the owner can also choose to reject the report. If he does so, he must pay \$2 to learn the true sale price of the object from an independent source. If he finds that the agent lied about the sale price, the owner receives the entire sale price (\$10) while the agent pays a fine of \$50 to the government.

Assume that the both the owner and the agent act so as to maximize their own expected profits from the sale of the object. Let y be the probability that the agent, having actually sold the object for \$10, claims it to have been worth nothing. Let x be the probability that the owner, having been told that the object was worth nothing, rejects the report. A Nash equilibrium in this situation is a pair (x^*, y^*) such that

i) If the agent lies with probability y^*, the owner's expected profits are maximized when he rejects with probability x^*.

ii) If the owner rejects with probability x^*, the agent's expected profits are maximized when he lies with probability y^*.

Find the Nash equilibrium for any R between 0 and 10. Find the expected profits of the owner and the agent for any R. What value of R (where $0 \leq R \leq 10$) maximizes the owner's expected profits? What are the owner's and the agent's expected profits under this value of R? Does the *sum* of the owner's and agent's expected profits equal the true expected value of the object?

20

Preference Revelation

Chapter 10 described the optimal quantity of a pure public good and argued that it would not be provided in a competitive environment. Attempts to provide the good privately are frustrated by free-riding, which is individually rational but ultimately self-defeating. The government plays a major role in the provision of these goods because it can eliminate free-riding by dictating the quantity provided and the manner of its financing.

Providing the right quantity of public goods is not something that the government can easily do. The optimal quantity of a public good depends upon the preferences of the people in the community, but these preferences are not immediately observable. The government must ask people to disclose the intensity of their desire for the public good. However, the people who benefit from the public good are also, by and large, the people who pay for it. If they believe that their disclosures will affect their taxes, they might strategically misrepresent their preferences. The government's decision would then be based upon inaccurate information.

The government can act correctly only if it can obtain truthful information about preferences, and this information might not be willingly revealed by the people who have it. This problem is called the **preference revelation** problem. This chapter examines a simple economy in which preferences might not be truthfully revealed, and discusses the means through which the government can circumvent the problem.

20.1 PREFERENCE REVELATION IN A SIMPLE ECONOMY

Imagine an economy in which there are n people. Each person's utility depends upon his own consumption of bread b, and the quantity of public good z. There are two types of people, differing only in the intensity of their liking for the public good. There are h people who have the utility function

$$u_H = \frac{\theta_H}{\alpha} (z)^\alpha + b$$

304

and $n - h$ people who have the utility function

$$u_L = \frac{\theta_L}{\alpha} (z)^\alpha + b$$

The parameters in the utility functions satisfy these restrictions:

$$0 < \alpha < 1$$

$$0 < \theta_L < \theta_H$$

People of the first type place a high value on public goods and will be called "type H." People of the second type place a low value on public goods and will be called "type L."

Each person is endowed with $\overline{b}$ units of bread, which is either consumed as bread or taxed away by the government. The government uses all of its tax revenue to provide the public good. One unit of bread is needed to produce one unit of public goods.

20.1.1 Lindahl Equilibrium

The Samuelson condition states that the optimal quantity of public goods is provided when the sum of the marginal rates of substitution is equal to the marginal rate of transformation.[1] Each person's marginal rate of substitution generally depends upon his consumption of both public and private goods. People can afford fewer private goods when they pay higher taxes, so each person's marginal rate of substitution is affected by *both* the quantity of public good provided *and* the manner in which it is financed. The optimal quantity of public goods can change as the burden of paying for the public good is shifted from one segment of society to another. Consequently, it is generally necessary to determine simultaneously the quantity and financing of the public good.

Lindahl equilibrium describes one way of simultaneously choosing the quantity of public good provided and assigning shares of its cost to the members of society. The quantity of public good is determined by the Samuelson condition. Each person is also assessed a **tax price** for the public good. His tax price is equal to his marginal rate of substitution, and his share of the cost of financing the public good is equal to his tax price multiplied by the number of units of public goods provided (z). Then

- The revenue raised by this scheme is z times as large as the sum of the tax prices. Alternatively, it is z times as large as the sum of the marginal rates of substitution.
- The cost of providing the public good is z times as large as the marginal rate of transformation.

[1] As in our earlier discussion of public goods, the marginal rate of substitution is the amount of bread that exactly compensates for the loss of one unit of public goods, and the marginal rate of transformation is the amount of bread gained by society when production of the public good is reduced by one unit.

Since the sum of the marginal rates of substitution is equal to the marginal rate of transformation when the Samuelson condition is satisfied, the tax revenue is exactly equal to the cost of providing the public good.

The Lindahl equilibrium in the economy described above is easily discovered because the marginal rates of substitution do *not* depend upon private consumption. The Samuelson condition for this economy is

$$hMRS_H + (n - h)MRS_L = 1$$

where MRS_H and MRS_L are the marginal rates of substitution of type H and type L people. Each marginal rate of substitution is the ratio of the partial derivatives of the utility function:

$$MRS_H = \theta_H(z)^{\alpha-1}$$
$$MRS_L = \theta_L(z)^{\alpha-1}$$

Substituting the marginal rates of substitution into the Samuelson condition and solving for z gives the optimal quantity of public good. That quantity depends upon the number of type H people in the economy:

$$z^*(h) = (h\theta_H + (n - h)\theta_L)^{1/(1-\alpha)}$$

The tax imposed upon each person depends upon his type and the quantity of public good produced. The taxes imposed on type H and type L people when z units of the public good are produced are

$$\tau_H(z) = MRS_H \times z = \theta_H(z)^\alpha$$
$$\tau_L(z) = MRS_L \times z = \theta_L(z)^\alpha$$

The Lindahl equilibrium, when there are h people of type H, involves the production of $z^*(h)$ units of public goods, and the imposition of taxes $\tau_H(z^*(h))$ and $\tau_L(z^*(h))$ on type H and type L people, respectively.

20.1.2 Can the Lindahl Equilibrium Be Implemented?

Imagine that the government knows that each person is either type L or type H, but that it does not know which people are type H. Indeed, it does not even know how many type H people there are in the economy. It cannot immediately implement the Lindahl equilibrium, because it does not know how many units of the public good should be produced, and it does not know which people should pay the higher tax. The government can implement the Lindahl equilibrium only if people reveal their types, but people reveal their types only if it is in their interest to do so.

Each person has two options: he can reveal his type or he can lie about it. His choice hinges upon the quantities of public good that would be produced if he told the truth and if he lied – and these quantities are determined by the claims made by every other person. Thus, preference revelation is a strategic game, in which each person's decision is influenced by every other person's decision.

The basic elements of the strategic game are

- Each person can claim to be either type H or type L.
- The government acts as if everyone truthfully reveals his type. That is, if $\widetilde{h}$ people claim to be type H, it provides $z^*(\widetilde{h})$ units of the public good, and imposes the taxes $\tau_H(z^*(\widetilde{h}))$ and $\tau_L(z^*(\widetilde{h}))$, respectively, on people who claim to be type H and type L.
- Each person anticipates the government's behaviour and knows every other person's claim. He is therefore able to calculate the utility that he would have if he told the truth and if he lied.
- A Nash equilibrium in this game consists of a claim for every person in the economy, such that (i) each person who truthfully reveals his type would not have a higher utility if he instead chose to lie, and (ii) each person who lies about his type would have a lower utility if he instead chose to tell the truth.[2]

The circumstances under which a person will tell the truth can be discovered by comparing his utility when he tells the truth to his utility when he lies. Let's consider each type of person in turn.

Behaviour of Type H People

Imagine that a type H person knows that $\widetilde{h} - 1$ of the other $n - 1$ people have claimed to be type H. If he reveals his own type, the government will produce $z^*(\widetilde{h})$ units of public goods and impose upon him the tax $\tau_H(z^*(\widetilde{h}))$. His utility will be

$$u_H = z^*(\widetilde{h}) \left[\frac{\theta_H}{\alpha} - \theta_H \right]$$

On the other hand, if he claims to be type L, the government will produce $z^*(\widetilde{h} - 1)$ units of public goods and impose upon him the tax $\tau_L(z^*(\widetilde{h} - 1))$. His utility would be

$$u_H = z^*(\widetilde{h} - 1) \left[\frac{\theta_H}{\alpha} - \theta_L \right]$$

His utility when he tells the truth is at least as great as his utility when he lies if

$$\frac{(\widetilde{h} - 1)\theta_H + (n - \widetilde{h} + 1)\theta_L}{\widetilde{h}\theta_H + (n - \widetilde{h})\theta_L} \leq \left[\frac{(1 - \alpha)\theta_H}{\theta_H - \alpha\theta_L} \right]^{(1-\alpha)/\alpha} \tag{20.1}$$

---

[2] I have actually deviated slightly from the formal concept of Nash equilibrium by requiring people to tell the truth if they are equally well off under either claim. (A true Nash equilibrium would allow them to lie if telling the truth does not make them better off.) This deviation simplifies the subsequent discussion, but does not significantly alter the results.

The right-hand side of this inequality does not depend upon $\widetilde{h}$, but the left-hand side rises as $\widetilde{h}$ rises.[3] It follows that any given type H person would tell the truth if many people are claiming to be type L.

Now imagine that a type H person knows that $\widetilde{h}$ (rather than $\widetilde{h} - 1$) of the other $n - 1$ people are claiming to be type H. An argument similar to the last one shows that lying about his type would give him a higher utility than telling the truth if

$$\left[\frac{(1 - \alpha)\theta_H}{\theta_H - \alpha\theta_L} \right]^{(1-\alpha)/\alpha} < \frac{(\widetilde{h})\theta_H + (n - \widetilde{h})\theta_L}{(\widetilde{h} + 1)\theta_H + (n - \widetilde{h} - 1)\theta_L} \tag{20.2}$$

The right-hand side of this inequality rises with $\widetilde{h}$, so any given type H person would lie if many people were claiming to be type H.

There is only one integer value of $\widetilde{h}$ that satisfies *both* (20.1) and (20.2). Call this integer k, and imagine that k people among the n people in the economy are claiming to be type H. Each type H person who is telling the truth would know that $k - 1$ of the other $n - 1$ people are claiming to be type H, and by (20.1), would not benefit by switching to a lie. Simultaneously, each type H who is not telling the truth would know that k of the other $n - 1$ people are claiming to be type H, and by (20.2), would be worse off it he told the truth. Thus, each type H person who is lying would continue to lie, and each type H person who is telling the truth would continue to tell the truth.

Behaviour of Type L People

Type L people do not lie about their types. To see why they don't lie, consider what happens to a type H person who switches from truth-telling to lying.

> The imposter's tax price immediately falls. If the government does not change the level of public good provision, his consumption of bread rises by z times the difference in the tax prices, leading to an equal rise in his utility. Since his tax price is now lower, he would be happy to see the government raise the level of public good provision. The government, finding that there is one fewer type H person and one more type L person, does just the opposite. That's a bad break, but so long as a lot of other people are claiming to be type H – so that public goods are still generously provided – the imposter's increased bread consumption more than compensates him for the loss of public goods. On the other hand, if not many other people are claiming to be type H, the quantity of public goods provided was small before he switched and is even smaller now. The additional bread consumption does not compensate him for the loss of public goods, and he regrets his decision.

A type L person who switches from truth-telling to lying is less fortunate.

---

[3] Each one-unit increase in $\widetilde{h}$ raises both the numerator and the denominator by $\theta_H - \theta_L$. Since the numerator is smaller than the denominator, the increase in the numerator is proportionally bigger than the increase in the denominator, causing the ratio to rise.

Table 20.1: The
Number of Truthful
High-Valuation People

α	k
3/4	2
7/8	3
15/16	8
31/32	9
63/64	15
127/128	26

The imposter's tax price rises, reducing his consumption of bread by z times the difference in the tax prices. There is an immediate drop in his utility. Since he is now paying a larger part of the cost of each unit of public good, he would like to see the government cut back on its provision of the public good. The government, responding to the signal that there is one more type H person and one fewer type L person, chooses instead to increase the provision of public goods. This adjustment makes the imposter even worse off than he was before.

Any individual who switches from truth-telling to lying will experience changes in his tax price and in public good provision. For a type H person, these changes have opposing effects on his utility. He might be better off, and he might be worse off. For a type L person, these changes unambiguously reduce welfare.

Nash Equilibrium

Describing the Nash equilibrium is now just a matter of putting the pieces together. Type L people tell the truth. If there are no more than k type H people in the economy, every one of them will also choose to tell the truth. However, if there are more than k type H people, exactly k of them will tell the truth and the remainder will lie.

Clearly, the likelihood of truthful revelation depends upon the value of k. If k is small, some people will lie – unless h happens to be even smaller. Let's find the value of k in some simple cases.

If θ_L is equal to zero, k is the integer that satisfies the condition

$$\frac{k-1}{k} \leq (1-\alpha)^{(1-\alpha)/\alpha} < \frac{k}{k+1}$$

Table 20.1 shows how this number varies with α. The results are not particularly encouraging. Truthful revelation occurs only when there is a very small number of type H people, or when the marginal utility of a unit of public goods declines very slowly. For example, if α is equal to 31/32, some type H people will lie if the economy contains more than nine people of that type.

Truthful revelation is even less likely when θ_L is positive. If θ_L is half as large as θ_H, k is the integer that satisfies the condition

$$\frac{n+k-1}{n+k} \leq \left[\frac{2-2\alpha}{2-\alpha}\right]^{(1-\alpha)/\alpha} < \frac{n+k}{n+k+1}$$

Although k rises with α, it is only large when α is very close to 1. For example, if α is equal to $127/128$, k is only $30 - n$ when n is less than 30, and it is 0 otherwise. The largest economy in which truthtelling is assured (i.e., in which $k \geq n$) contains only fifteen people.

20.1.3 An Alternative Tax Regime

A government attempting to implement the Lindahl equilibrium will almost certainly be unable to do so, because some type H people will claim to be type L, causing the quantity of public good provided to be smaller than is optimal. But does the revelation problem arise only with the Lindahl equilibrium, or will it also arise under other tax systems?

At first sight, it might seem as if people sometimes lie about their types under the Lindahl equilibrium because their claims determine their tax prices. If this were so, abandoning the Lindahl equilibrium, and instead assigning each person the same tax price, would remove the incentive to lie. People would truthfully reveal their types, allowing the government to provide the optimal quantity of public good. This argument turns out to be correct in the economy described above, but only because that economy is so simple. It is not correct in an economy that is very slightly more complicated.

If the cost of each unit of public good were shared equally across the n people living in the economy, each person's tax price would be $1/n$. The level of public goods provision that would make a person of type H as well off as possible is found by maximizing the utility

$$U_H = \left(\frac{\theta_H}{\alpha} \right) z^\alpha - \frac{z}{n}$$

It is

$$\widehat{z}_H \equiv (n\theta_H)^{1/(1-\alpha)}$$

Similarly, the level of public goods provision that would make a type L person as well off as possible is

$$\widehat{z}_L \equiv (n\theta_L)^{1/(1-\alpha)}$$

If the government uses the Samuelson condition to determine the quantity of public good actually provided, that quantity is $z^*(\widetilde{h})$ when $\widetilde{h}$ people claim to be type H. The government produces $\widehat{z}_L$ units when no one claims to be type H. It produces more units of the public good as the number of people claiming to be type H rises, and produces $\widehat{z}_H$ units when everyone claims to be type H.

Under this tax regime, any person who lies about his type would move the actual quantity of the public good farther away from the quantity that he most desires, making himself worse off. Consequently, each person truthfully reveals his type, allowing the government to determine the Pareto optimal quantity of the public good. There is no revelation problem.

Unfortunately, even a small change in the nature of the economy will resurrect the revelation problem. Suppose that there are three types of people in the economy: the two described above, and a type M (for "middle") whose utility function is

$$U_M = \left(\frac{\theta_M}{\alpha} \right) z^\alpha + b$$

Here, θ_M is a constant lying between θ_L and θ_H. If everyone has the same tax price, the quantity of public good most desired by a person of this type would be

$$\widehat{z}_M = (n\theta_M)^{1/(1-\alpha)}$$

Suppose, as before, that the government believes people's claims, and uses the Samuelson condition to determine the quantity of public good actually produced. If $\widetilde{h}$ people claim to be type H and $\widetilde{m}$ claim to be type M, the quantity produced is

$$z^{**} = \left(\widetilde{h}\theta_H + \widetilde{m}\theta_M + (n - \widetilde{h} - \widetilde{m})\theta_L \right)^{1/(1-\alpha)}$$

This quantity could be as low as $\widehat{z}_L$ or as high as $\widehat{z}_H$.

Will people of each type tell the truth? Certainly, people of types L and H will do so. Claiming to be a type other than their true type will push z^{**} farther away from their most desired quantity, making them worse off. It is likely, however, that some of the type M people will lie. Suppose that z^{**} is less than $\widehat{z}_M$ when everyone tells the truth. It might well be that the type M people would be better off if one or more of them were to claim to be type H, so that z^{**} is pulled toward $\widehat{z}_M$.[4] Similarly, if z^{**} is greater than $\widehat{z}_M$ when everyone tells the truth, the type M people might be better off if some of them were to claim to be type L.[5]

The revelation problem isn't solved by anything as simple as a uniform tax price, but it can be solved. Specifically, there are some tax systems, called **revelation mechanisms,** that induce truthtelling. One of these is examined below.

20.2 THE GROVES–CLARKE MECHANISM

Imagine an economy consisting of n people, identified by the integers from 1 to n. Person i has the utility function

$$u_i = \frac{\theta_i}{\alpha} (z)^\alpha + b_i$$

---

[4] There is no guarantee that some type M people will lie. It could be that, if just one type M lies, z^{**} rises so much above $\widehat{z}_M$ that the type M people are worse off. Every type M person would then tell the truth. What is important here is that there is also no guarantee that every type M will tell the truth.

[5] The Lindahl example, described earlier, is one in which too few units of the public good might be provided, but too many units would never be provided. This outcome accords with our notion of free-riding. Note, however, that the quantity of public good provided can be either too large or too small in the three-type example.

where θ_i is some positive finite number. Each person is endowed with $\bar{b}$ units of bread. Some of person i's endowment of bread will be used to pay his share of the cost of the public good, T_i, and the remainder will be consumed, implying

$$b_i = \bar{b} - T_i$$

One unit of bread is needed to produce each unit of the public good.

The government is aware that each person's utility function takes the above form, but the parameter θ_i is private information known only to person i. The task confronting the government is to induce each person to truthfully reveal this information, so that the government can provide the socially optimal quantity of public goods.

Clarke [16] and Groves and Loeb [30] describe a mechanism that solves the government's problem. Each person in the economy reports to the government the strength of his preferences for the public good. Specifically, person i reports that the parameter in his utility function is $\widetilde{\theta}_i$. He will report the true value of the parameter, θ_i, if he thinks that it is in his interest to do so; otherwise, he will attempt to advance his own interests by reporting some fictitious value. Under the Groves–Clarke (what happened to Loeb?) mechanism, the government determines the optimal quantity of public goods by applying the Samuelson rule under the assumption that these reports are true. The quantity of public goods provided then satisfies the condition

$$z^{\alpha-1} \sum_{j=1}^{n} \widetilde{\theta}_j = 1$$

Alternatively, it satisfies the condition

$$z^{\alpha-1} \left(\widetilde{\theta}_i + \widetilde{s}_i \right) = 1 \tag{20.3}$$

where $\widetilde{s}_i$ is the sum of the parameters reported by everyone other than person i:

$$\widetilde{s}_i = \widetilde{\theta}_1 + \widetilde{\theta}_2 + \cdots + \widetilde{\theta}_{i-1} + \widetilde{\theta}_{i+1} + \cdots + \widetilde{\theta}_n$$

The government then imposes a tax on each person. The tax T_i imposed on person i has two components:

$$T_i = \left[z - \left(\frac{\widetilde{s}_i}{\alpha} \right) z^{\alpha} \right] + f_i \tag{20.4}$$

The first component is equal to the total cost of the public goods, less the value of these goods to everyone other than person i. The second component is f_i, and for the moment, it is set equal to zero. Note that person i's tax depends upon his report $\widetilde{\theta}_i$ indirectly (because his report influences z) but not directly.

Now consider the behaviour of person i when he is confronted by the provision rule (20.3) and the tax rule (20.4). He can manipulate the quantity of public goods provided through his report $\widetilde{\theta}_i$, but there are tax consequences of doing so. Specifically, if he pushes z upwards, his taxes will rise by the difference between the cost of the additional public goods, and the value that everyone other than himself *claims* to place on these goods. If he places a high value on the additional public goods, he will be willing to bear the tax increase; but if he places only a small value on the additional public goods, he will not be willing to bear the tax increase. From the perspective of person i, the right quantity of public goods satisfies this condition:

The value that he places on one more unit of public goods is equal to the cost of an additional unit, less the sum of the values that individuals other than himself claim to place on an additional unit.

But the value that an individual places on a unit of public goods, measured in bread, is his marginal rate of substitution; and the cost of another unit of public goods, also measured in bread, is the marginal rate of transformation. Thus, this condition can also be expressed as

$$MRS_i = MRT - \sum_{j \neq i} \widetilde{MRS}_j \tag{20.5}$$

where MRS_i is person i's true marginal rate of substitution, and $\widetilde{MRS}_j$ is the *claimed* marginal rate of substitution of person j. The sum on the right-hand side includes the claimed marginal rate of substitution of every person other than person i. The government, on the other hand, chooses the quantity of public good in accordance with the rule

$$\widetilde{MRS}_i = MRT - \sum_{j \neq i} \widetilde{MRS}_j \tag{20.6}$$

Thus, under the Groves–Clarke mechanism, person i's rule for determining the quantity of public good that is best for himself is (20.5), while the rule used by the government to determine the actual quantity of public good is (20.6). These rules coincide if person i truthfully reveals his preferences to the government. That is, person i wants to tell the truth – and he will do so regardless of the choices made by the other people. Honesty really is the best policy.

Person i is just an arbitrarily chosen member of the society. What is true of him is true of everyone in the society. Every person wants to tell the truth, regardless of what every other person does, so everyone will ultimately tell the truth. Since every claim is a truthful claim, the government's decision rule leads to the provision of the socially optimal quantity of the public good.

The same argument can be made more precisely. Under the Groves–Clarke mechanism, person i's utility is

$$U_i = \left(\frac{\theta_i}{\alpha}\right) z^\alpha + \overline{b} - z + \left(\frac{\widetilde{s}_i}{\alpha}\right) z^\alpha \tag{20.7}$$

His utility is maximized when the quantity of public goods satisfies the condition

$$\frac{dU_i}{dz} = (\theta_i + \widetilde{s}_i) z^{\alpha-1} - 1 = 0 \tag{20.8}$$

The rule that the government actually uses to determine the quantity of public goods is (20.3). Comparing (20.3) and (20.8) shows that person i's preferred quantity of the public good is provided when he reports truthfully. The same is true for everyone in the economy, so everyone will be truthful, and consequently, the quantity of public good provided by the government satisfies the Samuelson condition.

Unfortunately, with f_i equal to zero for each person i, this mechanism does not raise enough revenue to pay for the public good. As observed earlier, the revenue raised just covers the cost of the public good when these conditions hold:

- Each person's tax price is equal to the cost of another unit of public goods, less the sum of every other person's marginal valuation of a unit of public goods.
- The optimal quantity of public goods is provided.

The Groves–Clarke mechanism ensures that the optimal quantity of public good is provided; but by (20.4), person i's tax price is set equal to the cost of a unit of public goods, less the sum of every other person's *average* valuation of the public goods provided.[6] Because each person's marginal utility of the public good declines as the quantity of the public good rises, each person's average valuation is always larger than his marginal valuation. Consequently, the Groves–Clarke mechanism sets each tax price too low to cover the cost of the public good.

This problem is resolved by the second component of the tax. Each person i is assigned an additional tax f_i, set so that total tax revenues are at least as large as the cost of the public good. Setting these taxes is somewhat tricky, because two opposing factors must be taken into account.

First, the revenue that must be raised by the second component of the tax is the difference between the total cost of the public good and the revenue raised by the first component of the tax. It is therefore determined by the reports of the people living in the economy, but these reports are sent *after* the tax system has been set out. That is, the second component of the tax must be set without knowing how much revenue it must raise. If the second component is lump sum, it must be set exorbitantly high to ensure that enough revenue is raised. A better solution is to make this component of the tax dependent upon the reports received.

Second, f_i cannot depend upon person i's report $\widetilde{\theta}_i$, either indirectly (through z) or directly. If it does, the incentive for truthtelling generated by the first component of the tax is lost.

This dilemma is resolved by making person i's tax component f_i depend only upon the reports sent by other people. In the example described here, for instance, each f_i could depend upon $\widetilde{s}_i$. Clarke [16] and Groves and Loeb [30] show that it is possible to construct functions f_i so that the revenue raised is at least as great as the cost of the public good.

---

[6] His total tax depends upon the others' *total* valuation of the public goods, so his tax price (i.e., his tax per unit of the public good) depends upon their average valuation.

Unfortunately, it is generally not possible to design functions that raise *exactly* the required revenue. Excess revenue is as much of a problem as insufficient revenue. If it is known that any excess revenue is rebated to the people living in the economy, each person will recognize that his report influences the amount of excess revenue, and hence the amount of the rebate. The incentive for truthtelling would again be lost. The only alternative is to "waste" the excess revenue. The efficient quantity of public good would be provided, but the economy would be operating inside the production possibility frontier. The amount of waste can be minimized if the government can make a fairly accurate guess of the optimal quantity of public good – but if it can, the Groves–Clarke mechanism isn't needed.

Groves and Ledyard [29] describe an alternative mechanism under which tax revenue is exactly equal to the cost of the public good. The Groves–Ledyard mechanism is somewhat more complicated, and somewhat less intuitive, than the Groves–Clarke mechanism, and will not be described here.

These mechanisms suffer from two shortcomings that limit their usefulness. First, they are difficult to understand, and people confronted with a mechanism that they don't understand are unlikely to respond in a predictable fashion.[7] Second, if there are many people in the economy, each person's decision has a very small impact on his tax payment and the quantity of public goods. It is therefore unlikely that people will devote much effort to their reports. They will be dishonest out of laziness rather than cunning.

20.3 PREFERENCE REVELATION IN PRACTICE

Governments seem to provide adequate quantities of police and fire protection, roads and bridges, and many other (impure) public goods. Should we conclude that preference revelation isn't an issue of great importance?

Let's be careful here. This conclusion would be justified if free-riding were the only sort of strategic behaviour, but it is not. The first example in this chapter is essentially a free-riding problem: people understate their preferences for the public good to avoid paying for the good. In the second (three-type) example, however, the character of the problem is quite different. People lie to change the quantity of public good provided, but the equilibrium quantity might be quite close to the optimal quantity, and it could be either above or below the optimal quantity. A public good can be either overprovided or underprovided.

Equally, an ample supply of any good is not evidence that the optimal quantity is supplied. The quantity of labour supplied in any economy is very large, but this observation does not imply that the welfare cost of the income tax is insignificant.

---

[7] For example the American president in the 2002 election was determined by a recount of the ballots in Palm Beach County, Florida. Several thousand voters in this county appeared to have unintentionally voted for a fringe candidate, and almost 20,000 voters invalidated their ballots by voting for more than one candidate. Events like this one suggest that a successful voting system has to be an extremely simple one.

Nevertheless, Johansen [35] has argued that there is no compelling evidence that the quantity of public goods provided differs greatly from the optimal quantity, and many economists have echoed this view. They argue that public goods are generally provided by governments, and that these governments are elected by the people who benefit from the public goods. The elections might then be viewed as a rough-and-ready preference revelation mechanism. Each person votes for the candidate whose views most closely resemble his own, and in doing so, might reveal as much information about his preferences as can practicably be collected.

QUESTIONS

1. Consider an economy consisting of three people – A, B, and C. Person i (where i is A, B, or C) has the utility function

$$U_i = z^{1/3}(c_i)^{2/3}$$

where z is the quantity of public good provided and c_i is person i's consumption of private goods. Person i's income y_i is divided between consumption of the private good and his contribution to the financing of the public good. Person i's contribution is the product of his "tax price" t_i and the quantity of the public good, so

$$c_i + t_i z = y_i$$

Person A's income is 90, person B's income is 120 and person C's income is 150. Twenty units of private good must be given up to produce each unit of public good. Find the Lindahl equilibrium.

2. Consider a three-type economy like the one described in Section 20.1.3. Assume that θ_H is 10, θ_M is 4 and θ_L is 2.
   a) Assume that there are 5 type H people, 15 type M people, and 10 type L people. Find a Nash equilibrium.
   b) Assume that there are no type H people, 15 type M people, and 15 type L people. Find a Nash equilibrium.

21

Regulation of a Natural Monopoly

It was argued in Section 18.2 that, if taxes are distortionary, the best policy for regulating a natural monopoly has three components:

- If the monopoly incurs a loss, the government should collect extra tax revenue to cover the loss.[1]
- If the monopoly earns a profit, the government should appropriate the profit and reduce the revenue raised through taxation by an equal amount.
- The pricing of the monopoly's output involves a trade-off. As the price rises above marginal cost, fewer units of the monopoly's good are purchased, and less consumer surplus is generated in the monopoly's market. However, the monopoly's profits rise, so less revenue needs to be raised through distortionary taxes. The decline in the welfare cost of the tax system means that more surplus is generated elsewhere in the economy. The regulator should choose the price that maximizes total surplus.

The model on which this policy was based neglects the role of management. Energetic and effective management will be reflected in lower costs, while lax management will result in higher costs. But if management is important, the policy described above is unlikely to be optimal. Why should the managers strive for greater profits, if profits are appropriated by the government? Why should they avoid losses, if losses are automatically covered by the government?

If the regulator can directly observe the managers' behaviour, the answer to these questions is easy: the regulator can induce the managers to work efficiently by punishing lax behaviour. But if the regulator cannot directly observe the managers' behaviour, the possibility of moral hazard arises. The managers are likely to focus on personal

---

[1] Society is better off when the monopoly operates than when it does not if the consumer surplus generated by the monopoly is greater than its costs. The government should then cover the monopoly's losses so that the monopoly can continue to operate. However, if the consumer surplus generated by the monopoly is less than its cost of production, the monopoly should be shut down.

317

satisfaction rather than society's interests. Laffont and Tirole [38] offer these examples of the kind of behaviour that the managers might adopt:

> The [monopoly] takes discretionary actions that affect its cost or the quality of its products. The generic label for such discretionary actions is **effort.** It stands for the number of office hours put in by a firm's managers or for the intensity of their work. But it should be interpreted more broadly. Managers' allocation of perks (hiring personnel to lighten their work loads, inattention to excessive inventories of inputs, etc.), indulgence in activities that privilege their career potential over efficiency, delay of distasteful actions (e.g., layoffs during periods of low activity), purchase of materials and equipment at high prices, and hoarding of engineers or machines not required under current contracts but useful for commercial profits or for winning future contracts are examples of "negative effort." (p. 1)

The regulator can limit this kind of behaviour by abandoning the policy outlined above, and adopting in its place a policy that provides cash incentives for the proper management of the firm. However, even the best policy of this kind is imperfect, in the sense that total surplus is smaller than it would be if the regulator were able to observe the managers' behaviour. The best policy fails in two ways. First, it does not always elicit the ideal amount of management effort. Second, it does not confiscate all of the profits, so that discretionary taxes are higher than they should be.

This chapter describes the nature of the regulator's best policy when the regulator cannot directly observe the managers' actions. The model used here is taken from the work of Laffont and Tirole ([38], pp. 131–137).

21.1 NATURAL MONOPOLY WITH A ROLE FOR MANAGEMENT

Imagine that the demand curve for the monopoly's output is linear:

$$p = a - q \tag{21.1}$$

Here, p is price, q is output, and a is a positive constant. Simple manipulations determine the elasticity of demand η:

$$\eta = \frac{p}{a - p} \tag{21.2}$$

There is a fixed cost of production, and there is a marginal cost of production that depends upon the intensity of the managers' cost control efforts. The cost equation is

$$c = \gamma + (m - e)q$$

where c is total cost, γ and $m - e$ are the fixed and marginal costs of production, and e is the effort expended by the monopoly's management. An increase in effort reduces marginal cost.

The managers' utility increases as their income rises, and falls as their effort rises.[2] Their utility U is

$$U = y - e^2$$

where y is the managers' income. This income is equal to the monopoly's profit (revenue less cost) plus a government transfer t:

$$y = pq - c + t$$

The transfer can be either positive or negative. If it is positive, the government must raise t additional dollars through distortionary taxes, and raising each of these dollars imposes upon the economy a welfare cost equal to z. If the transfer is negative (i.e., if money is transferred from the monopoly to the government), the revenue raised through distortionary taxes can be reduced by $-t$, with a consequent reduction in the welfare cost of the tax system.

The regulator is able to observe the firm's marginal cost μ, which is equal to $m - e$. If m were known to the regulator, the regulator would be able to infer the managers' effort from its observation of μ, and would therefore be able to control effort. However, if the regulator is unsure of the value of m, it cannot infer e from its observation of μ. There is then the possibility that laxness on the part of the managers will be undetected – that is, misinterpreted as a high value of m.

Since the purpose of this model is to discover exactly what the regulator can do to control the managers' behaviour when e cannot be observed or inferred, some uncertainty over the value of m is needed. It will be assumed that m takes one of two values, m_L or m_H, where m_L is less than m_H. The actual value of m is determined randomly: it is high with probability h and low with probability $1 - h$.

The regulator knows the values of m_L and m_H, and the probability with which each value is realized, but it does not know which value has occurred. The managers, however, do know which value has occurred. The outcome when information is restricted in this fashion is called the **asymmetric information equilibrium.**

Since our objective is to discover how well the regulator copes with this situation, we will need a benchmark against which the asymmetric information equilibrium can be compared. The standard benchmark is the **full information equilibrium,** which describes the outcome when both the regulator and the managers know which value of m has occurred.

21.2 FULL INFORMATION

Under full information, the regulator first observes the value taken by m, and then determines the appropriate price and quantity of the monopoly's output, and the

---

[2] Working harder, like working longer, is assumed to make people worse off. Indeed, it is assumed that the utility lost when effort is slightly increased rises with the level of effort, so that it is not socially desirable for the managers to work as hard as they possibly can.

appropriate effort and transfer. Since price and quantity are connected by the demand equation, it is sufficient for the regulator to determine quantity, effort, and the transfer.

The regulator maximizes society's welfare W, where

$$W = [V(q) - p(q)q] - (1 + z)t + U \tag{21.3}$$

Here, $V(q)$ is the value of q units of output to the consumer, and $p(q)$ is the highest price at which q units of output can be sold. The first two terms of this equation are the consumer surplus generated in the monopoly's market, and the surplus lost when the government imposes distortionary taxes to finance the transfer t. The third term is the surplus accruing to the managers as a result of their operation of the firm.[3]

The regulator needs the managers to operate the monopoly, so it cannot make choices under which the managers prefer not to do so. If the managers do not operate the monopoly – if they expend no effort, produce no goods and receive no transfer – their surplus is zero.[4] The regulator obtains the co-operation of the managers if their surplus is at least zero when they operate the monopoly. That is, the regulator must satisfy the constraint

$$U \geq 0$$

Given that it wishes to maximize society's welfare, how well off should the regulator make the managers? A \$1 increase in the transfer raises the managers' surplus by one dollar. This additional transfer is financed by distortionary taxes which reduce the surplus accruing elsewhere by $1 + z$ dollars. Thus, each dollar of transfers reduces society's welfare by z dollars. The best transfer is therefore the smallest possible transfer – the transfer that drives the managers' surplus to zero. This transfer compensates the managers for their effort and for any losses that they incur in the operation of the firm:

$$t = e^2 + \gamma + (m - e)q - p(q)q$$

When the regulator sets the transfer at this value, society's welfare depends only upon the quantity and effort chosen by the regulator, and upon the parameter m. It is

$$W = V(q) - p(q)q + (1 + z)\left[p(q)q - \gamma - (m - e)q - e^2\right]$$

The quantity and effort that maximize society's welfare satisfy the conditions

$$\frac{\partial W}{\partial q} = 0$$

$$\frac{\partial W}{\partial e} = 0$$

---

[3] Surplus and the managers' utility are measured in the same units: giving a dollar to a consumer raises his surplus by \$1, and giving a dollar of extra income to the managers raised their utility by a dollar. Consequently, the managers' utility and the managers' surplus are equivalent, and total surplus can be calculated by simply adding the managers' surplus to everyone else's surplus.

[4] It is assumed that the managers do not pay the fixed cost of production until they discover the value of β and learn the regulator's terms. If they are unhappy with the regulator's terms, they do nothing, earning a utility of zero.

The first condition states that, at the optimum, no small change in output (either upward or downward) will raise W. The second condition makes the same claim for small changes in effort.

Evaluating the partial derivative in the first condition yields, after some manipulation,

$$\frac{p - (m - e)}{p} = \frac{z}{1 + z}\frac{1}{\eta} \tag{21.4}$$

which is the Ramsey pricing rule derived in Section 18.2. Evaluating the partial derivative in the second condition yields

$$2e = q \tag{21.5}$$

The left-hand side is the marginal disutility of effort, and the right-hand side is the decrease in total cost (or equivalently, the increase in profit) generated by a marginal increase in effort. The managers should increase their effort until the profits generated by further effort are just offset by the disutility of further effort. That is, the optimal effort is the effort that the managers would freely choose if they were allowed to keep the monopoly's profits.

For each m, the optimal price, quantity, and effort are found by solving the three-equation system (21.1), (21.4), and (21.5). The transfer and the marginal cost are then calculated. The solution associated with m_L is

$$p_L^*, \ q_L^*, \ e_L^*, \ t_L^*, \ \mu_L^*$$

where an asterisk denotes an optimal value. The solution associated with m_H is

$$p_H^*, \ q_H^*, \ e_H^*, \ t_H^*, \ \mu_H^*$$

Let's compare these solutions.

Substituting (21.2) into (21.4), and (21.1) into (21.5), yields the two-equation system

$$p = \theta(m - e) + (1 - \theta)a$$

$$p = a - 2e$$

Here,

$$\frac{1}{2} < \theta \equiv \frac{1 + z}{1 + 2z} < 1$$

For each value of m, this system can be solved for p and e. These solutions are illustrated in Figure 21.1. It is evident that

$$p_H^* > p_L^*$$

$$e_H^* < e_L^*$$

By the definition of μ, the latter inequality implies that

$$\mu_H^* > \mu_L^*$$

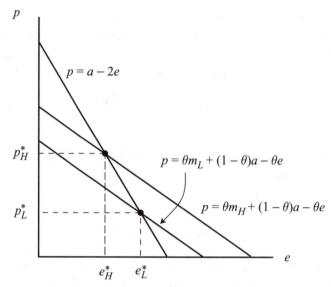

Figure 21.1: Price and Effort. The monopoly should produce and sell more goods when its marginal cost is innately low (i.e., m is equal to m_L). More goods can only be sold if the price is lower, so p_L^* is less than p_H^*. Also, producing more goods raises the benefit of additional effort, so e_L^* is greater than e_H^*.

Since the demand curve is downward sloping, the former inequality implies that

$$q_H^* < q_L^*$$

If m is low, the monopolist's good is produced cheaply. The regulator takes advantage of the low production costs by requiring a higher level of output when m is low than when it is high ($q_L^* > q_H^*$). A greater quantity of goods can only be sold if the price is reduced ($p_L^* > p_H^*$). Also, the benefit of additional effort is a reduction in the cost of producing *each* unit of goods, so the benefit of additional effort is greater when more goods are produced. Consequently, the regulator expects greater effort when m is low than when m is high ($e_L^* > e_H^*$).

21.3 THE CONSEQUENCES OF ASYMMETRIC INFORMATION

Under full information, the regulator observes the value of m before issuing instructions to the managers. For example, if the regulator wishes to bring about (or **implement**) the full information equilibrium, and if it finds that m is low, it issues the following instructions:

> If you produce, reduce marginal cost to μ_L^*. Set the price at p_L^*, and produce as many units of output as people want to buy. You will receive a transfer t_L^*.

It would issue a similar set of instructions if it finds that m is high. Since the regulator observes m before issuing instructions, it is able to dictate the managers' behaviour under each value of m.

By contrast, under asymmetric information, the regulator does not observe the value of m. Its instructions must consist of a list of options, or a **menu,** from which the managers choose one option after they have observed m. For example, a regulator that wishes to implement the full information equilibrium might try to do so by offering the following menu:

> If you produce, reduce marginal cost to either μ_L^* or μ_H^*. If you reduce marginal cost to μ_L^*, set the price at p_L^* and produce as many units as people want to buy. You will then receive a transfer of t_L^*. If you reduce marginal cost to μ_H^*, set the price at p_H^* and produce as many units as people want to buy. Your transfer in this case will be t_H^*.

Will this menu implement the full information equilibrium? It will if the managers always choose the option that the regulator intends them to choose – that is, if they reduce marginal cost to μ_L^* when m is low, and to μ_H^* when m is high. But the managers won't do so, and the full information equilibrium won't be implemented. To understand why, consider the managers' options under each value of m.

Suppose that m is high. If the managers reduce marginal cost to μ_H^*, their utility is zero. On the other hand, if they reduce marginal cost to μ_L^*, their utility is even lower. Here's why:

> If m were low, the managers would have to expend effort e_L^* to reduce marginal cost to μ_L^* and earn the transfer t_L^*. If they did so, their utility would be equal to zero. However, m is actually high, so the managers would have to expend greater effort to reduce marginal cost to μ_L^* and earn the transfer t_L^*. (Specifically, their effort would have to be $e_L^* + m_H - m_L$.) Since effort reduces utility, expending greater effort would drive the managers' utility below zero.

Thus, the managers' options are to attain a utility of zero by reducing marginal cost to μ_H^*, or to attain a negative utility by reducing marginal cost to μ_L^*. Since the managers act in their own interest, they reduce marginal cost only to μ_H^*. They behave as the regulator would like them to behave.

Now suppose that m is low. The managers can attain a utility of zero by making the choice that the regulator would like them to make, that is, by reducing marginal cost to μ_L^*. However, they can attain a higher utility by choosing the other option:

> If m were high, the managers could reduce marginal cost to μ_H^* by expending effort e_H^*. The managers would then receive the transfer t_H^* and attain a utility of zero. But m is actually low, so that the managers can reduce marginal cost to μ_H^* and earn the transfer t_H^* with less effort. (Specifically, the required effort is $e_H^* - m_H + m_L$.) Since expending less effort raises the managers' utility, their utility would be positive if they reduced marginal cost to μ_H^*.

The managers receive zero utility is they choose the option that the regulator wants them to choose, and they receive positive utility if they choose the option that the regulator does not want them to choose. The managers act in their own interests, so they choose the latter option.

The menu set out above fails to implement the full information equilibrium because the managers reduce marginal cost to μ_H^* under each value of m. Indeed, there is no set of instructions that will succeed. The regulator's inability to observe certain information reduces its options, and with fewer options, the regulator is unable to implement the full information allocation.

21.4 ADJUSTING THE MENU

The managers act in their own interests. The regulator must recognize this fact when it designs the menu, and construct the menu so that the managers will always choose the intended option. A menu with this property is said to be **incentive compatible,** and the regulator's problem is to find the best incentive compatible menu.

The nature of the best incentive compatible menu is derived in the appendix using a relatively formal methodology. It is also described, somewhat more casually, in this section. The approach used here involves two steps. The first step is to adjust the menu described in the last section in a very simple way to make it incentive compatible. The second step is to look for a welfare-improving way of adjusting the revised (incentive compatible) menu.

The original menu is not incentive compatible because, if m is low, the managers attain a positive utility by choosing the "wrong" option. The transfer t_H just compensates the managers for the effort required to reduce the marginal cost to μ_H when m is high. However, if m is low, the same marginal cost can be achieved with less effort, so that the transfer t_H represents more than adequate compensation for the managers.

The menu is made incentive compatible by adjusting the transfers. One possibility would be to reduce t_H by enough that the managers would not choose the "wrong" option if m were low. This change, however, would have a nasty side effect. The transfer t_H was originally set so that, if m were high and the managers chose the intended option, their utility would be zero. They would then be just willing to operate the firm. If t_H were smaller, the managers' utility would be pushed below zero and they would be unwilling to operate the firm.

If the "wrong" option cannot be made less attractive to the managers, the "right" option must be made more attractive. This is accomplished by raising t_L until the managers, if m is low, have as high a utility when they choose the intended option as they do when they choose the "wrong" option.

Note that the two transfers are now set in different ways: t_H is set to ensure that the managers are willing to operate the firm when m is high, and t_L is set to ensure that the managers choose the intended option when m is low.

Now the question becomes, can the *revised* menu be adjusted in a way that raise social welfare while retaining incentive compatibility? It can, and the pivotal adjustment is a reduction in the effort required of the managers when m is high.

Consider the effects of a slight reduction in e_H:

- The reduction in e_H has no effect on social welfare if m turns out to be high. The managers gain because they avoid effort, which is unpleasant to them, and society as a whole loses because more scarce resources are used up in the production of the monopolist's good. By (21.5), these changes are exactly offsetting.
- Once e_H has been reduced, the transfers can be adjusted in such a way that society's welfare will be greater if m turns out to be low. The transfer t_H compensates the managers for their effort, and for any losses that occur, when m is high. If e_H is reduced, t_H can also be reduced. The net effect of these changes is to make choosing the "wrong" option less attractive to the managers when m is low.[5] If the "wrong" option is less attractive, the "right" option can also be made less attractive – that is, t_L can be reduced. Since this transfer is financed through distortionary taxation, the deadweight loss of the tax system will decline, raising social welfare.

Thus, a slight reduction in e_H, accompanied by appropriate changes in the transfers, will not affect social welfare if m is high and will increase social welfare if m is low. It is therefore unambiguously beneficial to society.

21.5 CONCLUSIONS

The best outcome under asymmetric information involves a menu of options under which the managers put forth less than the optimal amount of effort if the monopoly's costs are high. There is an efficiency loss associated with this low level of effort. The regulator is aware of this efficiency loss, but can do nothing about it – every other menu would involve still greater efficiency losses. This outcome is typical of situations involving moral hazard. The efficiency loss can be controlled but not eliminated.

APPENDIX: OPTIMAL REGULATION UNDER ASYMMETRIC INFORMATION

The full information equilibrium represents the ideal outcome. It cannot be implemented under asymmetric information, so the regulator (and society) must settle for a less-than-ideal outcome.

The regulator will want to find the best of these less-than-ideal outcomes. To do so, it must maximize some measure of society's welfare while satisfying a number of inequalities. Let's look at the parts of the regulator's maximization problem.

---

[5] Let de_H be the amount by which e_H is reduced, and imagine that m is high. The managers' marginal disutility of effort is $2e_H^*$, so this reduction in effort allows the managers' transfer to be reduced by $(2e_H^*)de_H$. Now consider the effects of these changes on the managers' utility when m is low and the managers choose the "wrong" option. Their marginal disutility of effort is $2(e_H^* - m_L + m_H)$, so the reduction in effort causes their utility to rise by $2(e_H^* - m_L + m_H)de_H$. The reduction in the transfer causes their utility to fall by $(2e_H^*)de_H$. The net effect of these two changes is to reduce their utility. That is, choosing the "wrong" option when m is low has become less attractive.

The Regulator's Objective

A fully informed regulator would know how its choices affect social welfare, but under asymmetric information, the regulator does not know the value of m, and hence does not know the exact consequences of its choices. Rather than maximizing society's welfare, it must maximize society's **expected welfare.** Expected welfare, $E\,W$, is a weighted average of the possible outcomes, with each outcome weighted by the probability with which it occurs. Specifically, it is

$$E\,W = hW_H + (1 - h)W_L$$

where W_H and W_L measure society's welfare when m is high and low, respectively. Welfare under any given m is given by (21.3), so expected welfare can also be written as:

$$E\,W = h\left\{V(q_H) - (m_H - e_H)q_H - \gamma - zt_H - (e_H)^2\right\} + \qquad (21.6)$$
$$(1 - h)\left\{V(q_L) - (m_L - e_L)q_L - \gamma - zt_L - (e_L)^2\right\}$$

Constraints

The regulator does not observe the value of m, so it can only provide the managers with a menu of options, from which they will choose the one that maximizes their own utility. The regulator must anticipate the managers' behaviour when it designs the menu. Formally, the menu must satisfy two types of constraints, participation constraints and incentive compatibility constraints. The **participation constraints** ensure that the managers do not exercise their option not to work. The **incentive compatibility constraints** ensure that, under each value of m, the managers choose the option that the regulator intends them to choose.[6]

There is a participation constraint for each value of m. Each constraint states that, if the managers choose the option that the regulator intends them to choose, their utility will be at least as high as it would have been if they had not worked – that is, it will be non-negative. These constraints are

$$U_L \geq 0 \qquad (21.7)$$

$$U_H \geq 0 \qquad (21.8)$$

where U_L is the managers' utility when m is low and the managers choose the intended option, and U_H is defined analogously.

There is also an incentive compatibility constraint for each value of m. These constraints state that, under each value of m, the managers are better off choosing the option that the regulator intends them to choose, rather than the one that it does not

---

[6] Alternatively, these constraints state that the managers must have an incentive to choose the option that advances (or is compatible with) the regulator's objectives – hence the name.

intend them to choose. To obtain them, let the option intended for the low value of m be:

> If you produce, reduce marginal cost to μ_L. Set the price at p_L, and sell as many units as people want at this price. This amount will be q_L. You will receive a transfer of t_L; this transfer will raise your total income to y_L.

and let the option intended for the high value of m be:

> If you produce, reduce marginal cost to μ_H. Set the price at p_H, and sell as many units as people want at this price. This amount will be q_H. You will receive a transfer of t_H; this transfer will raise your total income to y_H.

Now suppose that the *actual* value of m is m_L. If the managers choose the intended option, they must expend effort e_L. If they choose the other option, their effort will be $m_L - \mu_H$, which is equal to $e_H + m_L - m_H$. Thus, the managers' utility when they choose the intended option is at least as high as it is when they do not, if

$$y_L - (e_L)^2 \geq y_H - (e_H + m_L - m_H)^2$$

This is the incentive compatibility constraint for m_L. Analogous reasoning shows that the incentive compatibility constraint for m_H is

$$y_H - (e_H)^2 \geq y_L - (e_L + m_H - m_L)^2$$

Note, however, that

$$U_L = y_L - (e_L)^2$$

$$U_H = y_H - (e_H)^2$$

so that the incentive compatibility constraints can also be written as

$$U_L \geq U_H + (e_H)^2 - (e_H + m_L - m_H)^2 \tag{21.9}$$

$$U_H \geq U_L + (e_L)^2 - (e_L + m_H - m_L)^2 \tag{21.10}$$

Solution

If the regulator were to maximize expected welfare subject to the participation constraints, he would find that the best outcome is the full information equilibrium. Asymmetric information matters because it imposes new constraints – the incentive compatibility constraints – upon the regulator.

If additional constraints are placed on a maximization problem, the value of the thing being maximized (expected welfare, in the case at hand) cannot rise. That value either falls or remains the same, depending upon whether the new constraints are binding or non-binding. A constraint on an agent is **non-binding** if it requires him to do something that he would have done anyway. A constraint is **binding** if it forces the agent to alter his behaviour. If *any* of the additional constraints are binding, the maximized value falls.[7]

Here, at least one of the new constraints is binding. In the absence of these constraints, the regulator would have chosen the full information equilibrium. This equilibrium violates the incentive compatibility constraint associated with the low value of m,[8] forcing an adjustment upon the regulator.

The best outcome (i.e., the asymmetric information equilibrium) is found by maximizing expected welfare subject to the four inequalities (21.7)–(21.10). Solving a problem of this kind is a little tricky. Binding constraints force the regulator to make adjustments, but the adjustments that he makes determine which constraints are binding. We don't know which constraints are binding until the problem has been solved.[9]

If we *did* know which constraints were ultimately binding, solving the maximization problem would be much easier. A binding constraint forces an adjustment, but the adjustment that is made is the smallest one consistent with satisfying the constraint. Consequently, the inequality symbol ($\geq$ or $\leq$) in a binding constraint can be replaced by the equality symbol ($=$). This fact has already been employed in the derivation of the full information equilibrium. In that derivation, social welfare was maximized subject to the constraint that the managers' utility be non-negative ($U \geq 0$). The regulator would like the managers to work for no income,[10] which would give the managers a negative utility. Since the managers will not work unless they receive a non-negative utility, the regulator gives them the smallest income that satisfies this condition. That is, the regulator allows the managers a utility of precisely zero.

If we did know which inequality constraints were binding, we could convert those inequalities into equalities. We could also throw away the non-binding constraints, because these constraints don't influence the regulator's choice. We would no longer be maximizing expected welfare subject to a set of inequality constraints; we would be maximizing expected welfare subject to a set of equality constraints, and we know how to solve problems of this kind.

---

[7] The constraint that you must breathe sometime today would be non-binding, because you would have done it anyway. The constraint that you must go on an African safari this year would probably be binding, and you would have to juggle the way in which you allocate your time and money to comply with it. This reallocation would make you worse off. You had already allocated your time and money in the best possible way. Since a trip to Africa was not in your plans, you had decided that you had better things to do. The constraint would force you to abandon your preferred plans in favour of an imposed plan.

[8] Recall that the role of the incentive compatibility constraint is to induce the managers to take the option intended for them. The full information equilibrium cannot be implemented under asymmetric information because, when m is low, the managers do not do so – so the full information allocation must violate the associated incentive compatibility constraint.

[9] There are formal methods of solving problems of this type, but they are beyond the scope of this book.

[10] Taking a dollar away from the managers allows the regulator to reduce the revenues raised through distortionary taxation by a dollar, generating a gain of z for society.

In the present case, we don't know which constraints will be binding, but we can make a very good – indeed, perfect – guess:

The regulator does not want to give the managers a higher utility than he has to, so one of (21.7) and (21.9) will be binding, as will one of (21.8) and (21.10). Since U_H cannot be negative, (21.9) states that U_L must be at least equal to some positive value. By contrast, (21.7) requires only that U_L be at least zero. Since (21.9) imposes a tighter restriction than (21.7), it will be binding and (21.7) will not be binding. Now consider (21.8) and (21.10). If (21.8) is binding (so that U_H is equal to zero), (21.10) will be satisfied but not binding as long as e_H is less than e_L, as it is under the full information equilibrium. That is, unless the relative sizes of e_H and e_L are reversed under asymmetric information (and they are not), (21.8) will be binding and (21.10) will not be binding.

If (21.8) and (21.9) are the only binding constraints, the constraints on the maximization problem can be written as

$$U_L = (e_H)^2 - (e_H + m_L - m_H)^2 \qquad (21.11)$$

$$U_H = 0$$

As under full information, these constraints can be used to eliminate the transfers from the measure of social welfare, thereby converting the constrained maximization problem into an unconstrained maximization problem.

The unconstrained problem is to choose two output levels and two effort levels to maximize

$$EW = hW_H + (1 - h)W_L$$

where[11]

$$W_H = V(q_H) - p(q_H)q_H + (1 + z)\left[p(q_H)q_H - \gamma - (m_H - e_H)q_H - (e_H)^2\right]$$

$$W_L = V(q_L) - p(q_L)q_L - z\left[(e_H)^2 - (e_H + m_L - m_H)^2\right] +$$
$$(1 + z)\left[p(q_L)q_L - \gamma - (m_L - e_L)q_L - (e_L)^2\right]$$

The optimal quantities under low and high values of m satisfy the conditions

$$\frac{\partial EW}{\partial q_L} = 0$$

$$\frac{\partial EW}{\partial q_H} = 0$$

Evaluating these partial derivatives leads to the conclusion that, under asymmetric information as under full information, prices should be determined by the Ramsey

---

[11] Note that the forms of W_L and W_H are different. The additional term in W_L is the social cost of raising the managers' utility from 0 to the level prescribed by (21.11).

pricing rule. The optimal efforts under the low and high values of m satisfy the conditions

$$\frac{\partial EW}{\partial e_L} = (1-h)(1+z)(q_L - 2e_L) = 0 \tag{21.12}$$

$$\frac{\partial EW}{\partial e_H} = h(1+z)(q_H - 2e_H) - 2z(1-h)(m_H - m_L) = 0 \tag{21.13}$$

The rule for determining effort when m is low is the same as the full information rule: the optimal effort is the effort that the managers would choose to expend if they were allowed to keep the monopoly's profits. However, a different rule determines effort when m is high. This rule requires the managers to expend *less* effort than they would if they were allowed to keep the monopoly's profits.

Comparing the Equilibria

Consider first the choices associated with m_L. Under both full and asymmetric information, the values of e_L, q_L, and p_L are determined by a three-equation system consisting of the demand equation and the rules for choosing effort and price. Since the same rules are optimal under both full and asymmetric information (so that the entire three-equation system is the same), these variables take the same values under both information structures:

$$\tilde{e}_L = e_L^*$$

$$\tilde{p}_L = p_L^*$$

$$\tilde{q}_L = q_L^*$$

The managers must have a higher utility under asymmetric information than under full information (to ensure incentive compatibility), and they can only attain this higher utility if they have a higher income. Since profits are the same under both information structures, their income will be higher only if their transfer is higher:

$$\tilde{t}_L > t_L^*$$

Now consider the choices associated with m_H. The values of e_H, q_H, and p_H are also determined by a three-equation system consisting of the demand equation and the rules for choosing price and effort. Two of these equations are the same under both information structures, but the effort rule changes. Specifically, the rule under asymmetric information requires a lower level of effort at every level of output than the rule under full information. This change in the rule alters the solution in a predictable fashion:

$$\tilde{e}_H < e_H^*$$

$$\tilde{p}_H > p_H^*$$

$$\tilde{q}_H < q_H^*$$

(Note that $\widetilde{e}_H$ is smaller than $\widetilde{e}_L$, as argued above.) The transfer must also be adjusted, to fix the managers' utility at zero, but the way in which it must change is difficult to determine.

QUESTIONS

A government employs a firm to produce a public good. The value of the public good depends upon the number of weeks that the firm operates the project. Specifically, the social value of the public good, measured in thousands of dollars, is $12e$ when the firm operates the project for e weeks. The social cost of producing the good, which is also measured in thousands of dollars, is θe^2, where θ is a random variable that takes the value 4 with probability 1/2 and the value 2 with probability 1/2. This cost is entirely borne by the firm, and the government compensates the firm by making a payment of M thousand dollars to the firm. This payment must at least cover the firm's costs, since the firm would otherwise refuse to participate. The welfare cost of raising the required M thousand dollars through taxation is $(1/2)M$ thousand dollars. The net social value of the public good is therefore

$$W = 12e - \theta e^2 - (1/2)M$$

a) Assume that the government can observe the value of θ. It will require e_L weeks of work and make a payment of M_L thousand dollars if θ is low, and it will require e_H weeks of work and make a payment M_H thousand dollars if θ is high. If the government wishes to maximize the net social value of the public good, what should the values of these four variables be?

b) Assume that the government cannot observe the value of θ, so that it must offer the firm a contract of this form:

> Work either e_L weeks or e_H weeks. If you work for e_L weeks, you will be paid M_L thousand dollars. If you work for e_H weeks, you will be paid M_H thousand dollars.

Here, e_L is the weeks of work that the government would like the firm to undertake if θ is low, and e_H is the weeks of work that the government would like the firm to undertake if θ is high. Explain why this contract is inefficient if the parameters of the contract take the values determined in a).

c) Assume that the government, unable to observe θ, tries to maximize the expected net social value of the public good:

$$EW = (1/2)\left[12e_L - 2(e_L)^2 - (1/2)M_L\right]$$
$$+ (1/2)\left[12e_H - 4(e_H)^2 - (1/2)M_H\right]$$

It induces the firm to behave in the intended manner by picking contract parameters that satisfy four constraints:

- The participation constraint for the low value of θ states that, if θ is low and the firm undertakes effort e_L, its profits will be at least zero.

- The participation constraint for the high value of θ states that, if θ is high and the firm undertakes effort e_H, its profits will be at least zero.
- The incentive compatibility constraint for the low value of θ states that, if θ is low, the firm's profits will be at least as high when it undertakes effort e_L as they are when it undertakes effort e_H.
- The incentive compatibility constraint for the high value of θ states that, if θ is high, the firm's profits will be at least as high when it undertakes effort e_H as they are when it undertakes effort e_L.

Express these constraints algebraically.

d) Under the best contract satisfying these four constraints, the participation constraint for the high value of θ and the incentive compatibility constraint for the low value of θ are binding, and the other constraints are not binding. Find the parameters of this contract.

22

Other Examples of Asymmetric Information

This chapter discusses three areas in which asymmetric information has substantial "real world" applications.

22.1 HEALTH CARE AND HEALTH CARE INSURANCE

There are many instances in which problems of adverse selection or moral hazard are resolved (or ameliorated) without government intervention. However, one sector in which these problems have been particularly profound, and have consequently prompted government intervention, is the provision of health care and health insurance. In Canada, as in many European countries, universal health care insurance and many forms of health care are provided by the government. In the United States, there is a smaller but nevertheless significant degree of government involvement. Let's look at the problems and their solutions.[1]

22.1.1 Adverse Selection

An insurance company is offering **actuarially fair** insurance if, in an average year, the premiums paid by the policy-holders are just equal to the payments made to the policy-holders. Risk-averse people would always accept actuarially fair insurance, and for the remainder of this section, we shall imagine that everyone is risk-averse.

Suppose that a group of companies offered health care insurance which would be actuarially fair if it were accepted by all of the residents of a region. Would everyone living in the region actually accept the insurance? Would the companies have an incentive to alter the terms on which they offer insurance?[2]

---

[1] The implications of asymmetric information for medical care were first studied by Arrow [5]. Research in this area, and in the study of insurance generally, tends to be abstract and is not easily accessed by those without a substantial grasp of mathematics.

[2] This discussion will ignore the costs of administering and marketing insurance plans, and an insurance company will be presumed to be profitable if it earns at least as much in premiums as it pays out in benefits.

The potential buyers will make predictions about their own need for health care. Those who believe that they are likely to accumulate large medical bills will be only too happy to purchase health care insurance at premiums which reflect the average person's medical bills rather than their own. Even those who believe that their medical bills will not be much different from the average person's bills will wish to purchase insurance. Insurance allows them to convert an uncertain stream of payments (the medical bills) into a certain stream of payments (the insurance premiums) so that they face less uncertainty in their lives. However, those who believe that they are likely to remain healthy, and who therefore expect relatively small medical bills, will choose not to purchase insurance. They, too, might like to reduce the uncertainty they face by converting an uncertain stream of medical bills into a certain stream of premiums, but not on these terms – not when the premiums are so much larger than their estimated medical bills.

These decisions reflect adverse selection in the market for health care insurance. The people who expect to have the largest medical bills accept the insurance while those who expect to have the lowest medical bills do not. The withdrawal of the people with the lowest expected claims means that the claims made to each insurer will exceed the premiums collected by that insurer. The insurers will experience losses, and will have to change their policies to avoid further losses. They will make several adjustments.

1. Premiums will be raised, and coverage might be curtailed, as the insurers attempt to balance their revenues and expenditures. These changes will induce some people to switch from being insured to being uninsured. Some of these people believe that their medical bills are likely to be low, and simply decide that the benefit of insurance no longer justifies its cost.[3] Others have no such expectation, but have such low incomes that health care insurance has become prohibitively expensive. The unemployed, the "working poor," and the elderly are likely to find themselves in this category.

2. The healthier part of the population will choose to be uninsured if the insurers continue to offer only one policy with everyone paying the same premium. However, these people constitute a potential market for an insurer who is willing to design a policy that will appeal to them. This policy will differ from the first in that its coverage is less complete[4] and its premiums (which are again actuarially fair) are smaller. The premiums are low because the coverage is less complete, and also because the policy is intended for relatively healthy people. Relatively unhealthy people prefer the original policy because they believe that they need the more complete coverage, but relatively healthy people are attracted to the new policy because its premiums are low. Thus, the insurer is able to offer two policies, each with actuarially fair rates, such that the healthier people choose one policy and the less healthy people choose the other. Fewer people are uninsured.

---

[3] Our earlier discussion of adverse selection suggests that the only premium at which the insurers are able to balance revenues and expenditures might be so large that no one accepts the insurance (so that both revenues and expenditures are equal to zero). Observation of real economies suggests that this does not occur, that there is an equilibrium in which some people are insured.

[4] Coverage can be made less complete by including coverage for a limited number of services, setting high deductibles, or offering only partial reimbursement for expenses.

There is no reason why this process should stop at two policies, particularly if insurers compete with each other. Each insurer will try to steal away the healthier part of the other insurers' customers by designing a new policy that those people prefer to the existing policies. Ultimately, there will be many insurance policies, with people choosing more or less complete (and more or less expensive) policies based upon their own evaluations of their health. This process, whereby people voluntarily separate themselves into groups based upon information known only to themselves, is called **self-selection.**

3. Insurers will offer insurance to particular groups (such as employee groups) on the condition that some (quite high) proportion of them accept it. This practice leaves little room for adverse selection, and makes it more difficult for competing insurers to poach clients. However, this practice also tends to exclude individuals who do not belong to particularly desirable groups, notably the unemployed and the elderly.

Thus, two characteristics of equilibrium in a private insurance market are that some people will not be insured and that coverage will tend to be incomplete. Some of the people with incomplete coverage would prefer to purchase *full* coverage if they could purchase it at actuarially fair premiums, but they cannot do so.[5] A person's health status is largely private information, and people do not have an incentive to honestly reveal this information to the insurer (they would always prefer the insurer to believe that they are healthier than they actually are). The insurer must therefore induce people to reveal this information through self-selection, and as argued above, this necessarily entails *incomplete* coverage. Thus, there is an inefficiency in the private market – not enough insurance is provided.

This inefficiency disappears when the government provides full-coverage health care insurance funded from general tax revenues. Everyone obtains full insurance which, as risk-averse individuals, is exactly what they want.

This policy also redistributes income from the healthier part of the population to the less healthy part of the population. The cost of the privately provided insurance varies, in a rough way, with a person's general health (revealed through self-selection), but the cost of the publicly provided insurance does not. Thus, a switch from private provision to public provision increases the cost of a healthy person's insurance and decreases the cost of an unhealthy person's insurance. However, such re-distribution of income has no efficiency consequences.

Many countries offer health care insurance of this type. The United States is an outlier, choosing to supplement the private insurance system by providing health care insurance to the elderly and the poor, and funding emergency care for the uninsured. This approach does not remove the inefficiencies caused by adverse selection.

---

[5] Some people have such low incomes that they would not purchase insurance even at actuarially fair rates. Although there is no inefficiency here that can be corrected by public insurance, their plight can still be used to justify public insurance on other grounds: equity, the presence of externalities in health care, and "spillovers" to other forms of government expenditure (someone who does not receive appropriate health care might be unable to work and end up collecting welfare). I will not consider these arguments further, not because they are unimportant, but because our focus is on the consequences of asymmetric information.

22.1.2 Moral Hazard

There are many opportunities for moral hazard in the relationship between a patient and his physician. The patient is not only badly informed about his illness and possible treatments, but is also making decisions under stressful conditions. This situation allows the physician a considerable degree of leeway in charting the course of treatment, and he might well employ unnecessary procedures. He might do so to reassure the patient that everything possible is being done, or because he wishes to develop a reputation for thoroughness (which might attract more patients at a later date). When the patient has extensive medical coverage, neither patient nor physician has an incentive to balance the cost of a treatment against its potential benefits, and treatment is likely to be pursued until the potential benefit of further treatment has been driven to zero.

Since the doctors are the informed party in this relationship, the incidence of moral hazard can be reduced only by changing the behaviour of doctors, perhaps by changing the way in which doctors are remunerated. Most doctors in Canada are currently paid on a **fee-for-service** basis (i.e., they get a little more money if they provide a little more treatment). This system might provide an incentive for unnecessary treatment, and it certainly provides no disincentive. An alternative system, currently employed in the United Kingdom, is **capitation.** Each doctor has a roster of patients, and is paid a fixed amount of money for each patient on his roster. He is then responsible for providing basic medical services to these patients, without further remuneration. He therefore bears the cost of additional procedures, and has an incentive (perhaps too strong an incentive) to avoid inappropriate treatment.

22.2 THE STANDARD DEBT CONTRACT

Investors often finance risky projects with borrowed money. The contract between the investor and the lender generally requires the investor to repay a fixed amount (representing principal plus accrued interest) by a fixed date. The contract also stipulates that ownership of the project is transferred to the lender if the investor fails to make the required payment. Why has this contract, among all of the possible contracts, become the customary contract between lenders and borrowers?[6]

Hidden information plays a central role in the explanation. Imagine that an investor must finance a project by borrowing a particular sum of money from a lender, and that both the investor and the lender are risk-neutral. The project has a one-time pay-off, or earnings, of s dollars. The value of s is not known to either the investor or the lender at the time that the financing is required. However, both the investor and the lender know that there is some uncertainty about what s will be, and both know the probability distribution of the possible values of s. Once the project is operating, its earnings are costlessly revealed to the investor. The lender, however, can only discover the earnings

---

[6]   The debt contract model presented here is a greatly simplified version of one presented by Gale and Hellwig [27]. Results from Williamson [66] are also used.

by hiring accountants to go through the books – a costly procedure that he would like to avoid.

Assume that the lender is willing to provide financing to the investor only if his expected return on the loan is R dollars.[7] The lender will insist that the investor sign a loan contract that ensures that he receives this expected return. However, the lender's inability to directly observe the project's earnings places some limitations on the structure of the contract. Here are some of their options:

- The investor could be required to make a fixed payment of R dollars under every eventuality. There is no better contract than this one if the project always earns at least R dollars. However, if there is a chance that the project's earnings will be less than R dollars, the lender would know that the investor might not be able to pay him the full amount. That is, he would know that this contract would sometimes earn him R dollars and sometimes earn him less than R dollars, and hence that its expected return is less than R dollars. The lender would not agree to such a contract.
- The lender could decide to audit the project, so that the project's earnings will be known to both the lender and the investor. The contract could then specify a repayment that depends upon the project's earnings. (Specifically, the contract could specify repayments smaller than R dollars when earnings are less than R dollars, and repayments greater than R dollars when earnings are greater than R dollars.) This contract turns out not to be a good one, as the cost of the audit has to come out of someone's pocket.
- The lender could decide not to audit the project, in which case the repayment can only depend upon the investor's *report* of the project's earnings. This kind of contract could create a moral hazard problem: the investor could have an incentive to lie about the project's earnings so as to minimize the repayment.

22.2.1 The Form of the Contract

The best possible contract turns out to be the **standard debt contract:**

> **The investor is required to pay $\widehat{R}$ dollars if he reports that his earnings are greater than or equal to $\widehat{R}$ dollars. If he reports earnings lower than $\widehat{R}$ dollars, the lender takes over the project, pays the auditing cost to find out what he's got, and takes the entire earnings of the project. $\widehat{R}$ is chosen so that the lender's expected return is equal to R dollars. If there is more than one $\widehat{R}$ with this property, the lowest one is chosen.**

An investor who reports earnings below $\widehat{R}$ is said to be **insolvent** or **bankrupt.**

---

[7] The word "expected" is used in this section to mean the "statistician's best guess of" rather than "anticipated."

This contract has two important characteristics. The first is that it is designed so that the lender cannot gain by lying about the project's outcome:

- The investor will not claim that his earnings are below $\widehat{R}$ when they are actually above it. Reporting earnings above $\widehat{R}$ obliges him to make the fixed payment but leaves him some profit, whereas claiming insolvency would trigger the lender's takeover of the project, leaving the investor with nothing.
- An investor who has earnings above $\widehat{R}$ could claim that his earnings are some *other* amount above $\widehat{R}$, but he cannot gain by doing so: the repayment is the same under both reports.
- An investor who has earnings below $\widehat{R}$ cannot gain by claiming that his earnings are some other amount below $\widehat{R}$, as his profits are zero under every such report. He cannot claim that his earnings are above $\widehat{R}$, as this claim would require him to repay an amount greater than his earnings.

The second feature of this contract is that it minimizes the likelihood of an audit.[8] Audits occur when the project's earnings are less than $\widehat{R}$ dollars, so minimizing the probability of an audit is equivalent to minimizing $\widehat{R}$. Since the lender's expected return is fixed (at R dollars), the more that he is paid when the project is insolvent, the less he must be paid when the project is solvent – that is, the lower is $\widehat{R}$. Assigning all of the project's earnings to the lender in the event of insolvency therefore yields the smallest $\widehat{R}$. But we have to be careful here: there might be more than one contract that induces truthful behaviour and assigns all earnings to the lender in the event of insolvency. The best of these contracts is the one with the lowest $\widehat{R}$ and therefore the lowest probability of insolvency.

The cost of ensuring truthful behaviour is lower when the investor can offer some other asset as **collateral.** The terms of a collateralized contract are the same as those described above, except that the lender acquires the ownership of *both* the project and the collateral if the investor fails to repay the loan. Since the presence of collateral reduces the investor's willingness to default on a loan, and increases the lender's return if he does, the lender's expected return is higher under any given fixed payment $\widehat{R}$. It follows that the lender will still be able to obtain the expected return R if the fixed payment is somewhat reduced.

22.2.2 Example

Suppose that the earnings s of each project are uniformly distributed on the unit interval, that investors must borrow an amount B to undertake the project, and that each lender requires an expected return R on such a loan. Assume that

$$B < R < 1/2$$

---

[8] The lender's expected return, net of audit costs, is fixed at R dollars, so auditing costs are ultimately paid by the investor. A contract that minimizes the likelihood of an audit is therefore beneficial to the investor.

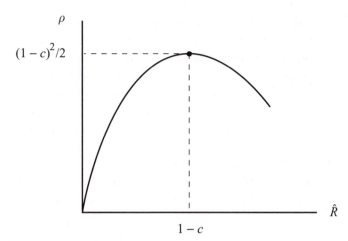

Figure 22.1: The Relationship between the Fixed Payment and the Lender's Expected Return. Raising the fixed payment gives the lender a greater return if the loan is repaid, but lowers the probability that it will be repaid. Consequently, the lender's expected return first rises and then falls as the fixed payment rises.

Let ρ be the lender's expected return on a standard debt contract, and let c be the cost of an audit.

The lender's expected return can be calculated as follows:

$\rho = \text{(probability of insolvency)} \times \text{(lender's expected return under insolvency)}$

$+ \text{(probability of solvency)} \times \text{(lender's return under solvency)}$

Each of these terms is readily evaluated:

- The probability that the investor will be insolvent is the probability that s is less than $\widehat{R}$. The assumption that s is uniformly distributed on the unit interval implies that this probability is $\widehat{R}$ itself.
- If the investor is insolvent, the lender receives the project's earnings less the cost of the audit. The statistical best guess of the project's earnings, given that those earnings are uniformly distributed on the unit interval *and* known to be less than $\widehat{R}$, is $\widehat{R}/2$. The best guess of the lender's net earnings when the investor is insolvent is therefore $\widehat{R}/2 - c$.
- The probability that the investor is *not* insolvent is $1 - \widehat{R}$.
- If the investor is not insolvent, the lender receives $\widehat{R}$.

Filling in the blanks gives

$$\rho = \widehat{R}\left[\frac{\widehat{R}}{2} - c\right] + (1 - \widehat{R})\widehat{R} = \widehat{R}(1 - c) - \left(\frac{1}{2}\right)\widehat{R}^2$$

The relationship between the expected return ρ and the fixed payment $\widehat{R}$ is shown in Figure 22.1. The expected return initially rises as $\widehat{R}$ rises, but eventually begins to fall. An increase in $\widehat{R}$ has both a cost and a benefit for the lender. The cost is that the probability of full repayment falls. The benefit is that the lender receives a greater repayment *if* he is repaid in full. The benefit of a marginal increase in $\widehat{R}$ is greater than the cost when $\widehat{R}$ is low and hence the probability of full repayment is high; and the benefit is less than the cost when $\widehat{R}$ is high and the probability of full repayment is low.

The highest value of ρ occurs when $\widehat{R}$ is equal to $1 - c$. Every value of $\widehat{R}$ greater than $1 - c$ gives the same expected return to the lender as some lower value of $\widehat{R}$. Since the lower value is preferred to the higher value, the standard debt contract will set $\widehat{R}$ somewhere between 0 and $1 - c$. The particular value of $\widehat{R}$ chosen will depend upon the expected return demanded by the lender: the contract will specify the value of $\widehat{R}$ that sets the lender's expected return ρ equal to his required expected return R.

22.2.3 Allocative Effects of Asymmetric Information

The asymmetry of information between the lender and the investor leads to an inefficient outcome. The nature of the resource misallocation can be inferred from the above example. The expected return of a project is exactly $1/2$. Assume that the lender's required return R is less than $1/2$, and that the investor is willing to undertake the project if his expected return is non-negative.

Full information in this context means that the lender can directly observe the project's earnings. The contract between the lender and the investor can therefore specify a repayment that varies with earnings. For example, the contract could require the investor to pay the lender the fraction $2R$ of the project's earnings. The lender's expected return would then be R and the investor's expected return would be $(1/2) - R$. Since the lender is able to get the return that he requires, and the investor gets a non-negative expected return, the project will be carried out. Furthermore, the project will not be audited.

By contrast, the best contract under asymmetric information is the standard debt contract. There are then two cases:

- If R is not greater than $(1 - c)^2/2$, there is a value of $\widehat{R}$ that allows the lender to earn his required return. There are some earnings under which the investor is solvent (because $\widehat{R}$ is less than one), so the investor's expected return is non-negative. The project will again be undertaken. However, an audit will be required if the project's earnings turn out to be low, and this audit will use up scarce resources.
- If R is between $(1 - c)^2/2$ and $1/2$, there is no value of $\widehat{R}$ that allows the lender to earn his required return. The requirement that the contract be structured so that the investor has no incentive to lie about the firm's earnings limits the size of the expected return that the investor can offer the lender. In this case, he simply cannot offer a large enough return to satisfy the lender, so the project is not undertaken.

Projects that are undertaken under full information might not be undertaken under asymmetric information, even though their expected earnings $(1/2)$ are greater than the value of the resources needed to undertake them (R). Even if projects are undertaken under asymmetric information, their social returns are lower than under full information, because costly audits will occasionally be necessary.

22.3 EFFICIENCY WAGES

Contracts between two parties in the presence of asymmetric information must take into account the **principal-agent problem.** The principal wishes his agent to perform some task for him, but cannot observe some aspect of the agent's performance. If there are situations in which the agent's interests diverge from those of his principal, how is the principal to ensure that the agent acts in the principal's interest rather than his own? The solution is to design the contract so that the agent's reward for pursuing the principal's interest exceeds the reward for pursuing his own interest. Payments to senior managers, for example, often include stock options.[9] These options are more valuable when the company is more profitable, so the managers have an incentive to work in the company's interest.

The problem of ensuring that employees work in the firm's interest is not confined to upper management. There are some instances in which the firm can easily discover whether its employees are working as hard as the firm would like. Assembly lines are one instance, and piece work is another. However, there are many instances in which the output of individual workers is not directly observable, or only sporadically observable. Shapiro and Stiglitz [58] argue that, in these situations, firms can ensure appropriate effort on the part of workers by paying **efficiency wages.** These wages are somewhat higher than the smallest wage that the worker would be willing to accept.

Imagine that each worker can choose the degree of diligence with which he performs his job. In particular, he can produce q units of goods each day by performing his job conscientiously, or he can produce no units of goods by shirking. The worker prefers to shirk, but there is some payment e which would just compensate him for working diligently on any given day.

Although the firm cannot gauge each worker's output perfectly, a worker who shirks is caught with probability p on any given day. A worker who shirks, but is not caught, will continue to be employed and will receive the same wage as a worker who does not shirk. The benefit of shirking on any given day is that the worker avoids the effort of diligent work. A worker who is found to be shirking is fired at the end of the day. Such a worker loses his wage income for an uncertain period of time, and must make the effort of searching out new employment, and runs the risk that his new wage will be lower than his current wage.[10] If L is the expected loss associated with the switch from

---

[9] Stock options allow the holder to acquire the stock of some company at a specified price at some future time. The holder of the option will exercise that right if the stock price rises above the specified price. The profit on each share purchased in this way is equal to the gap between the share price and the specified price.

[10] The new wage could, of course, be higher than his current wage, but it cannot be so much higher that the worker is willing to undergo the search to find it. If it were, he would quit today instead of waiting to be fired.

employment to unemployment, the best guess of the cost of shirking on any given day is pL.

The worker will be diligent if the benefit of shirking is not greater than its expected cost:

$$e \leq pL$$

The value of L is determined by several factors:

- The worker's current wage, w, which is measured in units of goods per day. The firing of the worker from his current job ends a stream of wage payments, and the higher is the wage rate, the greater the value of the lost wage earnings.
- The worker's best guess of the wage that he will earn on his next job, $\overline{w}$. The worker will eventually find another job, and the higher the new wage rate, the smaller will be the cost of losing his current job.
- The unemployment rate u. A higher unemployment rate implies more competition for available jobs, and therefore a longer period of unemployment. The longer the time before the worker can acquire another job, the greater the cost of losing his current job.

The relationship between L and its determinants can be represented by the function $\widehat{L}$:

$$L = \widehat{L}(w, \overline{w}, u)$$

where

$$\frac{\partial \widehat{L}}{\partial w} > 0, \qquad \frac{\partial \widehat{L}}{\partial \overline{w}} < 0, \qquad \frac{\partial \widehat{L}}{\partial u} > 0$$

A further restriction should be added:

$$\frac{\partial \widehat{L}}{\partial w} + \frac{\partial \widehat{L}}{\partial \overline{w}} > 0$$

The easiest way to understand this restriction is to imagine that w and $\overline{w}$ are equal, so that the worker, once he finds a new job, is as well off as he was before he lost his old job. Then $\widehat{L}$ represents only the effort of finding the new job and the wages lost during the search for that job. Equal increases in w and $\overline{w}$ change this cost by increasing the value of the wages lost during the search.

Each firm will, of course, wish to dissuade its workers from shirking. It can do so by raising L until pL is just equal to e. The firm cannot influence either the wages paid by other firms or the economy's unemployment rate, so it can only raise L by raising its own wage rate.

If there are a number of identical firms in the economy, and if each is attempting to ensure diligence on the part of its workers by adjusting its own wage rate, there will be a symmetric Nash equilibrium in which every firm pays the same wage. That wage is just high enough to dissuade workers from shirking:

$$e = p\widehat{L}(w, w, u)$$

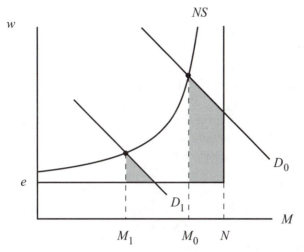

Figure 22.2: Labour Market Equilibrium under Full and Asymmetric Information. The "no shirking" locus shows the wage that firms must pay to avoid shirking at each level of employment. Hence, it is a kind of asymmetric information supply curve. The intersection of the "no shirking" locus and the demand curve determines the equilibrium.

If there are N workers in the economy and M of them are working, the unemployment rate is

$$u = \frac{N - M}{N}$$

and the equilibrium condition is

$$e = p\widehat{L}\left(w, w, \frac{N - M}{N}\right)$$

The pairs (M, w) that satisfy this condition form the "no shirking" locus (NS) shown in Figure 22.2. Its curvature has been inferred from the observations that

- As employment falls toward 0, the competition for jobs becomes desperate and the period of unemployment following a job loss becomes arbitrarily long. Workers cling to their current jobs, even if the wage w is only slightly above e.
- As employment rises toward N, the period of unemployment shrinks to almost nothing. The wages lost during this very short interval can only be a significant deterrent to shirking if the wage rate is very high.

This locus shows, for each level of employment, the market wage that firms must pay to ensure diligence on the part of their workers.

The "no shirking" locus lies above the labour supply curve that would prevail if effort could be freely observed by the firm. Any number of workers, up to a maximum on N, would then be willing to work diligently for the payment that just compensates them for their effort (e). This "full information" labour supply curve is also shown in Figure 22.2.

Now consider the demand for labour. Firms maximize their profits by hiring additional workers until the marginal product of labour, q, is just equal to the wage, w. Since the marginal product of labour falls as employment rises, the quantity of labour demanded by the firms falls as the wage rate rises. That is, the labour demand curve is downward sloping. Two possible positions of the labour demand curve are shown in Figure 22.2.

If effort is freely observed by the firm, equilibrium in the labour market occurs at the intersection of the labour demand curve and the full information labour supply curve. If worker effort is only sporadically observed, the equilibrium occurs at the intersection of the labour demand curve and the "no shirking" curve.

Employment is lower and the wage rate is higher under asymmetric information than under full information. The welfare cost of asymmetric information is calculated in the usual fashion. A one-unit reduction in employment reduces social welfare by the difference between the worker's output, q, and the value that the worker places on his labour, e. That is, it is the vertical distance between the labour demand curve and the full information labour supply curve. The welfare cost associated with asymmetric information is therefore the area bounded by these curves, and by the employment levels under full and asymmetric information. These welfare costs are shown as shaded areas in Figure 22.2.

QUESTIONS

1. An individual hires an agent to sell an asset for him. The market value of the asset is uncertain, and its owner knows only that the market value might be anything from 0 to 1. The agent will discover the asset's actual value when he sells it, but its actual sale price (denoted S) cannot be independently verified by the owner. The agent is therefore able to report any sale price that he likes, provided only that the reported price lies between 0 and 1 (inclusive). The deal between the owner and his agent is that the agent will sell the asset, report the sale price to the owner, and submit some part of the reported sale price to the owner. Any remaining money accrues to the agent as his commission. The schedule that relates the reported sale price of the asset, $\widehat{S}$, to the payment that the agent must remit to the owner, R, is determined by the owner before the asset is sold. He chooses this schedule to make himself as well off as possible. The only constraint on the structure of this schedule is that R must lie between 0 and $\widehat{S}$ (inclusive) for every $\widehat{S}$.

   a) Assume that the agent acts in his own interest. For each sale price S between 0 and 1, characterize the payment R that the owner will receive under any given contract.

   b) Now imagine that there is a chance π that the agent will be caught if he lies about the sale price. If he is not caught, the original agreement between the owner and the agent remains in effect. If he is caught, the entire amount of the sale is given to the owner, and as well, the agent is fined an amount P (which accrues to the government). Assume that the agent is risk neutral and acts in his own interest. Let an incentive compatible schedule be one under which the agent has no incentive to lie about the sale price. Find the incentive compatible contract that is most beneficial to the owner.

2. Consider the efficiency wage model described in Section 22.3. Assume that the initial position of the labour demand curve is such that there would be no unemployment under full information. Under asymmetric information, what are the effects of the following changes on the wage rate, employment, and the welfare cost of the informational asymmetry?

   a) The firms become more productive, in the sense that they can produce more goods with given inputs of capital and labour.

   b) Information about job openings becomes more readily available, reducing the length of time required for an unemployed worker to find a job.

Asymmetric Information and Income Redistribution

We have, to this point, concerned ourselves with the circumstances under which a system of free markets does not give rise to a Pareto optimal allocation – that is, with failures of the first fundamental theorem of welfare economics. We now turn to the second theorem, which argues that an appropriate redistribution of endowments will allow the economy to reach any desired Pareto optimal allocation. The implication of this theorem is that we need not passively accept whatever income distribution is ground out by a system of free markets. The income distribution can be altered through simple policies that guide the economy from one Pareto optimal allocation to another. There is no conflict, this theorem suggests, between economic efficiency and the attainment of an equitable distribution of income.

Our experience with redistribution programs suggests otherwise. A tax imposed to finance transfers to the poor is like every other tax: people alter their behaviour to avoid paying it, and their collective attempts to avoid the tax generate a deadweight loss. People also alter their behaviour to increase the transfers that they receive from the government, and these adjustments also generate a deadweight loss.

The claims of the second theorem diverge from our experience because some very strong assumptions underlie the second theorem. One of these assumptions is that the government has full information about the innate characteristics of the people living in the economy. If it had such knowledge, it could use these characteristics to determine each person's tax or subsidy. It could levy high taxes on people who are smart enough to become doctors or charismatic enough to get onto the cover of *People* magazine. It could recognize the people who have whatever peculiar combination of talents is needed to be on the leading edge of the next wave of popular music, and tax them heavily too. And it would provide subsidies to people who are at a disadvantage in a market economy. People with major physical and mental handicaps would be included in this group, as would people who are simply clumsy or absentminded. Because this program would be based on innate characteristics, people would be unable to influence the taxes that they pay or the transfers that they receive, and so would not engage in the kind of behaviour that gives rise to a deadweight loss.

Of course, governments don't have this kind of knowledge about individual characteristics. They are consequently forced to base their redistributive policies at least partially on actual market outcomes. They see who is relatively successful and who is relatively unsuccessful, and transfer income from one group to another. Policies of this kind are open to manipulation, and lead to deadweight losses.

The next few chapters acknowledge that governments are in fact unable to implement lump-sum transfers, and examine the consequences of this fact for redistributive policies. Chapter 23 briefly describes the determinants of the income distribution, and discusses some basic aspects of redistribution. It is followed by two chapters which discuss income redistribution in economies in which the second theorem does not apply. Chapter 24 shows how the adjustments that people make to redistributive policies increase the cost of redistribution, and ultimately limit the amount of redistribution that can occur. Chapter 25 looks at two kinds of policies (tagging and targeting) that moderate these adjustments, allowing more redistribution to occur, or the same amount of redistribution to occur with a smaller loss of efficiency.

23

The Distribution of Income

Each person's welfare under the market system is determined by three factors:

- *Tastes and needs.* Some people, such as the disabled and the chronically ill, need to consume large quantities of goods and services to maintain even a moderate level of economic welfare. On the other hand, healthy and free-spirited individuals might be quite content with few material possessions.
- *Prices.* Given his income, each person can buy more goods and services when prices are lower, and therefore prefers low prices to high prices. A fall in any given price, however, will impact each person to a different degree. A reduction in the price of prescription drugs, for example, will have little effect on the welfare of the healthy, but will greatly impact the chronically ill.
- *Income.* At given market prices, each person can afford to buy more goods and services when his income is higher.

Differences in these three factors across the population lead to disparities in economic welfare. Because disparities that arise from the first two causes can be offset by a redistribution of income (e.g., transfers to the chronically ill from the rest of the population), disparities in economic welfare can ultimately be ascribed to the distribution of income.

Just how unequal is the distribution of income? Pen [48] visualizes the income distribution as a parade.[1] Every income-earner in the economy marches in the parade, at such a rapid pace that they all pass in front of us over the course of one hour. The marchers are stretched or shrunk so that their height is proportional to their pre-tax income. People with average incomes have average height (say, 1.7 meters). People with smaller incomes are shrunk and people with higher incomes are stretched. The marchers are ordered by height, with the shortest first and the tallest last.

The first few marchers are underground, with "their feet on the ground and their heads deep in the earth." They are the entrepreneurs who have lost money over the course of the year. They are followed by occasional workers, such as high school students with

---

[1] The data roughly approximate the income distribution in the United States and the United Kingdom around 1970.

part-time jobs: they only come up to our (normal sized) ankles. The marchers' heights then increase quite sharply, to about one meter, as those elderly and disabled people who are dependent on government pensions pass by. Once they are gone, the heights of the marchers increase gradually – very gradually – until, with only twelve minutes left in the parade, the people of average height pass by. Now heights begin to grow more rapidly. With only a few minutes left in the parade, the doctors, lawyers, and accountants begin to pass by. The first of these are six meters tall. The heights of these and other professionals grow rapidly, and then the professionals give way to senior executives, whose heights can exceed 100 meters. Finally, within the last minute of the parade, the most senior executives give way to people who earn their incomes, not from the sale of their labour, but from the ownership of assets. The heads of the last few are hidden by cloud, and the very last marcher is so tall that airliners fly through his navel.

This chapter begins with a discussion of the reasons for such an extreme distribution of income. The reasons why income does not exactly reflect economic welfare are then briefly examined. Finally, the rationales for reducing income disparities through government policies, and the nature of these policies, are discussed.

23.1 DETERMINANTS OF INCOME

The two main kinds of income are labour income and asset income. **Labour income** is income received in exchange for the provision of labour. It generally takes the form of wages, salary, or commissions, and the discussion below focusses on these kinds of labour income. An entrepreneur, however, receives labour income in the form of profits, which are only tangentially discussed here. **Asset income** is the income earned from the ownership of assets, such as stocks, bonds, and commercial property.

Labour income can be thought of as the product of two factors: the rate at which income is earned when working, and the amount of time spent working. Wage income, for example, is the product of the hourly wage rate and the number of hours worked. These two factors will be considered in turn.

23.1.1 Rate of Pay

Under a system of competitive markets, each worker's wage rate is equal to the value of his marginal product (i.e., the value of the goods and services that he can produce in an hour). Each worker's value of marginal product depends upon his innate qualities, the training that he has received, and his job. The term "innate qualities" is used here to refer to a large number of attributes that influence the value of an individual to a firm. Among these attributes are intelligence, manual dexterity, strength, willingness to work hard, the ability to easily interact with others, and even the ability to get out of bed when the alarm clock rings.

The allocation of workers to jobs is the result of a sorting or matching process. Employers want to hire the most qualified worker for each job, and each worker wants to be hired for the job in which the value of his marginal product (and hence his wage) is highest. Ultimately, workers are matched with jobs such that no worker can find a better job and no employer can find a better worker. No worker can find a better job because the jobs in which his value of marginal product would be higher are occupied by people who are better qualified for those jobs. No employer can find a better worker for his job because the better workers already occupy jobs in which the values of their marginal products (and their wages) are higher than they would be in that job.

The consequence of this sorting process is that more able and better trained workers will occupy the jobs in which the value of any given worker's marginal product is higher, and hence will receive higher wages. For example, imagine that two jobs, one as a street cleaner and the other as a fireman, are available. Clean streets are aesthetically pleasing, and hence street cleaners have a positive value of marginal product, albeit a low one. An out-of-control fire, however, can have tragic consequences, so the fireman's value of marginal product is high. Imagine also that there are two candidates for these jobs, Charlie Plodder and Horatio Hero. Horatio is fitter and faster and smarter, and always pays attention to the in-flight safety demonstrations. He is altogether the more able of the two, and would perform each job better than would Charlie. Although Charlie would be the better paid of the two if he became the fireman and Horatio became the street cleaner, this allocation would not be maintained. Horatio would want the fireman's job and the fire department would want him to have it. Charlie would be fired and replaced by Horatio, leaving Charlie with Horatio's old street cleaning job. The new allocation would be consistent with the sorting process. The street cleaning department would rather have Horatio than Charlie, but wouldn't be able to get him because he would have a better paying job; Charlie would rather have the fireman's job, but wouldn't be able to get it because it would be occupied by a more able worker.

So, workers with greater innate ability and better training earn higher wages. This hypothesis goes some way toward explaining the distribution of wages, but it is still somewhat limited. Neither ability nor training can be measured along a single dimension, so it is not always possible to decide which worker has "greater" ability or "better" training. In these instances, the hypothesis has no predictive power. As well, the hypothesis does not offer much guidance if two jobs require radically different kinds of ability or training. It doesn't, for example, explain the wage differential between NFL linebackers and ballet dancers.

The sorting explanation is also limited in that it takes the characteristics of both workers and jobs as given. There are so many nurses, accountants, and wrestlers, and so many job openings for mechanics, bank tellers, and opera singers. Fitting workers to jobs is simply a matter of making all the pieces fit together, of solving a giant jigsaw puzzle, and the sorting explanation tells us what the puzzle will look like when its finished. Formulating the problem in this fashion, however, sets aside some crucial issues. What determines the number of people who choose to study nursing, and the number who choose to study accountancy? What determines the number of job openings for assembly line workers and for engineers?

On the supply side of the labour market, people look at their own attributes, and decide which career will, with appropriate training, offer the greatest promise. They are guided by their imperfect knowledge of the nature of various kinds of work, and by their equally imperfect forecast of what their earnings would be in those jobs.

On the demand side, diminishing marginal product plays a key role in determining the number of jobs of any given type. The value of the work done by one more employee of any given type declines as the number of employees of that type rises. As the number of accountants rises, the value to the firm of the work that could be done by one more accountant declines. When this value falls below the market-determined wage of accountants, the firm stops hiring accountants. Note that other market-determined wages and prices also influence this decision. If some of the work done by accountants is strictly mechanical, the firm will consider hiring, not another accountant, but a clerk who would take over the routine work of its accountancy department. If new and effective accountancy software is developed, the firm will consider replacing some of its accountants with a computer. Whether it makes these choices will depend upon the wages of accountants and clerks, and the price of greater automation.

This explanation of the determination of the pattern of wages can be extended in a number of ways.

Education

Most of the jobs available in the modern economy require at least some education, if only in basic reading, writing, and arithmetic. Many of them require quite advanced and specialized training. Individuals who acquire more formal education extend their capabilities, allowing them to compete for jobs that pay higher wages.

Spence [61] argues that further education can raise a worker's wage even if it does not extend the worker's abilities. An individual's innate qualities might not be immediately evident to potential employers. A person who graduates from college proves to potential employees that he has some qualities – those needed by successful college students – that people who have not gone to college might not have. Employers who want high-ability workers would therefore choose that person over someone who has not attended college, even if he acquired no job-relevant skills while at college. Knowing this, a person might attend college simply to demonstrate to potential employers that he has these attributes. This behaviour is called **signalling.**

The cost of acquiring an education places a lower bound on the amount by which education increases a person's salary. The major cost is forgone earnings. An individual who is attending school cannot hold down a full-time job, so he gives up a substantial amount of wage income.[2] As well, school attendance has significant direct costs (notably tuition fees and books). All of these costs are borne during the year of additional schooling. At the end of the year, the individual begins his working life. The additional education allows him to compete for better jobs, so his salary in every year of his

---

[2] It is perhaps worth noting that university enrollment rises when the economy goes into a recession. If you wouldn't have been able to get a job anyway, you're not giving up any earnings by going to university. This reduction in the cost of further education induces a significant number of people to continue their schooling.

working life will be higher than it would otherwise have been.[3] Additional education is a profitable venture if, and only if, the present discounted value of these salary differences exceeds the current cost of additional education.

If this present discounted value were to fall below the cost of education, few people would choose to attend school, and those few would do it for non-economic reasons. The number of trained people would fall. Competition for the services of the remaining trained workers would become more intense, driving the present discounted value of their salary premium above the opportunity cost of education, inducing more people to undertake training. Thus, the salary premium earned by educated workers acts as a sort of tap, ensuring a continuing flow of such workers.

The people who choose to acquire extensive educations tend to have innate qualities that employers want – they're smart, motivated, and able to make independent decisions. If their skills are observable by potential employers (so that Spence's argument does not apply), they would have earned higher wages than their less able counterparts even if they had not acquired an education. Their wages are also higher because they have, in fact, chosen to acquire an education, and must be compensated for its costs. Thus, more able people tend to have a double advantage over less able people: they earn higher wages because they are more able *and* because they tend to be better educated.

Hierarchies and Tournaments

Basic economic theory imagines that the internal structure of a competitive firm is relatively unimportant. It assumes that the firm employs each type of labour until its value of marginal product falls to its market-determined wage. The actual structure of most firms is more complicated, and can have important implications for the earnings distribution.

Large corporations often have a hierarchical structure. A manager might supervise a group of assistant managers, each of whom supervises a group of foremen, each of whom supervises a group of production workers. Workers who are higher up in the hierarchy must have a wider range of skills, or be more able, and are appropriately rewarded for these attributes.[4]

The firm often fills job openings in the hierarchy by promoting workers from lower positions in the hierarchy. There are two reasons for this strategy:

- No two firms operate in exactly the same way, so there is some degree of on-the-job learning in every job. If workers are promoted through the hierarchy, every job

---

[3] Of course, people cannot precisely forecast the amount by which additional education raises their future salaries, but they must make some kind of rough forecast in order to make an economically sensible decision.

[4] Workers might be required to have a strong knowledge of the skills exercised by their subordinates, and to carry out skills not needed by their subordinates. They are compensated for possessing these additional skills. Alternatively, it might be that workers who are higher up in the hieracharcy must display a greater degree of competence. A mistake by a production worker affects only his output, but a mistake by a foreman affects the output of every production worker in his group. Again, competence must be rewarded.

opening is filled by a worker who already understands the general procedures of the firm, and who is fully conversant with the roles of the workers who will be under his supervision.

- The firm's managers are not certain of the abilities of new workers. They place these workers in jobs at the bottom of the hierarchy, and learn about each worker's ability by observing his performance. When a job opening occurs at the next level of the hierarchy, the worker who has proven to be the most able is promoted to fill it. Likewise, the performance of the workers at each level provides the managers with more information about their abilities, and when a job opening occurs at the next level of the hierarchy, the best of the workers will be promoted to fill it. Workers advance upwards through the hierarchy as they prove their worth to the firm.

Under the first explanation, promoted workers are paid more because they have become better workers by acquiring important information about the firm. Under the second explanation, workers are initially paid less than they are worth, because they cannot prove their abilities to the firm. Their abilities are revealed to the firm over time, and as they are revealed, the workers are compensated for them.

Lazear and Rosen [39] argue that this hierarchical structure has the properties of a tournament. Demonstrating their abilities to the firm does not entitle the workers to promotion or even higher wages: they are promoted only if they are the best workers at their level of the hierarchy when a job opens in the next level of the hierarchy. Workers must compete with each other for promotion, just as the players compete with each other in a tennis or golf tournament.

One prominent example of a hierarchy is a professional sports team and its farm teams. In American baseball, each major league team is affiliated with a number of minor league teams. A player on an A team might be promoted to AA baseball, and from AA to AAA, and from AAA to the major leagues. He improves his skills at each step, but his promotion hinges both on his actual skills and on the managers' estimate of his potential. If he cannot persuade the managers that he is among the very best active players, his advancement will stop short of the major leagues.

Professional sports also illustrates another peculiarity of the wage structure. From the spectator's point of view, there is not much difference between AAA baseball and major league baseball. (Indeed, some people argue that AAA, with its smaller ballparks and less arrogant players, is the better of the two.) The caliber of the players is also fairly similar, and a young player might move between these leagues a number of times before establishing himself. Nevertheless, the salary differential is enormous. The top major league players earn something in the order of 100 times as much as the top AAA players. Rosen [52] argues that this extreme salary gradient is caused by economies of scale in production. A baseball game can be played as easily before 40,000 people as before one person. The same game can be presented to millions of viewers on television. Doing so creates very large rents that are divided between the television network, the team's owners and the team's players. However, presenting the same game to millions of viewers also means that relatively few baseball teams are needed, and hence the market value of players who are not quite the best is low. The same phenomenon occurs with musicians, actors, and authors.

Chance

Some people (including musicians, actors, and authors) consciously take big gambles that determine, for better or for worse, their lifetime earnings. Aspiring actors might recognize that most of the actors in Hollywood are waiting tables and washing floors, but they are drawn by that small chance of great fame and fortune. Their earnings will ultimately be either very high or very low, but they prefer this gamble to the more certain prospects of a career in insurance sales. Entrepreneurs are often making the same gamble: success will make them wealthy, but failure will bankrupt them.

Other people do not consciously gamble, but their earnings are nevertheless determined by an element of serendipity. The "computer geek" who is on the edge of a software revolution might be surprised to find himself a millionaire, and the prudent M.B.A. who graduates during an economic downturn might be equally surprised to find himself relatively poor.

Unions

The purpose of a union is to increase the welfare of its members. It is generally imagined that the union does so by pushing up the wage rate paid by a firm, even if this somewhat reduces the number of union members employed.[5]

The bargaining between a firm and its union can be modelled as a strategic game. In the simplest such game, the union is imagined to set a wage below which its members will not work. The firm agrees to pay this wage (it won't willingly pay more), but also adjusts employment so that the value of a worker's marginal product is just equal to the wage. Since the value of marginal product falls as employment rises, lower wages will be associated with higher levels of employment. This behaviour on the part of the firm implies that the union is choosing not a wage, but a combination of wage and employment. It chooses the combination that it believes to be best for its membership.

McDonald and Solow [42] argue that this depiction of bargaining is too simple, and that there might not be a negative relationship between wages and employment. As an illustration of their argument, imagine that there is initially no union, and that the firm hires h_0 units of labour at a wage rate w_0. Now the workers form a union, and bargaining proceeds in the manner described above. The union decides that it is willing to sacrifice employment for a higher wage, so it demands a higher wage w_1. The firm acquiesces, but (as expected) cuts employment to h_1. The union prefers the new combination of wage and employment to the old one. The firm prefers the old combination. The higher wage rate raises the firm's costs and lowers its profits. The ensuing cut in employment

---

[5] Arguably, the union's actions do not harm workers who lose their jobs. If the workers were paid the market-clearing wage in the absence of union activity, and if the union's attempts to drive up wages cause some workers to lose their jobs, the displaced workers will be able to find other work that pays the market-clearing wage.

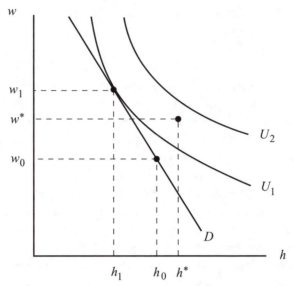

Figure 23.1: Bargaining between a Firm and a Union. Both the firm and the union might prefer the combination (h^*, w^*) to the combination (h_1, w_1). This combination can only be reached through a contract that specifies both wages and employment.

reduces costs more than it reduces revenue,[6] pushing up profits, but even then, the firm's profits are below its initial profits.

The bargain is illustrated in Figure 23.1. Here, D is the firm's labour demand curve. It shows the quantity of labour that the firm would choose to employ at any given wage rate. The union's preferences are indicated by a set of indifference curves. They slope downward, indicating that the firm is willing to sacrifice employment for a sufficiently large wage increase. The union prefers higher wages to lower wages, and more employment to less employment, so employment–wage combinations lying on indifference curves farther from the origin are preferred to combinations lying on indifference curves closer to the origin. The characteristic of (h_1, w_1) is that the union believes this combination to be better than any other combination lying on the firm's labour demand curve.

The question that McDonald and Solow ask is whether the bargaining would stop at this point. They argue that it would not, because there is an adjustment to the bargain that would make both the union and the firm better off. The key element of their argument is that the union and the firm should come to an agreement that specifies *both* wage and employment. This kind of bargaining leads to a very different outcome than the kind described above, in which the agreement specifies the wage and leaves the firm free to adjust employment in its own interests.

McDonald and Solow argue that the ultimate bargain might require the firm to employ h^* workers at the wage w^*. The union prefers (h^*, w^*) to (h_1, w_1) because (h^*, w^*) lies on a higher indifference curve. If h^* is not too high, the firm also prefers

---

[6] The firm is able to produce and sell fewer units of goods because it is employing fewer workers.

(h^*, w^*). The cut in wages (from w_1 to w^*) raises the firm's profits. Some of this increase in eroded away by the requirement that the firm hire more workers (h^* rather than h_1), but if h^* is not too great, the firm's profits will be larger at (h^*, w^*) than at (h_1, w_1).

In summary, if the firm's workers form a union, and if that union bargains effectively, the employment–wage combination will not change from (h_0, w_0) to (h_1, w_1), but from (h_0, w_0) to (h^*, w^*). Wages and employment will both increase. The union members will be made better off at the expense of the firm.[7]

Incentives

The firm can ensure that workers on an assembly line perform their jobs as expected. The speed with which they perform their jobs is determined by the speed of the line, and the quality of their performance can be controlled through monitoring. However, there are many other kinds of jobs under which the worker's performance is not so easily ascertained. The speed of his work is not easily monitored if, for example, he works on a series of tasks, each of which is somewhat different. A worker who appears to be slow might in fact be slow, or he might simply have encountered a series of time-consuming tasks. The quality of a worker's performance might also be difficult to determine if he does not work under direct supervision. In such situations, the firm might choose to offer extra compensation to ensure that the job is adequately performed.

One example of this behaviour, discussed at length in Section 22.3, is efficiency wages. If the firm can only imperfectly monitor the worker's behaviour, the firm might adopt the strategy of paying an unusually high wage and firing people who are found to be shirking. The worker then knows that he might get away with a poor performance, but that if he does not, it will cost him a relatively high paying job. This possibility might be enough to discourage him from shirking.

Another example is the stock options offered to executives, and in some instances, to every member of a firm. The executive's actions influence the value of the firm, but there is no assurance that the executive will try to maximize its value. He might have personal objectives which conflict with this goal, such as access to a corporate jet, or the formation of alliances with individuals who can advance his career. Including stock options as part of his salary package encourages him to put aside these objectives in favour of maximizing the firm's value, because the value of the stock options rise with the firm's value. The more that he advances the firm's interests, the more he advances his own.

23.1.2 Hours of Work

Perhaps the most crucial aspect of this issue is whether an individual can find work at all. In the current economy, highly skilled people tend to have little difficulty in finding work and keeping it. At worst, they might provide their services under a series of

---

[7] Note that unionization necessarily reduces the firm's profits, both because the firm must pay a higher wage and because it is pushed off its demand curve.

short-term contracts which, coupled together, provide them with full-time work. Such people might even be able to queue their contracts, so that they are certain of employment for some time into the future. People with relatively few skills – including people with no more than a high school education – are often less fortunate. Their jobs tend to be less secure, with relatively long periods of joblessness in between. They form queues for jobs, rather than the other way around. The likelihood that they will be unemployed for part of the year sharply reduces the number of hours that they are likely to work during the year. Since they earn low wages when they do work, their labour income will be small.

Of course, some people who work a small number of hours each year do so by choice. They are peripherally attached to the job market, working when necessary at relatively low wages. The behaviour of such people poses a chicken-and-egg problem. Is their lack of attachment to the labour force the result of their recognition that, without marketable skills, they have little prospect of a rewarding career? Or have they chosen to acquire few skills because they have so little interest in a traditional career?

Of those who can consistently find work, some are only able to work part-time. They might be taking care of children, or of elderly parents, or they might themselves have illnesses that preclude full-time work. Consequently, their labour income will be relatively low.

There are also people who systematically work many more hours than the average. Some of these people earn only low or moderate wages, and maintain reasonable incomes only by dint of long hours. However, people who intend to work long hours are likely to choose professions in which they will be well paid. A medical doctor, for example, invests heavily in his own career: his training period is very long, and the direct costs of a medical education are high. He expects to be compensated for these costs by working in a profession in which hourly earnings are high. The compensation is greatest, however, for people who couple the high hourly earnings with many hours of work, and hence people who intend to work long hours are more likely to undertake medical training. The same argument can be made for lawyers, accountants, and many other highly paid professions.

23.1.3 Asset Income

The income earned from assets supplements (and in some cases, replaces) labour income. The income from assets acquired through a long-term savings program can significantly augment an individual's consumption, but are unlikely to make him really prosperous. An individual's working lifetime is relatively short. For most people and for much of this time, a large part of income is devoted to paying a mortgage and raising children, so that it is difficult to acquire income-earning assets.

People who have large amounts of asset income are likely to have acquired it through luck or inheritance. One way of accumulating assets is to reinvest the income earned by assets, but at normal rates of return, this method is unlikely to generate substantial amounts of wealth over a few decades. However, people who invest in stocks are gambling. Many of these gambles will ultimately yield a return not much different from the rate of return on safer assets, such as bonds. Some will generate substantial losses, but happily, some will generate very large returns. The fortunate individuals who collect these returns are able to amass large amounts of wealth over quite short periods of time. Alternatively, assets accumulated by one person can be bequeathed to another. Substantial fortunes can be amassed in this way: small rates of return earned over several generations can yield the same fortunes as very large returns earned over short periods of time. Such bequests arise for two reasons. Some people deliberately choose to leave a bequest to their descendants. Others do not, but unable to predict the dates of their deaths, they do not spend it all before the grim reaper calls.

Some assets do not yield income, but nevertheless augment consumption, in the sense that their possession reduces or eliminates the need to make some kinds of expenditures. The most important of these is housing. The cost of accommodation is a substantial part of many people's monthly expenditures, but once a house has been bought and paid for, these expenditures are vastly reduced, freeing up income for other uses. Cottages, motor boats, and recreational vehicles also fall into this category.

It should also be noted that some people have negative assets, that is, debts. Rather than generating additional income, debts soak up part of an individual's income earnings, reducing his current consumption of goods and services.

23.2 INCOME AND WELFARE

Income is a good but incomplete indicator of welfare. There are a number of reasons why income and economic welfare are not perfectly correlated, and these are briefly discussed below.

Size of the Family Unit
The more dependents supported by a single income-earner, the lower will be the welfare of the members of that unit. For this reason, single parent families are disproportionately represented among the poor.

Needs and Disabilities
The chronically ill require more resources to meet their basic needs than do the healthier members of society, and hence their incomes overstate their welfare. By contrast, the incomes of the elderly tend to understate their welfare if they are healthy. They often live in their own homes, have few child-related expenses and no work-related expenses. Eventually, however, their health will fail, and their incomes will overstate their welfare – not because they are old, but because they are sick.

Life-Cycle Effects
Some differences in income arise simply from age. Students tend to have quite low incomes, and are worse off than people who are already holding full-time jobs. Wages tend to rise over the greater part of an individual's working life, so relatively young

workers are less well off than their older counterparts. People tend to be net debtors during the early part of their lives, and have positive net assets later in life, so that their asset income is initially negative and positive later.

It is perhaps the case that life-cycle effects should not concern us greatly. Arguably, there is no inherent unfairness in these differences because everyone is young once, and with a little luck old once. Consider, for example, the case of university students. They are choosing not to work so that they can enhance their future earning potential. Their poverty is both temporary and voluntary, and a decade after their graduation, they are likely to be earning incomes well above the average. If our measure of income disparity is current income, they are among the poorer segments of society, but if our measure is lifetime income, they are among the richer segments.

23.3 REASONS FOR INCOME REDISTRIBUTION

Most, if not all, competitive economies have adopted policies designed to raise the welfare of the least well-off members of society. These policies are generally justified by a belief that extreme differences in economic welfare are unethical. There are instances, however, in which redistribution also improves economic efficiency.[8]

23.3.1 Social Justice

This rationale applies the Golden Rule to the entire economy. It contends that economically advantaged people should treat economically disadvantaged people in the way that they would like to be treated if their roles were reversed.

Social justice is not a matter of preferences, but an ethical imperative, and hence does not appear in any individual's utility. Rather, it is an overarching criterion for evaluating possible configurations of individual utilities. The most common method for implementing such a criterion is to postulate a **Bergson–Samuelson social welfare function.** This function assigns a level of social welfare W to each list of the utilities of the people living in the society. For example, if there are n people living in the economy, identified by the integers from 1 to n, and if person i's utility is U_i, the social welfare function would be

$$W = \widetilde{W}(U_1, U_2, \ldots, U_n)$$

Lists of utilities that yield higher values of W are preferred by society to lists that yield lower values of W.

The function $\widetilde{W}$ is generally assumed to have two basic mathematical properties:

- It is a strongly increasing function (i.e., W rises when any of the utilities rise). An increase in any person's utility is assumed to make society better off, even if the

---

[8] See Boadway and Keen [12] for a more detailed discussion of the motives for redistribution.

person whose utility rises is already very well off. Envy is not allowed to influence social welfare.

- It is a symmetric function (i.e., every utility affects W in the same way). The social welfare function treats people as if they were anonymous – there is no "A" list.

One function with these properties is the **Benthamite social welfare function:**

$$W = U_1 + U_2 + \cdots + U_n$$

This function assigns no importance to the distribution of economic welfare. A third property must be added to obtain a social welfare function under which reducing inequality is an ethical imperative. Specifically, successive increases in any one person's utility must increase W by smaller and smaller amounts. Two social welfare functions with this property are

$$W = (U_1)^\alpha + (U_2)^\alpha + \cdots + (U_n)^\alpha \qquad (23.1)$$

$$W = (U_1)^\alpha \times (U_2)^\alpha \times \cdots \times (U_n)^\alpha$$

Here, α is a parameter lying between 0 and 1.

To understand the consequences of invoking a social welfare function, imagine an economy in which there are just three people. Person i (where i is 1, 2, or 3) is endowed with an income $\overline{Y}_i$. The three people have the same utility function and display diminishing marginal utility of income. Specifically, if U_i and Y_i are person i's utility and income,

$$U_i = (Y_i)^\beta \qquad (23.2)$$

where β is a parameter lying between 0 and 1. Assume that (23.1) is the social welfare function. Substituting (23.2) into (23.1) yields

$$W = (Y_1)^\gamma + (Y_2)^\gamma + (Y_3)^\gamma \qquad \gamma \equiv \alpha\beta$$

Note that the parameter γ also lies between 0 and 1.

If the government can transfer income from one person to another in a lump-sum fashion, social welfare is maximized by equalizing incomes. Indeed, this policy is optimal even if the social welfare function is Benthamite ($\alpha = 1$). The sum of utilities is increased by transferring dollars of income from the person who values them least to the person who values them most. With diminishing marginal utility of income, the poorest person values them most and the richest person values them least, so the sum of utilities can be increased by redistributing income from rich to poor. The socially optimal policy is to entirely eliminate differences in incomes. This policy remains optimal when society is averse to disparities in economic welfare ($0 < \alpha < 1$).

As argued previously, however, it is not possible to raise significant amounts of revenue in a lump-sum fashion. People will respond to the tax regime by altering their behaviour in ways that reduce economic efficiency. It is equally difficult to transfer revenue to people in a lump-sum fashion, because people will alter their behaviour in

Table 23.1: Optimal Redistribution

Endowed Incomes	Optimally Redistributed Incomes
$(7, 9, 14)$	$(7, 9, 14)$
$(5, 10, 15)$	$\left(6, 10, 13\frac{1}{2}\right)$
$(2, 10, 18)$	$\left(5\frac{3}{5}, 10, 12\frac{3}{5}\right)$
$\left(5\frac{1}{2}, 6\frac{1}{2}, 18\right)$	$\left(6\frac{6}{7}, 6\frac{6}{7}, 15\frac{4}{7}\right)$

ways that increase the transfers that they receive, again reducing economic efficiency. A simple way to model these inefficiencies is to imagine that, for every dollar taken from one person, another person can be given only k dollars, where k is less than one. The inefficiencies involved in redistribution limit the socially optimal amount of redistribution, even when society is quite averse to disparities in economic welfare.

If Y_P and Y_R be the incomes of the poorest and richest persons, social welfare is maximized by applying these rules[9]:

> If Y_P / Y_R is initially smaller than $k^{1/(1-\gamma)}$, redistribute income from rich to poor until Y_P / Y_R is equal to $k^{1/(1-\gamma)}$. If Y_P / Y_R is initially larger than $k^{1/(1-\gamma)}$, do not redistribute income.

The pressure to reduce disparities in income is greater when redistribution is less costly (k is larger), and when equality is more important to the society (α is smaller).[10]

The examples in Table 23.1 illustrate the application of these rules. They assume that γ is $1/2$ and k is $2/3$, so that $k^{1/(1-\gamma)}$ is equal to $4/9$. Each entry in the table is a list showing the income of each of the three people. The first list in each row shows the endowed incomes, and the second list shows the incomes after the socially optimal redistribution of income.

The first example shows that there won't necessarily be any redistribution of incomes. Here, the ratio of the poorest person's income to the richest person's income is initially so high that redistribution from rich to poor would actually reduce social welfare.

In the second example, the income ratio is low enough to justify some redistribution. One and a half dollars of income is taken from the richest person so that $1 can

---

[9] If $1 is taken away from the richest person so that k dollars can be given to the poorest person, the increase in social welfare Δ is

$$\Delta = \gamma k \gamma (Y_P)^{\gamma-1} - \gamma (Y_R)^{\gamma-1}$$

The first term is the social benefit of giving k dollars to the poorest person (this being k times $\partial W/\partial Y_P$), and the second term is the social cost of taking $1 from the richest person (this being the negative of $\partial W/\partial Y_R$). Re-arranging this expression shows that Δ is equal to zero when

$$\frac{Y_P}{Y_R} = k^{1/(1-\gamma)} < 1$$

If Y_P/Y_R takes a smaller value, Δ is positive and further redistributions from rich to poor are warranted. If Y_P/Y_R is larger than this critical value, Δ is negative and redistributions from rich to poor would reduce social welfare rather than raising it. Redistributions from poor to rich always reduce welfare.

[10] Remember that k is less than unity, so $k^{1/(1-\gamma)}$ rises when the exponent becomes smaller.

be given to the poorest person. These transfers raise the income ratio to the requisite four-ninths, precluding further redistribution. The remaining person is too poor to lose income and too rich to receive income, so his income does not change.

The endowments are even more unequal in the third example. The optimal transfers are quite large, and so is the amount of goods lost in the transfer process. Consequently, the poorest and richest people end up being worse off than they were under the less unequal endowment of the second example. Taken together, these three examples show that, *if goods are lost in the transfer process, the socially optimal distribution depends upon the initial distribution.*

In each of these examples, the transfers involve only the two people with extreme incomes. The fourth example differs from the third in that the endowments of the two poorest people are less unequal. Consequently, everyone is involved in the redistribution. The income of the poorest person is raised until it is just equal to the income of the second poorest person, and then both incomes are raised together. The cost of raising two incomes rather than one is so great that little redistribution occurs. The rich person loses only half as much income as he did in the third example, even though there are twice as many transfer recipients.

23.3.2 Efficiency

The deleterious incentive effects associated with income transfers cause economic efficiency to fall as redistribution becomes more extensive, but there are a number of other connections between redistribution and economic efficiency. Some of these connections cause economic efficiency to rise when income is redistributed from rich to poor. Consequently, it is sometimes possible to justify redistribution on the grounds that it increases economic efficiency.

The simplest of these arguments is that people simply prefer to live in a society in which there are no grave disparities of income. In such a society, income redistribution takes on the characteristics of a public good, and there is an optimal quantity of this public good as there is of any other public good. This possibility was examined in detail in Section 11.2.

Another possibility is that there is a greater incidence of crime in very unequal societies. The rich as well as the poor might then benefit from some degree of income redistribution. The poor benefit because their incomes are higher, and the rich benefit because they are less likely to be the target of criminal actions.

Stiglitz [63] argues that informational considerations also give rise to a relationship between income inequality and economic efficiency – although it is not certain whether a reduction in inequality will enhance or impair economic efficiency. He offers examples of both possibilities.

An example in which greater inequality increases economic efficiency is based upon the inefficiencies inherent in the loan market, as discussed in Section 22.2. An entrepreneur who finances his projects with borrowed money generally knows more about his project than does the lender. The lender must therefore protect himself against manipulation on the part of the entrepreneur. His contract with the entrepreneur – the standard debt contract – does prevent manipulation, but it also generates some degree of economic inefficiency. This inefficiency would be avoided if the distribution of income were "lumpier" (more rich people and fewer poor and moderately wealthy people) so that the same number of projects could be carried out with less recourse to borrowing.

An example in which greater inequality decreases economic efficiency is based upon sharecropping, an economic institution that is quite common in less developed countries. It arises when agricultural land is concentrated among a few individuals, rather than divided equally among the rural population. The landowners then require the help of the poorer farmers to work the land. The contract between a landowner and a farmer can take several forms. Here are two simple ones:

- *Fixed wage.* The landowner hires the farmer to work at an hourly wage. This contract is inefficient because the farmer, recognizing that the benefits of hard work accrue entirely to the landowner, moderates his efforts. The land, carelessly worked, is less productive than it could be.
- *Fixed rent.* The farmer pays the landowner a fixed rent for the right to work the land. The entire crop is retained by the farmer. Since the benefit of extra effort on the farmer's part accrues entirely to the farmer himself, the farmer will apply the optimal degree of effort to the task. The inefficiency described above is eliminated, but a new one is created. Agriculture is a risky business: some years the crops are good, and some years they are bad. This variability would not lead to economic inefficiency under the fixed wage contract, because the rich landowner could use his assets as a buffer against the variability of the harvest. He could mortgage his land to finance his consumption when the harvest is bad, and repay the mortgage when the harvest is good. The poor farmer does not have this option, so his consumption rises and falls with the success of his crop. The variability of his consumption makes him worse off.

The ideal contract would have the landowner bear the risk and the worker supply the optimal amount of effort, but there is no contract with these properties. The best compromise is often **sharecropping,** under which the farmer works for a fixed share of the crop. The farmer is still exposed to some risk, but not to as much as under the fixed rent contract. The farmer still shirks somewhat, but not by as much as under the fixed wage contract (because he receives part of the benefit of extra effort).

A degree of inefficiency remains under sharecropping, but this kind of contract is necessary only because of the unequal division of the land. If there were a more equal division of the land, there would be less need for such contracts.

23.4 POLICY OPTIONS

The government's basic tool for redistributing income is the tax-and-transfer program. People with high incomes are taxed at relatively high rates, so that people with low incomes can be taxed at low rates and people with very low incomes can be the recipients of cash transfers.

This tool is not quite the one that the government would like to have. Ideally, the government would like to base its tax-and-transfer program, not on people's incomes, but on their innate abilities to earn incomes. The government could then engineer any distribution of income that it wanted. It cannot do so under an income-contingent program, because people alter their behaviour to reduce the taxes that they pay or to increase the transfers that they receive. These adjustments ultimately limit the degree of redistribution that can occur. This issue is extensively discussed in Chapter 24.

Although complete information about innate abilities is not available to the government, the government can observe certain indicators that are correlated with ability, such as health and age. If the transfer is contingent upon these indicators (as well as or instead of income), a greater degree of redistribution can be achieved. This kind of policy is examined in Chapter 25.

Another option is to levy taxes so that goods and services can be provided to everyone. If everyone has equal access to these goods and services, but rich people pay a larger fraction of the cost than do poor people, the overall effect of this policy is to transfer consumption from the rich to the poor. This kind of policy is relatively common; for example, governments often provide education, medical services, and infrastructure, financed through progressive income taxes. Alternatively, the goods and services can be provided selectively, as is the case with social housing.

At one time, economists argued that transfers of cash were better than transfers of goods and services. There would be no difference in the effects of the two policies if the transfer recipient wanted the goods that would be given to him. (If he were given cash, he would use it to buy the goods. Giving him the goods simply saves him a trip to the mall.) However, he won't necessarily want these goods. For example, suppose that an individual is given free housing. If he had instead been given the value of that housing in cash, he might have purchased worse housing so that he could increase his spending on food and clothing. The decision to transfer "in kind" rather than "in cash" then leaves the individual less well off than he could have been.

Economists have now modified their views on this issue. If people with different characteristics have different demands for the transferred goods, transfers of goods rather than cash can be used to moderate the adjustments that they make to the tax-and-transfer program. Since it is these adjustments that limit the amount of redistribution that the government can engineer, the government is able to achieve a greater reduction in income disparity when its program involves a transfer of goods. This possibility is also examined in Chapter 25.

QUESTIONS

1. Consider negotiations between a firm and a union over the wage w and the level of employment h. The firm wishes to maximize its profits, these being the difference between output and wage costs:

$$\pi = 2h^{1/2} - wh$$

The union wishes to maximize its utility

$$U = (w - \overline{w})h \qquad w > \overline{w}$$

where $\overline{w}$ is a legally enforced minimum wage.

a) Sketch some representative indifference curves for the union in the (h, w) quadrant. Find an expression for the slope of the union's indifference curve.

b) If the firm takes the wage as given, it will demand the quantity of labour that maximizes its profits. The graph of the relationship between the wage and this quantity of labour is the firm's competitive demand curve. Find the equation for the competitive demand curve, and sketch it in the figure.

c) An iso-profit curve for the firm consists of the pairs (h, w) that yield the same level of profits. There is an iso-profit curve for every level of profits. We must determine the slope of an individual iso-profit curve, and the manner in which the iso-profit curves are stacked together:

i) Since a unit increase in h raises profits by $\partial \pi / \partial h$ and a unit increase in w raises profits by $\partial \pi / \partial w$, the firm's level of profits remains constant if each unit increase in h is accompanied by a wage reduction of $\partial \pi / \partial h \div \partial \pi / \partial w$ units. That is,

$$\text{slope of iso-profit curve} = -\left(\partial \pi / \partial h \div \partial \pi / \partial w\right)$$

Find an expression for the slope of an iso-profit curve. Show that every iso-profit curve is upward sloping to the left of the demand curve, flat as it crosses the demand curve, and downward sloping to the right of the demand curve. Sketch some representative iso-profit curves in the figure.

ii) Show that iso-profit curves that are lower in the figure correspond to higher levels of profits.

d) Consider an arbitrarily selected pair $(\widehat{h}, \widehat{w})$. Show that if the indifference curve and iso-profit curve passing through this point are not tangent to each other, there are other pairs at which both profits and utility are higher. Show that if these curves are tangent to each other, every other pair yields either lower profits or lower utility or both.

e) Pairs (h, w) at which the iso-profit and indifference curves are tangent to each other are efficient bargains – bargains at which one party (i.e., the firm or the union) can only gain at the expense of the other party. Prove that all of the efficient bargains lie on a vertical line segment ending at the point $(\overline{w}^{-2}, \overline{w})$.

2. Person 1 and person 2 are the only two residents of an economy. Person i (where i is either 1 or 2) has the utility function

$$U_i = (Y_i)^{\beta}$$

Here, Y_i is person i's income and β is parameter between 0 and 1. Assume that the social welfare function is

$$W = (U_1)^{\alpha}(U_2)^{\alpha}$$

where α is a parameter between 0 and 1. Initially, person 1's income is $\overline{Y}_1$ and person 2's income is $\overline{Y}_2$.

a) Express W in terms of Y_1 and Y_2. If a social indifference curve shows all the pairs (Y_1, Y_2) that yield the same value of W, what would a social indifference curve look like if it were drawn in the (Y_1, Y_2) quadrant? Find an algebraic expression for the slope of a social indifference curve.

b) Imagine that income redistribution is costless, in the sense that the economy can reach any pair (Y_1, Y_2) that satisfies the condition

$$Y_1 + Y_2 = \overline{Y}_1 + \overline{Y}_2$$

Draw a graph of the attainable pairs in the (Y_1, Y_2) quadrant. This set is called the "utility possibility frontier." Using this frontier and the social indifference curves, find the best attainable income distribution. Show that this distribution is the same for every initial distribution satisfying the condition

$$\overline{Y}_1 + \overline{Y}_2 = \overline{Y}$$

where $\overline{Y}$ is a constant. Show that the best attainable income distribution is income equality.

c) Now imagine that income redistribution is costly, in the sense that taking \$1 away from one person allows k dollars to be given to the other, where $0 < k < 1$. Draw a graph of the utility possibility frontier. Prove that

   i) If $k \leq \overline{Y}_2/\overline{Y}_1 \leq 1/k$, the optimal income redistribution policy is to do nothing.

   ii) If $\overline{Y}_2/\overline{Y}_1 < k$, the optimal policy is to redistribute income from person 1 to person 2 until Y_2 is equal to kY_1; and if $\overline{Y}_2/\overline{Y}_1 > 1/k$, the optimal policy is to redistribute income from person 2 to person 1 until Y_1 is equal to kY_2.

d) Finally, imagine that income redistribution is costly, in the sense that taking z dollars away from one person allows $f(z)$ dollars to be given to the other person, where the function f has these properties:

$$f(0) = 0$$

$$\left.\frac{df}{dz}\right|_{z=0} = 1$$

$$\frac{df}{dz} > 0$$

$$\frac{d^2 f}{dz^2} < 0$$

That is, taking the first dollar from one person allows \$1 to be given to the other person, but each successive dollar taken from the first person allows successively smaller amounts to be given to the second person. Show that income equality is optimal only if the initial income distribution is completely equal. Show that if the initial income distribution is not completely equal, some redistribution of income from rich to poor is always optimal.

The Limits to Income Redistribution

Suppose that a society believed that the distribution of income generated by competitive markets was too unequal. What kind of intervention would be needed to bring about greater economic equality?

The second theorem addresses precisely this issue. Its answer is that only very limited intervention is needed. The government does not need to worry about the quantities of cabbage and cheese that each person gets, or with any other details of the individual commodity bundles. It does not even have to ensure that sufficient resources are devoted to cabbage farming or cheese production or any other activity. A policy that simply redistributes purchasing power, and then allows people to trade in competitive markets, is as good as any policy can be.

The claim of the second theorem, like that of the first theorem, is valid only for economies that satisfy certain well-specified – and very restrictive – conditions. One of these conditions is that the government's redistribution of purchasing power be lump sum. Transfer recipients must not be able to increase their transfers by changing their behaviour, and taxpayers must not be able to reduce their tax payments or become transfer recipients by changing their behaviour. This requirement is very strong. It means that the redistribution cannot be from the rich to the poor: a person's income is determined in part by market behaviour (for example, by the quantity of labour offered for sale), and market behaviour can be changed. Instead, the redistribution must be from those whose innate characteristics would make them rich, to those whose innate characteristics would make them poor.

Since the government cannot discover each person's innate characteristics, let alone predict his market success on the basis of these characteristics, lump-sum redistribution is impossible. In practice, greater income redistribution leads to a greater deadweight loss. The deadweight loss can, in theory, become so large that further redistribution to the poor would be impossible. An attempt to give the poor a larger share of national income would cause national income to fall by so much that the poor would be made worse off. There is little evidence that actual economies have approached this theoretical limit of redistribution, and certainly, North American economies are far from it. The extent of redistribution appears to be limited, in practise, by the unwillingness of the relatively affluent to bear its cost. As their after-tax incomes fall, and the disincentive effects of the tax-and-transfer system become increasingly apparent to them, they become reluctant to support further redistribution.

It is nevertheless important that policymakers understand the factors that constrain their attempts to redistribute income. This chapter illustrates the problems associated with redistribution through a simple model in which people differ in only one way. If the government can base its redistributive policies upon this single characteristic, it is able to achieve complete income equality without incurring a deadweight loss. If it cannot base its policies on this characteristic, it can base them only on observed market income. In this case, the deadweight loss ultimately becomes so severe that incomes cannot be equalized.

24.1 AN ECONOMY WITH SELF-SELECTION

Imagine an economy in which there are a fixed number of workers, each providing a fixed number of hours of labour. These workers are employed in one of two industries. A worker employed in the high-wage industry produces w_H units of goods, and a worker employed in the low-wage industry produces w_L units of goods, where w_H is greater than w_L. The labour markets are competitive, so every worker is paid a wage equal to the amount of goods that he produces.

Every worker believes that jobs in the high-wage industry are intrinsically less desirable than jobs in the low-wage industry. Work in that industry is dirtier or more dangerous or more stressful, or in some other way more demanding, than work in the other industry. Nevertheless, some workers believe that the higher wage sufficiently compensates them for performing less desirable work, and choose to work in the high-wage industry. The workers who do so are the ones who are *least averse* to performing the undesirable work. An economist would say that these workers **self-select** for work in the high-wage industry.

We have to be quite specific about the workers' preferences if we are to determine which workers end up in which industry. Let θ be the amount of additional income that exactly compensates a worker for undertaking the less desirable work. Then

- The assumption that workers are averse to work in the high-wage industry is equivalent to assuming that θ is non-negative.
- The assumption that workers differ in the degree of their aversion is equivalent to assuming that θ differs across workers. For concreteness, assume that every θ lies between 0 and 1, and that the distribution of θ across workers is uniform within this interval.

The workers for whom θ is less than some critical value $\widehat{\theta}$ choose to work in the high-wage industry, and the workers for whom θ is greater than $\widehat{\theta}$ choose to work in the low-wage industry. A worker for whom θ is equal to $\widehat{\theta}$ is indifferent between work in the two industries. What determines $\widehat{\theta}$?

Since θ is the compensation needed to induce someone to work in the high-wage industry, and the wage gap $w_H - w_L$ is the compensation actually given, a worker is indifferent between work in the two industries if his θ is just equal to the wage gap. That is,

$$\widehat{\theta} = \Delta$$

where Δ is the wage gap $w_H - w_L$. If Δ is between 0 and 1, some but not all of the workers will choose to be in the high-wage industry.

Since the values of θ are uniformly distributed on the unit interval, a fraction $\widehat{\theta}$ of the workers have a θ which is smaller than $\widehat{\theta}$. Thus, $\widehat{\theta}$ is also the fraction of the economy's labour force that chooses to work in the high-wage industry. It follows that the distribution of income is entirely determined by the two wage rates. A fraction $w_H - w_L$ of the workers earns the wage w_H, and the remainder earn the wage w_L.

24.2 REDISTRIBUTIVE POLICIES

Now imagine that the government of this economy introduces a policy that redistributes income from the high-wage workers to the low-wage workers. The nature of the policy will depend upon the information available to the government. Let's consider two situations. In the first, the government is able to observe each worker's θ, so that it can link each worker's tax or subsidy to his θ. There is then no deadweight loss associated with redistribution, because no one can alter his behaviour so as to reduce the tax that he pays or increase the subsidy that he receives. In the second, the government is assumed to be unable to observe θ. It can observe only a worker's choice of employment, or equivalently, his income, and hence it can only link his tax or subsidy to these things. The government's policy will induce some workers to switch industries, generating a deadweight loss.

24.2.1 Lump-Sum Redistribution

A government that wishes to implement a more equal distribution of income must tax those who are initially earning the high wage and subsidize those who are initially earning the low wage. If it can observe each worker's θ, the government can make the tax or subsidy contingent on these values. Specifically, it will tax each worker whose θ is below the *initial* value of $\widehat{\theta}$, and subsidize each worker whose θ is above the *initial* value of $\widehat{\theta}$. Since individuals cannot change their taxes or subsidies by switching industries, this program will not induce anyone to switch industries and the value of $\widehat{\theta}$ will not change.

If all of the revenues obtained by taxing the rich are distributed as subsidies to the poor, the relationship between the tax τ and the subsidy σ is[1]

$$\tau\widehat{\theta} = \sigma(1 - \widehat{\theta})$$

[1] For example, if $\widehat{\theta}$ is $2/3$, the subsidy paid to each low-wage person is financed by the taxes paid by two high-wage people. Consequently, the subsidy is twice as large as the tax.

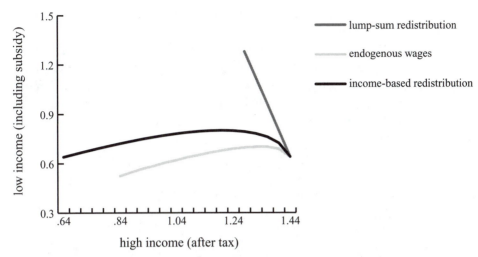

Figure 24.1: Incomes of the High- and Low-Wage Workers as the Tax Varies. The graphs show the effect of taking income away from the high-wage workers under several different taxes: a lump-sum tax, an income tax with fixed wages, and an income tax with wages that rise in response to a shortage of labour.

The after-tax income of a worker in the high-wage industry is

$$y_H = w_H - \tau \tag{24.1}$$

The subsidy-inclusive income of a worker in the low-wage industry is

$$y_L = w_L + \sigma = w_L + \frac{\tau\widehat{\theta}}{1 - \widehat{\theta}} \tag{24.2}$$

Increasing τ from zero reduces the after-tax income of the high-wage workers and raises the subsidy-inclusive income of the low-wage workers. When τ is equal to $\Delta(1 - \Delta)$, every worker's income is $w_L + \Delta^2$. Figure 24.1 shows the combinations of y_L and y_H that can be reached by varying τ, given that w_H and w_L are 1.44 and 0.64, respectively.

This policy carries with it *no deadweight loss*. The tax paid or the subsidy received by each person depends only upon his preferences. Since people cannot alter their taxes and subsidies by changing their behaviour, they don't change their behaviour, and no deadweight loss occurs.

24.2.2 Taxes and Subsidies Based upon Income

Now suppose that the government is unable to observe each worker's θ, so that it cannot link the transfers to these values. It must instead link the transfers to information that people freely reveal through their market behaviour (i.e., through self-selection). In the present case, that information is their choice of jobs, or equivalently, their income.

Suppose that the government imposes a tax τ on each individual who earns the income w_H and pays a subsidy σ to each individual who earns the income w_L. Equations (24.1) and (24.2) again describe the incomes of the two groups of workers in the presence of the transfer program. However, the introduction of the program will change the composition of these two groups.

It is still the case that workers with values of θ smaller than some $\widehat{\theta}$ choose to work in the high-wage industry, and that workers with values of θ larger than $\widehat{\theta}$ choose to work in the low-wage industry, but the manner in which $\widehat{\theta}$ is determined has changed. With the program in place, a worker is indifferent between work in the two industries if the after-transfer income differential exactly compensates him for taking the more demanding work:

$$\widehat{\theta} = y_H - y_L \tag{24.3}$$

Substituting (24.1) and (24.2) into this equation yields

$$\Delta - \tau - \frac{\tau\widehat{\theta}}{1 - \widehat{\theta}} = \widehat{\theta} \tag{24.4}$$

Thus, $\widehat{\theta}$ now depends upon the parameters of the government's tax-and-subsidy program as well as the wage gap.

Equation (24.4) is a quadratic function of the unknown $\widehat{\theta}$. It has two real solutions, only one of which makes economic sense. The sensible solution is

$$\widehat{\theta} = \frac{1}{2}\left\{(1 + \Delta) - \sqrt{(1 + \Delta)^2 - 4(\Delta - \tau)}\right\}$$

This solution has the following properties:

- $\widehat{\theta} = \Delta$ when $\tau = 0$, giving rise to the original distribution of income.
- $\widehat{\theta} = 0$ when $\tau = \Delta$. This tax is so high that everyone chooses to avoid it by working in the low-wage industry, so everyone earns the income w_L. Since no one is paying taxes, there is no tax revenue to distribute to the poor. Income has been equalized by reducing the income of the rich.
- As τ rises from 0 to Δ, $\widehat{\theta}$ falls from Δ to 0. Furthermore, if r is the ratio $\widehat{\theta}/(1 - \widehat{\theta})$,

$$\frac{dr}{d\tau} < 0$$

$$\frac{d^2 r}{d\tau^2} > 0$$

so that the relationship between r and τ is that shown in Figure 24.2.

The ratio r is the number of high-wage workers who support each low-wage worker. The subsidy σ is equal to τr, so it is also equal to the area of a rectangle with width τ and height r. Inspection of Figure 24.2 shows that this area is positive for all values of τ between 0 and Δ, but that it is equal to zero at the endpoints. It follows that an increase in the tax increases the subsidy when the tax is sufficiently close to 0, and that an increase in the tax reduces the subsidy when the tax is sufficiently close to Δ. No strong conclusions can be drawn about the relationship between the tax and the subsidy for intermediate levels of taxation.

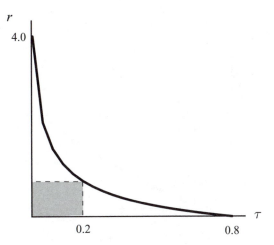

Figure 24.2: The Relationship between the Tax and the Subsidy. The tax paid by each high-wage worker (τ) is used to finance subsidies to low-wage workers. As the tax rises, the number of high-wage workers supporting each low-wage worker (r) falls. The subsidy paid to each low-wage worker (σ) is equal to $r\tau$, which can be represented by an area under the curve. For example, when the tax is equal to 0.2, the subsidy is equal to the shaded area shown in the figure.

Figure 24.1 shows the combinations of y_H and y_L that can be obtained when the transfers are linked to income. The subsidy paid to each poor person is $r\tau$. An increase in the tax with fixed employment makes the poor better off, but an increase in the tax causes some workers to move from high-wage employment to low-wage employment. There are then fewer taxpayers to support each transfer recipient, which makes the poor people worse off. The interaction between these two effects leads to the hump-shaped curve shown in Figure 24.1. Taxes can be simply too high, in the sense that the same subsidy to the poor can be implemented with lower taxes on the rich.

Another way to describe these contrary effects is that a higher tax increases the share of total output received by the poor, but it also causes some workers to move from the high-wage sector to the low-wage sector. Total output falls by $w_H - w_L$ units of goods for each worker who switches industries. Thus, a higher tax gives the poor a greater share of a smaller output.

24.2.3 Endogenous Wages

As a first approximation, it could be argued that the rich are rich because they take on jobs that not many people can do, and that the poor are poor because they take on jobs that all too many people can do. Our model, by contrast, imagines that the wages attached to the different kinds of jobs are independent of the number of workers seeking those jobs, and it might therefore overstate the potential for income redistribution. This possibility has been studied by Feldstein [24] and Allen [3]. Their results show that the scope for income redistribution might, or might not, be strongly influenced by wage adjustment. Let's look at an example in which it does prove to be important.

Imagine that the economy produces a single good, and that its production involves two types of work. Workers believe that the first kind of work is less desirable than the second, and will accept it only if the associated wage is sufficiently high. The workers self-select, in the manner described earlier, so that a fraction $\widehat{\theta}$ of the workers ultimately accept this type of work, and the remainder accept the second type. The production

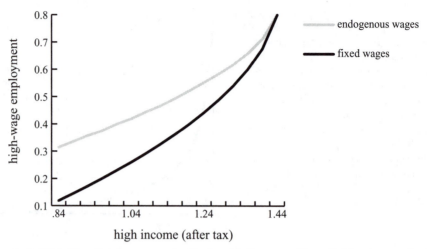

Figure 24.3: High-Wage Employment under Fixed and Endogenous Wages. Raising the taxes (and reducing the incomes) of high-wage workers induces some workers to move into low-wage employment. The incentive to move is smaller when wages are endogenous.

function is

$$q = k\left(\widehat{\theta}\right)^\alpha \left(1 - \widehat{\theta}\right)^{1-\alpha}$$

where q is output, k is a positive constant, and α is a constant between 0 and 1. The labour markets are competitive, so that the wage paid to each worker is equal to his marginal product. The wage of someone doing the less desirable work is

$$w_H = \alpha k \left(\frac{\widehat{\theta}}{1 - \widehat{\theta}}\right)^{\alpha-1} \tag{24.5}$$

and the wage of someone doing the more desirable work is

$$w_L = (1 - \alpha)k \left(\frac{\widehat{\theta}}{1 - \widehat{\theta}}\right)^{\alpha} \tag{24.6}$$

An equilibrium in the fixed wage economy was characterized by equations (24.1)–(24.3). An equilibrium in the endogenous wage economy is characterized by these equations and the wage equations (24.5) and (24.6). This system of five equations determines the two wages, the two incomes and the allocation of labour for any given tax.

If there is no tax, and if α is equal to 0.9, there is a value of k such that w_H and w_L are equal to 1.44 and 0.64, as they were in the earlier examples. Figures 24.1, 24.3, and 24.4 show the way in which the endogenous wage economy evolves as the tax rises from zero under these parameter values. It is apparent from Figure 24.1 that the potential for income redistribution is much smaller. The low income can be raised only by about 10%, and this increase is won at the cost of a 10% reduction in the high income. Each wealthy person must give up more than two units of goods in order to transfer one unit of goods to each poor person, even though the wealthy significantly outnumber the poor.

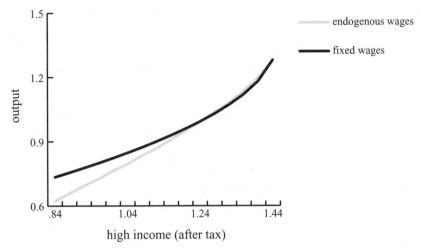

Figure 24.4: Output under Fixed and Endogenous Wages. A tax increase causes some workers to shift from more productive work to less productive work. Fewer workers shift when the wages are endogenous, so output falls less. However, the reduction in output when a single worker moves becomes progressively larger under endogenous wages, causing larger declines in output. The latter effect dominates when the tax is high.

What does wage adjustment do? Most obviously, it partially reverses the effects of the transfer program. A tax increase induces a reallocation of labour, so that w_H rises and w_L falls, widening the gap between the rich and the poor. Thus, market forces and government policy are altering the distribution of income in opposite directions.

The widening of the wage gap slows the movement of labour from one sector to another. Figure 24.3 shows that, for any given high income, more workers remain in the high-wage sector. There are more taxpayers supporting each subsidized worker, so that (other things being equal) the subsidized worker is better off. However, the widening of the wage gap also has an adverse effect. The amount of output lost when one worker moves between sectors is $w_H - w_L$. When the wages are fixed, the output lost with the movement of each worker is the same. When the wages are endogenous, the output lost with the movement of each worker rises as more and more workers move to low-wage employment.

Figure 24.4 shows the way in which output declines as the high income falls under both fixed and endogenous wages. The endogeneity of wages exerts two contrary effects on output: workers move more slowly between the two sectors, but the movement of workers generates progressively greater losses. The figure shows that the net effect is small when the income of the high-wage workers is still relatively high, but that the latter effect ultimately dominates.

24.3 WELFARE AND PARETO EFFICIENT TAXATION

Society is generally more concerned with the distribution of economic welfare than with the distribution of income. Changes in the income distribution are generally regarded as a means to achieving that end, rather than an end in itself. However, economic welfare is not directly observable. If we are to concern ourselves with its distribution, we must make assumptions about the choices that confront people, and then draw inferences about their well-being from the decisions that they make. For example, the fixed wage model described above is consistent with each of the following scenarios:

- Work in the low-wage industry does not lower any worker's utility (all of the low-wage jobs are at Club Med), but work in the high-wage industry is difficult. Indeed, anyone doing this work experiences a decline in utility which can be offset by θ units of additional income, where θ varies from person to person.
- Everyone dislikes high-wage work, and anyone doing this work experiences a decline in utility which can be offset by one unit of additional income. Attitudes toward low-wage income vary: anyone doing this work experiences a decline in utility which can be offset by $1 - \theta$ units of additional income, where θ varies from person to person.

In the first instance, the utilities of people engaged in high-wage and low-wage work can be expressed as

$$u_H = y_H - \theta$$

$$u_L = y_L$$

so that

$$u_H = u_L + \left(\widehat{\theta} - \theta\right)$$

Every person for whom θ is less than $\widehat{\theta}$ chooses high-wage employment, and has a higher utility than any low-wage worker. In the second instance, by contrast, the utilities can be expressed as

$$u_H = y_H - 1$$

$$u_L = y_L - (1 - \theta)$$

so that

$$u_L = u_H + (\theta - \widehat{\theta})$$

Every person for whom θ is greater than $\widehat{\theta}$ chooses low-wage employment, and has a higher utility than any high-wage worker.

We tend to believe that those with the lowest incomes are also the least well-off members of society, and hence we tend to believe that the first scenario is the more reasonable one. There are, however, certain choices which might be better characterized by the second scenario. Do people who opt for dangerous work, or work in isolated locations, have a special affinity for that work, or are they people for whom conventional modes of life yield less satisfaction? Are they opting into these jobs, or are they opting out of conventional jobs?

So, to understand the relationship between income and welfare, we must first explain why people ultimately earn different incomes. Mirrlees [44] offers one such explanation. He assumes that people differ only in their abilities, and that every person's wage rate is proportional to his abilities. Each person's utility rises with his own consumption of goods and leisure, and each person must work (i.e., forgo leisure) to earn the income with which to buy goods. Under certain simple assumptions, people with greater abilities will perform more work. They will have more consumption and less leisure than people with lesser abilities, and their utility will be higher. Thus, Mirlees imagines that the distribution of utility is determined by the distribution of abilities.

Suppose that the government wishes to maximize the sum of the utilities of the people living in this economy.[2] Since high-ability people have high incomes and high utilities, the government would like to design a tax system that reduces the consumption of high-ability people and raises the consumption of low-ability people. One such system is the **negative income tax,** under which each person is given a lump-sum transfer, and each person pays a tax which rises with his earned income. There will be some threshold income at which the tax is just equal to the transfer. Everyone with an income below this threshold benefits from the system, and everyone with an income above the threshold loses.

A tax system is said to be **progressive** if the ratio of the net payment (tax less transfer) to earned income rises with earned income. The degree of progressivity is determined by the speed with which this ratio rises with income. For example, a negative income tax system is mildly progressive if the lump-sum transfer is positive and a constant fraction of earned income is paid in taxes. It is highly progressive system if the **marginal tax rate** – the fraction of each additional dollar of income paid in taxes – rises rapidly with income.

Mirrlees shows that attempts to redistribute income are constrained by self-selection. The government would like to tax high-ability individuals more highly than low-ability individuals. It cannot, however, observe abilities, but must instead use incomes as a signal of ability. Each individual, knowing his own ability and the structure of the tax system, decides how much leisure he is willing to forgo to earn an income. So long as the marginal tax rates are not too high, the incomes that people choose to earn will rise with their abilities, so that the tax system reveals each worker's ability to the government. But now the government faces a dilemma. It wants to know the identities of the high-ability people so that it can impose high marginal tax rates upon them. However, high marginal tax rates induce people to work less, possibly so much less that their incomes are no

---

[2] A government with this goal is said to be **utilitarian** or **Benthamite.** Its intent is relatively modest. A government with a stronger interest in income redistribution might wish instead to maximize a weighted sum of utilities, with low utilities being weighted more strongly than high utilities. The limiting case is a **Rawlsian** government, which attempts to maximize the utility of the person with the lowest utility. (This objective does not necessarily lead to complete equality, as it might be necessary to raise the welfare of some relatively able people in order to benefit the least able. For example, doctors might be allowed high incomes in order to persuade some people to adopt this profession.)

greater than those earned by individuals of lesser ability. Incomes would then no longer reveal ability. That is, a government's attempt to exploit information about abilities can lead to the loss of that information.

The ideal tax system might not be very progressive even if the government's goal is to redistribute economic welfare. Higher ability individuals must be taxed at high marginal tax rates to achieve this end, but they must not be taxed so highly that incomes no longer reveal ability.

Of course, the nature of the "ideal" tax system depends upon the strength of the government's desire to redistribute economic welfare. A government with a stronger interest in redistribution will demand greater sacrifices from the wealthier members of society so that it can raise further the welfare of the poorer members. It is generally imagined, however, that governments do not pursue equality as an end in itself, and that they would not choose to lower the welfare of the wealthy unless there were *some* compensating increase in the welfare of the poor. The need to distinguish tax systems that satisfy this requirement from those that do not motivates Stiglitz's [62] concept of Pareto efficient taxation.

If the government could observe every person's ability, it could design a system of taxes and subsidies to achieve any desired distribution of economic welfare. Each person's tax or subsidy would depend only upon his own innate ability, so there would be no scope for evasion. However, if abilities are not directly observable, so that the taxes and subsidies must be based upon income, every tax system will have to cope with the problem of self-selection. Some distributions of economic welfare will no longer be attainable, and some of those that are attainable will be dominated by others that are "better" in the Pareto sense. A Pareto efficient tax system is one that is *not* dominated in the Pareto sense. That is, a tax system is Pareto efficient if there is no other tax system (raising an equal amount of revenue) such that someone is better off and no one is worse off.

Consider, for example, the fixed wage model set out earlier, and interpret θ in the manner described in (a). Imagine that the tax and subsidy are geared to income. An increase in the tax always reduces the high income, but successive increases in the tax first raise and then lower the low income. This observation gives rise to the humped curve in Figure 24.1. Any tax/subsidy system represented by a point on the downward-sloping part of the curve is Pareto efficient, while any point on the upward-sloping part of the curve is not. The former taxes are Pareto efficient because a somewhat lower tax will make low-θ people better off at the expense of high-θ people, and a slightly higher tax will make high-θ people better off at the expense of low-θ people, but no tax adjustment will raise someone's welfare without harming anyone. The latter taxes are not Pareto efficient, because there is a much lower tax at which y_H is higher and y_L is the same, and everyone is at least as well off under this lower tax.

24.4 CONCLUSIONS

Self-selection ultimately limits the extent to which income can be redistributed. A government which is intent on redistribution should design its policies so that these limits are pushed out as far as possible. Certainly, this design should include a tax system with the correct degree of progressivity, but it might have other characteristics that ease the self-selection problem. Two of these, tagging and targeting, are examined in the next chapter.

QUESTIONS

1. Consider an economy in which there are two industries. The wage income of a worker in one industry is \$10, while the wage income of a worker in the other industry is only \$4. The government, however, imposes a tax of τ dollars on each high-wage worker and provides a subsidy of σ dollars to each low-wage worker in order to reduce the income differential. The government's tax revenue is equal to the cost of the subsidies.

   One-quarter of the workers are qualified to work only in the low-wage industry. The remaining workers are able to work in either industry. These workers choose to work in the high-wage industry if the difference between the after-tax income of a high-wage worker (y_H) and the subsidy-inclusive income of a low-wage worker (y_L) is more than \$4. If this difference is less than \$4, they will choose to work in the low-wage industry. If it is exactly \$4, they do not care where they work, and any division of these workers between the two industries is possible.

   Find all of the pairs (y_H, y_L) that can occur in this economy.

2. Consider an economy like the one above, except that the wages paid in the high-wage industry fall as the number of workers in that industry rises. In particular, assume that each worker's wage income is

$$w_H = 4 + \frac{3}{p}$$

   where p is again the fraction of workers in that industry. The wage income of low-wage workers continues to be fixed at \$4. Find all of the pairs (y_H, y_L) that can occur in this economy.

Redistributing Income through
Tagging and Targeting

"Give alms to the deserving. Give alms to the undeserving." So counsels a Zen proverb. Unfortunately, governments cannot rely on such simple decision rules. There are economic and political constraints on the amount of revenue that a government can raise, so every dollar given to the undeserving is a dollar that cannot be given to the deserving. Separating the deserving from the undeserving is therefore an important consideration for any government.

This chapter discusses two kinds of policies that allow greater transfers to the deserving by separating them from the undeserving. The first is tagging, which was first suggested by Akerlof [2]. Under tagging, the government uses information about non-manipulable characteristics in its attempts to distinguish between these two groups. The second is targeting, proposed by Nichols and Zeckhauser [46] and Blackorby and Donaldson [8]. Here, the government distinguishes between the two groups by exploiting differences in the structure of their demands for goods and services.[1]

25.1 TAGGING

It was assumed, in the last chapter, that those in need of assistance could not be identified by innate characteristics, but that they could be identified by their incomes. Neither of these assumptions is entirely correct. Income does not reveal an individual's need for assistance if, for example, the individual has a disability which does not prevent him from working but which forces him to bear significant expenses not borne by others. As well, there are a number of traits that can be used to identify groups which are, *on average*, in need of assistance. These traits include age, health, disabilities, or the presence of a female head of household.

Tagging refers to a policy of using these traits to identify (or "tag") people who are likely to be needy, and providing the tagged individuals with a level of financial support beyond that available to untagged individuals. A higher level of financial support is

---

[1] These concepts have recently been extended in a number of different directions. The current research is neatly summarized by Boadway [10].

possible because tagging is based upon characteristics over which people have little or no control, so that there is little scope for self-selection.

The higher transfers to tagged individuals must be paid for by raising the taxes (or reducing the transfers) of untagged individuals. That is, a decision to tag some individuals will raise the welfare of those individuals at the expense of the untagged individuals.[2] It follows that the value of tagging hinges upon the degree of overlap between the tagged individuals and the needy individuals. People who are needy but not tagged are made worse off by the tagging policy. People who are tagged but not needy are made better off by the tagging policy, even though the resources devoted to them could have been used better elsewhere.

There are a number of reasons why there will not be complete overlap between the tagged group and the needy group[3]:

- The criteria for tagging might not be complete. For example, a policy that tags disabled people, but not female heads of households, will make the disabled better off at the expense of female heads of households.
- Members of tagged groups are generally needy but not always needy. For example, a program that tags the elderly will raise the welfare of every elderly person, even though many elderly people are in good health and have sufficient incomes.
- There might be unavoidable errors in deciding which people are members of tagged groups. A decision to tag people with chronic illnesses must be accompanied by very explicit criteria as to what constitutes chronic illness. Physicians charged with categorizing individuals might well make mistakes in implementing these rules.
- There can also be moral hazard problems. If unemployable people are tagged and generously supported, some people will attempt to persuade physicians that their bad backs make it impossible for them to work.
- Someone must do the tagging, and they must have an incentive to get it right. For example, social workers often regard themselves as the advocates of the needy. They might well resist a policy that requires them to categorize the needy into two groups, one of which will not receive government benefits.

A carefully designed policy can maximize the overlap, but tagging will not be perfect. Nevertheless, even an imperfect tagging policy might extend the government's ability to redistribute income.

---

[2] If the government spends more money on the group of tagged individuals, it must raise more money from the group of untagged individuals. The self-selection problem discussed in the last chapter implies that *every* untagged person must bear a share of the additional financial burden. Untagged taxpayers must pay higher taxes, and untagged transfer recipients must receive smaller transfers.

[3] Tagging is an exercise in statistical discrimination. The government infers that people are needy because they have certain characteristics. The government cannot precisely separate those who are needy from those who are not needy because some people who are poor do not have the designated characteristics and some people who have the characteristics are not poor. The former possibility is known as a "Type I" error: someone who is needy is not recognized as needy. The latter possibility is known as a "Type II" error: someone is incorrectly designated as needy.

25.2 TARGETING

Targeting is the strategy of coupling income transfers to the poor with restrictions on the commodity bundles consumed by the poor. Two forms of targeting will be discussed below. In the first, a restriction is placed on the income that can be earned by transfer recipients. This restriction is binding, in the sense that the intended transfer recipients are able to earn more income, and indeed would prefer to earn more income, but are nevertheless prevented from doing so. In the second, the transfer to the poor is partly cash and partly units of a particular good (called an **indicator good**). This policy ensures that the income recipients consume at least some minimum amount of the indicator good.

   If disadvantaged members of society could be identified by some innate attribute (such as ability or health), the latter policy would be unwise and the former would be idiotic. Economists have long argued that transferring goods rather than cash cannot raise the recipient's welfare and might well lower it. For example, a recipient of housing might have been happier if he had smaller accommodations but better food or clothing. Providing income rather than housing to him would allow him to make his own choices and would raise his welfare. As for the former policy, restricting the earned income of a person whose problem is that he doesn't earn enough income would be downright perverse.

   However, if the disadvantaged cannot be identified by innate characteristics, they must be identified by their market behaviour, specifically, by the incomes that they earn. The government's ability to raise the welfare of these people is then limited by the willingness of relatively well-off people to masquerade as people who are not well-off. A commodity bundle or earned income restriction makes sense if it harms the would-be imposters more than it harms the truly disadvantaged. The government, having discouraged masquerades, is able to impose higher taxes on the rich and offer bigger transfers to the poor. The greater transfers more than compensate the poor for the harm done to them by the restriction, so that the net effect of the policy is to increase their well-being.

25.2.1 A Restriction on Earned Income

Imagine an economy in which every person has the same utility function

$$u = c - \left(\frac{h}{2}\right)^2$$

Here, u is utility, c is consumption, and h is hours of work. Half of the population earns a high wage rate, w_H, and the other half earns a low wage rate, w_L. Each person who earns the wage rate w_i (where i is either H or L) has the budget constraint

$$c = w_i h$$

He chooses to work the number of hours that maximizes his utility subject to this budget constraint:

$$h_i = 2w_i$$

His income y_i and utility u_i are

$$y_i = 2 (w_i)^2$$
$$u_i = (w_i)^2$$

The initial difference in wage rates generates a disparity in incomes and in economic well-being.

The government can reduce income inequality by transferring income from the rich to the poor. If each person's wage rate is observable, the transfer can be conditioned on those wage rates: people earning the wage w_H pay a tax equal to τ and people earning the wage w_L receive a subsidy equal to τ. These transfers have no effect on anyone's hours of work. Each person extends his work hours until the disutility of another hour of work is just equal to the utility of the goods that can be purchased with an hour's wage earnings. Since neither the marginal disutility of work nor the marginal utility of consumption is affected by the transfer, hours of work h_i and earned income y_i do not change. Each person's consumption changes by the amount of the transfer. Then

$$u_H = (w_H)^2 - \tau$$
$$u_L = (w_L)^2 + \tau$$

The government could, if it wished, equalize utilities by implementing the transfer

$$\tau^* = \frac{1}{2} \left[(w_H)^2 - (w_L)^2 \right]$$

Suppose, however, that the government observes each person's income rather than his wage rate. The government's objective is still to transfer income from the high-wage workers to the low-wage workers, but its policy must now take this form:

Each person with an income of $\overline{y}$ or less receives a transfer equal to τ, and each person with an income higher than $\overline{y}$ pays a tax equal to τ.

The policy is exactly specified when the values of $\overline{y}$ and τ have been selected.

The government's choice of these values is not entirely unconstrained. The government can afford to implement this policy only if every high-wage worker acquiesces to paying the tax. A high-wage worker will do so only if he cannot raise his utility by reducing his hours of work until his income falls to $\overline{y}$ (so that he receives the transfer instead of paying the tax).

Let's call a person who behaves in this fashion – pretends to be disadvantaged when he really is not – an *imposter*. The imposter's utility is

$$\widehat{u} = \overline{y} + \tau - \left(\frac{\overline{y}}{2w_H} \right)^2 \qquad \overline{y} < y_H$$

The constraint confronting the government is that a high-wage earner must not benefit from becoming an imposter:

$$u_H \geq \widehat{u} \tag{25.1}$$

Lower values of $\overline{y}$ ease the constraint (reduce $\widehat{u}$) because they force an imposter to reduce his hours of work, even though he prefers *more* hours of work.[4]

For any given value of $\overline{y}$, the largest implementable transfer is the one that reduces u_H to $\widehat{u}$. Since $\widehat{u}$ is greater than u_L (because an imposter has to work fewer hours than a low-wage earner to earn any given income), the gap between u_H and u_L cannot be closed under *any* policy. The issue that we must consider is the character of the policy that raises the low-wage earner's utility as much as it can be raised.

A natural candidate for $\overline{y}$ is y_L, the income initially earned by low-wage earners. The largest implementable transfer is then

$$\tau^{\circ} = \frac{1}{2} \left[\frac{(w_H)^2 - (w_L)^2}{w_H} \right]^2$$

This transfer is only a fraction of the transfer that equalizes utility:

$$\frac{\tau^{\circ}}{\tau^*} = 1 - \left(\frac{w_L}{w_H} \right)^2$$

The observation that underlies targeting is that the utility of the poor could be raised further if $\overline{y}$ were set below y_L. The poor would be forced to reduce their hours of work to qualify for the transfer, but so would an imposter. The differential impact of the restriction on these two kinds of people would allow the government to increase its transfer.

The poor are working the optimal number of hours when they are earning y_L, and the characteristic of the optimum is that a small change in hours worked does not change utility. But by the same token, small changes in hours worked reduce utility by only a small amount when the number of hours worked is *near* to the optimal number.[5] It follows that a small reduction in $\overline{y}$ from y_L has an insignificant impact on the utility of the poor. However, for an imposter, the effect is severe. The imposter is working

---

4   That is, he would happily work more hours at the wage rate w_H, because he believes that the disutility of an hour's work is smaller than the utility of the goods that can be purchased with an hour's wages. However, doing so would push his income above $\overline{y}$, so that he pays the tax instead of receiving the transfer – and that is the outcome that the imposter is trying to avoid.

5   Graphing utility against hours worked would yield a hill-shaped curve. The optimal number of hours worked corresponds to the top of the hill, where the hill is flat. Any number of hours worked which is *near* to the optimal number corresponds to a part of the hill which is *near* to the top, and therefore *almost* flat.

far fewer hours than he would like when $\overline{y}$ is equal to y_L, so there is already a large gap between the disutility of another hour of work and the utility from consuming the goods that can be purchased with an hour's wages. Any further reduction in his hours of work causes a substantial decline in the imposter's utility. A decline in $\widehat{u}$ means that the constraint (25.1) is no longer binding, so τ can be increased. In fact, if the constraint was binding before the reduction in $\overline{y}$, τ can be increased by half of the fall in $\widehat{u}$. The consequent rise in the utility of the poor is almost as large as the increase in τ.

If $\overline{y}$ is pushed too far below y_L, the utility of the poor will begin to decline. The requirement that the poor work many fewer than the optimal number of hours causes their utility to decline substantially, and the increase in the transfer is not large enough to offset this decline. Nevertheless, it is certain that some restriction on the earned income of the poor will facilitate the redistribution of income and economic well-being.

25.2.2 A Restriction on the Consumption of Goods

People differ in their consumption behaviour, and a government might be able to exploit these differences in the design of its redistributive policies. In particular, the genuinely disadvantaged might consume larger quantities of some goods than would an imposter. Such goods are called **indicator goods.** The government can raise the utility of the poor by a greater amount if it transfers both cash and units of the indicator good. The example below assumes that disadvantaged people require more medical care than the rest of the population, so that medical care is an indicator good. Other plausible indicator goods are public housing, public schooling, and pensions. Workfare can also be analyzed within the targeting framework.

Imagine again that the population is divided into two equal groups. People in the first group have the utility function

$$u = c - \left(\frac{h}{2}\right)^2$$

and people in the second group have the utility function

$$u = c^{1/2}m^{1/2} - \left(\frac{h}{2}\right)^2$$

where m is consumption of health care, c is consumption of some other good, and h is hours worked. Everyone in the economy earns the wage rate w, and the prices of both goods are equal to one.

The people in the first group are destined to be the high-income, high-utility people, and are identified by the letter H. Their hours of work, income, and utility are

$$h_H = 2w$$

$$y_H = 2w^2$$

$$u_H = w^2$$

The people in the second group are the low-income, low-utility people (identified by the letter L). They also maximize their utilities subject to their budget constraints, choosing

$$h_L = w$$

$$y_L = w^2$$

$$m_L = c_L = w^2/2$$

Their utility is

$$u_L = w^2/4$$

If the government wishes to reduce economic inequality, but is unable to observe innate characteristics, it must once again resort to a transfer program based on income. Let's imagine that the government chooses not to restrict the income of the poor, instead making a transfer to everyone earning an income of w^2 or less, and collecting taxes from everyone earning more than w^2. The utilities in the presence of the tax are

$$u_H = w^2 - \tau$$

$$u_L = \frac{1}{4}w^2 + \frac{1}{2}\tau$$

The transfer must not be so great that well-off people prefer to pose as disadvantaged people. The utility of such an imposter would be

$$\widehat{u} = (y_L + \tau) - \left(\frac{y_L}{2w}\right)^2 = \frac{3}{4}w^2 + \tau$$

The largest implementable transfer equalizes u_H and $\widehat{u}$, and is equal to $w^2/8$. Substituting this transfer into the expressions for u_H and u_L shows that, under this transfer, the utility of the rich remains almost three times as great as the utility of the poor.

Now imagine that the government's transfer to each poor person consists of σ units of income and $\overline{m}$ units of health care. Health care must be consumed by the recipient: it cannot be sold or given to any other person. The transfer is financed by imposing a tax τ on each rich person, where

$$\tau = \overline{m} + \sigma$$

This modification of the transfer scheme does not alter the utility of the rich, who continue to pay taxes. It does, however, affect the utility of an imposter, since imposters place no value on health care. The imposter's utility under this scheme is

$$\widehat{u} = \frac{3}{4}w^2 + (\tau - \overline{m})$$

It does not change the utility of the poor if each of them would have purchased at least $\overline{m}$ units of health care anyway. Since the poor devote half of their incomes to the purchase of health care, this condition is satisfied if

$$\overline{m} \le (w^2 + \tau)/2$$

So long as this condition is satisfied, any increase in $\overline{m}$ (coupled with an equal decrease in σ) harms imposters without harming the disadvantaged. Having discouraged imposters, the government can impose a larger tax on each wealthy person, and make a larger transfer to each disadvantaged person. Thus, the requirement that each transfer recipient consume health care raises the welfare of the poor.

In this example, the largest implementable transfer occurs when the government transfers *only* medical care. It is $w^2/4$, which is twice the size of the largest implementable cash transfer, but small enough that the choices of the poor are not infringed. Substituting this transfer into the expressions for u_H and u_L shows that, under this transfer, the utility of the rich is exactly twice the utility of the poor. Transferring goods rather than cash permits greater equalization.

This example is quite extreme, in that the rich place no value on health care, but similar results would be obtained if the utility function of the rich were replaced with

$$u = m^\alpha c^{1-\alpha} - \left(\frac{h}{2}\right)^2$$

where α is between 0 and 1/2. Imagine that the government transfers only health care (so that τ is equal to $\overline{m}$). As α rises toward 1/2, the quantity of health care demanded by an imposter rises, causing the largest implementable transfer of health care to shrink. However, as long as the transfer is larger than the imposter's demand for health care, the largest transfer of health care is larger than the largest cash transfer. Once the imposter's demand exceeds the transfer, transferring health care rather than cash gives the government no additional leverage.

There are other possibilities that do not arise in this particular example. It will often be optimal to provide a transfer consisting of both cash and units of the indicator good, and it will sometimes be optimal to provide more units of the indicator good than the poor would have demanded, had they been free to allocate their augmented income as they pleased. The rationale for the latter outcome parallels that for the optimality of restricting the income of transfer recipients.

25.3 CONCLUSIONS

It was argued, not so long ago, that the ideal social assistance program was the negative income tax. Social assistance would be delivered, not through a maze of programs and services, but by adding a line to the income tax form. People with low incomes would receive cash transfers, and people with high incomes would pay taxes. Both benefits and taxes would vary with income. This ideal is no longer sustainable. Income redistribution under such a system is limited by self-selection. Once those limits have been reached, further redistribution can only take place through tools like tagging and targeting. The austere provisions of the negative income tax must be replaced by a network of special cases, rules, and restrictions.

QUESTIONS

1. Imagine that the government is initially transferring a fixed dollar amount to every person who is observed to have a low income. The government believes that everyone who is genuinely needy has a low income, but that only half of low-income people are genuinely needy. It decides to give a transfer only to people who have certain characteristics, such as advanced age and physical disabilities. The distribution of these characteristics has the following properties:
   - Everyone who has the characteristics is low income.
   - Half of the low-income people have the characteristics.
   - Eighty percent of the needy have the characteristics.

   The government also doubles the transfer given to each eligible person, so that the total amount of money that it transfers remains the same.

   The low-income population can be divided into four groups: genuinely needy with the required characteristics, genuinely needy without these characteristics, low-income with the required characteristics, and low income without the required characteristics. What percentage of the low-income group falls into each category? What fraction of the money transferred accrued to the people in each group under the old program, and what fraction accrues under the new program?

2. Consider an economy in which every person's utility function takes the form

$$u = c - \left(\frac{1}{2\theta}\right) h^2$$

   Here, c is consumption and h is hours of work. The parameter θ varies across individuals. Within the economy, θ is uniformly distributed on the unit interval. Each unit of consumption goods costs \$1, and the wage rate is \$2.

   a) Assume that there are no taxes or subsidies within the economy. How much work does a person of any type θ do? What is his consumption and what is his utility? If a lump-sum tax were imposed upon him, or a lump-sum subsidy given to him, how would that tax or subsidy affect his hours of work, consumption and utility?

   b) People with low values of θ find work difficult. (A low θ might be interpreted as a physical disability which hampers a person's ability to earn an income.) Suppose that the government decides to assist the people for whom θ is less than $1/4$. Unfortunately, it cannot directly observe each person's θ, so it instead adopts a policy of giving a subsidy of σ dollars to each person whose earned income is less than 1. This subsidy is paid for by imposing a tax of τ on each person whose earned income is greater than 1. This policy will induce some people who originally had earned income greater than 1 to reduce their hours of work and their earned incomes in order to qualify for the subsidy. If a person of type $\bar{\theta}$ is indifferent between paying the tax and receiving the subsidy, every person whose θ is smaller than $\bar{\theta}$ will elect to receive the subsidy and every person whose θ is above $\bar{\theta}$ will elect to pay the tax.

i) Find the equation that describes the value of $\bar{\theta}$ for which the cost of the subsidy is exactly equal to the revenue from the tax.

ii) Consider the behaviour of a person whose θ is greater than 1/4. What is his utility if he pays a tax τ? What is his utility if he reduces his hours of work so that he will receive a subsidy σ? Under what circumstances is he indifferent between receiving the subsidy and paying the tax? What equation describes $\bar{\theta}$ for arbitrarily chosen values of τ and σ?

iii) Assume that the government chooses σ and τ so that $\bar{\theta}$ is 3/8, and so that the cost of the subsidy is exactly covered by the revenue from the tax. Find σ and τ.

c) Now consider an alternative policy, which is also intended to assist the people for whom θ is less than 1/4. Under this policy, the people with earned incomes smaller than 3/4 receive the subsidy and the people with earned incomes larger than 3/4 pay the tax. Find the values of σ and τ such that $\bar{\theta}$ is 3/8 and the cost of the subsidy is exactly equal to the tax revenue. Compare the alternative policy with the original policy. In particular, show that every person whose θ is between 0 and 3/16 is better off, as is every person whose θ is between 3/16 and 1/4.

26

The Role of Government in a Market Economy

Competitive markets have contributed greatly to our material well-being, but they are not without their flaws. A still higher level of material welfare can be obtained if the government operates in consort with the market system, mending its flaws and moderating its harsher tendencies. The government has two well-defined functions in this partnership.

The government's first potential role follows from the observation that actual economies do not satisfy the requirements of the first theorem. Since this theorem describes the *least restrictive* conditions under which competitive markets are efficient, actual market economies must be inefficient. The allocation of resources in a market economy is imperfect, and the government might be able to improve it.

The second function follows from the observation that competitive markets can give rise to very unequal distributions of material welfare. There is a broad consensus in many societies that extremely unequal distributions are undesirable. Such extremes can be partially mitigated by charitable acts on the part of the rich, but charity has the attributes of a public good, and hence will be underprovided. If a consensus in favour of redistribution exists, adequate redistribution can occur only through government action.

26.1 REPAIR OF MARKET FAILURES

There are two ways in which the government can attempt to improve the allocation of resources: it can provide goods and services directly, and it can make laws that alter market outcomes. These interventions must be carefully targeted, of course, because wholesale intervention might reduce welfare rather than increase it.

The market economy does not provide adequate quantities of public goods. The government might be able to correct this failure by providing these goods itself. Its ability to finance their provision through general revenues implies that it is not hampered by "free riders," though it must still cope with the preference revelation problem. Examples of public goods provided by some level of government include defence, the legal system, the collection of statistics, parks and recreational facilities, roads and bridges, police and fire protection. Private goods with strong externalities are also good candidates for public provision, because self-interested individuals will purchase them in insufficient quantities. Goods in this category include education and public health measures (such as the inoculation of children). Finally, the government might also choose to provide goods produced under increasing returns to scale, such as mail service, water, and sanitation.

The government can also make and enforce laws. The laws passed by governments often allow it to regulate an industry, that is, to impose new operating standards from time to time. Two areas in which these powers are particularly important are the control of externalities (notably environmental pollution) and the regulation of goods produced under increasing returns to scale.

26.2 REDISTRIBUTION OF INCOME

The second theorem argues that, under certain conditions, the government can shift the economy from one efficient allocation to another by redistributing purchasing power. That is, redistribution can be accomplished without a loss of economic efficiency. But this theorem, too, is at odds with reality. It holds only if the redistribution is lump-sum. Lump-sum redistribution requires each person's tax or transfer to be based upon his innate characteristics, rather than his market behaviour. These characteristics are better known to the individuals themselves than to the government, however, and this asymmetry of information makes lump-sum redistribution impossible. A deadweight loss will result from any attempt to redistribute income.

The failure of the second theorem does not mean that income should not be re-distributed. It simply means that redistributing the pie also shrinks the pie, so that society will have to balance the perceived benefit of redistribution against its cost. It also suggests that the design of redistributive policies is extremely important. If the deadweight loss associated with transferring income between the rich and the poor can be reduced, greater redistribution is associated with any given deadweight loss, or a lower deadweight loss is associated with a given amount of redistribution.

One aspect of a least-cost policy of taxes and transfers is that there is a limit to its progressivity. The aim of a redistributive policy is to tax very able people so that less able people can be subsidized. But since ability cannot be directly observed by the government, it cannot be taxed. The government must instead base its taxes and transfers on market behaviour, taxing high-income earners and subsidizing low-income earners. People will respond to this kind of policy by altering their behaviour to reduce the taxes that they pay or increase the transfers that they receive. If the tax is too progressive, some high-ability people will be induced to behave like lower-ability people, and hence the taxes collected from them will be the taxes intended for the lower-ability people. That is, the government will fail in its attempt to tax these people more heavily than their less able counterparts.

Two policies that might assist the government in its attempts to redistribute income are tagging and targeting. Tagging redistributes income toward people who have char-acteristics (such as age or disability) that are strongly correlated with need. Targeting restricts some aspects of market behaviour in order to more accurately identify those in need. The government might, for example, restrict the income earned by transfer recipients, or require them to consume a certain amount of particular goods (such as health care or public housing). The government's decision to provide certain private goods can be viewed as an application of targeting.

26.3 THE LIMITS ON GOVERNMENT ACTION

Asymmetric information limits in several ways the government's ability to repair market failures and redistribute income:

- The government can provide the optimal quantity of a public good only if it has quite complete information about individual preferences, but it cannot directly observe this information. If it asks people about their preferences, they are likely to respond strategically rather than honestly. Hence, the quantity of public goods provided will differ somewhat from the optimal quantity.
- A lump-sum tax must be either entirely unconditional, or conditioned only on innate characteristics. Some revenue could be raised by imposing an unconditional tax on every citizen, but not the amount of revenue needed to finance a modern government. (The tax would be so large that some people would be unable to pay it, and others would be impoverished if they did.) The alternative, then, would be to base each person's tax on innate characteristics that indicate his ability to pay. The government, however, is unable to observe these characteristics and hence unable to levy lump-sum taxes. It must fall back upon distortionary taxes. Consequently, the social benefit of government policies undertaken to remedy market failures are to some extent offset by the social cost of financing them.
- The managers of a regulated firm will act in their own interests. These interests will often differ from those of society at large. Since the managers know more about the operation of the firm than the government does, there will be opportunities for the managers to advance their own interests (at society's expense) without being detected by the government. The government will try to eliminate these opportunities, but the social benefits of the firm's operation will nevertheless be smaller under asymmetric information than under full information. The government will face the same problem in dealing with government-owned firms and with the civil service, so there will be inefficiencies in the operation of these organizations as well.
- The government will sometimes find that social welfare can be increased by enacting laws that restrict individual behaviour. These laws will not necessarily obeyed, however, so some resources will be expended in enforcing these laws and prosecuting those who violate them. This use of scarce resources would not be necessary if the government could observe each individual's behaviour.

These arguments describe the constraints placed on the government's efforts to improve social welfare when the government is assumed to be an altruistic organization, dedicated to the public interest. But this assumption itself has often been called into question.

It must be acknowledged that, whatever the shortcomings of government might be, we would be less well off without it. An elected government is an instrument through which citizens engage in projects that manifestly improve their collective welfare. At the national level, for example, the government formulates law and organizes defence. At the local level, the government ensures that the law is enforced, clean water is available, garbage and sewage are removed, and public education provided.

Elected governments tend to be successful in this kind of activity for two reasons. First, the election of local representatives to a government assembly allows all voices to be heard. This assembly is then able to develop and implement acceptable compromises. Second, the government has the power to levy taxes, eliminating the free-rider problem that could paralyze projects that benefit the community as a whole.

Economists look at the market system and ask, not whether it works, but whether it could work better. They ask precisely the same question when they look at government, and they tend not to be reassured by what they find. The electorate is composed of self-interested individuals, and the people that they elect to represent them are also self-interested. What mechanism, if any, ensures that self-interested people act for the common good? If there is none, what mechanisms limit the damage that they cause?

One concern is that majority voting is subject to abuse. A majority vote can be used to sanction a project that benefits everyone, but it can also be used to advance the interests of one segment of society over another. Tullock [64] argues that redistribution is frequently the dominant element in a majority vote. Suppose, for example, that there are one hundred voters. A proposal that gave a benefit of B dollars to each of fifty-one voters, and was financed by a tax of C dollars imposed on each of the voters, would be approved so long as B exceeds C. There are two problems here. The first is that this kind of voting might reduce total surplus. (The project is undertaken if B is greater than C, but it only increases surplus if $51B$ is greater than $100C$.) The second is that the majority can arbitrarily expropriate the wealth of the minority.

Another concern is that an elected government, possessing as it does the power to tax and spend, is able to generate very large rents for itself and for its supporters. A self-interested government might focus on collecting these rents rather than on advancing the common good. Furthermore, the rent-seeking argument applies here: if an elected government can earn rents, would-be governments will expend scarce resources in an effort to be elected.

Three mechanisms that constrain the actions of elected governments are the structure of government, the act of voting, and the existence of alternatives in the public sector.

A system of "checks and balances" places some restrictions on what a government can achieve. An independent judiciary, for example, can prevent the government from overstepping legally established bounds. In a parliamentary system, an opposition party will expose any untoward government actions to public scrutiny. The American system requires the consent of the House of Representatives, the Senate and the President for most measures to be enacted.

Elections allow voters to assess the government's behaviour. If the government is too greedy, or if its program is too divisive, it will be tossed out of office. Moreover, elections set the course of the next government. For example, a political party will propose the privatization of government-owned firms if it is widely believed that these firms are operating inefficiently. If that party forms the next government, it will be aware that it is unlikely to retain the approval of the electorate if it does not carry through with the proposal. Also, a newly elected government is unlikely to continue unpopular programs initiated by the last government.

Voters can, through successive elections, expand or contract the scope of the government's activities. They are able to do so only because there are often private sector alternatives to the government's activities. A national health care system can be partially or totally replaced by private health care if it is believed to be inefficient. If a city's police force is judged to provide inadequate protection, private security firms stand ready to provide supplemental services. There are some economies of scale in having a municipality collect garbage, but private garbage collection is not uncommon. Parents can choose to send their children to a public school or a private school, and their decision will hinge upon the costs and qualities of each school. Governments provide support for the needy, but so do many private and religious organizations. If governments become too inefficient, the electorate will support parties that intend to narrow the scope of government by transferring some of the government's activities to the private sector.

It would be surprising if these mechanisms were capable of ensuring that the government always acted for the greater good. There are limits on what even the best government can achieve, and actual governments might well fall short of these limits.

A Note on Maximization

In this book, the maximum value of a function is almost always found by setting its first derivatives equal to zero. Solving a maximization problem is seldom so easy. This appendix describes some of the auxiliary issues associated with maximization problems, and explains why the maximization problems in this book can be so readily solved.

Maximizing a Function of One Variable

Let the value taken by some variable U be determined by another variable x, and let the relationship between U and x be described by the function u:

$$U = u(x)$$

Assume that x can be any number such that $a \leq x \leq b$, where a and b are real numbers. The set of admissible x is the function's **domain.**

Let x^* be the value of x that corresponds to the largest value of U. We wish to find x^*, or to be more exact, we wish to describe x^*. The procedure described below applies only to a restricted class of functions, specifically, to functions that are continuous and differentiable.

Continuity and Differentiability

There is no guarantee that an arbitrarily selected function $u(x)$ has a maximum value. Consider, for example, the following function:

$$U = \begin{cases} 2x & \text{if } 0 \leq x \leq 1 \\ 1/(x-1) & \text{if } 1 < x \leq 2 \end{cases} \qquad \text{(A1)}$$

Here, U becomes infinitely large as x falls toward 1, but when x finally reaches 1, the value of U suddenly falls to 2. For any imaginable value of x that is close to 1 but above it – so that U is very large – there is another x that is still closer to 1 and above it, so that U is larger still. Since there is some value of x that yields a bigger U than any value of x

395

that we choose to name, we cannot name x^*. That is, there is no value of x that has the property that we have ascribed to x^*.

If we are going to hunt for x^*, we want to be sure that it exists. Consequently, we restrict our attention to a class of functions – the continuous functions – for which x^* is certain to exist.[1] Continuity is defined as follows:

> Let $u(x)$ be a function with domain $a \leq x \leq b$. Then u is **continuous** if, for every $x°$ between a and b, **the gap between $u(x)$ and $u(x°)$ becomes arbitrarily small as x gets arbitrarily close to $x°$.**

That is, u is continuous if there are no breaks in the graph of u.

There is a break in the graph of (A1) where x is equal to 1, so this function is not continuous. To show that it is not continuous using the formal definition, let $x°$ be 1. If x rises toward 1, the gap between $u(x)$ and $u(1)$ is

$$u(x) - u(1) = 2x - 2$$

which shrinks to zero as x approaches 1. However, if x falls toward 1, the gap is

$$u(x) - u(1) = \frac{1}{x - 1} - 2$$

which *explodes* as x approaches 1. Thus, there is a value of $x°$ (namely, 1) for which the continuity requirement is not satisfied, implying that (A1) is not a continuous function.

By contrast, the following function is continuous:

$$U = \begin{cases} x & \text{if} \quad 0 \leq x \leq 1 \\ 1 & \text{if} \quad 1 < x \leq 2 \end{cases} \tag{A2}$$

If $x°$ is not greater than 1,

$$u(x) - u(x°) = \begin{cases} x - x° & \text{if} \quad 0 \leq x \leq 1 \\ 1 - x° & \text{if} \quad 1 < x \leq 2 \end{cases}$$

and if $x°$ is greater than 1,

$$u(x) - u(x°) = \begin{cases} x - 1 & \text{if} \quad 0 \leq x \leq 1 \\ 0 & \text{if} \quad 1 < x \leq 2 \end{cases}$$

In either case, the gap between $u(x)$ and $u(x°)$ falls to zero as x approaches $x°$.

If a function is continuous, and if its domain has certain elementary properties, it has a maximum. However, the methodology described below can be used to describe its maximum only if the graph of the function has a definite slope at every point in the

---

[1] The Weierstrass theorem, also known as the extreme value theorem, states that a continuous function has a maximum value if its domain has certain elementary properties which are satisfied here.

domain. A function with this property is said to be differentiable[2]:

> The function u is **differentiable** if it is continuous and if, for every $x°$ between a and b, the slope of the graph of u just to the left of $x°$ is the same as the slope of the graph just to the right of $x°$.

Consider, for example, the function (A2). It is continuous, but it is not differentiable. The slope of the function is 1 when x is less than 1, and it is 0 when x is greater than 1. Thus, there is an abrupt change of slope when x is equal to 1. By contrast, the following function is both continuous and differentiable:

$$U = \begin{cases} (1 - x)^2 + 1 & \text{if } 0 \leq x \leq 1 \\ 1 & \text{if } 1 < x \leq 2 \end{cases} \tag{A3}$$

There are no breaks in the graph of (A3), so it is continuous. Also, there are no abrupt changes in the slope of the function's graph, so it is differentiable. (Suppose, for example, that $x°$ is equal to 1. The slope of the graph is 0 at every x greater than 1, and it falls to 0 as x rises toward 1, so there are no abrupt changes of slope at this point.)

Stationary Points

A stationary point of the function u is a value of x at which its graph is flat.[3] If the function is differentiable, stationary points can be defined in terms of the derivative:

> Let $u(x)$ be a differentiable function. If the derivative du/dx is equal to zero when it is evaluated at $\widehat{x}$, then $\widehat{x}$ is a **stationary point** of u.

The value of x that maximizes U (which we called x^*) is frequently a stationary point. If x^* is not an endpoint of the domain – if it is neither a nor b – it lies in the interior of the domain and is said to be an **interior maximizer.** Every interior maximizer is a stationary point.

> Let $u(x)$ be a differentiable function with domain $a \leq x \leq b$, and let x^* maximize $u(x)$. If $a < x^* < b$, then x^* is a stationary point.

---

[2] This definition is usually couched in terms of left- and right-hand derivatives. The slope of the graph of u at any $x°$ is, by definition,

$$\frac{u(x) - u(x°)}{x - x°}$$

The numerical value of the slope depends upon x as well as $x°$. The idea of a derivative is to eliminate the slope's dependence on x by imagining that x is infinitely close to $x°$. But is x just above $x°$ or just below it? If x is just below $x°$, the derivative obtained is called the **left-hand derivative** (because $x°$ is approached from the left); and if it is just above $x°$, the derivative obtained is called the **right-hand derivative.** The derivative du/dx exists at $x°$ only if the right- and left-hand derivatives take the same value. The function is differentiable if the derivative exists at every $x°$ in the domain.

[3] When the graph of u is discussed, it is imagined that x is measured horizontally and U is measured vertically.

This result follows from the definition of the derivative. The derivative du/dx measures the amount by which U changes when x is changed by an arbitrarily small amount. A positive derivative implies that a small increase in x will cause U to increase. A negative derivative implies that a small decrease in x will cause U to rise. Thus, if the derivative at some interior point $x°$ is *not* equal to zero, there is some small change in x that causes U to rise, implying that $x°$ does not itself maximize U. Since a point at which du/dx is not equal to zero cannot be an interior maximizer, every interior maximizer must be a point at which du/dx is equal to zero.[4]

This result suggests that one way of finding x^* is to look for a stationary point, and this is the procedure that we will routinely use. It must, however, be used cautiously. An interior maximizer is always a stationary point, but not every interior stationary point is an interior maximizer.

> **Let $u(x)$ be a differentiable function with domain $a \leq x \leq b$, and let $\widehat{x}$ be a stationary point such that $a < \widehat{x} < b$. Then x^* is not necessarily equal to $\widehat{x}$.**

There are two reasons why x^* might not be equal to $\widehat{x}$:

- If x^* is in the interior of the domain, it corresponds to a stationary point. However, u might have several stationary points, and all but one of them will *not* be the interior maximizer. The remaining stationary points correspond to troughs or low peaks in the graph, or to "inflection points" (where the second derivative of the function changes sign).
- If x^* is not in the interior of the domain, it need not be a stationary point. In this case, every interior stationary point will mark a trough, a low peak, or an inflection point.

So, finding a stationary point isn't necessarily the same thing as finding the maximizer.

Concavity

There are methods for testing stationary points to determine whether they mark peaks, troughs, or inflection points,[5] and sketching the graph should help to determine whether

---

[4] Alternatively, if x^* is an interior maximum, no small movement away from x^* will raise the value of U, implying that du/dx is equal to zero.

[5] The method is to determine the sign of the second derivative of u at the stationary point. This derivative,

$$\frac{d^2u}{dx^2} \equiv \frac{d}{dx}\left[\frac{du}{dx}\right],$$

measures the speed with which the slope of the graph of u is changing. A **positive second derivative** indicates that the slope rises as x rises. Since the slope is zero at the stationary point itself, the slope must be negative to the left of the stationary point and positive to the right of it, indicating that the stationary point marks the bottom of a trough. A **negative second derivative** shows that the slope falls as x rises. The slope must therefore be positive to the left of the stationary point and negative to its right, so that the stationary point marks a peak. A **zero second derivative** suggests that the *second derivative* has just changed signs, and if so, the stationary point is an inflection point.

or not x^* lies in the interior of the domain. Consequently, it is possible to puzzle out whether any given stationary point maximizes the value of U. There is, however, a class of functions – the **concave functions** – for which we can be certain that any stationary point maximizes U. Specifically,

> Let $u(x)$ be a differentiable and concave function with domain $a \leq x \leq b$. If a stationary point exists, it is a maximizer. If no stationary point exists, U is maximized at one of the endpoints. Specifically, U is maximized at a if U decreases as x rises, and it is maximized by b if U rises as x rises.

Now, what exactly is a concave function? The most basic characterization relates to the function's graph:

> If, for any two points x_1 and x_2 in the domain of $u(x)$, a line segment connecting the points $(x_1, u(x_1))$ and $(x_2, u(x_2))$ lies everywhere on or below the graph of u, then u is a **concave function.**

A little experimentation should prove to you that this condition will be met only if the slope of the graph of u never increases as x rises. This observation yields a second characterization of a concave function:

> Let $u(x)$ be a differentiable function with domain $a \leq x \leq b$. If
>
> $$\frac{d^2 u}{dx^2} \leq 0$$
>
> at every x in the domain, u is a **concave function.**

Consider, for example, the function

$$U = x^a \qquad x \geq 0 \tag{A4}$$

Here, a is a constant. The first and second derivatives are

$$\frac{dU}{dx} = ax^{a-1}$$

$$\frac{d^2 U}{dx^2} = a(a-1)x^{a-2}$$

The second derivative is not positive for any x in the domain if $0 \leq a \leq 1$, and hence (A4) is concave for these values of the parameter a.

Strict Concavity

Some concave functions are also strictly concave functions. These functions are defined as follows:

> If, for any two points x_1 and x_2 in the domain of $u(x)$, a line segment connecting the points $(x_1, u(x_1))$ and $(x_2, u(x_2))$ lies everywhere below the graph of u, except at the endpoints, then u is **strictly concave.**

Alternatively,

Let $u(x)$ be a differentiable function with domain $a \leq x \leq b$. If

$$\frac{d^2 u}{dx^2} < 0$$

at every x in the domain, u is a **strictly concave function.**

The distinction between concave and strictly concave functions is illustrated by the figure below.

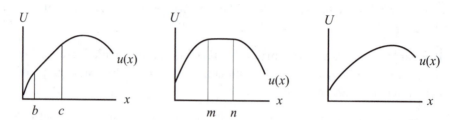

There can be straight sections on the graph of a concave function, but there can be no straight sections on the graph of a strictly concave function. The graph on the left is not strictly concave because there is a straight section on the upward sloping part of the graph. The graph in the middle is not strictly concave because there is a straight section at the top of the graph. The graph on the right is strictly concave.

Any stationary point of a concave function is a maximizer, but the maximizer need not be unique. The graph on the left has a unique maximizer, but the middle graph does not: every value of x between m and n is a stationary point and a maximizer. A strictly concave function, however, has at most one stationary point. Consequently, it has only one maximizer.

There are a number of examples in this book in which functions of one variable are maximized. The maximizer is almost always characterized as a stationary point, and the possibility that this stationary point might not be a maximizer – that it might correspond to a trough or a lesser peak or an inflection point – is seldom considered. Why can I get away with this? Because I have set up the problems so that only concave functions are maximized, so that any stationary point is a maximizer.[6]

Increasing and Decreasing Functions

A function is **increasing** if the value of the function does not decrease when any of its arguments increases. It is **strongly increasing** if the value of the function increases when any of its arguments increases. For example, (A2) is increasing but not strongly

---

[6] The model of permit trading (Section 7.3) contains a maximization problem in which one cannot blindly look for a stationary point. The maximizer is sometimes a stationary point and sometimes an endpoint.

increasing. Similarly, a function is **decreasing** if the value of the function does not increase when any of its arguments increases, and it is **strongly decreasing** if the value of the function decreases when any of its arguments increases.

Maximizing a Function of Two Variables

Now imagine that some function v relates the value of V to the values of x and y:

$$V = v(x, y)$$

For simplicity, let the domain of v be all the pairs of real numbers that satisfy the inequalities $a \leq x \leq b$ and $s \leq y \leq t$. We wish to find the pair (x^*, y^*) that maximizes the value of V.

The function v is assumed to be **continuous** (so that a maximum is certain to exist) and **differentiable** (so that the maximum can be described in terms of the function's derivatives). The formal definitions of these terms must be expanded to allow for functions of two variables, but their meanings are essentially unchanged. Imagine that the x and y axes are laid out on the ground at right angles (so that, for example, the x axis runs east–west and the y axis runs north–south). Measure the value of V as a vertical distance above the ground, so that the graph of v forms a sort of a canopy suspended above the ground. The function is continuous if there are no tears in the canopy. It is differentiable if there are no wrinkles or cusps in the canopy where its slope abruptly changes.

Stationary Points and Maximizers

A stationary point is a "flat spot" in the canopy, where small changes in either variable leave the value of V unchanged. Expressed in terms of the function's derivatives, a stationary point satisfies the conditions

$$\frac{\partial v}{\partial x} = 0$$

$$\frac{\partial v}{\partial y} = 0$$

The relationship between stationary points and the maximizer is essentially the same as it was for functions of one variable:

- If (x^*, y^*) lies in the interior (i.e., if neither x^* nor y^* is an endpoint of the domain), it is a stationary point.
- Not every stationary point in the interior is a maximizer. An interior stationary point could also mark the top of a minor peak, the bottom of a bowl, or be a saddle point.[7]

---

[7] The canopy forms a saddle if there is some point (called the saddle point) such that movements along one axis cause V to rise, while movements along another axis cause V to fall. You are at a saddle point when you have climbed to a mountain pass: the approaches to the pass lie behind and in front of you, while the mountain peaks lie on either side of you.

There are (again) simple tests to separate stationary points that mark peaks from those that mark bowls and saddles.

The relationship between stationary points and maximizers is much the same for concave functions of two variables as for concave functions of one variable. Specifically,

> Let $v(x, y)$ be a differentiable and concave function with domain $a \leq x \leq b$, $m \leq y \leq n$. If a stationary point exists, it is an interior maximizer. If no stationary point exists, V is maximized along an edge of the domain.

Furthermore, the test for concavity of a function of two variables is a direct extension of that for a function of one variable:

> If, for any two points (x_1, y_1) and (x_2, y_2) in the domain of $v(x, y)$, a line segment connecting the points $(x_1, y_1, v(x_1, y_1))$ and $(x_2, y_2, v(x_2, y_2))$ lies everywhere on or below the graph of v, then v is a concave function.

That is, for v to be concave, the canopy must be dome-shaped, with no depressions in its surface. There is a simple calculus test for concavity:

> Let $v(x, y)$ be a differentiable and concave function with domain $a \leq x \leq b$, $m \leq y \leq n$. If

$$\frac{\partial^2 v}{\partial x^2} \leq 0$$

$$\frac{\partial^2 v}{\partial x^2} \frac{\partial^2 v}{\partial y^2} - \left(\frac{\partial^2 v}{\partial x \partial y}\right)^2 \geq 0$$

> at every point in the domain, v is concave.

These results suggest an alternative to testing a stationary point to see whether it is actually a maximizer. Specifically, check to see whether the function is concave. If it is, any stationary point is a maximizer, and the absence of an interior stationary point indicates that the maximizer does not lie in the interior.

The idea of strict concavity can also be extended to functions of two variables:

> If, for any two points (x_1, y_1) and (x_2, y_2) in the domain of $v(x, y)$, a line segment connecting the points $(x_1, y_1, v(x_1, y_1))$ and $(x_2, y_2, v(x_2, y_2))$ lies everywhere below the graph of v, except at its endpoints, then v is a strictly concave function.

The calculus test for strict concavity is as follows:

> Let $v(x, y)$ be a differentiable and concave function with domain $a \leq x \leq b$, $m \leq y \leq n$. If

$$\frac{\partial^2 v}{\partial x^2} < 0$$

$$\frac{\partial^2 v}{\partial x^2} \frac{\partial^2 v}{\partial y^2} - \left(\frac{\partial^2 v}{\partial x \partial y}\right)^2 > 0$$

> at every point in the domain, v is strictly concave.

Strict concavity requires the graph of the function to be curved everywhere. Consequently, there is at most one stationary point and the maximizer is unique.

Again, when a function of two variables is maximized in this book, the function being maximized is concave, so a pair of interior maximizers can be found by setting the partial derivatives equal to zero.

This procedure could have been used in Chapter 4 to obtain the rules for hiring capital and labour in a competitive industry. For example, the ale industry's profits are (4.12). If f is concave (so that π_a is concave), and if the pair (K_a^*, L_a^*) that maximizes profits is in the interior, it is a stationary point. It satisfies the conditions

$$\frac{\partial \pi_a}{\partial K_a} = p \frac{\partial f}{\partial K_a} - r = 0$$

$$\frac{\partial \pi_a}{\partial L_a} = p \frac{\partial f}{\partial L_a} - w = 0$$

Noting that the partial derivatives correspond to marginal products gives the rules (4.13) and (4.14).

Adding a Linear Constraint

Now consider the problem of finding the pair (x^*, y^*) that maximizes $v(x, y)$ subject to the linear constraint

$$y = \alpha - \beta x$$

where the constants α and β are real numbers. The easiest way to deal with this problem is to use the constraint to eliminate one of the variables from v. This substitution changes the problem from a constrained maximization problem involving two variables to an unconstrained maximization problem involving one variable – and we already know how to deal with that problem.

Let $w(x)$ be the function obtained by eliminating y in this fashion:

$$w(x) \equiv v(x, \alpha - \beta x)$$

A stationary point of the new function w is a good candidate for x^*, and a stationary point satisfies the condition

$$\frac{dw}{dx} = 0$$

As with any other maximization problem, the issue is whether the stationary point is actually a maximizer. Are there circumstances under which we can be certain that the stationary point maximizes w? That is, are there circumstances under which we can be certain that the stationary point does not mark a lesser peak or a minimum, and that it is not an inflection point? Here is a useful result:

Let $v(x, y)$ be a concave function, and let α and β be real numbers. Then the function $w(x) \equiv v(x, \alpha - \beta x)$ is concave.

This result is useful because we already know about the relationship between the stationary points and maximizers of concave functions of one variable: if there is a stationary point, it is a maximizer. Of course, once x^* has been found, y^* can be found by substituting x^* into the constraint.

This technique could have been used in Chapter 3 to find the consumer's best attainable commodity bundle. Imagine that the individual's utility function is

$$U = u(a, b)$$

where a and b are his consumption of ale and bread, respectively. His budget constraint is

$$b = \bar{b} + p(\bar{a} - a)$$

where p is the market price of ale measured in bread, and $\bar{a}$ and $\bar{b}$ are his endowments of ale and bread. Substituting the constraint into the utility function gives

$$U = u\left(a, \bar{b} + p(\bar{a} - a)\right)$$

If u is concave, he is consuming his best attainable commodity bundle if the following condition is satisfied:

$$\frac{dU}{da} = \frac{\partial u}{\partial a} - \frac{\partial u}{\partial b}p = 0$$

Because

$$MRS \equiv \frac{\partial u}{\partial a} \div \frac{\partial u}{\partial b}$$

this condition can also be written in the familiar form

$$MRS = p$$

References

[1] Akerlof, George, 1970, The market for lemons, *Quarterly Journal of Economics* **84,** 488–500.

[2] Akerlof, George, 1978, The economics of 'tagging' as applied to the optimal income tax, welfare programs, and manpower training, *American Economic Review* **68,** 8–19.

[3] Allen, Franklin, 1982, Optimal linear income taxation with general equilibrium effects on wages, *Journal of Public Economics* **17,** 135–43.

[4] Arrow, Kenneth, 1962, Economic welfare and the allocation of resources for invention, in Richard Nelson, ed., *The Rate and Direction of Inventive Activity,* Princeton University Press.

[5] Arrow, Kenneth, 1963, Uncertainty and the welfare economics of medical care, *American Economic Review* **53.** Reprinted in P. Diamond and M. Rothschild, eds., *Uncertainty in Economics,* Academic Press (1978).

[6] Bator, Francis, 1957, The simple analytics of welfare maximization, *American Economic Review* **47.** Reprinted in Harry Townsend, ed., *Price Theory,* Penguin Books (1971).

[7] Becker, Gary, 1976, *The Economic Approach to Human Behavior,* University of Chicago Press.

[8] Blackorby, C., and D. Donaldson, 1988, Cash versus kind, self selection and efficient transfers, *American Economic Review* **78,** 691–700.

[9] Blinder, Alan, 1987, *Hard Heads, Soft Hearts: Tough-Minded Economics for a Just Society,* Addison-Wesley.

[10] Boadway, Robin, 1998, Redistributing smarter: Self-selection, targeting, and non-conventional policy instruments, *Canadian Public Policy* **24,** 363–69.

[11] Boadway, Robin, and Neil Bruce, 1984, *Welfare Economics,* Blackwell.

[12] Boadway, Robin, and Michael Keen, 2000, Redistribution, in A. B. Atkinson and F. Bourguignon, eds., *Handbook of Income Redistribution: Volume 1,* Elsevier Science.

[13] Buchanan, James, and Craig Stubblebine, 1962, Externality, *Economica* **N.S. 29,** 371–84.

[14] Buchanan, James, 1965, An economic theory of clubs, *Economica* **32,** 1–14.

[15] Carlson, Curtis, Dallas Burtraw, Maureen Cropper, and Karen Palmer, 2000, Sulphur dioxide control by electric utilities: What are the gains from trade? *Journal of Political Economy* **108,** 1292–1326.

[16] Clarke, E. H., 1971, Multi-part pricing of public goods, *Public Choice* **11,** 17–33.

[17] Coase, Ronald, 1960, The problem of social cost, *Journal of Law and Economics* **3,** 1–44.

[18] Cooper, Russell, 1999, *Coordination Games: Complementarities and Macroeconomics,* Cambridge University Press.

[19] Corlett, W., and D. Hague, 1953, Complementarity and the excess burden of taxation, *Review of Economic Studies* **21,** 21–30.

[20] Delong, J. Bradford, 1998, Robber barons, in Anders Aslund, ed., *Perspectives on Russian Economic Development,* Carnegie Endowment (Moscow).

[21] Diamond, Peter, 1984, *A Search-Equilibrium Approach to the Micro Foundations of Macroeconomics,* MIT Press.

[22] Diamond, Peter, and James Mirrlees, 1971, Optimal taxation and public production, I and II, *American Economic Review* **61,** 8–27 and 261–78.

[23] Dixit, Avinash, and Joseph Stiglitz, 1977, Monopolistic competition and optimum product diversity, *American Economic Review* **67,** 297–308.

[24] Feldstein, Martin, 1973, On the optimal progressivity of the income tax, *Journal of Public Economics* **2,** 356–76.

[25] Friedman, James, 1971, A noncooperative equilibrium in supergames, *Review of Economic Studies* **28,** 1–12.

[26] Friedman, James, 1977, *Oligopoly and the Theory of Games,* North-Holland.

[27] Gale, Douglas, and Martin Hellwig, 1985, Incentive-compatible debt contracts I: The one-period problem, *Review of Economic Studies* **52,** 647–64.

[28] Gordon, H. Scott, 1955, The economic theory of a common property resource: The fishery, *Journal of Political Economy* **63,** 116–24.

[29] Groves, Theodore, and John Ledyard, 1977, Optimal allocation of public goods: A solution to the free-rider problem, *Econometrica* **45,** 783–809.

[30] Groves, Theodore, and Martin Loeb, 1975, Incentives and public inputs, *Journal of Public Economics* **4,** 211–26.

[31] Harberger, Arnold, 1971, Three basic postulates of welfare economics, *Journal of Economic Literature* **9,** 785–97.

[32] Hicks, John, 1943, The four consumer's surpluses, *Review of Economic Studies* **11,** 31–41.

[33] Hicks, John, 1956, *A Revision of Demand Theory,* Oxford University Press.

[34] Hochman, Harold, and James Rodgers, 1969, Pareto optimal redistribution, *American Economic Review* **57,** 542–57.

[35] Johansen, L., 1977, The theory of public goods: Misplaced emphasis? *Journal of Public Economics* **7,** 147–52.

[36] Kreps, David, and Jose Scheinkman, 1983, Quantity precommittment and Bertrand competition yield Cournot outcomes, *Bell Journal of Economics* **14,** 326–37.

[37] Krueger, Anne, 1974, The political economy of the rent-seeking society, *American Economic Review* **64,** 291–303.

[38] Laffont, Jean-Jacques, and Jean Tirole, 1993, *A Theory of Incentives in Procurement and Regulation,* MIT Press.

[39] Lazear, Edward, and Sherwin Rosen, 1981, Rank-order tournaments as optimum labor contracts, *Journal of Political Economy* **89,** 841–64.

[40] Lipsey, Richard, 1996, *Economic growth, technological change, and Canadian economic policy,* C. D. Howe Institute.

[41] Lipsey, Richard, and Kelvin Lancaster, 1956–7, The general theory of second best, *Review of Economic Studies* **24,** 11–32.

[42] McDonald, Ian, and Robert Solow, 1981, Wage bargaining and employment, *American Economic Review* **71,** 896–908.

[43] Marshall, Alfred, 1920, *Principles of Economics,* 8th ed., Macmillan.

[44] Mirrlees, James, 1971, An exploration in the theory of optimal taxation, *Review of Economic Studies* **38,** 175–208.

[45] Ng, Yew-Kwang, 1973, The economic theory of clubs: Pareto optimality conditions, *Economica* **40,** 291–98.

[46] Nichols, A., and R. Zeckhauser, 1982, Targeting transfers through restrictions on recipients, *American Economic Review* **72,** 372–77.

[47] Oakland, William, 1972, Congestion, public goods, and welfare, *Journal of Public Economics* **1,** 339–57.

[48] Pen, Jan, 1971, *Income Distribution,* Praeger.

[49] Posner, Richard, 1975, The social costs of monopoly and regulation, *Journal of Political Economy* **83,** 807–27.

[50] Ramsey, F., 1927, A contribution to the theory of taxation, *Economic Journal* **37,** 47–61.

[51] Rogerson, William, 1982, The social costs of monopoly and regulation: A game-theoretic approach, *Bell Journal of Economics* **13,** 391–401.

[52] Rosen, Sherwin, 1981, The economics of superstars, *American Economic Review* **71,** 845–58.

[53] Samuelson, Paul, 1954, The pure theory of public expenditure, *Review of Economics and Statistics* **36,** 387–89.

[54] Samuelson, Paul, 1955, Diagrammatic exposition of the theory of public expenditure, *Review of Economics and Statistics* **37.** Reprinted in R. W. Houghton, ed., *Public Finance,* Penguin Books (1970).

[55] Samuelson, Paul, 1969, Pure theory of public expenditure and taxation, in J. Margolis and H. Guitton, *Public Economics,* St. Martin's Press.

[56] Sandmo, Agnar, 1973, Public goods and the technology of consumption, *Review of Economic Studies* **40,** 517–28.

[57] Sandmo, Agnar, 1974, A note on the structure of optimal taxation, *American Economic Review* **64,** 701–6.

[58] Shapiro, Carl, and Joseph Stiglitz, 1984, Equilibrium unemployment as a worker-discipline device, *American Economic Review* **74,** 433–44.

[59] Shibata, Hirofumi, 1971, A bargaining model of the pure theory of public expenditure, *Journal of Political Economy* **79,** 1–29.

[60] Solow, Robert, 1980, On theories of unemployment, *American Economic Review* **70,** 1–11.

[61] Spence, A. M., 1973, Job market signalling, *Quarterly Journal of Economics* **87,** 355–74.

[62] Stiglitz, Jospeh, 1982, Self-selection and Pareto efficient taxation, *Journal of Public Economics* **17,** 213–40.

[63] Stiglitz, Joseph, 1994, *Whither Socialism?* MIT Press.

[64] Tullock, Gordon, 1959, Some problems of majority voting, *Journal of Political Economy* **67,** 571–79.

[65] Warr, Peter, 1982, Pareto optimal redistribution and private charity, *Journal of Public Economics* **19,** 131–38.

[66] Williamson, Stephen, 1986, Costly monitoring, financial intermediation, and equilibrium credit rationing, *Journal of Monetary Economics* **97,** 89–108.

[67] Willig, Robert, 1976, Consumer's surplus without apology, *American Economic Review,* **66,** 589–97.

Index

A bold page number indicates that the index term is defined on that page.